THE LAST SAFETY NET

A handbook of minimum income protection in Europe

Thomas Bahle, Vanessa Hubl and Michaela Pfeifer

MZES
MANNHEIMER ZENTRUM FÜR
EUROPÄISCHE SOZIALFORSCHUNG

Hans **Böckler**
Stiftung

Fakten für eine faire Arbeitswelt.

First published in Great Britain in 2011 by

The Policy Press
University of Bristol
Fourth Floor
Beacon House
Queen's Road
Bristol BS8 1QU, UK
t: +44 (0)117 331 4054
f: +44 (0)117 331 4093
tpp-info@bristol.ac.uk
www.policypress.co.uk

North America office:
The Policy Press
c/o The University of Chicago Press
1427 East 60th Street
Chicago, IL 60637, USA
t: +1 773 702 7700
f: +1 773 702 9756
e:sales@press.uchicago.edu
www.press.uchicago.edu

British Library Cataloguing in Publication Data
A catalogue record for this book is available from the British Library.

Library of Congress Cataloging-in-Publication Data
A catalog record for this book has been requested.

ISBN 978 1 84742 725 0 (hardcover)

Cover design by Qube Design Associates, Bristol
Front cover: photograph kindly supplied by Nate Brelsford
Printed and bound by CPI Group (UK) Ltd, Croydon, CR0 4YY

Contents

List of tables and figures

Tables

Figures

List of abbreviations

AAH	Allocation aux adultes handicapés
ABW	Algemene bijstandswet
AER	Allocation equivalent retraite
AI	Allocation d'insertion
AIO	Aanvullende inkomensvoorziening ouderen
AKW	Algemene kinderbijslagwet
AO	Allocation ordinaire
AOW	Algemene ouderdomswet
API	Allocation de parent isolé
ARR	Allocation de remplacement de revenu
AS	Allocation spéciale
ASE	Aide au secours exceptionnel
ASI	Allocation supplémentaire d'invalidité
ASPA	Allocation de solidarité aux personnes âgées
ASS	Allocation de solidarité spécifique
ASV	Allocation supplémentaire vieillesse
AT	Austria
ATA	Allocation temporaire d'attente
AV	Allocation veuvage
AVTS	Allocation aux vieux travailleurs salariés
AW	Average worker's wage
BE	Belgium
BT	Bijzondere tegemoetkoming
CBA	Career beginners assistance
CCA	Child care allowance
CCF	Child care fee
CMU	Couverture maladie universelle
CRS	Child raising support
CSB	Centrum voor Social Beleid Herman Deleeck, University of Antwerp
CSI	Complemento solidario para idosos
CZ	Czech Republic
DE	Germany
DK	Denmark
EITC	Earned income tax credit
ES	Spain
ESA	Employment and support allowance
ESSPROS	European system of social protection statistics
EU	European Union
EUR PPS	Euro in purchasing power standards
FI	Finland

FR	France
GDP	Gross domestic product
GDR	German Democratic Republic
GI	Gewaarborgd inkomen voor bejaarden
GRAPA	Garantie de revenus aux personnes âgées
GT	Gewone tegemoetkoming
HLU	Hilfe zum Lebensunterhalt
HU	Hungary
HUF	Hungarian Forint
IAS	Indexante de apoios sociais
IE	Ireland
IGFSS	Instituto de Gestao Financeira da Segurança Social
IGO	Inkomensgarantie voor ouderen
ILO	International Labour Organization
IOAW	Inkomensvoorziening oudere en gedeeltelijk arbeidsongeschikte werkloze werknemers
IOAZ	Inkomensvoorziening oudere en gedeeltelijk arbeidsongeschikte gewezen zelfstandigen
IPREM	Indicador Público de Renta de Efectos Múltiples
IS	Income support
IT	Italy
IVT	Inkomensvervangende tegemoetkoming
JSA	Jobseekers' allowance
LISMI	Ley de Integración Social de las personas con discapacidad
MIG	Minimum income guarantee
Minimex	Minimum de moyens d'existence
MIP	Minimum income protection
MISSOC	Mutual information system on social protection in the member states of the European Union
MZES	Mannheimer Zentrum für Europäische Sozialforschung
NEI	Netherlands Economic Institute
NHS	National Health Service
NL	The Netherlands
NRR	Net replacement rate
OAA	Old age allowance
OECD	Organisation for Economic Co-operation and Development
OMC	Open method of coordination
ONAFTS	Office national d'allocations familiales pour travailleurs salariés
ONEM	Office national d'emploi
ONP	Office national de pensions
PAS	Pensiones asistenciales
PL	Poland
PNC	Pensiones no contributivas
PPP	Purchasing power parities

PPS	Purchasing power standards
PT	Portugal
RG	Revenu garanti aux personnes âgées
RIS	Revenu d'integration sociale
RMG	Rendimento mínimo garantido
RMI	Reddito minimo d'inserimento (in Italy)
RMI	Rentas mínimas de inserción (in Spain)
RMI	Revenu minimum d'insertion (in France)
RSA	Revenu de solidarité active (in France)
RSA	Regular social assistance (in Hungary)
RSI	Rendimento social de inserção
RSO	Revenu de solidarité
RWW	Rijksgroepsregeling voor werkloze werknemers
SaMip	Social Assistance and Minimum Income Protection database
SE	Sweden
SGIM	Subsidio de garantía de ingresos mínimos
SK	Slovakia
SMI	Salario Mínimo Interprofessional
SOFI	Institutet för social forskning, Stockholm
SPF	Service public fédéral
SPP	Service public fédéral de programmation
SS	Spouse supplement
SVB	Sociale Verzekeringsbank
SWA	Supplementary welfare allowance
TW	Toeslagenwet
UA	Unemployment assistance
UB	Unemployment benefit
UK	United Kingdom
UNDP	United Nations Development Programme
UWV	Uitvoeringsinstituut Werknemersverzekeringen
Wajong	Wet arbeidsongeschiktheidsvoorziening jonggehandicapten
WFTC	Working families tax credit
WIK	Wet inkomensvoorziening kunstenaars
WJI	Wet investeren in jongeren
WTC	Working tax credit
WW	Werkloosheidswet
WWB	Wet werk en bijstand
WWIK	Wet werk en inkomen kunstenaars

Acknowledgements

The last safety net presents results from a project on minimum income protection in Europe that has received generous financial support from the Hans-Böckler-Stiftung (HBS) in Düsseldorf. The HBS project was coordinated by Bernhard Ebbinghaus and Claus Wendt as well as by an advisory board with scientific experts and union representatives who provided helpful suggestions throughout. We are also grateful to the Mannheim Centre for European Social Research (MZES) at the University of Mannheim for supporting the project with its own resources and providing an excellent research environment. We were fortunate that in the framework of the EQUALSOC Network of Excellence, funded by the European Union, we had ample opportunity to work with other scholars of welfare state comparison and, more specifically, minimum income protection. We would like to thank Christian Albrekt Larsen, Jonathan Bradshaw, Susan Kuivalainen, Bertrand Maître, Ive Marx, Natascha van Mechelen, and Kenneth Nelson, among many others, for their helpful and stimulating comments.

The comparison of minimum income protection (MIP) schemes of 17 countries profited from intellectual exchange with a number of colleagues. We thank in particular our colleagues from Eastern Europe who contributed to this book and provided us with the data for their countries. While we gladly acknowledge their support, any shortcomings in the book, including unaddressed critique and comments, are entirely our own. The funding from both the HBS and the MZES also allowed us to involve student assistants in the project, some of whom decided to write their BA or MA theses in this field. Part of the data collection and other tasks would not have been possible without their help. To that end, we wish to thank Nico Müller and Regina Jutz as well as Ryan DeLaney, who proofread the manuscript. Our additional thanks go to Christian Melbeck for the IT support he provided in building up the EuMin database and to Franz Kraus, who advised us with respect to the data collection and international data sources. We also thank Marlene Alle, Beate Rossi, and Marianne Schneider for administrative and IT support at the MZES. Finally, we are grateful for the support by The Policy Press team around Emily Watt, who believed in the project throughout the lengthy process of finishing the manuscript.

Thomas Bahle
Vanessa Hubl
Michaela Pfeifer

Introduction

Minimum income protection in the welfare state

The European welfare states have developed the most extensive systems of social protection in the world. Europe's citizens are covered by social insurance schemes providing protection against sickness, unemployment, invalidity, and old age. Pensions and healthcare services are available for the vast majority of the population. Many countries also have well-developed benefits and services for families with children and for older persons in need of care. Nonetheless, poverty has never disappeared, and means-tested minimum income protection (MIP) has thereby remained a necessity. Large population groups receive MIP benefits in a number of European countries. More than 20% of older persons in Ireland and in the United Kingdom (UK) depended on MIP in 2007; in the same year in Germany, more than 10% of the adult working-age population was in receipt of MIP benefits. These figures show that MIP systems include sizeable proportions of the population, despite the fact that they are considered the residual last safety net that serves only in cases of need, when people's rights to all other kinds of social benefits are exhausted or do not suffice to guarantee a social minimum.

The residual character of MIP in the architecture of social protection systems was a widely shared assumption during the '*trentes glorieuses*' – the thirty years after World War II. The post-war European welfare states were built on the promise of comprehensive social protection for workers and citizens. The spectacular growth of social insurance coverage and social expenditure was indeed one of the most profound changes in most European societies from the early 1950s to the late 1970s (Flora, 1986–7). The goal of a comprehensive social protection system was linked to another great promise of post-war welfare capitalism: full employment. In many European countries, however, neither of these promises was ever really fulfilled.

The situation has significantly changed since then. The slowdown of economic growth beginning in the early 1980s and the erosion of social protection in the era of welfare state retrenchment have left increasing numbers of citizens in the margins of society with insufficient protection. Moreover, new social risks have emerged that are not adequately covered by traditional welfare state institutions (Marx, 2007). Increasing family instability and changing labour markets are among the most significant catalysts of social problems in European societies. Single parents need support that traditional social protection systems often do not provide. In addition, employment structures have changed profoundly with the secular shift from industrial to service economies, and low-skilled labour has faced a growing risk of unemployment, low pay, and precarious employment. The erosion of decent living wages for growing numbers of adults of prime working age is among the most important factors for high child poverty rates and has long-term consequences for individual pension prospects and income security in old age. In this changed context, MIP has gained a new relevance in guaranteeing a minimum standard of living for a larger number of citizens.

In Eastern Europe, a more profound and sudden shift occurred with the transition from socialist regimes to democracy and a market economy after 1989. During socialism, there was officially no unemployment or poverty. The socialist welfare system was characterised by a very strong link between employment and social protection instead of a universal concept of social citizenship (Inglot, 2008). MIP either did not exist or was targeted at marginalised population groups. Full employment, social benefits tied to the workplace, and heavy state subsidies for basic goods such as nutrition, housing, and public transport provided a tight protective and restrictive net for the vast majority of the population. This net was torn to pieces within an unprecedentedly short time after 1989. Rising unemployment and the breakdown of workplace-based social benefits made new protection arrangements necessary. Following this shift, therefore, most Eastern European countries introduced new schemes of unemployment insurance and minimum income protection.

These shifts emphasise that the role of MIP in the welfare state is twofold: it is both residual and fundamental. The role is residual because MIP enters only after all other social benefits are exhausted or if they do not suffice to guarantee a socially accepted minimum standard of living. In this sense, MIP provides the last safety net in the welfare state and constitutes the last resort for persons in need. The role of MIP is also fundamental because it provides the foundation of social citizenship rights. MIP guarantees the minimum standard of living below which no one in society should be allowed to fall (Leibfried, 1992). In this sense, it constitutes the foundation of the welfare state.

In both senses, MIP systems face new challenges today. Over the past 15 years, many European countries have cut back on their systems of unemployment protection and pension benefits. At the same time, the overarching paradigm of activation gained prominence among policymakers aiming to enhance labour market inclusion through both incentives and sanctions for most MIP and unemployment benefit recipients. Lower protection and stronger activation requirements have altered the conditions under which social security systems operate.

The described developments in social risks and social security are two interacting processes. While more and more persons are not adequately covered by 'old social rights', there is a shift in the overall construct of social rights. The new focus on the reciprocity of citizens' rights and duties and the fact that previous labour market achievements have lost value (as reflected by lower replacement rates and shorter benefit duration) changes the face of social citizenship rights. MIP, as a part of this construct, might see a change in its functioning logic as well. At the same time, its role in quantitative terms might grow, when, for instance, more people actually have to top up low wages or pensions with MIP, or when rights to other forms of social protection become more exclusive.

The economic crisis that began in 2008 has put additional pressure on social protection systems, including MIP. Their protectiveness is put to the test in the face of amplified social risks for large parts of the population. Can social protection systems adequately deal with these problems, or do large population groups fall through their protective arrangements into the last safety net of MIP? Systems are still highly protective in some countries, at least for some population groups, implying that few persons need MIP benefits. The protectiveness of social insurance has become much weaker in other countries, however, especially for the unemployed, leading to a growing need for MIP. In this case, the additional question of whether there are actually MIP systems in place that adequately cover those population groups arises. Does MIP provide comprehensive, accessible, and adequate benefits for all those members of society who cannot make their own living, or do they exclude certain categories of persons? In some countries, the last safety net is strong and dense, and represents a true social citizenship right for the whole population. In others, it is patchy and full of holes.

Comparative research on MIP systems

An up-to-date comparative assessment of MIP systems is needed in order to study these questions. Studies of MIP, however, have been a minor branch in comparative welfare state research. Most analyses have focused on social insurance and non-means-tested benefits, while MIP has often been neglected. Moreover, studies that have dealt with MIP have usually applied a rather limited perspective in several aspects. First of all, their focus in most cases has been on only one general MIP scheme in each country, not taking into account that most countries have several schemes covering different population groups. This limitation is misleading because it does not consider functionally equivalent institutions. It is also inadequate for assessing the real size and significance of MIP systems in each country. Second, most studies have looked solely at guaranteed benefit levels provided by this (one) MIP scheme, without acknowledging the numbers of recipients or expenditure levels. Therefore, significant dimensions of MIP systems remain unstudied, although the issue of how many persons in each country actually depend on MIP benefits is crucial from a social policy point of view. Third, the relationships between MIP and higher-tier social protection arrangements in each country have also not been studied systematically.

MIP systems have certainly attracted new interest in social policy circles and welfare state research because of the fundamental change in the social and economic conditions of European societies. With this renewed interest in the last safety net, the existing knowledge gaps and lack of comparative data have become apparent. The European welfare states vary widely in the role that MIP plays in overall social security systems, but these variations are not fully captured and understood by social policy researchers. This is true despite the European Union's longstanding interest in MIP. Beginning in the 1980s, the European Union (EU) launched several programmes on poverty and various initiatives culminating in the 2010 European Year for Combating Poverty and Social Exclusion. The EU was very active in developing and supporting practical social policies aiming at combating poverty. It was also successful in improving the database and knowledge of poverty through research programmes and data-collecting activities. Today, the focus has become much wider than in the original poverty programmes. The concept of social inclusion covers many aspects of life situations beyond income status. In this sense, social inclusion has become an important theme for the open method of coordination (OMC), by which member states seek to discuss, exchange, and coordinate their activities in combating social exclusion, including monetary poverty.

The main focus of interest in these activities has been on poverty and social inclusion indicators and on national policies that can be used or developed to improve the life situation of persons at risk (Marlier et al, 2007). Only recently have MIP systems themselves, come into the focus of these activities. In 2009, the EU Network of Independent Experts on Social Inclusion produced a synthesis report on 'Minimum income schemes across EU member states' (Frazer and Marlier, 2009) based on the national reports prepared by the independent experts. These reports provide an assessment and critical evaluation of MIP schemes for the non-disabled working-age population and display a focus on the issues of labour market integration and 'activation'. Two shortcomings of the study are that other categorical schemes are only mentioned in passing and that the synthesis report does not provide straightforward comparative indicators. Only for some countries is more differentiated information given. Nonetheless, this study is a very valuable up-to-date source for assessing the institutional complexities and variations of MIP systems in EU member states. The mutual information system on social protection in the member states of the European Union (MISSOC) (European Commission, 2010) also regularly produces comparative overviews of MIP schemes in EU countries. The focus, however, was mainly on the general last safety net whereas other categorical schemes only started to be compared more systematically in 2010.

The OECD has also produced a number of reports dealing with MIP. Among the first was a relatively comprehensive two-volume study on 'the battle against exclusion' (OECD 1998a; 1998b). This study investigated social assistance arrangements in eight countries (Volume 1: Australia, Finland, Sweden, and the United Kingdom; Volume 2: Belgium, the Czech Republic, the Netherlands, and Norway). The perspective was twofold: the institutional arrangements were analysed, and the situation of a number of groups at risk was studied, including the unemployed, single parents, young persons, and immigrants. The study also included data on benefit receipt. The focus of the subsequent OECD reports has increasingly shifted towards the issues of labour market integration and activation. Population groups with problems in access to paid work are of primary interest in this respect, especially the long-term unemployed and single parents (Immervoll, 2010). In most cases, however, the OECD studies focus on entitlement conditions for various groups, on benefit levels and work incentives, and on activation requirements. The whole spectrum of MIP benefits is not analysed in any of these publications, neither is there a systematic collection of data on recipients of MIP benefits.

The OECD and the Dutch NEI Labour and Education institute at Rotterdam undertook a comparative study on benefit receipt on behalf of the Netherlands Ministry of Social Affairs and Employment (Cluitmans et al, 2001; Moor et al, 2002). This study investigated benefit dependency at working age, including unemployment benefits, disability, and MIP benefits, although the MIP benefits, themselves, were not always clearly defined. Various existing categorical programmes were omitted, for the focus was on the general last safety net. Moreover, the problem of double-counting beneficiaries occurs when mixing different kinds of benefits and MIP schemes if administrative statistics are adopted without correction for benefit combination. This approach is explained and justified by the focus of these studies on target groups rather than benefit systems. Carcillo and Grubb (2006) expanded these time series on benefit receipt up to 2004, building on the Dutch study and using similar definitions (see also OECD, 2003, for a detailed description of the methodology; for a study on benefit coverage rates for different household types building on the same data, see Immervoll et al, 2004). While very valuable as a data source and for analysing the situation of specific target groups, the data share the limitations of the initial Dutch study. In order to avoid the problem of double-counting in our own study and at the same time arrive at a comprehensive assessment of MIP schemes, we focus on benefits that are mutually exclusive because they serve the same basic function of MIP. No other comparable study with more recent data has been undertaken to our knowledge.

The International Labour Organization (ILO) also produced a number of studies on minimum income schemes. In a study on such schemes in Europe (Standing, 2003), in-depth country reports and analyses for France, Portugal, Italy, Ireland, Finland, Belgium, and Greece were published. Again, as in many studies of this kind, the country information is very valuable, but the scope of comparison is limited. In more recent ILO studies, the focus has been shifted to the institutionalisation of safety nets in developing nations and countries at the take-off level. A concise overview of this process is given by Barrientos and Holmes (2006) and Leisering (2008). This worldwide perspective is not further explored in this book.

MIP played a minor role in mainstream comparative social policy research until recently, although a close analysis and understanding of the welfare state is impossible without taking the last safety net into account. This is especially true if the focus is on social citizenship rights. Among the comparative studies of MIP, a few major themes and perspectives are prominent. The vast majority of studies have focused solely on MIP benefit levels compared with wages or the relative poverty threshold. The database for this kind of analysis has been greatly improved in recent years due to the activities of the Organisation for Economic Co-operation and Development (OECD) and a number of research projects, among which those of the Social Science Research Institute (SOFI) at the University of Stockholm and of the Centre for Social Policy (CSB) at the University of Antwerp are the most important. The OECD provides model income calculations (tax benefit models) that include the case of social assistance recipients for each year from 2001 until 2008 (at the time of writing), based on existing national regulations (OECD, various years). At the SOFI, Nelson established the SaMip (social assistance and minimum income protection) database, which provides an alternative to the OECD models for the case of social assistance recipients (Nelson, 2007a, 2010). It covers more countries over a longer period of time and applies an alternative method for estimating housing costs and housing benefits. These differences in approach have a strong impact on the results of the model estimates on MIP benefit levels because housing costs are often fully covered by schemes. The first section of Chapter Four provides a detailed description of the two alternative approaches. The CSB has also undertaken a number of studies on benefit levels in social assistance based on project-related data gathered by national informants (Cantillon et al, 2008). Jonathan Bradshaw and his research team at the Social Policy Research Unit at the University of York were the pioneers of the model family approach, and they have published extensively on the methodology and the results of this method in various social-policy fields.

The results of the studies mentioned differ in many respects because the databases are different and some crucial assumptions of the model calculations also differ. However, the results do agree on a number of important aspects. First of all, they show huge international variations in estimated MIP benefit levels. Second, they show that MIP benefits do not lift recipients above the relative at-risk-of-poverty line of 60% of the median net equivalent household income in most countries, even though all existing legal benefits in these models are assumed to be fully taken up by entitled persons and completely granted by welfare administrations. This assumption is, of course, heroic in the sense that many survey-based studies have shown that real take-up rates vary between 40% and 70% (see also Behrendt, 2002). This aspect is further discussed in Chapter Four. Third, the studies on benefit levels show great variations in the treatment of different household and family types that are not always internationally consistent. In most countries families with children are treated better than single persons in terms of standardised income levels. Van Mechelen (2009) provides a sound and detailed methodological assessment of the different approaches and compares the results of various studies in this field.

The number of studies dealing with the conditionality of MIP benefits has also grown in recent years. Most significantly, activation requirements have become an important element of research in MIP systems. These studies have investigated the shifting balance between social rights and individual duties within MIP systems. One of the first important contributions in comparative perspective was the study *'An offer you can't refuse':Workfare in international perspective* by Lødemel and Trickey (2001). In this volume, the authors distinguish between highly visible centralised programmes with many beneficiaries and a high degree of unity on the one hand and more localised and less visible programmes on the other. Other studies have parallel differences in emphasis of either 'workfare' elements or human capital development (eg Jensen, 1999).

Additionally, edited volumes with detailed country studies on activation have been published by Serrano Pascual and Magnusson (2007) and Eichhorst et al (2008). Both volumes cover Denmark, France, Germany, the Netherlands, Sweden, and the UK. The first volume also includes Spain, Portugal, and the Czech Republic, while the second additionally investigated Switzerland and the US. While the dimension of activation constitutes an important element of MIP schemes, we do not systematically investigate this dimension because of the large existing body of specialised literature in this field (for recent efforts to classify countries and develop comparative quantitative indicators, see Dingeldey, 2007; Serrano Pascual, 2007; Aurich, 2011).

A third type of study has focused on institutional aspects of MIP systems, for example, on the impact of centralisation and decentralisation on benefit levels. Here, Hölsch and Kraus (2004) have made an important contribution, investigating the relationship between (de-)centralisation and the (re-)distributive impact of social assistance schemes. Their results show that this relation is by no means clear. In a second study published in 2006, Hölsch and Kraus investigated how other institutional aspects of social assistance schemes affect their performance, effectiveness, and efficiency in reducing poverty. According to their results, a high share of social assistance in the population often complements greater distributive effectiveness, whereas a higher budget for social assistance or even higher benefit levels do not always stand for high effectiveness and efficiency at reducing poverty.

In addition, there are a number of studies that provide rich, in-depth information on MIP systems in a smaller number of cases. In a study on social assistance dynamics in Europe (Saraceno, 2002), the last safety net is analysed at the local level in six European countries (Sweden, France, Italy, Spain, Germany, and Portugal). The study investigates the implementation of the residual MIP scheme at the local level, focusing on high-risk population groups such as single parents and immigrants. The rich information provided in this study, however, is limited to the general last safety net and does not look at other categorical programmes that are often regulated at the national rather than local level. A number of studies have focused on similar country cases, allowing for a finer and more detailed differential analysis. Kuivalainen (2004a) studied the Nordic countries in great depth, providing a historical comparative analysis of the development of the general last safety net in these states compared with some other European countries, such as the Netherlands and Britain. The focus is on the institutionalisation of (nationally defined) social citizenship rights in contrast to or in combination with locally organised systems of poor relief. The balance between the two poles is important for the institutional setup of the last safety net. This balance has been shifting towards the state, but it differs greatly between countries. Today, one can observe a partial shift back towards local discretion in some cases. Cerami (2006) analysed Eastern European countries and found that most of these countries introduced social assistance schemes early during the transition, usually in the form of a general last safety net, but the level of provision varies greatly and is often low in terms of benefit levels and access. Southern European countries are the latecomers in the institutionalisation of last safety nets. This fact and the causes and problems related to it are studied in the book *Welfare state reform in Southern Europe*, edited by Ferrera (2005). The study provides in-depth analyses of MIP systems in Italy, Spain, Portugal, and Greece on their difficult paths to establishing basic general social citizenship rights.

MIP research has doubtless gained ground in recent years, for the problems of persisting poverty and the failure to guarantee a minimum standard of living to all European citizens have become pertinent. However, a comprehensive, up-to-date comparative study of whole MIP systems in relation to the wider welfare state has been missing until now. To our knowledge, the major reference in the field is still the first comprehensive comparative study on MIP undertaken by *Eardley* et al in the mid-1990s (1996), describing the situation at the beginning of the 1990s. This study was also a major reference for our own project. The main results of this study are referred to in Chapter Four with respect to the different types of social assistance regimes that were identified by the authors.

Since 1992, however, MIP systems have significantly changed in many European countries. Some countries have introduced new MIP schemes; other schemes were abolished or integrated into other schemes. Portugal introduced a general last safety net in 1996, and Austria established national standards for the regionally organised MIP systems in 2010. In Germany, a new MIP scheme for the unemployed was established in 2005 and included almost 8% of the total population by 2010. These examples show that a great deal of change has happened in the field of MIP. Therefore, a comparative, up-to-date assessment of MIP systems in Europe is urgently needed.

Even though Eardley and his colleagues' study served as our starting point, there are two important differences between that study and our own approach. First of all, Eardley et al's study compared social assistance systems by applying a wide definition to this kind of benefit. The definition covered almost all means-tested benefits, including minimum income guarantees (as do we) as well as means-tested family and housing benefits, other more specifically targeted benefits, and benefits with an income test designed to filter out only the richest persons. Our own definition is more limited (see Chapter One for details): it covers only those schemes that guarantee a basic income amount, which is not the case with family or housing benefits. These benefits are often received in addition to a basic income guarantee and therefore have to be included in calculating actual benefit rates, but they do not themselves constitute an MIP guarantee. This distinction is crucial for an adequate assessment of MIP recipient data. The second major difference between the two studies is that the former entailed richer institutional and policy information than does our project, but it did not aim at developing comparative indicators. The focus of our study is on a few main indicators, but it also provides the necessary institutional background information for each country.

Plan of the book

The book provides a comprehensive and up-to-date comparative assessment of MIP systems in 17 European countries, covering the period from 1992 to 2010. It is the result of a research project that was funded by the Hans-Böckler-Stiftung and the Mannheimer Zentrum für Europäische Sozialforschung (MZES) in Germany. The data provided in the book and most of the analyses are based on the newly developed project database on MIP systems that is available to the public for scientific use.

The project's approach is distinctive and original in a number of respects. First, the perspective on MIP is comprehensive and covers all schemes existing in each country. Therefore, it provides a complete analysis of national MIP systems, including general and categorical programmes for different population groups. Second, the project looks into the relationships between MIP systems and overall social protection arrangements in a comparative perspective. The function that MIP systems fulfil for different population groups can only be adequately understood if social protection arrangements above the level of the last safety net are considered. There is great international variation in that respect, which has a strong impact on the need for MIP and the salience of MIP schemes. Third, the project combines the analysis of country-specific institutional arrangements, with a straightforward comparative approach based on quantitative and qualitative indicators that are also available in the database. Fourth, the book analyses comparative data on various aspects and dimensions of MIP systems, and it provides a comprehensive assessment that includes not only benefit levels but also the number of recipients, expenditure data, and the categorical differentiation of MIP systems.

A detailed description of the data sources and the methods applied for calculating the comparative indicators is given in Chapter One. Since most studies have focused on the issue of benefit levels and at the same time been limited to the general scheme in each country, our approach is a significant step forward for a comparative assessment of MIP systems. The data we provide offer a complete picture of MIP in each country, including all benefits that can be subsumed under this category. This is quite important because the general MIP scheme often only covers a small proportion of those persons who actually depend on any kind of MIP. Even more important are the issues of benefit receipt and expenditure on MIP. So far, no comparative data on benefit receipt and social expenditure on MIP benefits are available. Data on numbers of recipients are only available at the national and institutional levels, making international comparison rather difficult. In our comparative database, we have calculated national aggregates based on various official data sources in each country. Expenditure data on means-tested social benefits are provided by both Eurostat (2010) (European System of Social Protection Statistics) and the OECD (Social Expenditure Database; OECD, 2010a). However, most MIP schemes in both data systems are included among a catch-all residual statistical category with very different kinds of benefits, not all of which can be regarded as MIP. At the same time, some MIP schemes are subsumed in other categories of benefits, for example, in the old-age function. For our database, we collected expenditure data from various national sources at the institutional level and calculated national aggregates for MIP systems for comparative purposes on that basis.

This book addresses three main questions:

- What are the similarities and differences between MIP systems in EU countries?
- How are these similarities and differences related to variations in overall social security systems?
- What developments and trends can be observed for European MIP systems?

These questions are analysed in the following way. The first two chapters set the scene for the subsequent empirical analysis by delineating the meaning of MIP and placing it into the wider welfare state context. Chapter One develops a comparative definition of MIP and distinguishes it from other kinds of social benefits. This is not always an easy task because the boundaries are sometimes shifting or ambiguous. In addition, Chapter One describes the main characteristics of the database on which this book's analysis is based. Chapter Two studies the welfare state context in which MIP systems are institutionally embedded. The focus is on social arrangements for three population groups: older persons, unemployed people, and single parents. These groups have a high risk of falling into the last safety net if other social provisions fail to protect them adequately. The chapter concludes with hypotheses on the role and salience of MIP systems that are derived from these inter-country variations in the protectiveness of social security systems.

The empirical analysis of the book consists of two main parts. The first part (Chapter Three) provides a country-by-country analysis of MIP systems. Each of these country studies first gives a brief overview of the welfare state context for MIP systems and then analyses their institutional setting and main structural developments with a focus on recipient numbers. The second part (Chapter Four) presents the results of inter-country analyses based on comparative indicators, using national aggregate data for comparison. The sections focus on benefit levels, the number of recipients, social expenditure, and categorical differentiation of MIP systems. The final section of Chapter Four provides a summarising cluster analysis of cross-national patterns of European MIP systems.

The conclusion summarises the results by looking at three main themes. The first is the broad comparative pattern that shows up in the analysis. Is it possible to identify different 'families of nations' of MIP systems in Europe? If so, how are these patterns related to the overall welfare state context? The second theme is developments over time. Is it possible to identify common trends among all countries, or do different developments in different country groups prevail, thus lending support to the concept of path dependency? If so, what have been the causes for these common or different developments? The third and final section of the conclusion presents a preliminary analysis of the impact of the current

(2008–10) crisis on MIP systems. Most of the comparative analyses in the previous sections cover the period of 1990–2008 (sometimes also including 2009) due to the usual time lag in the production and publication of administrative data in most countries. However, for some cases, we have more recent data up to 2009 or 2010, which allow for a partial analysis of the crisis' impact on the institutional structure of MIP systems and benefit receipt. A central intent is to relate past and present developments and to draw conclusions on the future of the identified patterns of MIP in Europe.

ONE

Defining and measuring minimum income protection

This chapter introduces the conceptual and empirical basis of the project. The first section provides the project's definition of minimum income protection (MIP) and delineates the object of investigation. The second part gives an overview of the data sources and the structure of the database that forms the empirical foundation of the study.

Defining MIP

Each country's social security system is unique in its institutional architecture and in the relationships between its constituting elements. The design of MIP systems and their role within the welfare state vary both internationally and over time. The first major challenge is therefore to develop a common definition of MIP for all countries that is applicable to different contexts. As argued in the Introduction to this book, MIP is characterised by a twofold function: to provide the residual last safety net and to guarantee the social minimum below which no one in society should be allowed to fall.

From the residual character follows the first defining element of MIP schemes: the means test. MIP benefits are granted when all other social benefits are either not provided or exhausted, or if they do not satisfy basic needs. From the social minimum character follows the second defining element: the minimum income guarantee. MIP benefits can be distinguished from other kinds of social benefits on this basis as shown in Table 1.1.

MIP benefits provide a social minimum based on a means test. Tied benefits are different from MIP because they do not provide a social minimum. Examples of tied benefits include means-tested family allowances and housing benefits. These benefits do not qualify as MIP because they are provided for specific purposes

Table 1.1: The character of MIP benefits

Test of means	Guarantee of social minimum	
	Yes	No
Yes	MIP (e.g. income support)	Tied benefits (e.g. housing benefit)
No	Basic benefits (e.g. basic pension)	Wage-related benefits (e.g. sick pay)

Source: Authors' depiction.

and do not aim at covering all the basic needs of a person or household. However, tied benefits are often part of the MIP benefit package because they are provided in addition to MIP in specific situations of need. In these cases, tied benefits are an element of MIP but should not be confused with the basic MIP benefit, itself. This point is especially relevant for calculating MIP recipient rates among the population. Since the receipt of the two benefit types partly overlaps, the recipient data cannot be added up. Moreover, the extent of overlap cannot usually be seen from administrative statistics. There are also cases when tied benefits are granted without parallel receipt of MIP benefits. In combination with recipients' own earnings or other social benefits (apart from MIP), tied benefits do not fulfil the criterion for a residual benefit, either.

Basic benefits differ from MIP because they are not based on a means test and therefore do not fulfil the criterion for a residual benefit. Basic pensions are provided to all older persons, not just to those in need without means. Although basic pensions provide a guaranteed income for older persons in society, they do not require need. This is a fundamental difference to MIP. MIP is strongly based on rights in most European countries today, distinguishing it from the old poor laws, but the means test continues to be an important element that emphasises the residual character of these schemes.

The distinction between MIP and wage-related benefits is clear in both dimensions. If social benefits are provided on the basis of (previous) individual earnings, the aim is to guarantee not a social minimum but rather individual living standards or status. Moreover, usually no means test is applied, showing that these benefits are not designed specifically for needy persons. This dimension has important consequences for the design of benefits. MIP benefits are not provided on an individual basis in most cases, but they take into account the family or household constellation in which a claimant lives. This is not the case for the majority of wage-related benefits. With respect to need, MIP benefits usually vary by size and composition of the family or household, whereas wage-related benefits usually vary by individual wages and do not take into account household or family needs. With respect to the means test, MIP benefits usually also take into account the resources of the whole household or family unit; this is not the case for wage-related benefits.

Although these distinctions seem to be rather straightforward theoretically, in practice there are borderline areas that require case-by-case decisions. In general, the project follows a strict rule of definition, meaning that the preference is to exclude the respective benefit from the scope of MIP in ambiguous cases. The rule of strictness ensures that only those benefits that clearly fulfil the definition are included. The results of the book therefore tend to underestimate the scope and salience of MIP in some countries rather than to provide exaggerated data. Since one hypothesis of the book is the growing relevance of MIP, this rule of thumb is a conservative mode of testing the assumption.

The borderline cases can be situated in three different areas. The first two areas concern social benefits that are either means-tested or aim to provide a guaranteed minimum and thus fulfil one of the two defining characteristics of

MIP, the second one being ambiguous. The third area concerns cases in which both defining elements are fulfilled but additional conditions beyond need are required by claimants. For each of these areas, the most important cases and the decision that is taken in the project are briefly discussed.

The first borderline area springs from the fact that the level of the guaranteed social minimum can vary substantially between different population groups. The social minimum for unemployed people may be set at a different income level from those for older persons or for persons who have not been attached to the labour market. In these cases, we apply a rule of thumb. We generally include all these different categorical benefits if they are mutually exclusive because the different levels then clearly stand for different categorical social minima depending on social status. This information also holds highly relevant implications for the perspective of social citizenship rights in the welfare state. If such categorical differences exist, there are also different levels of basic social citizenship rights in a country (see Chapter Four).

The second area with problems of demarcation can be attributed to the varying extent and scope of means-testing. Extent in this case means the number of persons who are included in the test, whereas scope refers to the income components that are taken into consideration. In both respects, the means test varies widely between countries and between MIP schemes. The more household or family members are taken into account, the stricter the means test is. This is usually the case for the most residual last safety net in a country. The means test is applied in its mildest form if only one component of individual income is considered. These varying relationships and the decisions that are applied by the project with respect to delineating MIP are shown in Table 1.2.

Table 1.2 shows only the most extreme cases in a simplified way. In fact, the two dimensions are actually more differentiated because there are different grades of means-testing in between. The general rule is that we include only such benefits among MIP if most income components are taken into account in the means test. Only then does the scheme have a strongly residual character. This is not the case for basic pensions in Sweden and Finland. Since the early 2000s, these basic pensions have been income-tested, but only against individual earnings and individual pension income from statutory occupational schemes. Therefore, these mildly means-tested pensions are not included among MIP benefits (Chapter Two). The general rule for inclusion is that the means test is applied to the family or household, or that it takes into account most income components.

Table 1.2: The means test in MIP schemes

Extent of means test	Scope of means test	
	One component	All components
Individual	Not MIP	MIP
All household members	(Not relevant)	Strongly MIP

Source: Authors' depiction.

The third group of borderline cases is usually easier to decide upon. Here, the two defining conditions for MIP (the means test and social minimum) are fulfilled, but a third condition that makes the benefit more exclusive is also required. In some countries, means-tested MIP benefits exist for recipients of social insurance pensions or for long-term unemployed persons. In Austria and Spain, pensioners can get a means-tested pension supplement if their income falls below the legally defined minimum threshold. In France, long-term unemployed people with long work histories are entitled to a means-tested unemployment assistance benefit after their entitlements to wage-related unemployment insurance benefits are exhausted. These cases are all included among MIP benefits as special categorical schemes. The main difference from other categorical MIP schemes is that an additional condition is required – in most cases, social insurance status and long work records.

A fourth important distinction often raises a great deal of discussion. A few countries have the rare combination of wage-related and means-tested benefits, above all for long-term unemployment. This is the case in Austria and was the case in Germany until 2004. Long-term unemployed persons with long insurance records who had previously received insurance benefits are entitled to wage-related unemployment assistance if their income falls below a certain threshold. The wage replacement rate is lower than in first-tier unemployment insurance, but in principle, the benefit is still related to individual wages rather than to actual household or family needs. Therefore, this type of benefit is excluded from the scope of MIP. It does not provide a social minimum. If the wage-related benefit exceeds the guaranteed minimum, it is no MIP benefit. If, by contrast, it falls below the guaranteed amount for the household, the recipients are entitled to additional MIP benefits that lift their household's income to the guaranteed minimum level (for Austria, see Chapter Three).

These grey areas and ambiguous cases have been described in some detail because they show that the distinction between MIP and other social benefits is far from self evident. The decisions that are made by the project have consequences for the comparative assessment and measurement provided in the book. In general, we include the categorically differentiated schemes but exclude benefits that only apply a mild form of means test. We also exclude benefits that do not provide a social minimum and therefore can often be combined with a truly residual MIP benefit. This rule is most relevant for calculating the share of the population that lives on MIP benefits in each country. Recipient data are crucial for both key aspects of MIP: the residual character and the guarantee of a social minimum in society.

Data

The analyses in this book are based on the EuMin database, which was developed under the research project Social Assistance in Europe. Indicators of Minimum Income Security Schemes at the MZES. The project was funded by the

Hans-Böckler-Stiftung from 2008 to 2010, and one of its major aims was the development of a database containing institutional, quantitative, and comparative indicators of MIP. At the end of the project in December 2010, the database included 17 member states of the European Union and covered the period 1992–2009. Most of the data that this book draws on refer to a core period between 1995 and 2007. Information for the early 1990s and for more recent years was not fully available in every country, but for the core period the data allow for sound comparisons both between countries and over time.

The contents of the database spring from multiple sources. The purpose was to compile existing information available from various international resources into one framework of comparative variables and to enrich the picture with more detailed information on institutional settings and quantitative facts on caseloads and expenditure. Benefit rates were adopted from the OECD Benefits and Wages database (OECD, various years), SaMip (Nelson, 2007a, 2010), and MISSOC (European Commission, 2010). MISSOC data also offer information on the regulation of MIP, but statements are often vague and not easily comparable between countries. The most important data sources for EuMin, therefore, were statistics and legal documents available at the websites of national governments, statistical offices, and the administrating bodies of benefit schemes. This approach has led to a vast number of data resources, even for a single country, but a detailed analysis of these resources would go beyond the scope of this book. The EuMin database is available as an online service for researchers and policymakers as of September 2011 via the MZES website.[1] A complete documentation of all data sources is available at the same webpage. EuMin will thereby be given as reference for national data in the book. International resources will, however, be quoted where relevant.

Another reason that made the use of manifold data sources necessary is in the nature of the national MIP systems themselves. In many cases, the last safety net is a composition of several MIP benefits for different target groups. These schemes are often administered by various agencies at different government levels, and data reporting is seldom standardised for the whole of a national MIP system. Determining the total of beneficiaries and expenditure in a country therefore requires the sighting and integration of several statistical sources. The following sections describe how problems arising from this complexity were solved methodologically in the process of data collection. First, the structure of the database is presented; then the issues of comparability and lack of data are addressed.

The structure of the EuMin database

The EuMin database is organised into three sections that cover institutional data, quantitative data, and comparative indicators for 13 observation years (1992, 1995, 1998, and 2000–9) in 17 countries. An overview of the database structure is given in Table 1.3.

The first part of the database contains institutional information on the countries' main schemes of MIP. This limitation was inevitable because the level

Table 1.3: Structure of EuMin

Case definition:		
– Country		
– Year		
Subject area:		
Institutional information		
– Regulation		
– Eligibility		
– Subsidiarity		
– Activation		
– Benefit rates		
– Income models		
Quantitative information		
Data on recipients, beneficiaries, and expenditure at the:		
– System level		
– Aggregate level		
Comparative indicators		
– Categorical differentiation		
– Benefit levels		
– Scope		
– Expenditure		

Source: Authors' depiction.

of fragmentation of MIP varied strongly between countries. The number of MIP schemes ranges from only one in the Czech Republic and Slovakia to as many as 13 in Ireland. In many cases, it is neither useful nor feasible to quantify all institutional nuances and gradations of all of the schemes that exist in one country. Instead, the most relevant scheme was selected along two criteria: 1) a significant weight within the overall MIP system in terms of expenditure and beneficiaries and 2) a central role in the protection of a minimum income for broad segments of the population. Hence, even if MIP for older or disabled persons plays a bigger role in quantitative terms in some countries, such as Spain or Belgium, the priority was given to the more general benefit schemes for the working-age population[2].

Regarding content, the first part of EuMin covers basic data on the name, founding year, and organisational and financing principles of the main benefit as well as more detailed information on target groups, eligibility conditions, and the subsidiary and activating character of the scheme. A substantial part of this section is dedicated to the household income that can be attained by means of MIP benefits. For this purpose, the official benefit rates are complemented with income models that also take family benefits and housing allowances into account. Benefit rates and income models are furthermore presented for four household types: single and couple households, both with and without dependent children.

The second part of the database includes information on expenditure and the number of persons receiving MIP benefits. The latter distinguishes between the number of claimants alone (recipients) and claimants including their dependent household members (beneficiaries). The data is issued on two levels of aggregation:

On the system level, the data is issued separately for every benefit scheme existent in one country. The sum of recipients, beneficiaries, and expenditure for every country is provided at the aggregate level.

The last section of EuMin is a set of quantitative indicators designed to facilitate the comparison of European MIP systems. Next to information on the categorical differentiation of the overall system, this set of data contains mainly comparative indicators on the guaranteed income levels, the scope of benefit receipt, and expenditure in relation to a series of reference parameters. The benefit levels are related to the 50% and 60% poverty thresholds of equivalised median income and to minimum wages (if applicable) in order to relate them to national income distributions and wage scales. The benefit levels are also given as both a percentage of the GDP per capita and of Purchasing Power Parities to give an impression of their economic significance for different types of households. When looking at the scope of MIP, it is important to identify the impact MIP has on different parts of the population. Therefore, the total number of beneficiaries (that is, recipients and their household members) is related to the total size of the population. The number of recipients, on the other hand, is used when the significance of MIP for certain subgroups of the population is assessed, namely the working-age population, the unemployed, and the population above age 65. Finally, indicators on expenditure differentiate between MIP's salience in the welfare state, measured as its share of total social spending, and its significance in economic terms by relating MIP expenditure to the GDP.

Problems of comparability

During the process of data collection, several obstacles to achieving data comparability occurred. Due to the complexity of MIP systems and their embeddedness in very different welfare state contexts, particular difficulties arose in the adequate presentation of caseloads and benefit levels. Data availability was also an issue in some countries, primarily for the years prior to 2000.

When analysing MIP transfers, it is essential to keep in mind that the benefit rates officially published by government departments or MISSOC (European Commission, 2010) do not always correspond to the actual disposable income of beneficiaries. Denmark, for example, publishes benefit rates that surpass the rates of all other European countries, but these are gross amounts that are subject to income tax. Benefits are also taxable in the Netherlands, but the rates published by the government represent net values. Further problems of comparability stem from the issue of family benefits, which are sometimes included in the regular MIP rate for family households. In other cases, they are paid additionally or are deducted from the official amount. Housing benefits can cause the resulting household income to differ considerably from the basic guaranteed income amounts. In this case, regional variation in housing costs within countries is also a factor that complicates the assessment of minimum income levels. Moreover, some countries only have framework legislation, leaving specific decisions about housing allowances to the regional or municipal level, sometimes even on a case-by-case basis.

In order to make balanced statements about the income situation of households on benefits, EuMin includes income models that make use of different assumptions for estimating the actual level of MIP. The models of the SaMip database (Nelson, 2007a, 2010) are available in EuMin for the years 1992 to 2009. The calculations of SaMip are based primarily on the approach of Eardley et al (1996) but include a higher number of countries. Because the data on housing benefits in SaMip are not always comparable across countries and because there is no information given on the situation of couple households without children, the income models of OECD Benefits and Wages (OECD, various years) are also included in the database. Here, consistent assumptions about housing costs are made across countries. Nevertheless, these can also lead to over- or underestimations of housing allowances (cp Chapter 4.1).

Further difficulties arise when information on the scope of benefit receipt is gathered. Although most MIP transfers are oriented at the financial situation of households, in some countries, only the heads of households are captured by administrative statistics, while in others, all household members are counted. Reporting data on all beneficiaries of MIP is certainly the more interesting variant from a sociological perspective, and wherever possible, their number was estimated when solely recipient numbers were available from administrations. In most of these cases, official population statistics on the average household size of recipients and the size of households in different income groups served as the basis for estimations. However, as stated previously, both recipients and beneficiaries were included in the database because both flowed into the comparative data section in different ways according to the purpose of the respective indicators.

Finally, the problem of missing data needs to be solved in order to reach a stage at which indicators can be adequately interpreted. Essential information on various topics is not available for some countries and years. This does not affect all parts of the database to the same extent, but the issue should not be overlooked, especially in the quantitative and comparative sections. The problem may concern recipient, beneficiary, or expenditure data for one or more MIP systems at a time, but it also applies to reference data used for computing the comparative indicators (for example, median income). As in the case of beneficiary numbers, estimates were made where possible. However, some cells needed to be left empty. Wherever indicators might be biased by partly missing data or estimation procedures, this was made recognisable in the database. Details on these matters are included in the documentation of the dataset, which is available at the EuMin website.

For the analysis of this book, the second and third part of the database will primarily be used. Chapter Three mostly draws on quantitative data on the system level while Chapter Four draws on comparative quantitative indicators as well as on income models and information on the categorical differentiation of MIP schemes.

Notes

[1] www.mzes.uni-mannheim.de.

[2] The following schemes are defined as main benefit in the EuMin database:

AT: *Sozialhilfe der Länder*

BE: *Revenu d'integration sociale/Leefloon* (before 2003: *Minimum de moyens d'existence/ bestaansminimum*)

CZ: *Hmotná nouze* (before 2007: *Sociální potřebnost*)

DE: *Grundsicherung für Arbeitsuchende* (before 2005: *Sozialhilfe*)

DK: *Kontanthjælp* (before 2005: *Social bistand*)

ES: As an institutional example of the regional '*rentas mínimas*': *Renta mínima de inserción de la Comunidad de Madrid* (before 2002: *Ingreso Madrileño de Integración*)

FI: *Toimeentulotuki*

FR: *Revenu minimum d'insertion*

HU: *Rendszeres szociális segély* (RSZS)

IE: Supplementary welfare allowance

NL: *Algemene bijstand* (before 1996: *Sociale bijstand*)

PL: *Zasilek Okresowy*

PT: *Rendimento social de inserção* (before 2004: *Rendimento minimo garantido*)

SE: *Ekonomiskt bistånd* (before 2002: *Social bidrag*)

SK: *Pomoc v hmotnej núdzi* (1998–2003: *Sociálna pomoc; before 1998: Sociálna starostlivost*)

UK: Income support

TWO

Welfare state contexts

Introduction

MIP is a means of securing a basic standard of living for those population groups that are not adequately covered and protected by social insurance or general non-means-tested benefits. Hence, the role of MIP in the welfare state context can be interpreted as residual. On the other hand, a close look at the margins of the welfare state gives insights into the contents and limits of social citizenship rights as defined by Marshall in 1950 (Leibfried, 1992; Marshall and Bottomore, 1992). Even if residual in quantitative terms, MIP is a central policy instrument for promoting citizens' chances to participate in society. Nonetheless, European welfare states have institutionalised their last safety nets in different ways. While most countries in the study sample have a centrally organised, general MIP scheme, many also rely on categorical benefits for specific groups, such as older and disabled persons or refugees. Some countries' MIP schemes are more decentralised, with varying benefit levels and degrees of discretion at the regional or local level. In legal terms, MIP does not always take the form of a subjective citizenship right but rests on a more general notion about social support for the poor, leaving room for interpretation and coverage gaps. Regardless of its formal status, MIP frequently remains an 'incomplete social right' (Saraceno, 2010, p 171) and can only be understood in context with other forms of income protection.

According to Miller (1976, 1999), the right to benefits is based on statements of social justice that depend on the various kinds of relationships that connect people in society. He distinguishes three modes of relationship: 1) solidaric community; 2) instrumental association; and 3) citizenship. A solidaric community is characterised by its stability over time and the shared identity and culture of its members. It is the basic type of relationship in families or religious communities. Need is the main principle of distribution based on solidarity, and entitlements depend on how closely linked persons are to the community. An instrumental association exists when people collaborate in order to achieve a common aim, as they do, for example, in a market relationship or organisation. The criterion of justice in this case is desert: members who have contributed more to the association's goals are eligible to more social support. The third kind of relation is labelled citizenship and springs from the fact that members of modern societies are also connected politically, as equal citizens. Hence, the principle of justice following from citizenship is equality. While solidaric communities and instrumental associations have been shaping social justice throughout history, citizenship is a relatively new concept, at least in the way it is understood today. For a long time, a person's status as a citizen was defined not by equality but by certain characteristics, such as birth rights, gender, property, or some kind of desert. It is only in the past three centuries that civil, political, and lastly social citizenship rights have been generalised. The purest form of welfare provision based on citizenship is therefore universal benefits. Nevertheless, the principles of desert and need have not vanished from the scene, as they are present in modern welfare states in the form of contribution- and wage-related social insurance schemes and MIP as an expression of national solidarity.

In order to understand the role of MIP in a country, it is essential to know which principles of distribution dominate the overall welfare state context. Here, a look at welfare state typologies is promising, since many use welfare ideology as an explanatory variable (Abrahamson 1999). The regime types distinguished by Esping-Andersen (1990), for example, are labelled after the main sociopolitical ideas that historically shaped welfare states. Their redistributive impact can be measured by their effects on social stratification and the level of decommodification. Both concepts can be interpreted as indicators of social citizenship rights, since the first measures the equalising effect of income redistribution while the second stands for the degree to which incomes can be secured independently from the market (for an overview on the measurement of social rights and available sources, see Stephens, 2010). In a liberal welfare regime, public social protection is usually granted when the market and the family fail to provide a sufficient income. Social policy is poverty oriented and strongly depends on means-tested benefits, while social insurance and universal benefits are limited. Accordingly, other scholars, such as Titmuss (1974) and Leibfried (1992), would label this welfare model 'residual'. Esping-Andersen's second regime type is the conservative-corporatist welfare state that, in Titmuss' terms, would have been called an 'achievement-performance model'. Here, social rights are attached to labour-market performance and status, and are granted within a corporatist and employment-based social insurance system that is based on accrued rights and excludes parts of the population. The social democratic welfare regime type, on the other hand, is characterised by inclusive social insurance and universal, citizenship-based social rights. Decommodification is highest in this type of welfare state, and welfare state institutions strongly counterbalance market inequalities.

Returning to social justice, it is evident that the citizenship-based principle of equality is strongest in the social democratic welfare regime type. Here, MIP systems should be universal but also residual and actually very limited. Social distribution in the corporate-conservative welfare regime is influenced more by judgements on desert and merit, because entitlements to social benefits largely rest on rights accrued through the payment of contributions during economic activity. MIP systems should be categorical and residual for certain groups rather than universal, and their size should also depend to a certain extent on labour market structures and developments. The poverty orientation of liberal welfare states should lead to a focus on need and therefore on MIP and other means-tested benefits. The status of MIP as a social citizenship right should somehow be limited since priority is given to income distribution via the market. This limitation should be reflected by low replacement rates and highly fluctuating recipient numbers in line with business cycles.

In the first comprehensive comparative study of social assistance in OECD countries, Eardley et al (1996) and Gough et al (1997) did not find such a nice neat pattern among the countries; rather, the authors noted strong variations in Esping-Andersen's liberal and conservative regime types, while the social-democratic world was relatively homogeneous. The authors actually identified seven social assistance types, five of which included EU countries (see Chapter Four), yet the marked differences in MIP systems in both the liberal and the conservative welfare states are not explained. Such an explanation could come from two directions. First, a threefold typology might be insufficient for analysing a specific welfare state area in detail (Abrahamson, 1999). Considering the Southern European countries as a distinct welfare state regime type might shed light on the variations in the conservative-corporatist group of countries. With regard to MIP, it is important to know that social security in the Mediterranean countries is more fragmented than in other Continental European countries, with stronger contrasts between well-protected and under- or non-protected social groups. Moreover, the family and the third sector play a strong institutionalised part as providers of welfare and social services (Ferrera, 1996, 2005). Another major point of discussion is whether the Central and Eastern European countries can be perceived as a distinct group of their own. Political and economic transition has led to 'a "layering" of inherited communist, revived Bismarckian, and market-oriented elements' (Cook, 2010, p 672) in these countries' welfare states. The position of MIP in these 'hybrid' welfare regimes might be a central one, as in the liberal welfare states, but it could also be more residual if social insurance systems work effectively.

The second explanation for the marked differences in MIP systems in both the liberal and conservative welfare states assesses institutional aspects that come short in many typologies but are essential for understanding the risk of being dependent on state transfers. The worker-oriented perspective on income replacement is blind to many aspects of new social risks. For social risk groups such as lone mothers or low-qualified persons, it is not only the right to decommodification that is essential, for the chances for commodification in the first place influence whether these risk groups can profit from employment-based rights or if they have to rely on MIP and more informal forms of social support. It is also important to recognise MIP itself as a basic social right and, therefore, as an essential part of every developed welfare state, and not, as Esping-Andersen's approach suggests, mainly a characteristic of the liberal model (Sainsbury and Morissens, 2002; Stephens, 2010). Hence, instead of making statements about the general ideological baseline of a welfare system, the right to a minimum income must be set into context more specifically with other forms of social rights. For this purpose, the institutional characteristics of adjacent welfare state areas to MIP need to be analysed in a detailed manner.

Since relationships between people are not clearly delineated but are complex and overlapping, welfare institutions often have to balance conflicting claims and resources (Miller, 1999). As a result, different principles of social justice may be applied to different target groups within the same area of welfare provision. This chapter looks specifically into the distributive principles guiding three welfare state areas that are most relevant for MIP systems: unemployment protection, old-age security, and family policy. These policy areas and their variations are crucial for MIP systems because they provide a 'security filter' for those population groups that have the greatest risks of becoming dependent on MIP. Unemployed persons (particularly long-term unemployed people), older persons, and single-parent families are among the most vulnerable population groups in this respect. Their income position depends to a large extent on welfare state institutions and benefits (Sainsbury and Morissens, 2002).

All three areas of welfare that are the focus of this chapter do incorporate principles of equality, desert, and need. Public pensions, for example, can be citizenship based and flat rate, or employment based and wage related, or a combination of both. In most cases, they include a minimum pension level that is sometimes granted unconditionally, but it may also require a means test (Goedemé and Van Lancker, 2009). If so, means-testing might only affect pension income, but it can also stretch to all sorts of incomes of the pensioner and even of his or her entire household. As a result, national pension systems cover all of the three principles of social justice that have been discussed previously. Institutionally, categorical MIP for older persons is often incorporated or closely linked to the overall pension system. In some cases, however, it is granted and administered separately from other old-age benefits, to some degree separating the citizenship- or contribution-based social rights from the needs-based right to MIP. The level of old-age MIP is another indicator of the difference in social rights. Usually, benefit levels are higher than in general MIP and apply a 'softer' means test. Only in some cases, however, do such 'social pensions' reach the minimum level of contributory pensions.

Unemployment benefits generally rest on entitlements that have been gained through employment. Both the time contributions paid to unemployment insurance and the level of former wages play a role in defining benefit amounts. But social rights based on employment are no longer sufficient to secure an income for broad parts of the population. Groups affected by 'new social risks' include, for example, low-qualified and low-paid persons, especially families with children and lone parents who have to reconcile childcare and paid work. Long-term unemployment or interrupted employment careers hinder many from gaining the 'old social right' of unemployment insurance. The importance of MIP for the unemployed is therefore highly dependent on how easily such rights are built and how quickly insurance claims are exhausted after a time of unemployment. In some countries, an intermediate level of social protection between insurance and MIP exists: unemployment assistance is principally a benefit based on desert, but it incorporates elements of need and acts as a buffer to the last safety net. A central question from the social rights perspective is to what extent recipients of unemployment insurance and assistance are treated differently to unemployed MIP claimants.

When looking at family policy, the perspective is twofold on cash transfers and on childcare arrangements. Family benefits are an important measure to reduce child poverty (Bradshaw and Finch, 2010). In many countries, such transfers are equalising, citizenship-based rights, but there are also contributory forms, and in some cases benefits are targeted at low-income families only. Moreover, how these transfers are treated in the means test is of great importance for households dependent on MIP. These factors have a considerable impact on the extent to which children's social citizenship rights are dependent on their families' status. The service perspective needs to be taken into account for a reason that has already been identified in the Introduction and earlier in this chapter: in contrast to the *trentes glorieuses*, male employment alone does not secure a household's income situation, and marriage no longer grants automatic access to income and care redistribution (Saraceno, 2010). Women's ability to access paid employment and to reconcile family and work obligations must therefore be considered as a fundamental social right (Stephens, 2010). Access to care services or leave arrangements gives women the chance to be independent from solidarity-based transfers of the family and the state while gaining employment- and contribution-based social protection rights of their own.

The brief discussion of the three welfare areas demonstrates that it is necessary to look deeper into the specific institutional arrangements of social protection in order to properly assess the role of MIP systems. Table 2.1 summarises the elements that define how higher-tier benefits operate as security filters above MIP and points out their relevance for social rights. Eligibility conditions are a result of the principles of social justice that define access to social rights. The more the higher-tier social benefits incorporate principles of equality and/or need, the less important the last safety net in a given country should be. Replacement rates and generosity, as well as benefit duration, are an expression of how strongly the social right is valued. When universal or wage-related social rights are strong, few people need to rely on MIP. Both dimensions influence how comprehensive the coverage of higher-tier benefits among the population is and how inclusive social rights effectively are. The wider the coverage of unemployment and old-age protection systems among the total population is and the higher benefit levels are – especially for low-wage earners – the less likely individuals are to fall into

Table 2.1: Social security protection filters

Dimensions of social rights	Corresponding elements of social security
Principles of social justice Strength of social right	Eligibility conditions Replacement rates and generosity
Inclusiveness of social right	Coverage

Source: Authors' depiction.

the last safety net. The same holds true for family transfers, although in this case other policy elements such as childcare need to be taken into account as well.

In terms of the 'filtering outcome' of higher-tier benefits for the significance of MIP in the overall welfare state, the three forementioned dimensions interact. For example, if insurance coverage is wide among population groups at risk and benefits are high, social protection is somewhat comprehensive and the role of MIP is marginal. The opposite constellation (narrow coverage and low benefits) indicates a rudimentary social protection system that is linked with MIP having a potentially important role. If coverage is narrow but benefits for the insured population are high, social protection is rather selective and leaves ample room for a sizeable MIP for those persons who are excluded from insurance entitlement. Then again, a wide coverage combined with low benefits may also require a sizeable MIP if benefits are too low to lift incomes to the guaranteed minimum.

The next sections analyse these broad patterns of variation between countries in the three policy areas mentioned earlier. The focus is on the potential impact of these variations on the role of MIP in the overall social security system.

Unemployment protection

In most countries unemployment insurance was introduced as the last of the four main social insurance systems providing security against major social risks: industrial accidents (and occupational diseases), old age (and invalidity), sickness (and health), and unemployment (Alber, 1982; Schmidt, 2005). One reason for this final development was that unemployment insurance implied a severe break with liberal traditions and was the most direct intervention in the labour market among all types of social insurance (Flora and Heidenheimer, 1995). Another reason was that unemployment protection was often organised by trade unions on an industry-wide or regional and local basis. Later, this voluntary insurance often became subsidised and regulated by public authorities and the state. This structure is well known as the Ghent system of unemployment protection. Today, however, most European countries have compulsory public social insurance against the risk of unemployment for the major part of the workforce. Only Denmark, Finland, and Sweden have kept subsidised voluntary insurance based on trade union membership, yet even these systems have high coverage rates. Whether voluntary or compulsory, unemployment insurance systems have kept to their main rationale of desert-oriented social distribution based on accrued rights. Elements of need and equality have nevertheless been incorporated over time in the form of assistance schemes and maximum or minimum benefit amounts.

In many countries, the rise of non-standard employment such as part-time or temporary work raises significant questions about the adequacy of social protection for growing parts of the workforce. A number of studies have shown that unemployment protection has been eroded among socially vulnerable groups in which young adults and women are largely overrepresented (Leschke, 2008). One aspect that makes many non-standard types of employment precarious is that 'classic' employment-based rights are weaker or non-existent for affected employees. If a person with non-standard employment conditions loses his or her job, he or she is often not entitled to unemployment insurance benefits. Even if the person succeeds in entering the system, benefits are often too low to secure a decent livelihood due to low wages earlier on.

The following analysis focuses on three institutional aspects of unemployment insurance that are particularly relevant for the social rights of the marginal workforce: access to insurance benefits, benefit levels for low-wage earners, and the duration of benefits for persons who only fulfil the minimum eligibility conditions. Variations in these three dimensions indicate how open and generous unemployment protection is for the most vulnerable groups among the workforce, and this openness has major consequences for the filtering function of unemployment insurance with respect to MIP.

In most countries today, insurance against unemployment is compulsory for workers above a certain income level or with a minimum of work hours. Only in Sweden, Denmark, and Finland is membership in insurance funds voluntary, but participation is very high. Yet even if a person is principally covered, he or she might not actually fulfil the necessary conditions for establishing a right to benefits in case of unemployment. Most insurance systems require a minimum period of insurance (minimum record) prior to the advent of unemployment. Many persons on temporary contracts or with spells of interrupted employment may not fulfil these requirements, even if they have paid insurance contributions over a certain period. This minimum insurance record usually has to be fulfilled within a certain reference period. In general, the higher the required minimum record is, the less protective a system for vulnerable groups is. At the same time, the longer the reference period is, the more room for interrupted forms of employment exists, which is – *ceteris paribus* – more desirable for these groups.

Figure 2.1 shows the variation between countries with respect to minimum insurance records and reference periods for 2007. The two variables have a direct impact on the inclusiveness of unemployment protection since they express how narrowly or widely the right to insurance benefits is defined. From the early 1990s onwards, regulations have become stricter in most countries.

The most important variable is the minimum insurance record, which is displayed on the vertical axis in Figure 2.1. There are three groups of countries that show rather similar regulations with respect to this indicator. Only some cases are in between or outlying. The first group clusters around six months (26 weeks) and includes the Netherlands, Ireland, Sweden, and France. France seems to have the most accessible system among this group because the minimum record can be acquired over the longest reference period of 22 months. This is favourable for persons with interrupted work histories. In the Swedish case, the employment requirement is only six months, but membership in the voluntary insurance fund has to be at least 12 months. The second group clusters around one year (54 weeks) and includes Austria, Germany, the United Kingdom, Italy, the Czech Republic, and Denmark. For this group, the reference period is, of course, longer at about

Figure 2.1: Eligibility for unemployment insurance benefits, 2007

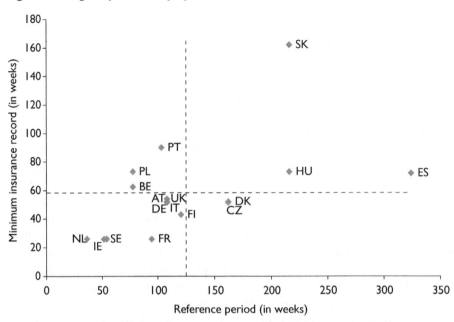

Source: OECD Benefits and Wages database (OECD, various years); authors' calculations.

two years, or even three years in Denmark and the Czech Republic. Finland is close, with somewhat more favourable conditions. The third group clusters around 72 weeks of minimum record but varies widely in the reference period. Overall, these countries, which include Eastern Europe (except the Czech Republic) and Southern Europe, have the most difficult access conditions to unemployment insurance. Slovakia has by far the most restrictive regulations, which require an employment record of as much as 3 years.

Second to access comes the question of how much is paid to unemployed persons. A standard measure in this respect is the net wage replacement rate, which is shown in Figure 2.2 for a single person and a couple with two children. The assumption in both cases is that there was only one earner prior to unemployment and that earnings were low at two thirds of the average wage (OECD standard). This low-income group is most likely to fall back on MIP even when unemployment benefits are received. Low replacement rates may require additional MIP benefits in order to reach the guaranteed minimum income for the household, especially in the case of a family with children. For them, the extent to which the family's greater needs are considered in unemployment insurance is essential.

Figure 2.2 shows a number of interesting comparative patterns. First, the ranking of countries deviates from the familiar welfare state clusters. While Denmark and Sweden are generally at the top, Portugal, Belgium, and Spain also have quite high replacement rates in the case of a single person. These are countries in which access to insurance is more difficult, but benefits are quite generous for those who fulfil

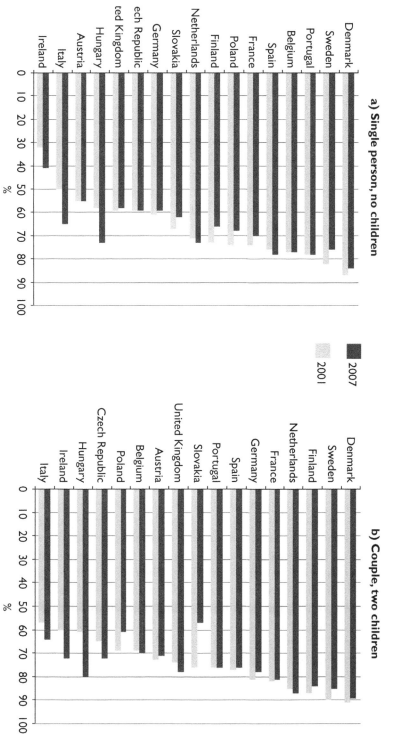

Figure 2.2: Net wage replacement rate at initial phase of unemployment (67% of average wage), 2001 and 2007

a) Single person, no children

b) Couple, two children

■ 2007

▨ 2001

the conditions. This pattern may be symptomatic of a highly segmented labour market. At the bottom end of the ranking, among the countries with the lowest replacement rates, are some cases with relatively easy access, such as Ireland and the United Kingdom. In these countries, unemployment compensation is highly accessible but is rather low; in the two mentioned cases, it is actually not higher than MIP benefits. A second important pattern to be observed in Figure 2.2 is a slight trend of convergence between countries over time, primarily explained by increasing benefit rates among the least generous countries and a small decrease in rates in the leading nations. The majority of countries slightly decreased their replacement rates between 2001 and 2007, showing a partial retrenchment effort.

The third interesting feature is that in most countries, replacement rates for the family are significantly higher than for the single person. It should be noted that neither family benefits nor possible MIP top-ups are taken into account in this calculation. Therefore, these figures represent the 'pure' effects of the unemployment insurance system. If one included the mentioned additional benefits, the situation would turn out even more favourable for families. The ranking of countries in the case of the family deviates in some places from the single person ranking. While Denmark and Sweden are still on top, a number of countries have significantly higher replacement rates for families than for singles: the Netherlands, France, Germany, the United Kingdom, and Austria. In the other countries, the difference between the two rates is smaller, and in a few cases, the relationship is even reversed, as in Belgium, which reports a higher replacement rate for the single person. However, in this case, additional family benefits (which are not included in this calculation) play a significant role.

A final critical issue is the duration of benefits. The shorter the period of payment is, the higher is the risk of unemployed persons falling back on MIP. The duration of unemployment benefits usually varies a great deal by age and employment or insurance record, and there is often a wide span between the minimum and the maximum duration. While the maximum is of great interest to older employees with long employment histories, the minimum is important for more vulnerable groups among the workforce. Figure 2.3 shows the minimum benefit duration for those who just meet the minimum insurance conditions and (again) the respective level of benefits (the average net replacement rate for the average of the family types at 67% of average worker's wage (AW)). The two indicators together show the generosity of unemployment insurance in terms of both level and time.

The Nordic countries and Belgium are the most generous, offering a high level of benefits for a long period of time; Denmark is by far the most generous country in both respects. Relatively high benefits are also provided in the Netherlands, Spain, Portugal, France, and Hungary, yet their minimum duration is rather limited. The remaining countries combine both low net replacement rates and a short duration. Ireland falls a bit outside this group because it has very low benefits but a more extended duration.

As noted earlier, the replacement rates are calculated for a low-wage earner, and benefit duration is the minimum for persons who fulfil only the minimum

Figure 2.3: Generosity of unemployment insurance benefits, 2007

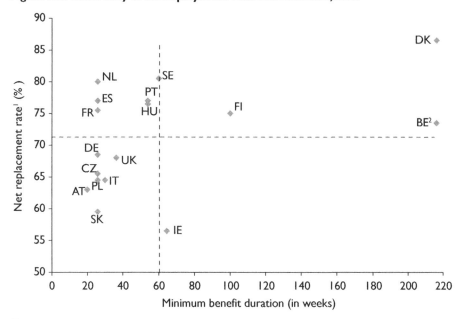

Notes:
[1] At the initial phase of unemployment, after earning 67% of the average wage; [2] Unlimited insurance benefits.
Source: OECD Benefits and Wages database (OECD, various years); authors' calculations.

insurance conditions. In most countries, benefit rates vary by income group, and duration varies by age and/or insurance record. In terms of benefit levels, the Anglophone countries are the most egalitarian because they provide flat-rate benefits for everyone from the first day of unemployment. The duration of benefits does not vary either. In the United Kingdom, for example, all unemployed persons are shifted from insurance-based benefits to the means-tested jobseeker's allowance after six months. Therefore, the UK represents the most unified system, treating all unemployed persons equally.

The maximum duration of unemployment benefits displays great international variation, ranging from six months in the United Kingdom to indefinite in Belgium, although the replacement rate in the latter case is significantly reduced after the first year. In a number of countries, the maximum period has been reduced since the early 1990s, as in Sweden (from 28 to 14 months), Denmark (from 108 to 48), the United Kingdom (from 12 to 6), and Germany (from 32 to 12; recently prolonged to 15). On the one hand, the distance between minimum and maximum duration has become smaller on average, which means that older workers and persons with longer work histories in full-time jobs have lost some of their additional benefits and privileges as systems moved towards greater equality. On the other hand, the crucial difference between this group and the non-standard workers with short employment histories is still access to insurance, which is often very limited for the most vulnerable groups.

If an unemployed person has no access to unemployment insurance or if the wage-related benefit is too low or exhausted after a short while, he or she may become dependent on MIP if the means test is passed successfully. In some cases, at very low wages, insurance benefits need to be supplemented by MIP from the start. Yet in between insurance benefits and MIP, some countries have established a special assistance scheme for the unemployed. If these schemes provide both means-tested and flat-rate benefits, they are included in the scope of MIP as we define it, but if one of the conditions is violated, they are excluded. In Spain and Portugal, unemployment assistance is limited in time and income-tested, but the possible income of every single household member is already at a much higher income level than MIP benefits for entire households. Moreover, the Spanish benefit is provided as a lump sum and does not take the needs of the complete family household into account. These unemployment assistance schemes are therefore not included in our project as MIP benefits. Nonetheless, these schemes represent important functional alternatives to MIP for the long-term unemployed.

Some unemployment assistance schemes combine means tests with wage-related rather than flat-rate benefits. This was the case in Germany until 2004. As of 2010, Austria is the only country that still has a wage-related and means-tested scheme for the long-term unemployed; this is certainly one reason why the MIP recipient rate for the working-age population is lower in that country (see Chapter Four). For Belgium, unemployment insurance provides unlimited benefits, though at a significantly lower level after the first year. This also implies a potentially lower MIP recipient ratio.

Summarising the main features of unemployment protection for workers at risk in the different country groups shows significant variations both between and within country clusters. The Nordic countries on average have relatively 'open' systems of unemployment protection that provide quite generous benefits for an extended period of time; however, the differences between individual countries are high. Denmark is by far the most protective country not only in this group but overall. The Continental European countries have more restricted access conditions to insurance, provide lower benefits, and have shorter periods of payment. At the same time, insurance conditions in these countries are better for persons with longer work histories. Average benefit replacement rates for low-income earners vary particularly within this group, ranging from less than 65% in Austria to about 80% in the Netherlands. Additionally, the duration of payment varies, but none of these countries has a very long duration except Belgium. For Austria, the specific unemployment assistance scheme has to be taken into account. Among the Continental group, the Netherlands and France show a higher level of protectiveness for the unemployed covered by social insurance, while Germany shows the lowest. Austria and Belgium have quite selective systems due to their institutional specificities. The Anglophone countries provide only limited insurance against unemployment, but under relatively equal conditions. Benefit rates are flat rate and modest, and the payment of benefits is very limited, especially in the United Kingdom. The British benefits are higher than the Irish ones but are provided for a shorter period. After six months of insurance-based jobseeker's allowance, the means-tested allowance is granted, which is also provided to all non-insured persons who are able to work. One can generally say that unemployment insurance is almost completely provided at the level of MIP, with the crucial distinction that no means test is applied for the first six months.

Conditions are more difficult for vulnerable groups in Southern and Eastern European countries. On average, their unemployment insurance systems have the most restrictive access conditions, requiring lengthy periods of previous employment. Moreover, benefit levels are very low but have strong variations. The minimum duration of payments is also quite short on average. Among these two country groups, Slovakia has by far the least protective system, whereas Portugal and Spain do better and the Czech Republic, Poland, and Italy are in between. In some of these countries, MIP is also very limited and not available for all needy population groups. Italy, Spain, and Poland have rudimentary last safety nets. In Portugal, the Czech Republic, and Slovakia, MIP systems are more inclusive, but access is difficult in the two Eastern countries due to specific institutional regulations, which particularly tend to exclude minority ethnic groups. This aspect is further elaborated in Chapter Three.

Old-age security

Historically, older people were among the population groups at the highest risk of poverty. Yet most old poor-law systems regarded them as 'deserving' if they were unable to work due to age, sickness, or invalidity. For most older people, especially those among the working classes, the situation only improved substantially after public pension programmes had been introduced. This process started at the end of the 19th century in some pioneer countries and was completed in all European countries after World War II. It is a prime example of the gradual introduction and extension of social citizenship rights.

Public pension schemes have evolved along two basic models that are commonly referred to as the 'Bismarckian' and 'Beveridgean' types. The underlying logics of these systems are almost diametrically opposed. In the Bismarckian tradition, pensions are provided within the institutional framework of social insurance and cover workers and employees, and in some cases also the self-employed. Pensions are usually earnings related and financed from social contributions, in most cases jointly by employees and employers. This is a typical case of social distribution based on accrued rights. The primary goal of these systems has been to provide earnings replacement in cases of old age or invalidity. The first country that introduced a compulsory pension insurance system for workers was Germany (1889), soon followed by other Continental European countries such as Austria (1906), France (1895), Belgium (1900), and Italy (1898) (Bahle et al, 2010a). The Netherlands had initially followed the Bismarck path (from 1913), but then introduced a Beveridge-type pension system after World War II.

In the Beveridge model, the primary goal of public pensions has been to provide a minimum level of income for all older citizens as a means of preventing poverty. Pensions are usually flat rate and financed from general taxation or sometimes also from national insurance. Strictly speaking, the origins of this model go back to the years before Beveridge developed his insurance plan for Britain in 1942. The precursors of this model were introduced as early as 1891 in Denmark and Iceland, soon followed by New Zealand (1898), the United Kingdom, Ireland, and Australia (1908), Sweden (1913), and Norway and Finland (1936). These systems provided means-tested flat-rate pensions for citizens; in the UK and Ireland coverage was limited to economically active persons. With these schemes, older people were effectively freed from the poor-law tradition. The means test was usually set at a level that excluded the rich rather than one that stigmatised the poor, as had been the case before. In most of these countries, the means test was further relaxed over time, transforming these systems into almost universal pension schemes for nearly all citizens.

While the two systems were quite different during their initial stages of development, an institutional convergence to mixed systems has taken place. On the side of the Bismarck model, the link to employment was relaxed by granting pension credits for certain periods outside work, such as education, childcare, and care for older people. Persons who never worked still have no pension claims but may be entitled to survivors pensions. The second mechanism of convergence from the side of the Bismarck systems was the introduction of minimum pensions within earnings-related schemes. This required a relatively long insurance and employment record for individuals in most countries, but it actually covers a sizeable share of the retired workforce. With these gradual changes, many Bismarckian countries extended their coverage and incorporated an effective means of basic security into their systems. They became more inclusive and egalitarian – features that had always been the major characteristics of the Beveridge model.

The Beveridge systems have meanwhile moved closer to the Bismarck model by introducing an additional earnings-related pension tier on top of their basic pensions. This has become obligatory in some countries while in others it is subject to collective bargaining or remains in the realms of voluntary private initiative. Only three countries established a compulsory second public tier with earnings-related benefits: Sweden (1959), Finland (1961), and Norway (1966). Denmark and the Netherlands stuck to their public basic pensions and introduced additional occupational pensions regulated by collective agreements. In Britain, a public earnings-related scheme was introduced as late as 1975, but the option of contracting out to employer-funded occupational schemes and even to private savings plans has remained.

Through these institutional changes, the two originally distinct models developed into mixed pension systems aiming at both basic security and income maintenance for large population groups. Yet there are still big differences with respect to population coverage and the mix of the two pension tiers granting basic and income-related benefits, respectively. This is shown in Table 2.2, which is based on the typology of social security systems by Palme (1990) and Korpi and Palme (1998).

Table 2.2 classifies the pension systems of countries according to their actual fulfilment of two fundamental goals: basic security (based on equality) and income security (based on accrued rights). In this classification, the actual performance of pension systems is taken into account, such as the level of benefits compared with standardised average income. This approach explains why two of the Beveridge countries (Ireland and the United Kingdom) lack both forms of security. In principle, they have a basic pension for a high share of the population, but the amount provided does not effectively prevent poverty, nor is income security guaranteed by the state, because the occupational pillar is largely privatised. Therefore, this scheme is considered a residual pension system. By contrast, the Nordic welfare states (except Denmark) effectively provide for both forms of security. This is called the institutional model. Denmark and the Netherlands have successful poverty-preventing citizenship pensions, but their earnings-related tiers are based on occupational pensions regulated by collective agreements rather than by public social rights. Therefore, the state grants only basic security. These three models (country groups) all originate from the historical Beveridge legacy. By contrast, all original Bismarck-type countries still fall under the income security model in this classification. The Southern European and two of the East European countries (Hungary and Poland) may also be included in this group, whereas the Czech Republic fits into the basic security model and Slovakia into the residual group (see note to Table 2.2).

From the perspective of MIP, the aim of basic security is most important. If the pension system fails to provide a basic security level for significant parts of the population, a higher need for MIP should be observed. Based on the

Table 2.2: Old-age pension systems

		Basic security	
		No	Yes
Income security	No	**Residual** Ireland United Kingdom (USA)	**Basic security** Denmark Netherlands (Canada)
	Yes	**Income security** Austria Belgium Germany Italy France (Japan)	**Institutional** Finland Sweden (Norway)

Note: Eastern European countries were not classified in the sources but can be tentatively added to the models as follows: Czech Republic (basic security); Hungary and Poland (income security); Slovakia (residual). Portugal and Spain can be classified as income security.

Sources: Palme (1990), adapted from Bahle et al. (2010a).

table, one would expect a relatively well-operating protective filter for older people in Denmark, the Netherlands, Finland, Sweden, and probably also the Czech Republic. In these countries, equality is the guiding principle of pension provision. The situation should be worse in the income security group, where some segments of the older population are not effectively protected by – or are even excluded from – the pension system. These are the systems of old-age security for which desert is the most important criterion of resource distribution. The situation would be worst in Ireland and the United Kingdom, where public pensions are generally low and often have to be topped up by MIP. Judgements of need thereby play an important part in income protection for older people in these countries.

Yet all the countries under study combine different principles of social justice in their pension systems. The Bismarck-type countries in particular show wide variations. As mentioned earlier, some have extended their insurance systems more than others, and some countries have introduced minimum pensions in their earnings-related schemes while others have not. In Table 2.3 the focus is on the component of basic security. Basic security can be provided in the form of general basic pensions for the vast majority of the population. This is the institutional characteristic of Beveridge-type systems. In most of these countries, entitlement to pensions is based on citizenship or permanent residence; in the United Kingdom and Ireland it is based on contributions to national insurance. Interestingly, however, the three Nordic countries apply an income test to their basic pensions or at least to part of them (as in Denmark). In Finland and Sweden, this test was introduced at the beginning of the 2000s, when the whole pension system was turned upside down. Before that point the earnings-related tier provided an addition to the universal basic pension. Since then, the basic pension is only granted if earnings-related pensions fall below the level of the guaranteed basic pension. This is a mild form of means test, however, because it takes only individual pensions and not household income into account. These schemes are therefore not regarded as MIP schemes according to the definition of this book. Sweden and Finland do also have means-tested benefits of last resort for those not fulfilling the residence requirements for the full basic pension, which correspond to our definition of MIP (see Chapter Three). In Table 2.3 these benefits are included in the last column under 'assistance schemes'. The British and Irish contributory state pensions are granted without a means test, but they do not cover the whole population and are so low that older people with no other income have to supplement their pensions with means-tested social assistance (around 23% in Britain). Only the Dutch scheme is both universal and non-means-tested and offers a pension level that effectively prevents a fallback on the last safety net. As can be seen by the coverage rates, almost all older people in the Netherlands receive the general pension, and the number of those on social assistance can be ignored.[1] In Scandinavia, the percentage of persons who receive the income-tested basic pension is quite high as well, but the figures are expected to decline due to the gradual extension of the earnings-related pension schemes.

Table 2.3: Minimum pension schemes

	Pensions			Assistance schemes
	Eligibility conditions	Means test	Coverage rate[1] (2006)	Coverage rate[1] (2006)
Basic pensions				
Denmark[2]	Residence	Yes	98	–
Finland[3]	Residence	Yes	53	2
Sweden[4]	Residence	Yes	55	<1
United Kingdom[5]	Contributions	No	97	23
Ireland[6]	Contributions	No	72	28
Netherlands[7]	Residence	No	~100	–
Minimum pensions				
Austria[8]	Contributions	Yes	11	–
Belgium[9]	Contributions 30 years	No	11	5
France[10]	Contributions	No	36	5
Italy[11]	Contributions	Yes	32	5
Spain[12]	Contributions 15 years	Yes	24	7
Portugal[13]	Contributions 15 years	No	60	6
Czech Republic[14]	Contributions 15 years	No	~100	<1
Hungary[15]	Contributions 20 years	No	2	1
Poland[16]	Contributions 25 years	No	12	n.a.
No provisions				
Germany[17]	X	X	X	2
Slovakia[18]	X	X	X	1

Notes:

n.a. No data available.

1   As a percentage of the population 65+. For BE, FR, and PL: as a percentage of pensioners (for pensions). For PT and FI: as a percentage of pensioners (for both coverage rates). For IT, ES, and HU: as a percentage of population 60+.

2   *Folkepension.*

3   National pension: income-tested for statutory pension income (since 2001). MIP: Social assistance.

4   *Garantipension*: income-tested for statutory pension income (since 2003). MIP: *Äldreförsörjningsstöd.*

5   Basic state pension. MIP: Pension credit (data for 2005).

6   Contributory state pension. MIP: means-tested (non contributory) state pension.

7   *Algemene Ouderdomswet.*

8   *Ausgleichszulage.*

9   MIP: *Garantie de Revenu aux personnes âgées.*

10   MIP: *Minimum vieillesse.*

11   Abolished for newly insured from 1996 (retiring as of 2030). MIP: *Pensione sociale.*

12   MIP: Non-contributory pension.

13   Means test in pension scheme: From 2006, the means-tested solidarity supplement for older people has gradually been phased in for those not reaching the minimum contribution record. MIP: Social pension.

14   Minimum pension amount. MIP: Subsistence level guarantee.

15   MIP: Old-age allowance.

16   No data on assistance schemes.

17   MIP: *Grundsicherung im Alter und bei Erwerbsminderung.*

18   MIP: General social assistance scheme (aid in material need).

Sources: Social Protection Committee (2006); OECD (2009b); authors' compilation.

Another variant of basic security is a minimum pension granted within earnings-related pension schemes. Most countries that originally had Bismarck-type pension systems have introduced minimum pensions at levels that are usually well above the social assistance thresholds. These provisions often require a very long insurance record of more than 15 years (sometimes as long as 30 years). Interestingly, in most cases, these minimum pensions are not means-tested, which distinguishes them from the basic pensions in most Beveridge-type systems. This feature clearly expresses the still different assumptions about pension entitlements in the two historical models: in the Bismarck tradition, both standard and minimum pensions are seen as earned benefits from work; in the Beveridge tradition, these pensions are regarded as a public benefit based on citizenship or need. In fact, most Beveridge-type systems have never completely broken with the old poor-law legacy of means-testing basic pensions, and some countries such as Sweden and Finland have even recently reintroduced some of these elements. The Netherlands is the only exception in this respect.

None of the basic pension arrangements applies to the definition of MIP used in this study because they are not means-tested or apply a very mild form of means test. By contrast, some of the minimum pensions in the insurance arrangements of the Bismarck-type pension systems are truly means-tested, and therefore defined as MIP. Variants of such benefits exist in Austria, Italy, Spain, and, since 2006, also in Portugal. All other arrangements are regarded as institutional alternatives to MIP within the broader welfare state.

As can be seen in the figures on coverage rates, insurance-based minimum pensions play an important role in many Bismarck-type countries. In France and in Southern Europe, high proportions of the older population benefit from these provisions. These benefits fulfil the function of guaranteeing a social minimum for older people to a significant extent and offer a strong security filter for subsequent MIP systems. Therefore, the proportion of older people who fall back into social assistance (either into special programmes for older people or into the general last safety net) in most of these countries is relatively small compared with that in Ireland and Britain. It seems that earnings-related pension systems combined with effective minimum pensions for the insured population provide relatively good protection against the risk of falling into the last safety net. This observation is even more striking for a country such as Germany, which is one of the two countries in the sample that did not introduce any form of minimum pension in the pension system. Instead, before 2003, older people with low incomes had to apply for general social assistance; since 2003, there has been a special MIP scheme for older people and for those who are permanently unable to work. The conditions and requirements in this special MIP scheme are more relaxed than in the system for the working-age population, but still only about 2% of the older population receives these benefits. Of course, problems of non-take-up, which are particularly severe for older people, play a role in this fact, but this low figure is also a positive sign of the great success of a mature Bismarck-type pension system's prevention of poverty among older people – even if reducing inequality was not the primary intention of these schemes.

In summarising these findings for the different country groups, the following aspects stand out. In the Nordic countries, a decent minimum income level is effectively provided for the whole older population, but in Finland and Sweden, the basic pension has recently become income-tested against individual pension income from compulsory earnings-related pensions (second pillar). Since the basic pension is provided without a means test on further household income, this system can still be considered a universal basic pension and not part of MIP. The percentage of older people who fall back on benefits of last resort is therefore marginal. The same holds for the Netherlands, which has the most generous basic pension system of all the countries under study. By contrast, the basic pensions in the Anglophone countries do not provide effective protection above MIP. A high proportion of older people in both Ireland and the United Kingdom depend on means-tested benefits during retirement. This is especially the case for those who have no additional income beside the very low basic pension. As in the field of unemployment, MIP is not a last safety net but an essential part and component of old-age security in these countries.

In most countries with Bismarck-type pension schemes, minimum old-age pensions for the insured population provide an effective security net above MIP for many older persons. However, significant parts of the older population are not effectively protected because they have no insurance claims. Hence, MIP plays a certain complementary role for the population not covered by old-age insurance. Although MIP is not as important as in the Anglophone countries, its share among the older population is still higher than in Scandinavia. There are big differences among the individual Bismarck-type nations. The proportion of minimum pensioners among all pensioners is significantly higher in France and in Southern Europe compared to Austria, Belgium, Hungary, and Poland. This fact also shows the high inequality among pensioners in these countries. For many of them, pensions would be deplorably low if no minimum benefits were provided. This observation reflects general social inequalities and often highly segmented labour markets that leave many persons with inadequate pension credits that need to be supplemented by a guaranteed minimum pension.

Family policy

Family policy differs from the two policy areas previously described in several respects. In most countries, family policies were introduced comparatively late and have never been as integrated, explicit, and coherent as the other two areas. Many countries still lack an explicit and institutionally integrated family policy due to ideological and political reasons or simple neglect. For the welfare states of Continental and Southern Europe, this lack is largely due to the particular historical evolution of welfare provision based on subsidiarity and a strongly gendered division of labour. Men were the breadwinners, with employment in the labour market, and women were largely responsible for care work at home. Social rights attached to employment were therefore largely the social rights of male workers. Women participated in these rights only indirectly, and relatively generous cash benefits of the welfare state met the greater financial needs of families, especially in Continental Europe. The gradual erosion of the male breadwinner model, however, resulted in a whole cascade of follow-up problems, such as women's difficulties in reconciling paid employment and the demands of family life. Only very recently have these problems been taken up by the welfare state, with an increased emphasis on services for families.

Second, the aims of family policy often conflict and show quite different patterns in different countries. In some countries, the primary goal has been to prevent poverty among families and children (need) while others have aimed towards financial redistribution away from childless households and towards families with children, including the middle classes (equality). Alongside cash benefits, services and benefits in kind have become a major part of family policy in many countries. This development has been most important in housing, health, childcare, and preschool education. Childcare is of especially great relevance for female employment, for it helps to improve the compatibility of work and family. This enables women to gain employment-based social security rights independently of their spouses. The Nordic welfare states developed a strong service component early on, thereby freeing women from their family duties to some degree (providing 'defamilisation', to use Esping-Andersen's (1999) term) and providing an institutional framework conducive to paid employment for women with children.

The third important difference between family policy compared with old-age security and unemployment protection is that family policy has never had the function of wage replacement. Benefits in favour of families are usually too low to replace income from work. Only gradually has parental leave as a right been combined with wage-replacing benefits such as the German Elterngeld, which replaces around two thirds of the net wage prior to leave. The service components actually encourage and enable work rather than provide income replacement. Nonetheless, family policy – in the form of cash benefits as well as service arrangements – is important for alleviating the risk of poverty among families either by supplementing income from work or by supporting employment opportunities. Family benefits and services enhance households' incomes and are therefore important security filters above MIP, particularly for single-parent families who have a very high risk of poverty.

This section looks at different nations' broad family policy patterns that might affect the relevance of the last safety net for families with children, particularly single-parent families. We look at both the transfer and the service side of family policy. While the first acts as a more direct protection filter, the second works indirectly, facilitating access to the labour market and thus to higher-tier protection. A first rough indicator is social spending on families, as shown in Figure 2.4. This figure is split into expenditure on benefits and on services in order to detect the

Figure 2.4: Social spending on families, 2005

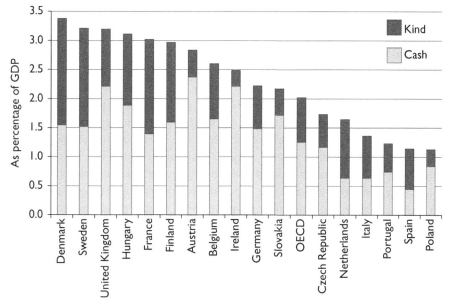

Source: (OECD, 2010a); authors' calculations.

general effort that countries invest in monetary redistribution versus empowering families' potential to generate incomes of their own.

Social spending on families varies between about 1% of the GDP in Poland to almost 3.5% in Denmark. All the Nordic countries are well above the OECD average, with Sweden and Denmark at the top. On the opposite side, all Southern European countries rank at the bottom of the distribution. There is no such clear pattern for the other country groups. The United Kingdom ranks surprisingly high (in third position), while Ireland is towards the middle. Among the Eastern European countries, Poland holds the lowest position whereas Hungary is one of the highest spenders. The Continental European countries all hold positions in the middle but with significant variation between France (3.0%) and Austria (2.8%) on one side and the Netherlands (1.6%) on the other.

The relative shares of financial aid and services (including benefits in kind) also vary widely. The Nordic countries and France all belong to the top spenders and have relatively high shares of spending on services. Services are actually more important than financial aid in the Nordic countries. By contrast, in the United Kingdom, Austria, Belgium, Ireland, and Germany, financial aid is much more important than services. Austria is on top if one considers only this financial family policy component. This shows that the Nordic welfare states put more emphasis on the provision of public services whereas the Continental European nations primarily support families by financial means.

All Eastern European countries show a pattern that comes close to the Continental European one, which may be surprising given their socialist history, with strong emphasis on female employment and public services. In one respect, this was a significant policy shift in these countries that can be explained by a deliberate break with the socialist past. Yet in another respect, this similarity with Continental Europe also shows that the Eastern European countries have originally shared the same historical traditions with respect to the relations between the state and the family (Inglot, 2008).

The service component is not only relatively high among the top spenders but also among the low spenders. In the Netherlands, Italy, and Spain, services also clearly predominate. This fact can be explained by a structural effect: In these countries, financial aid for families is very low and often targeted at low-income families. Services therefore receive a higher share of spending. The lack of public family policy forces families to keep and actually strengthen their role as providers of care, social security, and income, especially for the young (Ferrera, 2005).

A better insight into the different patterns of family policy can be gained by looking at the financial and service sides separately and by focusing on redistributive patterns in favour of families in more depth. The model family type approach is often used for this purpose. In this approach, the impact of the tax and transfer system in each country is simulated for different family types for which a number of standard assumptions are made, for example, concerning income levels from work and the number and age of children. This approach allows for a differentiated comparative analysis of policy instruments but does not reflect real living conditions in each respective country. Moreover, it is limited to an analysis of the income situation before and after taxes and transfers, and views employment and wages as exogenous conditions.

Since the income situation of families is influenced by a large number of policy instruments, including income tax, social security contributions, family benefits, and other social benefits, the focus here is on the overall package provided to families by social policies, taking together all kinds of benefits. The result is the so-called child benefit package for each country. The package is defined as the income difference between a certain family type and a similar household without children. It is therefore an indicator for the impact of children on the overall income situation of a household. The data are taken from a comparative study directed by Jonathan Bradshaw that describes the situation in 2001 (Bradshaw and Finch, 2002). There is no more recent study available that would offer the same analytical depth.

In the following analysis (see Figure 2.5), the child benefit package for a couple with two children (compared with a couple without children) and for a single-parent family with one child (also compared with a couple without children) is shown. In the first case, the standardised assumption is that there is only one earner, with average male earnings. In the second case, the assumption is one earner at average female earnings, also for the couple. For both cases, the child benefit package is shown in two components: first, after including all taxes, social contributions, and transfers (the purely financial side); and second, after also taking into account the impact of housing (both the costs and the transfers for housing)

Figure 2.5: The value of the child benefit package, 2001

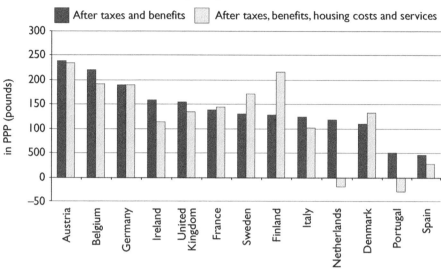

a) Couple with two children

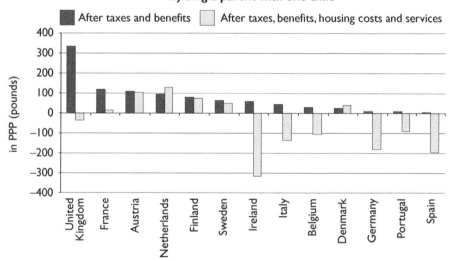

b) Single parent with one child

Source: Bradshaw and Finch (2002); authors' depiction.

and services, particularly childcare (again, both the costs and transfers linked to childcare). For the couple, it is assumed that no extra-familial childcare is needed because there is only one earner. For the single parent, a full-day place in childcare is assumed. In Figure 2.5 amounts are given in purchasing power parities (PPPs) in British pounds. Countries are ranked from the left to the right by the size of the package after taxes and cash benefits.

In financial terms, the Continental European countries provide the most support to couple families. Austria, Belgium, and Germany have the highest child benefit packages after taxes and transfers, followed by the two Anglophone countries, which is a bit of a surprise. One reason for this may be that the scale is measured in British pounds, which have a high currency value. The relatively high wage level in Ireland at the time should also be borne in mind. Nonetheless, complete families are supported quite well in both Anglophone countries. The lowest level of financial support is found in Southern Europe, the Netherlands, and – also surprisingly – in Denmark. Indeed, in purely financial terms, the Scandinavian countries are found in the middle and lower end of the ranking. Yet their package actually grows if housing and services are taken into consideration, whereas the package for most other countries remains stable or even decreases. This again shows the emphasis put on services in the Nordic countries. When including these components, Finland moves up to the second position (after Austria), and Sweden is almost equal to Belgium and Germany (in second and third positions, respectively). In Spain and Portugal, parents have less absolute income than a couple without children. In Portugal, but also in the Netherlands, the package turns out to be negative after taking housing and services into account.

For single parents with one child, the situation looks very different and indeed much worse compared with a couple family household that has the same level of work income at its disposal. In financial terms, the United Kingdom offers by far the most generous benefit package, but after housing and services are included the value becomes slightly negative. In this case and in Ireland, the fall in the value of the benefit package is dramatic and almost completely explained by the exceptionally high costs of childcare, which is most often provided by private for-profit agencies. In half of all countries, single parents end up with less in their pockets than a couple at the same earnings level does, whereas in the other countries, the (positive) difference is rather small. The main reason is that in these countries (France, Austria, the Netherlands, Finland, Sweden, and Denmark), the housing and service component does not have a negative impact – which indicates a relatively good infrastructure for employed single parents and low costs for publicly provided childcare.

The model family approach has a major disadvantage: It is not representative of the family structure in all countries. Since the child benefit packages vary between different family types, one solution to this problem is to look at a number of different cases and to calculate overall averages. This is, of course, still not statistically and empirically representative, but it paints a more balanced picture because various family types and income constellations are considered. Figure 2.6 shows the most representative measure for overall child support and is based on the average values for 34 individual model family cases in which problematic constellations such as single parenthood or low income are not over-represented. Moreover, the value of the child benefit package in this case is not measured in terms of PPP but in relation to average (national) earnings. Hence, these data can

Figure 2.6: The average value of the child support package, 2001

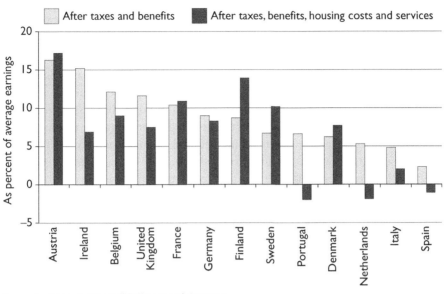

Source: Bradshaw and Finch (2002); authors' depiction.

be interpreted as an overall measure for generosity towards children (and families) compared with the national income.

Again, the picture is very different if one looks at the purely financial side or takes housing and services into consideration. In terms of financial support, the Continental European and the Anglophone countries are clearly the most generous while the Nordic nations are in the middle and the Netherlands and Southern Europe do the least for families; only Portugal is a bit more generous. If one includes housing and services, the picture changes drastically. Austria remains on top but is now followed by Finland, France, and Sweden, whereas Ireland, the United Kingdom, and Belgium fall back to a medium position. Taking all policy areas into consideration, Austria, Finland, France, and Sweden appear as the most generous supporters of families – two Nordic and two advanced (Catholic) Continental European countries with long traditions of family policy. The least support is provided in the Southern European countries and in the Netherlands – countries that have always been laggards in family policy in both financial and service components. It seems that the old historical patterns are still visible in actual benefit structures (Bahle, 2008).

Childcare services not only have a (sometimes negative) impact on the income situation of families; they are also of vital importance for the chances of parents' labour market participation and their ability to access employment-related social protection schemes. European countries still differ a great deal in the availability (and affordability) of childcare for parents with preschool children. The differences are greatest for children below the age of three, whereas for children between three and six years of age, the situation is much better and less unequal (Plantenga et al, 2008; Bahle, 2009).

Taken together, the profile of family policies from the perspective of MIP can be summarised as follows. The Nordic countries are generally characterised by high overall social spending on families and a high share of services. The value of the child benefit package is medium if only transfers and taxation are considered but is significantly higher after including housing and services, though still not in top position. The package offers medium social transfers but high and mostly universal services and is generally oriented towards increasing the employability of parents, especially single parents. Enrolment in childcare is very high for the youngest age group and fairly high for children aged three to six. This family policy profile provides relatively favourable conditions for families with children. There is also a significant within-group variation. Denmark offers fewer social transfers and invests more in services whereas Finland shows a reverse pattern within the general Nordic profile. Hence, with respect to the overall (average) child benefit package described in Figure 2.6, Finland ranks second after Austria, whereas Denmark is in a medium position. Here, policy is less oriented towards compensating families for the costs of children than towards activating the labour market and earnings capabilities by providing heavily subsidised childcare.

The two Anglophone countries also show a relatively homogeneous pattern that only sometimes partly deviates. Social spending on families is relatively high (although not the highest among the countries studied), but the value of the child benefit package varies considerably. For couples, both countries are fairly equal, but single parents are much more supported in the United Kingdom. Nonetheless, taking the costs (and benefits) for housing and childcare into account, both countries show a negative balance for single parents due to exceptionally high costs of childcare. On average, families are not supported very well financially and conditions for taking up employment are not especially favourable. This situation is above all true for single parents.

The Southern European countries in most indicators show a rather homogeneous pattern as well. They spend very little on families, have very low and often negative child benefit packages, and provide modest childcare except for children aged three to five, for whom coverage is fairly high. In all these countries, family policy is only rudimentary and financial support is especially weak. This does not necessarily mean that families bear a higher risk of poverty; some of the gaps in social security may be closed by family solidarity. Still, overall poverty rates and child poverty are high in Southern Europe, and parents' employment is also not supported. The relatively high amount of childcare for older children is primarily the result of educational aims rather than deliberate family policy efforts. The conclusion is that families in this part of Europe are mostly left to themselves and cannot expect significant public support in financial or in service terms. Children's social rights here are highly dependent on the status of their family members. Portugal is the only country that deviates from the others in one crucial respect: childcare for children below the age of three is

---

highly developed here due to the high female labour force participation that has long characterised this country.

The Continental European countries show the most heterogeneous pattern. All countries in this group have medium total social expenditures for families, but the more detailed patterns differ. One can probably broadly distinguish between a German-speaking variant and a French- (and Flemish-) speaking variant. Austria and Germany put more emphasis on financial transfers whereas Belgium and France have more services, particularly childcare facilities. Austria is the most generous country with regard to the (average) child benefit package, both in purely financial terms and after considering housing and services. France and Belgium have the most developed childcare and preschool system for children aged three to five in Europe, better than the system in Scandinavia, and also very high levels of enrolment for the younger age group, much ahead of Austria or Germany. It might therefore seem that employability plays a greater role in the French- and Flemish-speaking countries than in the German-speaking ones.

Finally, Eastern European countries do not form a homogeneous group either. In terms of overall spending on families, Hungary is among the top spenders in Europe (relative to the national GDP) while Poland is in the lowest position in the ranking. Unfortunately, these countries were not part of the Bradshaw study on the child benefit package (Bradshaw and Finch, 2002), so they cannot be compared here. All Eastern European countries share one important aspect: their childcare systems are very limited, especially for children younger than three, and they are not much better for preschool children. Poland is the only country in which enrolment for children between three and six does not exceed 40%, and the other three countries show quite modest figures. This indicates that the socialist idea of the female citizen-worker, which was not fully realised under the old regime, seems to have disappeared and been replaced by the still older conservative pattern of family policy based on the principle of subsidiarity. The former socialist Central European countries have thereby moved closer to the 'old' Continental European pattern.

Conclusions

Summarising and integrating the results of the three policy areas (old-age security, unemployment protection, and family policy), the following international pattern of institutional filters above the MIP level emerges. In Table 2.4, the degree of protectiveness for each country and policy area is ranked as high, medium, or low, based on the analysis presented earlier.

Older people are among the best protected groups in most countries, being protected either by general basic pensions or by minimum pensions in insurance-related systems. The clear exceptions are Ireland and the United Kingdom, where basic pensions are too low to secure a decent livelihood in old age. For families and the unemployed, the degree of protectiveness varies more between countries and is lower on average.

Table 2.4: The protectiveness of social security systems above the MIP level

	Unemployment	Old age	Family support Income	Work
Nordic				
Denmark	+	+	O	+
Finland	+	+	+	O
Sweden	+	+	O	+
Continental				
Austria	+	+	+	–
Belgium	+	O	+	+
France	O	O	+	+
Germany	–	O	O	–
Netherlands	O	+	–	O
Anglophone				
Ireland	–	–	O	–
United Kingdom	–	–	O	–
Southern				
Italy	–	+	–	–
Portugal	O	O	–	+
Spain	–	O	–	–
Eastern				
Czech Republic	O	+	(n.a.)	–
Hungary	–	O	+	–
Poland	–	O	(n.a.)	–
Slovakia	–	–	(n.a.)	–

Notes:
+ = high; O = medium; – = low.
Underlined: countries with three or more positive spells.
Italics: countries with three or more negative spells.

Source: Authors' depiction.

The Nordic countries show the highest degree of protectiveness for all groups except in income support for families, where they perform only at a medium level. However, families are supported by a very good infrastructure of services that allows for combining paid work and family care for both parents in couple families and for single parents. Hence, social rights are highly inclusive in these countries. Only Finland deviates from the pattern by having a higher level of income support and less developed childcare services.

The Continental countries show a heterogeneous pattern. Austria and Belgium are highly protective due to their specific arrangements for unemployed persons and their high level of income support for families. France is also quite protective, especially for families, while Germany and the Netherlands lag behind. In

Germany, family income support is at an average level, but the protectiveness for unemployed persons has been quite low since the 2005 reform. In the Netherlands, older people are very well protected due to high basic pensions, but families receive much less support.

The Anglophone countries have the lowest degree of protectiveness of all the countries studied except in the area of family income support, where they provide a medium level. The Southern European countries do quite well in protecting older people (mainly in insurance-related systems) but perform very poorly for families, in terms of both income support and employment-related policies. Overall, social protection rights are more selective than inclusive. The extreme case here is Italy, whereas Portugal shows a more balanced pattern. The Eastern European countries show a similar picture, which points to a great deviation from the socialist past in which working families received much better support than did pensioners. Today, the pattern has almost become reversed. The Czech Republic is something of an outlier among the Eastern countries because it has a relatively high level of protection for pensioners and for unemployed persons.

From this pattern, MIP should play a marginal role in the social security systems in the Nordic countries while it takes on a crucial position in the Anglophone countries regarding all three risk groups. In Southern and Eastern Europe, MIP should also play an important role, especially for the unemployed and for families – yet here there are no fully developed last safety nets (see Chapters Three and Four). The pattern is more varied in the Continental countries. Old people will seldom be dependent on MIP in all Continental countries, while for the unemployed and for families, differences are greater. In Austria and Belgium, both groups will only rarely fall into MIP, whereas in Germany and the Netherlands MIP is more important. France should range in between and have a lower significance of MIP, especially for families.

Notes

[1] For the small number of persons over 65 that are in need of MIP, benefits are available at the level of the basic pension. Between 2006 and 2010 the responsibility for these recipients has been gradually shifted from the municipalities to the Social Insurance Bank and outsourced into a new system (AIO, see Chapter Three).

THREE

Country analyses[1]

This chapter studies the institutional structure and quantitative development of national MIP systems. Each of the 17 countries is presented in a separate section, which is organised as follows: the first part analyses the role of MIP in the overall social security system in a historical perspective. The second part describes the present welfare state context of MIP systems in three policy areas: old-age pensions, unemployment insurance, and family policies. This second part relates to the comparative analysis of the welfare state presented in Chapter Two. The third part gives a concise overview of each country's MIP system. It shows which schemes exist, when they were introduced, who the major target groups are, and how these schemes can be generally characterised. For each country, a summary table presents the main components of the MIP system. The fourth and final part analyses the development of MIP receipt from 1992 to 2010 (or until the last year for which data are available). For each country, a figure shows the development of recipient numbers in the main MIP schemes. In addition, the total and the long-term unemployment rates are included in the figure. This approach allows for the explanation of the development of MIP receipt in the context of problem pressures, for which unemployment is a key indicator. Data on recipients are taken from the EuMin database, which was built up during the project and is described in Chapter One. The original data sources are too numerous and diverse to be mentioned here, but they are documented in the database, which is now available for public use. Data on unemployment are taken from Eurostat official websites (Eurostat, 2010).

Austria

Austria is a highly developed conservative-type welfare state. Total social spending amounted to 28% of the GDP, the sixth highest level in the EU in 2007 after France, Sweden, Belgium, Denmark, and the Netherlands. The welfare state is dominated by employment-related social insurance protecting against major social risks, whereas means-tested benefits and especially the last safety net play residual roles.

The distribution of legal and administrative functions for both areas of welfare between the different levels of government follows this dualistic structure. While social insurance is legislated at the federal level and administered by tripartite corporatist bodies, social assistance belongs to the legislative competencies of the nine Austrian provinces (*Länder*) and is administered by municipalities. The provincial schemes themselves were only introduced in the nine provinces between 1971 and 1978. Before that, the system had been highly decentralised and discretionary. In September 2010 a new system of needs-based MIP (*bedarfsorientierte Mindestsicherung*) was introduced by an agreement between the federal state and the nine provinces.

One reason for this belated and very limited development of MIP in Austria is the highly inclusive social insurance system that provides protection for the majority of the population, including the self-employed and family dependants. Moreover, there are categorical benefits for persons with low pensions and for long-term unemployed people. Hence, the number of persons who depend on the last safety net of provincial social assistance has stayed relatively low. Despite rising numbers during the past decade, this last safety net has remained residual by international standards. In 2008, it covered only around 2% of the population.

The welfare state context

Social insurance has been the institutional core of the Austrian welfare state from its beginnings in the late 19th century (Weigel and Amann, 1987). Insurance is mainly based on employment and financed by social contributions. It provides earnings-related benefits and is organised in separate schemes for different employment status groups such as industrial workers, employees, public servants, and special groups (Obinger and Tálos, 2006). Despite this organisational fragmentation, social insurance in Austria after World War II developed into a more encompassing and socially inclusive system than in most other conservative welfare states. With the addition of compulsory social insurance for farmers in 1965 and for the self-employed in 1966, the system has covered almost the whole economically active population, including family dependants. Under this encompassing system, special benefits for the insured have protected many persons from falling into the last safety net.

Pension insurance in Austria is based on economic activity and provides earnings-related benefits based on social contributions. The relation between pensions and earnings (contributions) is strong due to the equivalence principle, but there is an important element of MIP in the pension system. Low old-age, work incapacity, and survivors' pensions are increased to a legally defined minimum if the income of pensioners (including partner income, but excluding other household members) falls below the minimum (*Ausgleichszulage*). The *Ausgleichszulage* is thus an important element of MIP for the insured population and their survivors (described in the next section). Since social insurance is highly inclusive, the system actually covers the vast majority of the population.

Unemployment insurance covers the employed workforce except for civil servants. Since 2009, the self-employed are able to opt in voluntarily. Persons with very low earnings (below the contributory minimum of €350 per month), however, are not covered. Unemployment insurance benefits depend on previous earnings. Eligibility is based on a contribution record of at least one year before unemployment or 28 weeks in the case of repeated spells of unemployment. In

2009, the standard (basic) benefit amounted to 55% of previous net earnings from employment. This amount increases to 60% of previous earnings (80% for persons with children) if the standard benefit amount falls under the level set by the *Ausgleichszulagenrichtsatz* (legal minimum) in pension insurance for the respective household type. However, the benefit in this case also remains linked to previous earnings and is not topped up to the legal minimum. This is a major difference from pension insurance, where the minimum is actually guaranteed. The length of unemployment benefit payments varies by employment record and age. In 2009, the minimum period was 20 weeks, the maximum 52 weeks (for workers from age 50 and an insurance record of at least 468 weeks during the past 15 years).

Another specific feature of the Austrian system of unemployment protection is the existence of an unemployment assistance scheme for the long-term unemployed (*Notstandshilfe*). This scheme was introduced in 1977 in order to cope with increasing long-term unemployment following the first oil shock. It steps in after entitlements to unemployment insurance benefits have expired. Yet it should be noted that the system is relatively open. It is, for example, accessible for labour market entrants and (since 2009) for self-employed persons (voluntarily). Benefits are means-tested against total household income. The benefit level is fixed as a percentage of the previous unemployment benefit (UB). In 2009, the standard rate was 92% of UB (standard amount, that is, without increases for low-income earners). If the standard amount is lower than the *Ausgleichszulagenrichtsatz* in pension insurance, the percentage is increased to 95%. Even if this benefit does not reach the *Ausgleichszulagenrichtsatz* after the increase, it is not topped up to that level. If the benefit falls below the income threshold set by provincial social assistance, people are also entitled to these benefits of last resort. Indeed, in recent years the number of unemployment assistance recipients who need additional social assistance has grown significantly (to be discussed later).

In **family policy**, Austria belongs to the top social spenders in Europe, especially in terms of financial support. Austrian family policy has been strongly oriented towards cash benefits rather than services and has supported a traditional male-breadwinner model. The Austrian child benefit package provided by the tax and transfer system is actually the most generous in Europe on average (Bradshaw and Finch, 2002). By contrast, social services are less developed and childcare in particular is rather limited. In 2007, the childcare enrolment rate was only about 70% for children aged three to five (below European average) and about 10% for children younger than three – one of the lowest in Europe.

The Austrian system of MIP

The Austrian system of MIP consists of three main components: aid to victims of war and crime, the income-tested pension minimum, and the provincial schemes of social assistance, which have become more harmonised by the needs-based social minimum introduced in 2010 (Table 3.1). As argued earlier, the *Notstandshilfe*

Table 3.1: MIP schemes in Austria, around 2010

Year of introduction (abolition)	Name (in German)	Major target group	Main characteristics
1947/1957 and 1972	Kriegsopferfürsorge, Fürsorge für Verbrechensopfer (aid to victims of war and crime)	Victims of war, victims of crime (1972)	Minimum income provisions for specific target group; categorical benefit
1955	Ausgleichszulage in Pensionsversicherung (pension minimum)	Social insurance pensioners and survivors (work incapacity, old-age and survivors' pensions)	Minimum is fixed by law and income-tested (pensioner plus partner); no asset test
1971/1978 (9 provincial laws)	Sozialhilfe (offene Sozialhilfe) (social assistance provided to private households; replaces former regulations)	All people in need meeting requirements	Entitlement conditions and benefit levels vary widely between provinces; usually means-tested against total household income (and assets) with low asset and earnings disregards
2010	Bedarfsorientierte Mindestsicherung (needs-based social minimum)	All people in need meeting requirements	Nationally harmonised minimum standards for provincial social assistance schemes

Source: Authors' compilation.

(unemployment assistance) cannot be considered MIP in our definition because it does not provide a minimum on its own.

Aid to victims of war (*Kriegsopferversorgung*) was introduced in 1947 as an emergency measure in order to deal with the consequences of war. It was formerly a large system, but is very limited today; in 1972, another scheme for victims of crime was added (*Opferfürsorge*).

The pension minimum (*Ausgleichszulage*) was introduced in 1955 by the general social insurance law, which fully reinstituted social insurance in post-war Austria. The system provides an income-tested pension minimum for the insured population in cases of work incapacity, old age, or death (survivors). The *Ausgleichszulage* pays the difference between the actual income of the pensioner together with his/her partner and the legally guaranteed amount (the *Ausgleichszulagenrichtsatz*) for the respective household type. Assets and other household incomes are not taken into account. Where there is need, recipients may also claim special housing benefits, but these are not considered part of MIP. The pension minimum is set at a higher rate than the social assistance thresholds fixed under the nine provincial schemes of last resort.

Social assistance (*Sozialhilfe*), introduced comparatively late by provincial legislation between 1971 and 1978, can be considered the oldest scheme of MIP because the system builds on a long history of poor relief (*Fürsorge*) going back to imperial Austria. Until 2010, Austria was one of the few European countries without a nationally harmonised system of last resort benefits (Fink and Grand, 2009). The residual and very limited nature of social assistance also resulted in a very low take-up rate due to the stigmatising character of rules and procedures.

Regulations and benefits widely varied between the nine Austrian provinces until 2010 (Fink and Grand, 2009). The means test was generally rather strict, and benefits were comparatively low. There was almost no earnings disregard, and the complete household income apart from the long-term care benefit and family benefits was taken into account in the means test. The absence of earnings disregards may be partly explained by the fact that most long-term unemployed persons were covered by the special unemployment assistance scheme; therefore social assistance was rather residual and marginal. Another factor concerns the strictness of means-testing: for example, recipients also had to repay their 'debts' due to social assistance payments if they succeeded in leaving the system and getting a better income. Overall, the system was rather strict, stigmatising, and highly discretionary. Nonetheless, there was growing need, and the number of claimants rose steadily. The increasing pressure on the system led to the major reform in 2010, under which the new needs-based social minimum (*bedarfsorientierte Mindestsicherung*) was introduced.

The new system is based on an agreement between the federal state and the nine provinces. It introduced nationally uniform basic benefit levels for the first time. The institutional basis of the system thus remains at the provincial level, while at the federal level standard rules and minimum benefit amounts are defined. These nationally defined minimum rates are now also related to the pension minimum (*Ausgleichszulagenrichtsatz*). Hence, the system has also harmonised benefit levels between the different MIP schemes. The basic rate in 2010 was €744 per month for a single person, which includes a share of 25%, which is calculated for housing costs, but provinces may add further supplements on a discretionary basis. In addition, a number of improvements for recipients have been introduced. For example, benefits for single-parent families have been significantly increased, and the option of claiming benefits at labour market offices rather than at the municipality makes the system more open and less stigmatising, and the family's maintenance duties have been limited. At the same time, recipients of the *bedarfsorientierte Mindestsicherung* are now also 'activated' in similar ways to recipients of unemployment assistance. Additionally, some earnings disregards have been introduced in order to make work more attractive. No work requirements exist for persons who take care of those in need of long-term care or those who care for children under three. In addition, all recipients are fully covered by health insurance, which was not the case before.

Structural developments

In 2008, the resident population of Austria amounted to around 8.3 million persons; of those, about 430,000 persons received a minimum income benefit (5.2% of the total population). In comparative terms, this is a low figure and comes close to that of Scandinavian welfare states. In the same year, around 78,000 persons received the *Notstandshilfe* (which is not considered part of MIP), and another 114,000 received unemployment insurance benefits. Both figures were relatively low because unemployment in Austria, particularly long-term unemployment, was also at a comparatively low level.

Even if Austria does not have a 'real' legal minimum pension for all older citizens and no 'real' subsistence minimum provided by unemployment insurance and unemployment assistance, the inclusiveness of the social insurance system and the existence of both the *Ausgleichszulage* and the *Notstandshilfe* explain why fewer people fall back into the last safety net of provincial social assistance than in other countries. The pension minimum plays an especially significant role. In 2008, for example, 19% of work incapacity pensions, 5.4% of old-age pensions, and 16.8% of widows' and widowers' pensions were topped up to the legal minimum.

Nonetheless, interesting structural developments can be observed over time (Figure 3.1). The most important MIP system in terms of benefit receipt has

Figure 3.1: MIP receipt in Austria, 1992–2010[1]

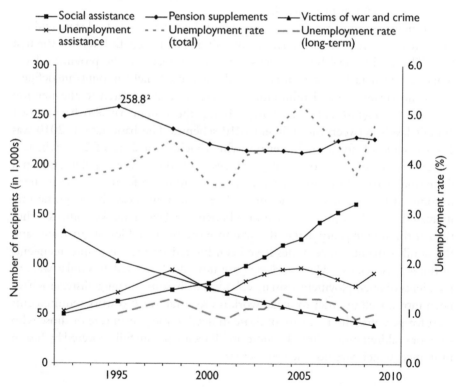

Notes:
[1] The number of MIP recipients is displayed by the solid lines which refer to the left vertical axis. The dashed lines depict the unemployment rates (total and long-term) and refer to the right vertical axis.
[2] By way of illustration, in 1995, 258,800 people received pension supplements which represents 3.26% of the total population.

Sources: EuMin database; Eurostat (2010); ILO (2010).

been the pension minimum. Although figures fell slightly until 2005 after a peak in 1995, the trend has since been reversed, with an increase in the most recent period. It should be noted that these figures are based on individual pensions at the end of a calendar year and do not include household dependants. As noted earlier, the pension minimum is very important for work incapacity and survivors' pensions, whereas only about 5% of old-age pensions are topped up to the legal minimum. Compared with this system, the schemes for victims of war and crime have been in constant decline. In 2008, more than 43,000 persons received one of these benefits after being measured on an individual pension basis at the beginning of a calendar year.

The number of beneficiaries of provincial social assistance has been increasing rapidly over the period, from fewer than 50,000 persons in the early 1990s to more than 160,000 in the late 2000s (Pratscher, 2009, 2010). More than half of all beneficiaries live in Vienna, the capital. However, these figures are calculated differently from the other data. Social assistance data include all persons living on benefits at any one point during a calendar year. Hence, figures are cumulated over the year and include all household dependants. Unfortunately, Austrian statistics do not allow for an estimation of annual averages, nor is it possible to break down recipients to comparable age groups for all nine provinces. The figure also shows that the increase in the social assistance caseload is not linked to fluctuations in unemployment rates. The unemployment assistance scheme therefore still seems to 'buffer' the social risks of long-term unemployed to a large extent.

Belgium

Under the Belgian welfare state, which has one of the largest budgets in Europe (relative to the GDP, surpassed only by Sweden and France), MIP plays a minor role in terms of expenditure. In 2006, only 1.7% of social spending flowed into MIP, while a remarkable 11.4% was allocated to unemployment protection. Higher figures in this domain can be found only in Spain (Eurostat, 2010). This stems from the fact that Belgium's welfare state is mainly based on compulsory social insurance. MIP principally plays the role of last resort for those who are unable to build up sufficient insurance claims.

The MIP system is rather fragmented in Belgium, which can be ascribed to its stepwise development. Programmes for older people and people with disabilities were already set in place in 1969. A general guarantee of an existence minimum (*minimum de moyens d'exixtence*, or *minimex/bestaansminimum*) was not introduced until 1974. At first, only Belgian nationals were eligible for these programmes until the law passed on 8 July 1976 proclaimed a general right for a decent standard of living and support by the social service centres, which are obligated to 'grant persons and families the kind of support that their community owes them'; 'this support can be of material, social, medical, socio-medical or psychological kind' (Moniteur Belge, 1976).

The welfare state context

The first pillar of the Belgian **pension system** is organised into separate branches for employees in the private sector, the self-employed, and civil servants. The maximum benefits in these systems can be topped up by occupational and private pensions as well as minor employment income. Furthermore, pension levels may not fall below a fixed minimum amount. If they do, social assistance for older people (GRAPA, discussed later) can be claimed, which serves the purpose of guaranteeing an adequate standard of living for pensioners. The minimum pension age is 65, but one may take early retirement at the age of 60 or after 35 years of employment. The full pension amount can only be achieved after 45 years of contribution for men and 44 years for women. However, periods of insured unemployment are recognised as contribution periods, and late retirement is also possible in order to compensate for career gaps (SPF Sécurité sociale, 2008; OECD, 2009b).

Belgium, as the country of origin of the so-called Ghent system, has a long tradition of **unemployment protection**, but it was the social pact of 1944 that shaped today's system by introducing compulsory unemployment insurance for all employees. The long-term increase in structural unemployment, caused by the 1973 oil crisis as well as the increasing labour market risks for women and young adults, led to a gradual change from securing former incomes to a principle of minimum income protection within unemployment insurance. If eligibility criteria are met, benefit duration is virtually unlimited, leading to a high coverage of unemployment insurance among the non-disabled population, while social assistance focuses more on other social groups. As a result, reintegration into the labour market is mainly a task for unemployment insurance. Here, activation in the form of work- or qualification measures are obligatory for most of the benefit recipients (Cantillon and Marx, 2008; ONEM, 2009).

The central element of Belgium's **family policy** is the general family benefit system, established in 1930 on the basis of firm- and sector-based benefits that had been introduced in the previous decades. Benefit levels are progressively designed according to the number of children in a household, a feature that aims at helping larger families make ends meet. Mothers have the legal entitlement to 15 weeks of maternity leave, and since 2001, fathers may take 10 days of paternity leave. In the field of childcare, Belgium has a long tradition of preschools, but day care for children under the age of three was institutionalised only in the 1970s. For parents of young children, a three-month parental leave (*congé parental/ouderschapsverlof*) is also possible and may be prolonged by a subsidised job interruption of up to five years (*crédit temps/tijdskrediet*; until 2001: *interruption de carrière/loopbaanonderbreking*). It is mainly women that make use of this option (Leitner, 2005; ONAFTS, 2005; SPF Emploi, Travail et Concertation sociale, 2008).

The Belgian system of MIP

Today's MIP system in Belgium contains six programmes for different target groups (see Table 3.2). They can be summarised into three categories:

1) general MIP
2) MIP for persons with disabilities
3) MIP for older persons.

The integration income (*revenu d'integration sociale* (RIS)/*leefloon*) is the central element of category 1). It is regulated by the social integration law (*droit à l'integration social/recht op maatschappelijke integratie*) of 26 May 2002, which defined the right of every person to so social inclusion, unlike its precursor, *minimex*, which concentrated on the right to a minimum income. Labour market integration is seen as the central element for preventing social exclusion and fostering participation in society.[2] Therefore, the right to work and to have a minimum standard of living are of equal importance in the new legislation. According to this logic, not only are monetary benefits paid to persons in need, but specific, labour market-oriented integration measures are also pursued. The implementation and administration of these measures lie in the hands of the communal social service centres.

Table 3.2: MIP schemes in Belgium, around 2010

Year of introduction (abolition)	Name (in French)	Major target group	Main characteristics
2002	*Revenu d'integration sociale* (RIS), formerly *minimex*	Non-disabled persons from 18 to 65	Part of the *droit à l'integration social*. Activation measures obligatory for beneficiaries under the age of 25
1976	*Aide financière*	Non-disabled persons from 18 to 65	Equivalent to the RIS. Paid out to persons who do not meet all eligibility criteria of the *droit à l'integration social*.
1969	*Revenu garanti aux personnes âgées* (RG)	People over 65	Expiring old-age pension guarantee
2002	*Garantie de revenus aux personnes âgées* (GRAPA)	People over 65	Current old-age pension guarantee
1969	*Allocation ordinaire/ allocation spéciale* (AO/AS)	Disabled persons from 18 to 65	Expiring programmes. Distinction between different types of disabilities.
1987	*Allocation de remplacement de revenu* (ARR)	Disabled persons from 18 to 65	Current legislation. Tops up income to the average level of a comparable employee without disabilities.

Source: Authors' compilation.

Persons in need who are unable to make any claims for other types of social benefits have the option of applying for financial aid (*aide financière/financiële steun*), whose benefit levels correspond to those of the integration income (SPP Intégration Sociale, Lutte contre la Pauvreté, Economie Sociale et Politique des Grandes Villes, 2003). Today, only very marginal groups have to apply for financial aid, for example, foreign nationals who have a residence permit without being officially registered. Prior to 2002, access conditions to *minimex* were more restrictive. The most important change concerns the omission of nationality-based constraints on benefit eligibility, leading to the inclusion of all registered residents of Belgium.

Benefits of category 2) are mainly based on the legislation passed on 27 February 1987. The income replacement allowance (*allocation de remplacement de revenu* (ARR)/ *inkomensvervangende tegemoetkoming* (IVT)) aims at replacing salaries that a person has to forgo because of his or her disability. It is granted to persons whose income totals less than one third of what comparable employees without disabilities could achieve in the labour market. The general directorate for persons with disabilities is in charge of the implementation of this MIP programme. It also pays out benefits falling under the former legislation (*allocation ordinaire* (AO)/*gewone tegemoetkoming* (GT) and *allocation spéciale* (AS)/*bijzondere tegemoetkoming* (BT)). Under certain conditions, persons who began receiving benefits before the 1987 reform are still eligible for these benefits if the new regulation would worsen their financial situation (DG Personnes handicapées, 2006). On average, 40% of ARR recipients also receive an integration allowance (*allocation d'integration/ingegratietegemoetkomin*), an additional benefit aimed at preventing social exclusion by compensating for the costs of diminished autonomy. For the expiring programmes, benefits comparable to the integration allowance are available and there are special allowances for persons at pension age (see, for example, DG Personnes handicapées, 2006).

Eligibility for benefits of category 3) is granted if every other possible claim of retirement provision is exhausted or if regular contributory pensions are very low. For beneficiaries of the integration income or the replacement allowance, reaching the age of 65 automatically leads to an eligibility check for this income guarantee for older people (*garantie de revenus aux personnes âgées* (GRAPA)/ *inkomensgarantie voor ouderen* (IGO)). The guaranteed pension is managed by the national pension office, which is also in charge of contributory pensions for employees and self-employed persons. This facilitates the verification of possible claims under any other pension system before granting the guaranteed pension income. Therefore, an application for GRAPA also counts as an application for other possible retirement benefits. Besides GRAPA, there are still benefits being paid out according to the old regulation (*revenu garanti aux peronnes âgées* (RG)/ *gewaarborgd inkomen voor bejaarden* (GI)), which is being gradually phased out. Important differences between GRAPA and its precursor are the change of the female age limit to match that of males, as well as the equal treatment of married and unmarried couples (ONP, 2010).

In addition to the actual MIP benefit, all MIP recipients can be exempted from health insurance contributions and benefit from higher reimbursements for treatments and reduced hospitalisation fees (European Commission, 2010). Moreover, social rates for telecommunication, electricity, heating, and public transport apply. For families, general and guaranteed family benefits (*prestations familiales garanties/gewaarborgde gezinsbijslag*) form an important part of the benefit package, as the benefit rates within the *Revenu d'integration* are the same for couples and family households. In 2006, 39.7% of all households on the integration income also received guaranteed family benefits (ONAFTS, 2007).

Structural developments

At the beginning of the period studied, support for older persons played the biggest role in Belgium's MIP system. Today, the old *revenu garanti* is gradually reaching the low numbers of the expiring systems for disabled people, which play only a marginal role in the Belgian system. Recipient numbers of the current disability scheme, however, have increased over time (see Figure 3.2). Since 2006, persons receiving ARR outnumber recipients of all other benefit types.

Figure 3.2: MIP receipt in Belgium, 1992–2010[1]

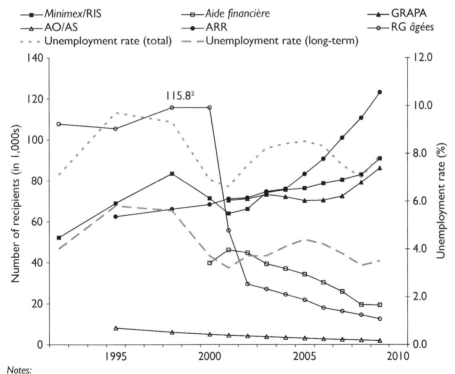

Notes:
[1] The number of MIP recipients is displayed by the solid lines which refer to the left vertical axis. The dashed lines depict the unemployment rates (total and long-term) and refer to the right vertical axis.
[2] By way of illustration, in 1998, 115,765 people received RG *âgées* which represents 1.14% of the total population.

Sources: EuMin database; Eurostat (2010); ILO (2010).

Minimex and the integration income have gained in importance as well, but recipient numbers have fluctuated more and seem to be linked to labour market dynamics. In particular, the peak in recipient numbers in the 1990s and the most recent increase in growth rates mirror developments in unemployment figures. Financial aid granted by the social service centres as an equivalent to the integration income has been in decline since 2002. This is most certainly an effect of the more inclusive character of the integration income compared with *minimex* in terms of access conditions linked to nationality, since the number of Belgians and nationals of other EU countries claiming integration income remained relatively stable while the number of foreign nationals from outside the EU began to increase rapidly with the adoption of the *droit à l'intégration sociale* (SPP Intégration Sociale, Lutte contre la Pauvreté, Economie Sociale et Politique des Grandes Villes, 2009).

The Czech Republic

by Tomáš Sirovátka

The Czech welfare state represents a mixed system in which some elements inherited from the pre-war conservative Bismarckian model (Cerami, 2006; Inglot, 2008) have been changed by the more uniform communist model and further modified by post-communist governments, which have implemented rather modest social standards with many targeted measures. Yet in the Czech Republic, these targeted policies differ from the liberal model in that they are generous enough to prevent poverty. According to Eurostat, the at-risk-of poverty rate did not go above 10% in the Czech Republic until 2007, which is one of the lowest rates in the EU (Sirovátka and Mareš, 2006). Nonetheless, the Czech welfare state has moved step by step into a more liberal, residual direction – for example, by not increasing benefit levels (or ceilings) and with a series of reforms (Saxonberg and Sirovátka, 2009). This can be seen as a trajectory towards a 'low social expenditure' welfare state (see Armingeon and Bonoli, 2006).

The welfare state context

The strategy of 'socialising' living costs during the communist regime was based on full enforced employment, free-of-charge public services, wage equalisation in favour of unskilled labour, and massive state subsidies for housing, food, and selected consumer goods. This strategy could not be sustained during the transition to the market economy, yet the protection of large population groups from the social risks of transformation became one of the main concerns of the new political elites. This led to the creation of a new last safety net (a minimum income guarantee) and a redesign of most social security schemes into an extended social safety net providing low average replacement rates but sufficient protection against poverty. Minimum pensions and minimum wages, the indexation of benefits, and the subjection of most family-related benefits to income testing provided sizeable population segments with an effective safety net.

In the area of **pensions**, the pay-as-you-go public pillar is supplemented by a widespread private pension scheme that is not yet important in terms of pension claims. The present public pillar is built on the pre-1989 scheme, but the 1995 Pension Act introduced a new pension formula. Since then, the pension has been composed of a basic (non-means-tested and universal) flat-rate component (which is about 20% of the average pension) and an earnings-related component amounting to 1.5% of the calculation base for each working year. Strong reduction rules are imposed on above-average earnings when computing the earnings-related component. The replacement rate of the net pension to gross wage was 70.3% for median earnings in 2004 but 98.8% for earnings at half the average wage (OECD, 2007a). Above all, the system protects against poverty rather than securing individual living standards.

On the other hand, the Czech system of **unemployment protection** is rather strict and close to the 'liberal' labour market regime (as defined by Gallie and Paugam, 2000b). Since 1992, unemployment benefits are provided for only six months at a replacement rate of 60% (for the first three months) and 50% thereafter (changed in 1998 to 50% and 40%, respectively) with a low ceiling. Fully unemployed households as well as households of unemployed breadwinners thus fall very quickly into the social assistance system. In 2004, the replacement rate was increased to 45% in the second three months, and support for those over 50 years was prolonged to a period of 9 months and for those over 55 for a period of 12 months. In 2008, the compensation period was cut by one month, and the benefit in the first two months increased to 65%.

In the area of **family policy**, the child benefit became income-tested in 1996, and other benefits for low-income groups were introduced: the social supplementary benefit, housing benefit, and commuting benefit. Additionally, rent and heating benefits were temporarily applied due to a sudden increase in housing costs. In practice, the social supplementary benefit represents a second child benefit targeted at low-income households. The benefit level decreases with increasing household income (a negative tax principle). The housing benefit was based on the same principle but was only about half of the social supplementary benefit. These family-related benefits seem to be highly effective at eliminating poverty.

The Czech system of MIP

MIP was not well developed under the communist regime, but some foundations for a later extension had been laid. As a result of research and proposals by the Standard of Living Research Institute (Výzkumný ústav životní úrovně), a minimum old-age pension for single persons and couples was established in 1970. This threshold was used in 1985 to calculate discretionary benefits for low-income households under Government Decree No. 149/1985 Coll. of the

Ministry of Labour and Social Affairs. Local authorities were entrusted to execute this programme.

In November 1991, the Living Minimum Act[3] and Act on Social Need[4] introduced social assistance benefits where income was below the amount of the living minimum (Table 3.3). This scheme responded quite well to the impact of the transformation and was comparable to other European countries. With regard to expected inflation in 1991, the level of the living minimum was set so that the real drop in value would not exceed 10% during 1991–2, whereas real incomes fell on average by 25%. At the same time, a rule for indexation was introduced (Dlouhý, 1997). This scheme was (with small adjustments) in effect until 2006. The system was supervised by the Ministry of Labour and Social Affairs, but the social departments of entrusted municipalities provided benefits and services as well as other emergency measures.

Citizens residing in the country since 1991 were eligible for social assistance in cases of need. The provision of emergency assistance in 'extraordinary cases' remained possible for non-adult citizens not residing in the country, if a person's health or education was endangered. The benefit is means-tested for total income below the fixed level of the living minimum. Moreover, there should be no possibility of increasing one's income through work or selling property. The work requirement does not exist for pensioners and persons older than 65, for parents caring for a child younger than four or for three or more children (from which one is younger than 10) or for a helpless person.

Since 1991, social assistance has provided a sum equal to the difference between the household's income and the statutory living minimum. Until 2006, the living minimum was composed of two components: 1) the contribution to personal needs provided to each individual household member differentiated by age, and 2) the contribution to the household's needs (for instance, housing), differentiated according to household size. The amounts were fixed by national legislation, but it remained possible to increase the amount, especially the household component with respect to real housing costs. Finally, some special discretionary benefits covered special situations, such as special nutritional needs and benefits for people with disabilities to modify a flat or for special tools. The costs of children's needs

Table 3.3: MIP schemes in the Czech Republic, around 2010

Year of introduction (abolition)	Name (in Czech)	Major target group	Main characteristics
1991–2006	*Sociální potřebnost*	Citizens residing in the country and in need	General social assistance scheme related to statutory living minimum
2006	*Hmotná nouze*	EU citizens residing in the country for at least three months and some other categories in need	General social assistance scheme related to basic personal needs

Source: Authors' compilation.

were typically of primary concern and included, for example, lump sums for clothes or contributions to leisure activities organised by schools.

Because of some widely acknowledged problems with this scheme (such as rising real housing costs, multiple causes of social exclusion, and welfare dependency due to lack of work incentives), there was an ongoing movement for reform (Víšek, 1998). The Research Institute of Labour and Social Affairs was asked to examine the adequacy of the subsistence minimum and made a recommendation for new legislation (Baštýř et al, 2003). EU membership was another catalyst for implementing a new law in 2006.

The new 2006 legislation was an attempt to reflect the broader context of social exclusion and provide an adequate minimum guarantee while increasing incentives to work by 'activating' welfare recipients (see Vládní návrh zákona o pomoci o pomoci v hmotné nouzi, 2005). Eligibility has been expanded in several respects and includes EU citizens with a registered residence in the Czech Republic of at least three months, beneficiaries of refugee or subsidiary protection status, and persons protected by international treaties (European Social Charter). Extraordinary immediate assistance can also be provided to persons residing legally in the Czech Republic and – as an exception in a case of serious threat to health – even to persons residing illegally.

The key change in 2006 was that the national living minimum was made to include only the costs of basic personal needs of household members; this amount has since been augmented, however. The protection of the living standard in the sphere of housing was solved both in the system of 'state social support' by redesigning the housing benefit (*příspěvek na bydlení*) and by implementing a supplement for housing (*doplatek na bydlení*) into the system of social assistance (under the 2006 Act on Material Need). Housing needs are first considered in the system of state social support. If housing costs are higher than 30% (35% in Prague) of the income of the household, the difference between the 30/35% of household income and the 'normative housing costs' (considered legitimate since corresponding to common costs in the locality) is repaid by the housing benefit. Only after applying this benefit is the entitlement under the system of social assistance assessed and a contribution towards housing costs (*doplatek na bydlení*) granted, but only if housing costs are recognised as 'reasonable'. There is no exemption for healthcare fees.

In addition to this living minimum, an 'existence minimum' (covering the basic personal needs at a level enabling survival) was implemented. This amounts to about two thirds of the living minimum for a single person. It is applied in cases where willingness to work or cooperation is assessed as deficient and also applied to a child's legal representative when a child fails compulsory school attendance. The latter condition is in practice mainly applied to Roma children, and aims to compel parents to send their children to school.

Since 2006, eligibility conditions have become tighter for young people: adult children and their parents who share accommodations are considered as one household in the means test for the living minimum – which practically excludes many young persons from entitlement. The living standard of such families is endangered in many cases. All persons living in the flat are considered for the housing supplement.

In 2006, positive incentives to work were also implemented. Only 70% of income from work and 80% of income from sickness and unemployment benefits is taken into account when testing means of subsistence. However, this incentive is not entirely effective because the level of the living minimum for a single person is only about 15% of the average wage. Thus, even persons with a minimum wage (close to 40% of the average wage) receive amounts higher than the level of the living minimum and cannot take advantage of the measure; the only exception is large families.

Since 1996, the revaluation of social assistance had been linked solely to the consumer price index; subsequent revaluations had been delayed, leading to a substantial drop in benefit levels. In 2007, the automatic revaluation of subsistence and existence minima was cancelled and is now at the discretion of national government. As of January 2009, recipients of social assistance are only entitled to the 'existence minimum' instead of the 'living minimum' after six months. Only if they participate in public work programmes for between 20 and 30 hours a month are they still entitled to the living minimum. If they work more than 30 hours, they receive an additional bonus. Places, however, are rather limited and often unavailable.

Structural developments

The number of social assistance recipients increased steadily from the scheme's implementation in 1991 until 2000. Although consistent data on the long-term development of recipient numbers and structure do not exist, it is evident that numbers increased during 1997–2000, when the unemployment rate went up from about 5% to nearly 10% and remained at this level until 2005, when it started to drop (see Figure 3.3).

Interestingly, the number of recipients (individuals) increased about threefold, which is more than the growth in unemployment from 1994 to 2005. The number of recipient families did not increase very much, despite increasing unemployment. Data on average numbers of beneficiaries (and expenditure) provided by the Czech Ministry of Labour and Social Affairs since 2003 (various years) document that numbers have actually been decreasing in recent years (2003–6). This trend may be explained by decreasing unemployment rates and increasing real incomes as well as by tightened eligibility conditions: the 2004 Employment Act relaxed the definition of a suitable job and imposed stricter sanctions if there is misconduct (exclusion from the register for six months). However, the number of single persons was still about twice the number of families with children among recipients.

The key reforms of social assistance were implemented in 2006 and afterwards. The data show that the number of recipients decreased in total by about 60%

Figure 3.3: MIP receipt in the Czech Republic, 1992–2010[1]

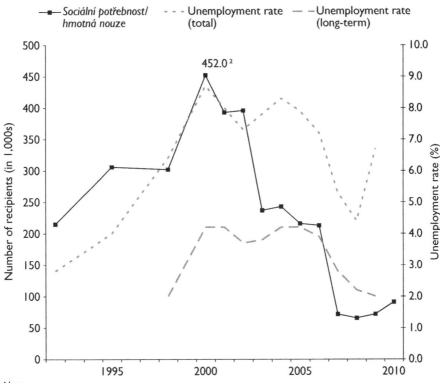

Notes:
[1] The number of MIP recipients is displayed by the solid lines which refer to the left vertical axis. The dashed lines depict the unemployment rates (total and long-term) and refer to the right vertical axis.
[2] By way of illustration, in 2000, 452,000 people received *sociální potřebnost*, which represents 4.4% of the total population.

Sources: EuMin database; Eurostat (2010); ILO (2010).

due to the impact of the Act on Material Need and the 2006 Act on Living and Existence Minimum, which restricted eligibility.

Individuals still represent more than half of the total recipients, while families with children represent about 38%, and incomplete families still prevail among them. The middle age categories constitute the largest group of recipients, of whom 8% are below 25, 22% are 26–35, 27% are 36–45, 28% are 46–55, 14% are 56–65, and only 1% are above 65 (Jahoda et al, 2009). No new data exist on the share of the unemployed, but we assume that their share has not changed much since 2006 when – according to statistics by the Ministry of Labour and Social Affairs – they represented the majority of social assistance recipients.

Denmark

With an average total social expenditure of 27.5% of the GDP between 2003 and 2005, Denmark is the third largest welfare spender in Europe after France and

Sweden (OECD, 2010a). The country thus ranks among the 'highly developed' welfare states of the OECD world and is usually classified as a Scandinavian or social-democratic universalist welfare state. The bulk of its spending goes towards healthcare, pensions, and unemployment benefits. Between 2003 and 2005, as little as 0.9% of the GDP was directed towards social assistance for the working-age population, and the figure is even lower in the longer run, with 0.8% on average from 2003 to 2009.

Denmark has a long history of public responsibility for the poor. A poor law was introduced in 1803, which established a parish-level administrative body responsible for poor relief, the poor's committee. Benefits were mostly given in kind, and every inhabitant of the parish had to contribute to the treasury for the poor (Jonasen, 2009). In 1891, a means-tested old-age pension for older and disabled people was introduced. Between 1891 and 1907, accident, sickness, and unemployment insurance came into existence, largely voluntary and either based on private effort or administered by the trade unions in the case of unemployment (Esping-Andersen and Korpi, 1987). In 1933, the earlier poor laws were replaced by a new law on public assistance that established the right to cash benefits in situations not covered by other social security schemes.

After World War II, the means test attached to basic pensions was gradually transformed to filter out only the richest pensioners, and coverage has remained at around 98% for several decades now. Today, the benefits provided by 'upstream' social security schemes such as pensions and unemployment insurance are relatively generous and encompassing, and therefore only a few people have to rely on means-tested social assistance. There is one general scheme that caters to the bulk of those in need, and several very small schemes for asylum seekers and recent immigrants to Denmark.

The welfare state context

The Danish **pension system** has three pillars. The first pillar is the state pension, which provides the so-called *Folkepension*, a programme with near-universal components dependent on long-term residency in Denmark (Green-Pedersen, 2006). Income from *Folkepension* has several components: first, there is a basic pension (*grundbeløb*), which amounts to around DKK63,050, or €8,500, annually (as at 2009). It is income-tested against individual work income, but income from other sources is not taken into account. Consequently, nearly all pensioners receive the benefit. Second, there is an income-tested pension supplement to the *grundbeløb* called the *pensionstillæg*, for which a stricter means test is applied than for the *grundbeløb*. In comparison with MIP programmes, however, there is a substantial disregard of income – currently, more than €8,000 for single people and more than €16,000 for couples (2009). If pensioners have an income above this threshold, the benefit is reduced by 30% of the excess income. Only if the income rises above around €37,000 does the benefit cease altogether. With the maturation of occupational and private pension plans, receipt of the full supplementary benefit dropped from 69% in 1993 to 57% in 2007 (Goul Andersen, 2011; see also Green-Pedersen and Baggesen Klitgaard, 2008). Several tied pension supplements are available after a stricter needs test, for example for expenditure related to health, heating and housing. There is also a personal supplement (*personligt tillæg*), a discretionary benefit particularly relevant for immigrants with an incomplete *folkepension*. In 2003, a supplementary pension benefit (*supplerende pensionsydelse*; colloquially also called *ældrecheck*) was introduced; it amounts to around €1,400 annually, available after a means test. Due to the disregard of owner-occupied dwellings, about 27% of pensioners receive the benefit (Goul Andersen, 2011).

The second pillar of the pension system builds on fully funded employment-based supplementary pensions (*arbejdsmarkedets tillægspension* (ATP)) and achieves near-universal coverage. As a third pillar, capital income, for example from private pension plans, plays a large role in Denmark and accounts for around 30% of retirement incomes.

Unemployment insurance is administered by the trade unions, and membership in the unemployment insurance fund is voluntary (Benner and Bundgaard Vad, 2000). Around 70% of the Danish workforce are members of a so called '*A-Kasse*' (Anker et al, 2009). Denmark has one of the most generous systems in Europe. Benefits last up to four years and replace between 80% and 90% of previous wages. A ceiling to the benefit ensures that those with lower earnings receive a generous benefit while the replacement rates for those with higher wages are considerably lower. The scheme supports around 85% of the unemployed. As there is little employment protection legislation, the long duration of the benefit helps people to accept the flexible labour market ('flexicurity').

Denmark is a true Scandinavian welfare state with regard to its **family policy**. It provides good conditions for both parents to combine work and family life, thus enhancing family incomes. Families are supported through heavily subsidised childcare to which they are legally entitled. These institutions also cater to children under three (Mahon, 2002). Moreover, there are generous leave schemes and universal child allowances.

The Danish system of MIP

Due to the inclusive nature of social security benefits, the system of MIP is relatively unified. *Kontanthjælp* is the most general programme, and there are three programmes targeted at foreigners at different stages of the integration process (see Table 3.4).

Kontanthjælp was introduced in 2002 under the law on active social policy and replaced the old *social bistand* programme that dated back to 1974. *Kontanthjælp* targets longer-term residents of Denmark, as residency – independent of citizenship – during seven out of the last eight years is one of the main entitlement criteria. The benefit is intended to provide an income for persons who temporarily cannot pay their own way due to a contingency such as the loss of a job (if they do not

Table 3.4: MIP schemes in Denmark, around 2010

Year of introduction (abolition)	Name (in Danish)	Major target group	Main characteristics
2002	*Kontanthjælp*	People meeting the residency requirements	Benefit levels are differentiated according to age. Activation is compulsory
1983, amended several times	*Kontante ydelse til asylansøgere*	Asylum seekers	Benefit levels are very low and contingent upon the status of the asylum application
2002	*Introduktionsydelse*	Foreigners from non-EU and non-Nordic countries and asylum seekers who do not fulfil the pre-conditions of residency	Benefit receipt is connected to participation in three-year integration courses and activation
2002	*Starthjælp*	Foreigners who do not meet the residence requirement and have completed their three-year integration course; asylum seekers after their three-year integration course	Benefits are substantially lower than *Kontanthjælp*

Source: Authors' compilation.

have the right to unemployment benefits), illness, the birth of a child, separation, or divorce. To receive the benefit, claimants must have no income or assets that can be used to cover their needs. One also needs to register as unemployed and be ready to take a job and take part in activation measures.

While it is a general principle of the Danish scheme that everyone is responsible for their own welfare and should be available to participate in the labour market, these conditions are not applicable to all recipients. The municipalities group claimants according to their distance from the labour market in so-called 'match groups', where group 1 is close to the labour market and expected to work, and group 5 is the most distant. Here, activation is not compulsory, and claimants of this group do not have to be available for the labour market. *Kontanthjælp* is intended to cover all expenditure, including those for food, clothing, and housing. For high housing costs, supplementary tied benefits are available. The benefit is taxable, and benefit levels are highly differentiated according to the age and family situation of the claimant. Single people below the age of 25 receive around 35% less than those over 25. After six months of continuous benefit receipt, the benefit is capped. The goal of the ceiling (*loftet*) is to make sure that it is always more attractive to take up a paid job than to live on benefit. Not all components of the benefit are taken into account in calculating the individual threshold above which the benefit is cut. Earned income is not calculated against it; therefore, the ceiling does not prevent recipients from working. The benefit can be reduced by between one sixth and one fifth of the initial rate paid out (Civil Affairs Agency, 2009).

Moreover, there is a '300-hours rule' (after 1 July 2009 the '450-hours rule', with a transition period until 1 July 2011), which is directed towards married couples where one or both of the partners receive *kontanthjælp*. It makes continuous benefit receipt contingent upon each of the spouses having worked at least 300 hours (or 450 hours, respectively) during the last two years. This equates to something less than three hours per week (or 5 hours under the 450-hours rule). As soon as one of the spouses does not fulfil this requirement, one partner loses the right to receive *kontanthjælp* (Danish Ministry of Employment, 2009).

Taking these rules into account, conditionality, an emphasis on activation and work incentives, seems to be relatively strong in the Danish social assistance scheme. The idea of activation was put into law in 1998, making it compulsory, and strongly emphasising recipients' obligations (Green-Pedersen and Baggesen Klitgaard, 2008, p 159).

In addition to *kontanthjælp*, there is a programme that is intended for asylum seekers. They receive support in kind and cash (*kontante ydelse*) after the Alien Act, depending on a number of preconditions and the status of their application. There are three types of cash benefits: First, the basic allowance, which is intended to cover costs for food and daily personal hygiene. Second, a supplementary allowance is available to those asylum seekers over 18 who comply with the contract they have entered into with regard to activation measures and participation in integration courses. Third, there is a caregiver allowance for parents, which is available for up to two children. The amounts paid out vary according to the status of the application. Once the application is processed in Denmark, benefit amounts are higher. Applicants whose applications are deemed 'manifestly unfounded' cannot receive the supplementary allowance, and their basic benefits are somewhat lower. If the application is rejected altogether and applicants prepare to leave the country, benefits are reduced.

The introductory benefit (*introduktionsydelse*) is paid to immigrants from non-EU and non-Nordic countries and asylum seekers during the first three years of their stay in Denmark after they have gained a residence permit. In order to be entitled to the benefit, claimants need to be unable to fend for themselves and ineligible for other social security benefits. They also have to take part in a three-year integration programme designed by the municipalities, usually comprising a language course, information on Danish customs and society, and labour market activation measures. The basis for their participation in the programme is the *integrationskontrakt*, in which concrete personal measures for education and activation are agreed upon. If beneficiaries fail to participate in the programme, their benefit may be either reduced or cancelled altogether. Additional preconditions to entitlement are that applicants register with the employment agency, actively look for a job, and post their CV online at www.jobnet.dk. An additional income of up to DKK33.10 (€4.50) per hour is allowed alongside of the *introduktionsydelse*, but income above this threshold is deducted from the benefit (www.borger.dk, 2009).

Starthjælp is a new programme that applies to all foreigners who arrived in Denmark after 1 July 2002. The programme targets people who are from neither Nordic nor EU countries and who have completed their three-year integration programme but do not fulfil the residency requirement of 'seven out of the last eight years'. This also applies to Danes who have not lived in Denmark or in another EU country for the same period. Further conditions for the receipt of the benefit include participation in activation measures and registering with labour market authorities. Benefit levels are the same as for *introduktionsydelse*, and the same rules for child allowances and additional income apply. Immigrants who arrived before 1 July 2002 receive *kontanthjælp till flygtninge*, a benefit essentially identical to *kontanthjælp*. The benefits *introduktionsydelse* and *starthjælp* are around 35% lower than *kontanthjælp*, and their introduction thus meant a substantial cutback in benefits available to immigrants (Rosholm and Vejlin, 2010).

Healthcare in Denmark is organised in a national health service, and its services are free of charge for residents. To cover co-payments for medicines, special supplements are available for recipients of *kontanthjælp*, and benefit receipt therefore entails access to comprehensive healthcare.

Structural developments

In 2007, the total Danish population was around 5.5 million persons. Approximately 107,000 households or around 214,000 persons, including dependent household members, lived on MIP benefits, equalling around 4.2% of the total population. The cost for MIP benefits totalled €1.5 billion – around 0.7% of the GDP. *Kontanthjaelp* was the most expensive MIP programme and accounted for almost the whole cost of MIP schemes. Both *starthjælp* and *introduktionsydelse*, and their forerunners, are today very small in terms of beneficiaries and expenditure. The number of beneficiaries in the predecessor to these programmes, *kontanthjælp till flygtninge*, peaked at around 29,000 in 1998, probably due to a large influx of refugees from the wars in Iraq and former Yugoslavia (see Figure 3.4).

The level of recipients of *kontanthjælp* seems coupled with the development of the Danish labour market: 85% of the unemployed are supported by the unemployment benefit offered by the *A-Kassen*, but those not covered have to rely on social assistance immediately after losing a job. As there is little employment protection legislation in Denmark, the Danish economy reacts much faster to crises (with layoffs) and to economic recovery (by hiring) than do the economies of other European countries, and the number of beneficiaries in *kontanthjælp* follows this development. Comparatively high unemployment levels above 5% in 2003 and 2004 corresponded to the highest levels of benefit receipt in the period under analysis. The following economic recovery, with unemployment levels at 3.6% in 2007, saw the lowest figures of beneficiaries. The recent jump in annual unemployment rates from 3.1% in 2008 to 6% in 2009, with the last quarter of 2009 seeing a peak of 7.1% of unemployment (OECD, 2010b), was followed by an 18% rise in the number of recipients of *kontanthjælp* from 2008 to 2009. The impact of labour market developments on benefit receipt in *kontanthjælp* thus seems considerable.

In terms of the social structure of beneficiaries, *kontanthjælp* is dominated by relatively young people and single households. In 2006, 40% of recipients were

Figure 3.4: MIP receipt in Denmark, 1992–2010[1]

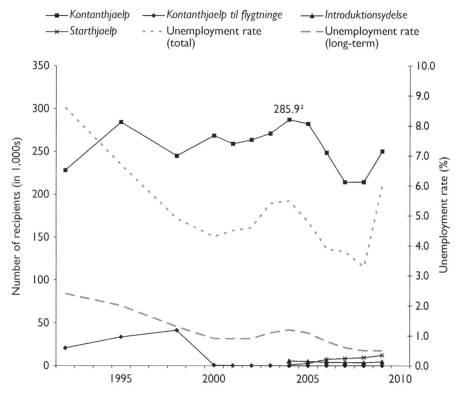

Notes:
[1] The number of MIP recipients is displayed by the sold lines which refer to the left vertical axis. The dashed lines depict the unemployment rates (total and long-term) and refer to the right vertical axis.
[2] By way of illustration, in 2004, 285,888 people received *kontanthjælp* which represents 5.3% of the total population.

Sources: EuMin database; Eurostat (2010); ILO (2010).

younger than 30 and around 65% were younger than 40. Single people made up 56% of households in receipt of benefit, followed by single parents, who made up around 26% of recipients of MIP benefits. Only around 17% were couples with or without children.

Finland

Between 2003 and 2005, Finland's average social expenditure amounted to around 26% of its GDP (OECD, 2010a). Thus, the country ranks behind the top five OECD spenders Sweden, France, Denmark, Germany, and Austria in regard to social spending. Even though Finland is often classified as a social-democratic welfare state, it incorporates elements of the conservative type and has always been a contested case with regard to its type of welfare state regime. Social spending on earnings-related pensions, healthcare, and social services for the municipalities accounted for around two thirds of total social spending in 2007 (Ruoppila and Lamminmäki, 2009), whereas social assistance cost as little as around 0.3% of the GDP.

Finland was a part of Sweden until 1809 and, as a result of the Napoleonic wars, an autonomous Russian grand duchy from 1809 to 1917. Throughout the period, the country maintained an institutional system similar to the Swedish one. In 1852, a poor law was established that made local taxation and local boards for poor relief mandatory. In 1865, poor relief was transferred from the parishes to the municipalities. A new poor law was introduced in 1879, which granted relief to the 'deserving poor' (such as orphaned children, the insane, the incurably sick, and infirm older persons), while help for the able-bodied was only available in the workhouse. After independence from Russia in 1917 and the resulting civil war in 1918, a new Act on Poor Relief was put in force in 1922. It extended the entitlement to relief to new groups and preferred cash benefits. Still, the institutionalisation of the poor was possible under this act, and control by the authorities continued (Esping-Andersen and Korpi, 1987; Markkola, 2007). Social assistance was reformed in 1956. From then on, the municipalities were responsible for supporting those in need, but the reform did not entail a modern understanding of social assistance. The poor could still be institutionalised, recipients were obliged to pay back the money they had received until 1970, and outdoor relief was prominent (Kuivalainen, 2004a, p 46). Only in 1984 was the modern programme that continues to operate until today introduced.

As a result of Russian imperial rule, social insurance developed slower in Finland than in other European countries. In the 1890s, there were efforts to establish social insurance to help the growing class of factory workers. Semi-compulsory work-accident insurance was established in 1895. As there was no legislation on sickness, unemployment, or old age, mutual trust societies were founded. Unemployment insurance was fully established in 1917 on a voluntary basis and administered by the unions. Old-age pensions were finally introduced in 1937, and sickness insurance came about as late as 1963 (Esping-Andersen and Korpi, 1987). Today, these benefits have become quite encompassing. Thus, social assistance is residual and comparatively unified.

The welfare state context

The Finnish **pension system** has two main components. First, there is the national pension (*kansaneläke*), which today provides a residence-based basic pension income to each citizen after a means test. Second, there are the so called 'legislated pensions' (Kangas, 2007), statutory earnings-related pensions that were introduced in the 1960s. These mandatory pensions are organised as occupational schemes.

The maturation of the legislated pensions greatly changed the role of the national pension. Up to the 1970s, spending on national pensions accounted for more than half of overall pension expenditure. This share has been declining ever since, and today national pensions account for only around 15% of total spending on pensions. Until 1996, the national pension had a component means-tested against income from legislated pensions and a universal component paid out to each pensioner after residency in Finland of at least five years. Consequently, around 92% of pensioners received some benefit from the national pension scheme. From 1996 onwards, the universal component was abolished and the whole national pension tested against income from legislated pensions. This means test and the maturation of the legislated pensions led to a decline of the number of recipients of a full national pension (Kangas, 2007).

In 2007, around 53.5% of Finnish pensioners received at least a partial national old-age pension. Approximately 10% of older persons, mainly very old women without a work history and persons without claims against the occupation schemes due to early incapacity received a full national pension, qualifying by their age, unemployment, or disability (Kangas and Luna, 2011). The full benefit amounted to €584 for single persons and €518 for each member of a couple. The national pension ceased once the income from statutory pensions was higher than around €1,200 for single persons and €1,075 for a member of a couple (KELA, 2010). While Finnish pensions are generally taxed, there is an income deduction at the level of the full national pension that may therefore be regarded as tax free.

Finland has three different schemes for **unemployment protection**. The basic benefit (*peruspäiväraha*) is intended for those who are not members of an unemployment insurance fund but still fulfil the condition of having worked 43 weeks during the last 28 months. In 2008, the basic benefit amounted to around €540 per month. Additional child supplements – around €100 per month for the first child and around twice as much for three children – are available. To receive the earnings–related benefit (*ansioperusteinen työttömyyspäiväraha*), 10 months of membership and contributions to an unemployment insurance fund are necessary. This benefit consists of the basic benefit amount plus an earnings-related component. The latter component is designed to provide generous net replacement rates for those at the lower end of the income distribution, while those with high earnings need to cope with lower replacement rates. Thanks to the child supplements, families are treated quite generously in comparison with persons without children (for details, see the description in OECD, 2008a). The net replacement rate for a single person with previous average production worker earnings amounted to 51%. A single-breadwinner married couple with two children would receive a replacement of 73% (OECD, 2010c). Both benefits are taxable but exempt from social security contributions except health insurance; the support lasts for 100 weeks at most.

Labour market support (*työmarkkinatuki*) is available after the exhaustion of the first-tier benefits for an unlimited time and is also accessible for those without a work history (such as first-time labour market entrants) after a five-month waiting period for most groups. This taxable benefit equals the basic benefit, and the same child supplements are available. It is income-tested against the income of the recipient and their partner. Comparatively generous disregards apply: in 2008, the disregard was €253 for a single person and €848 for a couple; in addition, €536 of

---

the spouse's income was not considered; for each dependent child, another €106 of income was not counted. Moreover, benefits such as child allowance, home care allowance, maintenance support, and housing allowance were not taken into account. For families, the benefit was reduced by 50% of the income in excess of the disregard. For single persons, the reduction amounted to 75%. Assets do not play a role (for details, see OECD, 2008a). Labour market support is thus not intended as a benefit of last resort and does not top up recipients' income to a certain level (Heikkilä and Kuivalainen, 2004). Rather, this support filters out those among the unemployed who definitely do not need support and provides some help to those who do.

Finland provides generous **family benefits**. First, there is a universal child allowance. For childcare, the state supports three options: first, parents have the option of using heavily subsidised municipal day care centres. Second, a home care allowance (*lasten kotihoidon tuki*) is available for those who want to take care of their child at home. It has a universal component amounting to around €300 in 2008 and an income-related component worth around €170. For a family of four, the benefit is reduced by around 8% for each percentage point of income in excess of 1,700 €. Third, financial support is also available for the cost of private day care (*lasten yksityisen hoidon tuki*). Similar to the home care allowance, there is a universal component and an income-tested supplement (OECD, 2008a).

The Finnish system of MIP

The Finnish MIP system is special insofar as there is only one general assistance scheme for the working-age population, *toimeentulotuki*, and no categorical schemes (see Table 3.5). While other benefits such as the home care allowances or the labour market subsidy include elements of means-testing, these provisions are not intended to top up claimants' income to a minimum level. Only *toimeentulotuki* aims to provide 'last-resort financial support'.

Toimeentulotuki was introduced in 1984. Every legal resident of Finland is eligible for the benefit. Neither citizenship nor duration of residency plays a role. Additionally, asylum seekers and refugees are entitled to social assistance even though their benefits are lowered during their stay in accommodation centres (Heikkilä and Kuivalainen, 2004).

Table 3.5: MIP schemes in Finland, around 2010

Year of introduction (abolition)	Name (in Finnish)	Major target group	Main characteristics
1984 (amended 1998, 2001, 2006)	*toimeentulotuki*	Those without sufficient means	General benefit accessible to all in need
2002	*maahanmuuttajan erityistuki*	Disabled or older immigrants who do not qualify for a full national pension	Means-tested against claimant's and partner's disposable income

Source: Authors' compilation.

The benefit has several components. First, there is a basic amount intended to cover the cost for a basket of goods deemed indispensable for well-being, such as food, clothing, medicine, public transport, TV licence, internet, and other small costs. The level of the basic rate is differentiated for single persons and couples, and there are also specific rates for children, depending on their age and number. Second, supplementary allowances, such as those for medical care, childcare fees, funeral costs, and housing, are available. The latter supplement covers the difference between the housing benefit (*yleinen asumistuki*), which maximally pays 80% of the housing cost, and the actual cost of accommodation. Moreover, preventive assistance (*ehkäisevä toimeentulotuki*) is intended to cover one-off needs and payments. It is paid out at the discretion of local authorities. Benefit levels are set at the national level and linked to the national pension index, which in turn is related to the cost of living. The municipalities are responsible for the administration of the scheme. Since 2006, the cost of the basic component of the benefit is shared equally between the state and the municipalities (Heikkilä and Kuivalainen, 2004; OECD, 2008a).

Toimeentulotuki is available after a means test, which includes both incomes and assets. All the disposable income of claimants is taken into account. Since 2002, 20% of work income up to 150 € per month and household may be disregarded in order to provide work incentives. Income from some benefits is exempt from the means test – mainly those intended for specific purposes, such as maternity benefit and housing allowance. Child allowances have been part of the claimant's income since 1994, but specific social assistance rates for children were introduced to offset the lower benefit. Owner-occupied accommodation is exempt from asset-testing, but otherwise all assets apart from small savings are taken into account. This may mean that a car has to be sold, for example (Ruoppila and Lamminmäki, 2009).

Since 2001, beneficiaries have had to register as unemployed and actively look for work. Moreover, the municipalities have to offer active labour market measures. Rejection of a job offer or an active measure may lead to a 20% reduction in the basic benefit for two months. A repeated rejection of such an offer may be sanctioned with a 40% reduction for two months (Ruoppila and Lamminmäki, 2009).

Apart from *toimeentulotuki*, there is a categorical MIP benefit in Finland that is targeted at persons of pensionable age. The *maahanmuuttajan erityistuki* is intended for immigrants who have lived in Finland for at least five years but have not acquired the right to a full national old-age or disability pension due to not meeting the residency requirement (40 years). In contrast to the national pension, the benefit is means-tested against the disposable income of both the claimant and the partner. Some types of benefit are exempt from the means test, such as general housing assistance. The yearly income of a single person may not exceed €6,935 (€12,360 for a married or cohabiting couple) in order to be eligible for the benefit. The full benefit is equal to a full national old-age or disability pension.

The Finnish healthcare system covers all residents. Only small fees have to be paid for these services and to cover their cost special supplements are available to recipients of *toimeentulotuki*.

Structural developments

In 2007, the Finnish total population was around 5.3 million persons, and on average, approximately 104,000 households, or around 163,000 persons including dependent household members, lived on MIP benefits (annual averages; STAKES, 2008). This equates to around 3.2% of the total population and around 3.6% of the population under 65 years of age. The cost for MIP benefits totalled €0.5 billion, around 0.3% of the GDP (STAKES, 2008, table 9). Experts estimate take-up to be as low as 50% due to the complicated administrative procedures and the stigma of claiming (Ruoppila and Lamminmäki, 2009, citing Kuivalainen, 2007). *Toimeentulotuki* was the most expensive MIP programme and accounted for 96% of the cost of all MIP schemes. The special assistance for immigrants (*maahanmuuttajan erityistuki*) is very small both in terms of beneficiaries and expenditure.

The receipt of *toimeentulotuki* is relatively closely coupled to the labour market situation (see Figure 3.5). In 2007, as many as 86% of recipients were unemployed, and around 40% received social assistance as a top-up to the labour market subsidy

Figure 3.5: MIP receipt in Finland, 1992–2010[1]

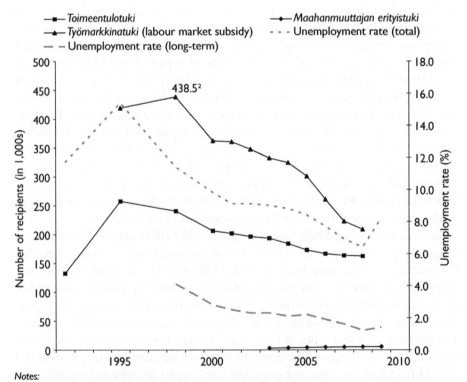

Notes:
[1] The number of MIP recipients is displayed by the sold lines which refer to the left vertical axis. The dashed lines depict the unemployment rates (total and long-term) and refer to the right vertical axis.
[2] By way of illustration, in 1998, 438,521 people received *työmarkkinatuki* which represents 8.52% of the total population.

Sources: EuMin database; Eurostat (2010); ILO (2010).

(*työmarkkinatuki*) (STAKES, 2008, appendix, table 24). The latter benefit is shown in the graph to illustrate the connection with the labour market; persons who receive both *toimeentulotuki* and *työmarkkinatuki* are counted in both programmes. The Finnish economical crisis from 1991 to 1993 caused unemployment to sky-rocket to 16% in 1994. Social assistance receipt peaked in 1996–7. Since then, the economy has gradually recovered, and employment returned to its pre-crisis level in 2007. This development also became evident in the steadily falling numbers of beneficiaries of both the labour market subsidy and social assistance. While there are no official statistics available for 2009 at the time of writing, the recent financial crisis has led to a 20% increase in the demand for social assistance, according to a 2009 survey of the municipalities, especially in urban communities. In more rural areas, the increase was smaller (Moilanen, 2009).

In terms of the social structure of beneficiaries, *toimeentulotuki* is dominated by relatively young persons and single households. During 2007, 51% of recipients were younger than 30 and around 65% were younger than 40 (STAKES, 2008, appendix, table 4). Approximately 71% of households in receipt of benefit were occupied by single persons, followed by single parents – around 12% of recipients of MIP benefits. Only around 17% were couples with or without children (STAKES, 2008, appendix, table 5).

France

In 2009, the French MIP system consisted of 10 non-contributory means-tested benefits. This second most categorically differentiated MIP system in Europe is the result of a complex historical development. The French National Assembly proclaimed an individual right to public assistance as early as 1793, making France the world's first country to do so, but this ambitious aim was not realised until very recently. In practice, poor relief remained locally and mainly religiously organised for a long time. During industrialisation, social insurance for workers was largely based on subsidised voluntary insurance and mutualism. The strong role of the state in welfare provision became firmly institutionalised only after World War II (Kaufmann, 2003).

Due to the late development of compulsory social insurance, France developed a complex system of national benefits for specific population groups based on the solidarity principle (*solidarité nationale*). These categorical benefits were established at the national level and became an important second pillar of the French welfare state. Benefits were granted only to specific groups, especially to older people and people with disabilities. Only in 1988 – 200 years after the proclamation of a universal right to public assistance by the National Assembly – was this categorical system made comprehensive with the introduction of the *revenu minimum d'insertion* (RMI) as the benefit of last resort for all persons above 25 not covered by a categorical scheme. Finally, in 2009, the RMI was replaced by the new *revenu de solidarité active* (RSA), which has a broader coverage and aims primarily at higher incentives to work by granting both out-of-work and in-work benefits with higher income disregards.

The welfare state context

In 2007, total social expenditure in France amounted to 30.5% of the GDP, the highest ratio in Europe, yet from this amount, only 14% was spent on means-tested benefits, including MIP. The complex categorical system of MIP complements a highly developed welfare state based on social insurance. Pensions and unemployment insurance provide wage-related benefits, but flat-rate minima for insured workers in both branches guarantee a floor for persons with long insurance records (de Montalembert, 2008).

The French **old-age security system** consists of two major employment-related tiers and is supplemented by a legally guaranteed means-tested social minimum for all older citizens. The first public pension tier provides wage-related pensions. Within this tier, there is a non-means-tested minimum pension for persons with long insurance records. In 2006, about 36% of all pensioners received this minimum pension. At the same time, the French pension system has a compulsory second occupational tier also providing wage-related benefits. Together, these two tiers provide rather generous benefits for the majority of the retired workforce.

Since both components started relatively late due to the belated development of French social security, securing a minimum income to older pensioner cohorts was necessary. Therefore, a means-tested pension for retired workers was introduced in 1941, the allowance for retired workers, or *allocation aux vieux travailleurs salariés* (AVTS). In 1956, MIP in old-age was extended to all French people. The AVTS (which was limited to insured and employed persons) was supplemented by the supplementary old-age allowance, or *allocation supplémentaire vieillesse* (ASV), which provided a means-tested legal minimum to all older citizens. Since 2007, both benefits have been integrated into the new solidarity allowance for older persons, the *allocation de solidarité aux personnes âgées* (ASPA), which now grants the legal old-age minimum income (*minimum vieillesse*). Yet there are still two kinds of minima: the minimum pension for the long-time insured population (non means-tested) and the general guaranteed minimum income for older persons (means-tested).

The French system of **unemployment protection** consists of three tiers. In the first tier, unemployment insurance benefits are wage-related, but there is also a flat-rate minimum component for workers with long insurance records. Unemployment insurance is also highly inclusive in the sense that entitlement is based on only six months of contributions in the 22 months preceding unemployment (in 2007). The benefit depends on previous wages but with various components providing better protection for lower earners. The duration of benefits depends on both insurance record and age. The variation is extraordinary. In 2008, for example, benefits were paid for seven months for persons under 50 years with an insurance record of six months (during the past 22 months). By contrast, benefits were paid for 23 months for persons with an insurance record of 16 months (during the past 26 months). For persons above 50 years, the respective figures were 27 and 36 months. For all the long-term insured unemployed who have exhausted their claims to unemployment benefits, the means–tested solidarity allowance, *allocation de solidarité spécifique* (ASS) enters as the second tier of protection. The ASS is part of the MIP system because it provides means–tested minimum benefits. Finally, for all those unemployed persons who qualify neither for unemployment benefit nor for the ASS, the RMI served as the third tier and last safety net. As of June 2009, the RMI was replaced by the RSA (discussed later).

Finally, in **family policy** France has a highly developed system of benefits and services. France has been a pioneer of family policy and provides high benefits, especially for families with three or more children. The childcare system is one of the most developed in Europe. In 2007, more than 30% of children below three were covered, and preschool enrolment for children from two and a half years old to compulsory school age is almost universal.

Even within this highly developed welfare state, MIP plays an important role. Sizeable population groups are excluded from social insurance because coverage continues to rely on employment. In combination with a highly segmented labour market, this produces persons who are 'excluded' from insurance benefits and for whom MIP is important.

The French MIP system

The French MIP system comprised 10 benefits for different population groups until June 2009 and nine thereafter. Table 3.6 lists the most important ones (see also Legros, 2009 and Nauze-Fichet, 2008).

The main benefits can be grouped into four categories:

1) Benefits for older persons (beginning in 1941 and 1956) and for disabled former workers (beginning in 1957); both are MIP elements within social insurance;
2) Benefits for persons who are unable to work: disabled persons (from 1975), single parents with children below three (beginning in 1976), older unemployed persons above 60 (2002–9);
3) Benefits for the long-term insured unemployed (beginning in 1979 and 1984);
4) The (general) minimum insertion income for persons above 25 (beginning in 1988 with the RMI and continued from 2009 by the RSA on a broader scale, including employed persons with low earnings).

In category 1), the minimum income guarantee for the elderly has the longest history. In 1941, a means-tested basic pension was introduced for workers with working careers of at least 25 years (the AVTS). This first tier of MIP for older persons was supplemented by a second one in 1956, the ASV, which guarantees a means-tested minimum for all older persons, regardless of previous employment record. Both benefits have been integrated into the new ASPA since 2007.

Benefits under category 2) cover a second group with a long history of entitlement to MIP: incapacitated workers. The ASI for insured employed persons

Table 3.6: MIP schemes in France, around 2010[a]

Year of introduction (abolition)	Name (in French)	Major target groups	Main characteristics
1941–2007 1956–2007 2007	Allocation aux vieux travailleurs salariés (AVTS) Allocation supplémentaire vieillesse (ASV) Allocation de solidarité aux personnes âgées (ASPA)	Insured retired employees with low pensions People 65+, or 60+ if unable to work	Income-tested social pension for former workers Legally guaranteed minimum for all older citizens (residents)
1957	Allocation supplémentaire d'invalidité (ASI)	Disabled/insured formerly employed persons below 60	Legally guaranteed minimum for disabled formerly employed
1975	Allocation aux adultes handicapés (AAH)	All disabled adult persons below pension age	MIP allowance paid by family branch of social insurance
1976–2009	Allocation de parent isolé (API) From 2009 integrated into RSA	Single parents with a child below three (plus a maximum of 11 additional months)	MIP allowance paid by family branch of social insurance
1979–84 1984	Aide au secours exceptionnel (ASE) Allocation de solidarité spécifique (ASS)	Long-term unemployed with exhausted insurance benefits; precondition for ASS: five years of work within the last 10 years	Second tier of unemployment protection; unlimited payments for eligible persons
1984–2006 2006	Allocation d'insertion (AI) Allocation temporaire d'attente (ATA)	Asylum seekers, refugees, unemployed released prisoners, and others without insurance entitlements	Insertion benefit paid for a maximum of one year
1988–2009	Revenu minimum d'insertion (RMI) From 2009 integrated into RSA	Insertion income for persons above 25. Eligibility for younger people only if caring for a child	Third tier of unemployment protection; general insertion income for persons above 25
2002–9	Allocation équivalent-retraite (AER)	Long-term unemployed persons over 60	Pre-retirement allowance for the older unemployed
2009	Revenu de solidarité active (RSA) Integrates RMI and API from 2009	Insertion income for persons above 25. People below 25 are eligible if caring for a child or having worked for two years during past three years	Insertion income for persons above 25 Paid as in-work and/or out-of-work benefit

Note:
[a] In addition to the MIP benefits listed in the table, there is the AV (*allocation veuvage*; widows' minimum income benefit) introduced in 1980, with very few beneficiaries, as well as the RSO (*revenu de solidarité*; solidarity income) introduced in 2001 in the French overseas departments. Neither is considered here.

Source: Authors' compilation.

---

was introduced in 1957 and guarantees a legal minimum for incapacitated former workers. Since 2000, it has only been available for persons below 60; older persons automatically receive the minimum for the elderly.

About 20 years later, two additional minimum income benefits were introduced for population groups with no or difficult access to the labour market: the AAH in 1975 for disabled persons and the API in 1976 for single parents with children below three. Since 2009, the API has been integrated into the new RSA, but with a higher benefit level preserving their special condition.

In 1984, the ASS was introduced for unemployed persons who had exhausted entitlements to wage-related unemployment insurance benefits, which make up our category 3). The ASS depends on applicants having been employed for at least five years in the past 10 years. It is an insurance-based but means-tested flat-rate benefit. The AI was also introduced in 1984 and is granted to former prisoners as well as refugees and asylum seekers without insurance entitlements. It is limited to one year in order to facilitate integration into the labour market. In 2006, the AI was replaced by the ATA, which has similar features.

The widest gap in the French system was only closed in 1988 with category 4), the RMI, a non-categorical benefit that secured a minimum income for all residents older than 25 and for younger adults with children (Lelièvre and Nauze-Fichet, 2008). Since 2003, the benefit has been linked to an individual insertion contract (*contrat d'insertion*) between the recipient and the benefit agency in which reciprocal rights and duties are laid down. The aim of the benefit was to integrate beneficiaries into work, but the means and duties depended on individual circumstances. Entitlement to the benefit was based on legal residence. Nationals from outside the EU and the European Economic Area (EEA) had to prove residence of at least five years. Recognised refugees and accepted asylum seekers were also entitled (others were transferred to AI or ATA). The means test for the RMI was very strict because all sources of income of all household members were assessed.

In 2009, the RMI was replaced by the RSA. The RSA integrates the former RMI and API, as well as other benefits for low-wage earners, such as the *prime pour l'emploi* (employment subsidy), which is not part of MIP. The RSA is both an out-of-work and an in-work benefit. It has a flat-rate component (which is also the legal minimum for those without any earnings) and a wage-related component. The wage-related component has the effect of an earnings disregard of 62% for RSA recipients within a band of incomes, leading to very high work incentives. The minimum benefit is higher for single parents with a child below the age of three. Eligibility for RSA is broader compared to the former RMI: entitlement to RSA is based on legal residence and age (minimum 25), but young persons below 25 are also entitled if they are caring for a child or have worked for at least two years within the past three years. EU and EEA nationals must have lived in France for at least three months directly prior to the application.

In France, the categorical differentiation of the MIP system has direct consequences for the income conditions of the different target groups because regulations and benefit levels vary widely. First of all, the means test is applied in different ways. For example, for the AAH and the former API (the benefits for disabled persons and single parents), the test was applied on an individual basis and did not take into account the income of other household members. By contrast, for the former RMI and the ASS, the household was the unit of the means test. Moreover, benefit levels differ substantially. In 2009, for example, the guaranteed minimum for a single person was around €320 in the case of ATA/AI, €455 for RMI or ASS, €584 for API (not including the child component), €633 for ASPA, and €653 for AAH. Hence, single parents and older and disabled persons especially have received much higher payments than the unemployed or non-disabled adults of active age. These differences persist with the new RSA, although the potential for additional earnings for RSA recipients has been improved significantly.

Structural developments

In 2006, the total population of France was about 63 million persons. In the same year, roughly 3.5 million persons received MIP benefits. If one includes dependent household members, one could say that around 6.4 million persons, about 10% of the population, lived on MIP. Total costs for all benefits amounted to about €19 billion in 2006. In the same year, the RMI and the AAH together represented about 60% of total expenditure. Recipients of MIP benefits are usually also entitled to means-tested housing allowances. In 2006, about 2.2 million households received these benefits, at a cost of €4.3 billion, which is roughly as high as one quarter of total MIP expenditure.

Despite cyclical fluctuations in the economy and the labour market, the total number of beneficiaries and household dependants has not changed significantly since the early 1990s. Yet there have been major structural changes within the group of recipients (Figure 3.6).

The major structural change within recipients is reflected in two adverse trends: First, the number of beneficiaries in the ASV, which used to be the most important MIP scheme until the mid-1990s, has declined from 1.2 million in 1990 to around 600,000 in 2007. This decline is due to the maturation of the French pension system and the fact that younger pensioner cohorts have better pensions than the older cohorts.

Second, the number of RMI recipients has doubled from around 500,000 in 1990 to around 1.1 million in 2007. These rising figures of RMI recipients show a major problem in the French labour market, namely high barriers to first-time labour market entrants and those with irregular work histories. Although many young adults below 25 are excluded from the RMI, the structure of recipients is nonetheless dominated by relatively young persons and single-person households: In 2006, more than half of recipients were younger than 40, and more than 700,000 were single (out of a total of 1.2 million); 300,000 were single parents, and only 200,000 were couples with or without children.

Figure 3.6: MIP receipt in France, 1992–2010[1]

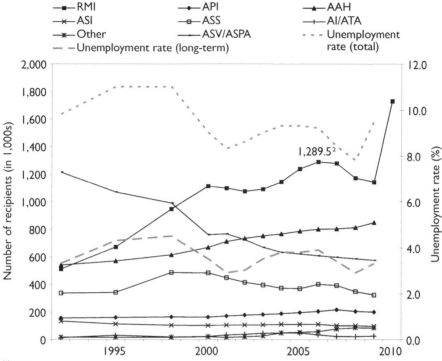

Notes:
[1] The number of MIP recipients is displayed by the solid lines which refer to the left vertical axis. The dashed lines depict the unemployment rates (total and long-term) and refer to the right vertical axis.
[2] By way of illustration, in 2006, 1,289,540 people received RMI which represents 2.04% of the total population.

Sources: EuMin database; Eurostat (2010); ILO (2010).

Compared to the benefits for older people and the RMI, the number of recipients in the other schemes has remained surprisingly constant. Even the potentially highly volatile benefit for the long-term unemployed, the ASS, has shown great stability over time. This means that the majority of the employed workforce with longer insurance records are relatively well secured, whereas the 'outsiders' who are only entitled to the RMI face significantly more problems.

The figures for single parents receiving the API are similarly stable. This may come as a surprise because France has one of the highest rates of out-of-wedlock births and single parenthood in Europe, close to Scandinavia and Britain. Yet there are two reasons for this stability. First, the API is limited to single parents with children below the age of three. Indeed, many single parents with older children received the RMI instead (around 300,000 in 2006). If one adds to this the number of API recipients, about 500,000 single-parent families lived on one of the major minimum income benefits. Secondly, as argued in the introduction to this section, France has a highly developed family policy and is one of the countries with the most extensive childcare systems. It should also be pointed out that preschools (*écoles maternelles*) are part of the educational system and therefore free of charge for parents. Compared with the situation in many other countries, this is very positive for the social integration of all population groups. In fact, although there is no formal obligation to participate, almost all children attend preschools from the age of two and a half. This family policy enables lone parents to take on paid jobs instead of falling into the last safety net. Still, many of them do depend on MIP, whereas complete families are rarely found among recipients.

With the introduction of the new RSA, the situation has changed slightly. In December 2008, there were 1,141,900 recipients of RMI and 200,400 recipients of API. Both benefits were integrated into RSA in June 2009. In December 2009, the RSA was received by 1,697,000 persons. Hence, the number is substantially higher than the sum of the two former benefits. One reason is that the scope of the RSA is wider. The RSA also includes a high number of low–wage earners. For example, in December 2009, 1,117,000 persons received only the flat-rate minimum benefit component (*RSA socle*), which means that they had no personal income. At the same time, however, about 404,000 persons received only the wage-related benefit component, which means that their income was above the threshold for the guaranteed minimum (*RSA activité*). The rest (176,000) received a combined benefit. Hence, more than one quarter of RSA recipients are persons in work who receive an earnings supplement.

Germany

The long history of the German welfare state has been characterised by the paramount importance given to employment-related social insurance. Germany was the first country in the world to introduce compulsory social insurance for industrial workers against major social risks (in the 1880s). Though the scope of social insurance was limited and benefits were flat-rate and meagre at the beginning, the insurance principle was extended to larger population groups, and benefits became earnings-related over the course of more than 120 years of institutional development (Alber, 1982; Schmidt, 2005).

Besides this dominant historical stream, social assistance has always fulfilled an important function, but its scope declined with the gradual extension of social insurance. While social insurance was legislated by the central/federal state, local authorities long held large competencies in social assistance. Until the end of the 19th century, poor relief was guided by the rule of 'place of birth', meaning that relief had to be provided by the community of origin instead of the community of residence. This was still the case even when mass labour migration into the new industrial centres was at its zenith. Although subsequent legislation in the Weimar Republic led to more national homogeneity, the principle of local poor relief was kept. At the same time, however, two categorical MIP schemes were introduced: one for victims of war and another one for social insurance pensioners. This was necessary because most insurance capital funds had been erased after the hyperinflation of the early 1920s. During the Great Depression, a special assistance scheme for the unemployed was added.

The categorical and local approach to social assistance came to an end in the early 1960s. In 1962, the *Sozialhilfe* was introduced by federal legislation as a general social assistance programme covering the whole population. Although the law established a federal framework, financing and administration were left in the hands of the states and local authorities. Nonetheless, the *Sozialhilfe* provided a general minimum income guarantee for all citizens. In the 2000s, the German MIP system was again fundamentally reformed. The minimum income guarantee for all citizens has remained, but the overall system has become a categorical one in which different population groups have access to different MIP schemes with partly deviating regulations but largely similar benefit rates.

The welfare state context

Given the predominance of employment-based and earnings-related social insurance in the German welfare state, social assistance has played a residual role as the last safety net for persons with no access to insurance or with low benefits. An important feature of social insurance is that it does not provide guaranteed minima for pensions or for unemployment (an exception being work-accident insurance). This means that persons with low insurance benefits due to short working careers or low earnings may have had to apply for social assistance in order to reach the legally guaranteed minimum income.

The German **pension system** has remained strongly earnings-related and still does not provide a minimum pension. Nonetheless, the large scope of insurance coverage, as well as relatively generous replacement rates and survivors' pensions, have so far prevented many older persons from falling into poverty. Indeed, Germany has continually had one of the lowest old-age poverty rates in Europe. Still, older persons have been a major recipient group for social assistance for long-term care services, which were mainly financed by social assistance until the introduction of long-term care insurance in 1995.

For the unemployed, there was a two-tier system of **unemployment protection** until 2004. The first-tier scheme of unemployment insurance (*Arbeitslosenversicherung*) provided earnings-related benefits for a limited time after the beginning of unemployment, depending on age. The second-tier scheme of unemployment assistance (*Arbeitslosenhilfe*) stepped in after people had exhausted their first-tier benefits and passed an income test applied to the household. This test, however, was less strict than in social assistance. Benefits were earnings-related, though at a lower level than in unemployment insurance. Hence, the system was closed to labour market entrants and those with no access to social insurance due to interrupted working careers or short working hours. The self-employed were also excluded. Since benefits were paid without time limit, only a few unemployed persons had to rely on social assistance. The German labour market had to struggle with an increasing long-term unemployment rate, especially after reunification.

This was one of the reasons for the major reform of unemployment protection enacted in 2004. This reform replaced the *Arbeitslosenhilfe* by a new means-tested MIP scheme for all long-term unemployed persons and new jobseekers, including persons without employment or insurance records (to be discussed later), whereas the unemployment insurance system remained in place (Mohr, 2007).

German **family policy** traditionally provides a relatively high level of financial transfers and tax subsidies for couples and families, but Germany is a latecomer in the field of childcare services and policies that help combining employment and family work. Single-parent families face difficulties in earning a livelihood. If private maintenance obligations (after divorce) do not suffice, many single-parent families have to rely on social assistance because they face huge obstacles in entering the labour market. Only recently have childcare services been extended into a larger scale. The goal is to provide a place for every third child below the age of three until 2013. This will improve the compatibility of family and work, a goal that is still problematic today.

The German system of MIP

The present German MIP system consists of five schemes: four categorical ones and a general scheme (see Table 3.7). Until the early 1990s, the system had been unified by the *Sozialhilfe* (general social assistance) introduced in 1962. Only the *Kriegsopferfürsorge* (relief for victims of war) existed in parallel to this general programme. Then, three categorical schemes were introduced: the *Asylbewerberleistungen* (scheme for asylum seekers) in 1993, the *Grundsicherung im Alter und bei Erwerbsminderung* (scheme for older persons and those permanently unable to work) in 2003, and finally the *Grundsicherung für Arbeitsuchende* (scheme for the unemployed and jobseekers) in 2005. The *Sozialhilfe* was thereby transformed into a minor residual scheme. The regulations and procedures differ between the schemes, for example with respect to the means test, but the benefits are at the same level, with the exception of the scheme for asylum seekers, for which benefits are much lower and mainly provided in kind.

The *Kriegsopferfürsorge* (relief for victims of war) is the oldest and most generous of the existing schemes. Today, it is not only available to soldiers and their families but also to victims of crime and to political prisoners of the former GDR.

Sozialhilfe (social assistance) replaced the former *Sozialfürsorge* (welfare relief) and established a general system of last resort for the whole population. This new system not only included means-tested cash benefits but also provided a variety of in-kind benefits and services in situations of special needs, for example disability or long-term care. In fact, the share of spending flowing into these special benefits increased constantly and even exceeded cash transfers. This changed, however, with the introduction of long-term care social insurance in 1995. Moreover, the establishment of the categorical MIP schemes for older persons and for unemployed people reduced *Sozialhilfe* to a very limited scheme.

Table 3.7: MIP schemes in Germany, around 2010

Year of introduction (abolition)	Name (in German)	Major target group	Main characteristics
1950	*Kriegsopferfürsorge*	Persons (mainly older people) who were impaired during military operations and their relatives; victims of war, violence, and crime; victims of political persecution in the former GDR	Compensatory pension for victims of war and violence and their families; mainly for older persons
1962	*Sozialhilfe; Hilfe zum Lebensunterhalt (außerhalb von Einrichtungen)*	General scheme. Today (after introduction of categorical schemes – since 2003 and 2005): mainly for persons below 65 with temporarily reduced earning capacity who are not cohabiting with employable persons	General social assistance. Today: residual
1993	*Asylbewerberleistungen*	Asylum seekers and refugees	Minimum support for asylum seekers and refugees and their dependants
2003	*Grundsicherung im Alter und bei Erwerbsminderung*	Persons 18+ with permanently and fully reduced earning capacity, or persons over 65	Minimum pension for older persons or the permanently impaired who are not required to work
2005	*Grundsicherung für Arbeitsuchende*	Employable persons 15–65 (unemployment benefit II) and non-employable persons who cohabitate with them (*Sozialgeld*)	Minimum income for employable jobseekers and their dependants

Source: Authors' compilation.

The major programme today in quantitative terms is the *Grundsicherung für Arbeitsuchende* (scheme for unemployed and jobseekers) introduced in 2005 (Huster et al, 2009). Recipient figures far outnumber the other schemes. This scheme is also in the centre of a highly controversial debate on MIP in Germany. It integrates the former unemployment assistance with the employable population among the *Sozialhilfe* recipients. As a consequence, the long-term unemployed who have exhausted their claims to wage-related unemployment insurance benefits and all other jobseekers who are able to work are covered by one scheme today. Another important feature of the new scheme is that benefits can also be received as top-ups to (low) work incomes. It therefore also functions as an in-work benefit similar to tax credits in other countries.

The *Grundsicherung im Alter und bei Erwerbsminderung*, a special scheme covering those among the former *Sozialhilfe* recipients who are too old or unable to work, was introduced in 2003. Compared with the old system and the parallel scheme for the unemployed, conditions for recipients are more favourable in this scheme. For example, private maintenance duties of family members (children or grandchildren) are no longer enforced, except for those on higher incomes.

Moreover, the means test is more relaxed, with higher disregards on property. One major goal of the 2003 reform was to remove the barriers which had impeded many entitled older persons from actually claiming assistance benefits. Many feared stigmatisation or that local authorities would hold their children or grandchildren liable to pay for them. Moreover, the new scheme established an important complement to the existing earnings-related pension system in the form of a guaranteed income for older persons. Still, however, this income guarantee is based on a means test, and there is no minimum pension in social insurance. For the recipient of the MIP benefits just described, housing costs (rent, heating) are normally covered in full if both the size of the flat and the rent level are considered reasonable. Healthcare is free of charge for MIP recipients, apart from a fee (€10) for each first visit to a doctor in a quarter.

A separate scheme for asylum seekers was established in 1993. The early 1990s was a period with high numbers of refugees seeking asylum in Germany. The scheme was intended to make this form of migration less 'attractive' by implementing much lower benefits than those provided under general social assistance. In particular, asylum seekers have received most support in kind rather than in cash; they get only a small amount of pocket money.

Overall, the German MIP system has developed from a general system established in the early 1960s into a categorical one in which specific regulations apply to different population groups. The former *Sozialhilfe* was not abolished, however, and remains the general last safety net for all those not covered by one of the categorical schemes.

Structural developments

The major changes in German MIP become especially apparent when looking at the development of caseloads. The reforms in the early 2000s have led to an MIP system that covers around 10% of the total population today. Before, only around 3% of the population was dependent on MIP (see Chapter Four). This increase was caused by the abolition of the former unemployment assistance scheme. Today, MIP is no longer a residual safety net in cases of individual need but has developed into a mass system, in particular for unemployed people and jobseekers. The quantitative growth has been accompanied by a strong institutionalisation by the federal state, even though the housing components of benefits and their financing rest with local authorities.

The structural development of MIP is shown in Figure 3.7 for the total number of beneficiaries, that is, entitled persons plus dependent family members.

The *Sozialhilfe* was the dominant scheme until 2004, covering almost 3 million beneficiaries at a relatively constant level. Fluctuations in unemployment rates were not reflected in the number of recipients because most of the long-term unemployed were covered by unemployment assistance. However, and perhaps surprisingly, such fluctuations are also not reflected by recipient numbers of unemployment assistance (which is not part of MIP). Instead, the data show

Figure 3.7: MIP receipt in Germany, 1992–2010[1]

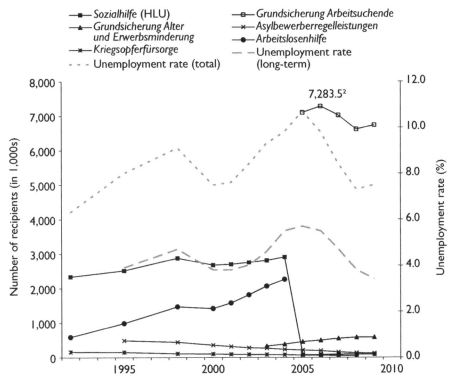

Notes:
[1] The number of MIP recipients is displayed by the solid lines which refer to the left vertical axis. The dashed lines depict the unemployment rates (total and long-term) and refer to the right vertical axis.
[2] By way of illustration, in 2006, 7,283,493 people received *Grundsicherung für Arbeitsuchende* which represents 8.84% of the total population.

Sources: EuMin database; Eurostat (2010); ILO (2010).

a continuous growth to more than 2 million persons in 2004. This anomaly is explained by the increasing problem of structural long-term unemployment in the German labour market. From 2005 onwards, the new *Grundsicherung für Arbeitsuchende* has been by far the largest MIP scheme in terms of beneficiaries. Overall, more than 7 million persons depend on this scheme, including family members of unemployed people.

Compared with this large scheme, the other MIP schemes are of a modest size. As mentioned, the *Sozialhilfe* today only covers around 100,000 persons, even fewer than the small system for asylum seekers, which has shown a constant decline in numbers. Only the scheme for older persons and those unable to work is of a significant size, with about 800,000 persons, and shows an increasing trend. The vast majority of pensioners still have an income above the guaranteed minimum. However, this is about to change dramatically for future pensioner cohorts who will face more difficulties than present pensioners. Today's employment careers are interrupted more often by periods of unemployment than before, and Germany's high long-term unemployment over the last decades will certainly result in more persons depending on MIP during their old age in coming years.

Hungary

by Mónika Bálint, Zsuzsanna Szabó and Dániel Horn

Hungary is a Central European country that switched to democracy and became a market economy during the early 1990s. The economic shock of the post-communist transition has meant that average well-being has deteriorated and income inequality has increased. Employment has dropped, and there has been an unprecedented rise in unemployment. During the socialist era, a variety of social benefits existed that have been greatly modified during the last decade because they have not provided a minimum level of well-being and were not sustainable in the long run (Hungarian Central Statistical Office, 2007a).[5] Officially, some parts of the Hungarian MIP system were already in place before the post-communist transition, but they did not fulfil their designated function. After the regime change, the system had to be reformed and was given a new character. The amount of social protection allowances is minimal, and it often does not effectively reach the desired target groups. Moreover, there are population groups (such as labour market entrants) that are not covered by any of the existing MIP schemes.

The welfare state context

The present Hungarian **pension system** is made up of three pillars: social insurance, private schemes, and voluntary savings (Hungarian Central Statistical Office, 2007a). Most older persons today receive a social insurance pension thanks to the formally full-employment situation during the socialist era, even though many of these pensions are very small. Since today's employment rate is very low, this situation will change in the near future (Holzer, 2010). Until 1997, persons for whom pensions did not cover minimum living expenses could apply for a spouse supplement (discussed later). Since the termination of this benefit in 1997 there has been no equivalent allowance. Persons reaching retirement age are only entitled to a pension if they fulfil the minimum insurance record; if not, they can receive an old-age allowance, which is an MIP benefit (discussed later). The minimal amount of insurance-based pension – received by many who were employed during the socialist era – and the old-age allowance are almost the same, both being relatively low.

In 1991, the Employment Promotion and Unemployment Benefits Act established insurance-based **unemployment benefits**. During the communist regime, unemployment and poverty were not officially recognised. There was no unemployment support and only very limited social assistance (Magyar-Nemzetközi Kék Szalag Bizottság, 1994). After the transition, unemployed persons were protected by two systems: the insurance-based allowance and means-tested unemployment assistance (later the regular social assistance). Entitlement to the allowances is based on whether sufficient time has been spent in work. The length of provision depends on how long the person worked, and the amount is linked to individual salary, with both a minimum and a maximum amount. Between 1992 and 2000, unemployed persons could receive unemployment assistance (UA) after they had exhausted their insurance-based allowance. At the beginning, UA was paid indefinitely, but after 1995, it was limited to two years. It was replaced by regular social assistance (RSA) in May 2000 (discussed later). The system of unemployment provision was significantly changed again in both 2005 and 2009. In 2005, the UA was replaced by job-search assistance, which aimed to motivate individuals to efficient job searching and cooperation with employment offices. In 2009, those entitled to regular social assistance were divided into two groups: Persons with physical and mental disabilities still received RSA, while physically eligible and long-term unemployed persons received availability support and had to be available for public work.

Hungary has a sophisticated **family benefit system** in which some benefits are universal and others are tied to the payment of contributions or are income-dependent. Some of these benefits are important for low-income families (Albert, 2009). All parents are entitled to family benefit (*családi pótlék*), child care allowance (CCA, *gyermekgondozási segély*), and child raising support (CRS, *gyermeknevelési támogatás*), whereas the maternity allowance (MA, *terhességi-gyermekágyi segély*) and the childcare fee (CCF, *gyermekgondozási díj*) are based on employment prior to childbirth. Families in need can apply for additional allowances (such as child protection allowance, *gyermekvédelmi támogatás*) at the local government level (Hungarian Central Statistical Office, 2007a).

The Hungarian system of MIP

The Hungarian system of MIP consists of benefits for three main target groups: older persons; unemployed school-leavers and the unemployed who have exhausted claims to wage-related benefits; and the disabled (see Table 3.8).

Benefits for older people include the spouse supplement (SS, *házastársi pótlék*) and the old-age allowance (OAA, *időskorúak járadéka*). The SS was introduced in 1990 and was provided to a pensioner's spouse (old-age or disability pensioner) living in the same household. The amount depended on age and income level as well as type of disability, but no new entitlements were issued after 31 December 1997. The OAA was introduced in 1998 for older people who had not been employed long enough to be entitled to an old-age pension and who had no other source of income. Entitlement criteria were changed on 1 January 2006, at which time persons over the age of 75 living alone received higher amounts. The goal of this change was to help single women living in small-settlement rural areas (Hungarian Central Statistical Office, 2007a, p 170).

Benefits for the unemployed include unemployment assistance (UA, *munkanélküliek jövedelempótló támogatása*), career beginners' assistance (CBA, *pályakezdők munkanélküli segélye*), and regular social assistance (RSA, *rendszeres*

Table 3.8: MIP schemes in Hungary, around 2010

Year of introduction (abolition)	Name (in Hungarian)	Major target group	Main characteristics
1990–7	Spouse supplement, SS (*házastársi pótlék*)	Pensioners (only couples)	Minimum benefits for low-income pensioner couples
1992–2000	Unemployment assistance, UA (*munkanélküliek jövedelempótló támogatása*)	Long-term unemployed	Minimum income for those who have exhausted their insurance-based unemployment benefits or are not entitled to them
1991–6	Career beginners' assistance, CBA (*pályakezdők munkanélküli segélye*)	Unemployed labour market entrants with secondary or tertiary education	Minimum income to cover costs of living
1997	Regular social assistance, RSA (*rendszeres szociális segely*), from 2009: benefit for persons of active age (*aktív korúak ellátása*)	Active-age disabled or non-employed persons	Minimum income to cover costs of living
1998	Old-age allowance, OAA (*időskorúak járadéka*)	Persons 62+	Minimum income to cover costs of living; depends on household type and age

Source: Authors' compilation.

szociális segély). Between 1992 and 2000, UA was provided by local governments for unemployed persons who had exhausted their insurance-based allowance. Entitlement was means-tested, and the per capita family income had to be below 80% of the minimum old-age pension. Irrespective of previous wages, the UA was a flat-rate benefit equal to 80% of the minimum old-age pension. Initially, duration was indefinite, but in 1995, it was limited to two years (IEHAS and NEF 2002b, p 162). After having exhausted UA, persons could receive RSA after 1 January 1997, when entitlement to social assistance was extended to the active-age unemployed. As of 2000, the RSA has become the only type of assistance for the long-term unemployed (IEHAS and NEF 2002a, p 192). From 1991 to 1996, first-time jobseekers could receive CBA if they had completed at least two years of vocational secondary school. They were entitled to 75% of the minimum wage for a maximum of six months until 1995, when the amount was changed to 80% of the minimum old-age pension (IEHAS and NEF 2002b, p 162). The CBA was replaced by the 'Start' programme, which also included lesser-educated persons, to help career beginners find employment.

Criteria for the receipt of RSA include earning an insufficient income, being of active age but not employed, and not being entitled to or having exhausted entitlements to UB or UA. The level of income (providing subsistence) was set at 80% of the minimum old-age pension, and the per capita family income had to be under this limit. Neither the recipient nor family members were allowed to own any property. This regulation was valid until 1 January 2006, at which point the RSA's entitlement conditions and benefit amounts were changed to take better account of family composition. The benefit is now calculated on the basis of income per consumption unit instead of per capita and depends on the aggregate income of the family. The benefit complements family income up to the entitlement limit, which is 90% of the minimum amount of old-age pension, and the duration is indefinite.

A major gap in the RSA system is that it is only for persons who have exhausted UA. Others outside the labour market (such as labour-market entrants or those living off the black market) can receive the RSA only after having cooperated with the labour market authorities[6] for at least a year (or at least two years before May 2000). In 2006, this rule was changed; those who have previously received regular monetary support (such as a childcare fee, child protection allowance, and so on) and do not receive any income only need to cooperate with the authorities for three months before being entitled to RSA.

The RSA was again renamed and reformed in 2009, becoming the benefit for persons in active age, and has two parts: The availability support (*rendelkezésre állási támogatás*) was designated for those who are able to work, whereas the RSA (same name, different programme) is given only to the disabled. Persons must be registered and sign an agreement that they intend to work in order to be entitled to availability support. They must also take part in public works, and those under 35 who did not complete their basic education must also participate in further education. The amount of availability support is fixed; it is independent of the size or composition of the family and equal to the minimum level of old-age pension (Albert, 2009, p 5). Again, the system does not cover labour market entrants because they have to show at least one year of cooperation with the authorities in order to be entitled if they do not fit into any other system (Albert, 2009, p 7). The RSA is additionally available to the disabled.

Structural developments

The caseload of the different benefits has changed significantly throughout the period under study (see Figure 3.8). The number of older persons receiving SS has been gradually declining every year because no new entitlements have been issued since 31 December 1997. An average of 53,000 households received SS in 1998, a figure that was down to around 31,000 in 2007. However, the number of households receiving SS is still significant, with 29,000 in January 2008 (0.3% of the population; 99% of the beneficiaries are women). The amount of the spouse supplement is the lowest of all pensions or pension-like benefits, amounting to 7,645 HUF per month in 1998 and to 14,394 HUF per month in 2007 (Hungarian Central Statistical Office, 2007a). The OAA was given to 8,900 persons in 1998, and this number declined continuously until 2006, when about 6,500 persons received the benefit. The higher support for persons over 75 living alone is evident in their receipt of 34% of the total amount. In 2006–7 around 2,100 persons received this increased amount (Hungarian Central Statistical Office, 2008).

Figure 3.8: MIP receipt in Hungary, 1992–2010[1]

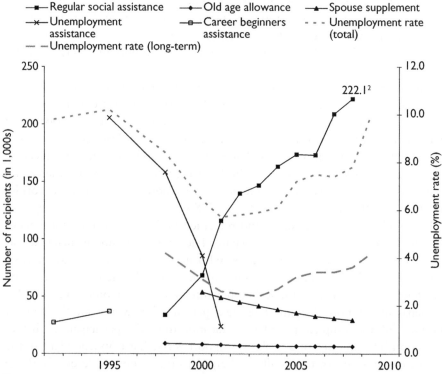

Notes:
[1] The number of MIP recipients is displayed by the solid lines which refer to the left vertical axis. The dashed lines depict the unemployment rates (total and long-term) and refer to the right vertical axis.
[2] By way of illustration, in 2008, 222,074 people received regular social assistance which represents 2.21% of the total population.

Sources: EuMin database; Eurostat (2010); ILO (2010).

The number of unemployed people receiving UA has been declining since 1995, dropping by 40% in 2000 and again by 70% in 2001. The ratio between women and men has been constant at about 40% to 60%, respectively. By contrast, the number of persons receiving RSA has been increasing due to the declining number of persons receiving UA. In 1997, only 13,500 persons received RSA compared to more than 173,000 persons in 2005. Another reason for the increase is the growing number of disabled persons receiving RSA. In 1997, their number was around 8,300 and grew to a little above 9,000 in 2005. In 2008, disabled persons made up 4.4% of all RSA recipients.

In 2007, entitlement conditions for RSA were changed. The main goals included the termination of long-term benefit dependency and enhancing the motivation to work. The scope of RSA beneficiaries was widened to the so-called subsidised jobseekers on 1 January 2007. Those receiving allowances – apart form persons with health problems – are obligated to cooperate with organisations assigned by the local government as a precondition of payment. This change is visible in the caseload numbers. The average monthly number of persons receiving the assistance was 173,000 in 2006, increasing to 209,000 in 2007 (with an additional 2,000 HUF increase in the amount) and to 222,000 in 2008. In short, the number of persons receiving RSA has sextupled between 1998 and 2007. The increase in the number of recipients has lowered the proportion of women in the group, which stood at around 52% in 1998 and reduced to 45% in 2007. Additionally, 58% of those entitled live alone, while 46% have at least one child (Hungarian Central Statistical Office, 2008). In 2008, 93% of recipients were unemployed, 3% were supported 'job-hunters' (cooperating with the labour market authorities), and 4% were disabled people. The median age group is 45–61 among disabled people, 30–44 among the 'job-hunters', and 18–29 among unemployed people.

Expenditure on these four MIP benefits (SS, OAA, UA, and RSA) amounted to 0.3% of the GDP in 1995. This ratio remained more or less constant, but the distribution between the four allowances has changed greatly. Between 1995 and 2001, the UA was the largest, with 0.19–0.15%, but after its abolition, the RSA has become the dominant allowance. The majority of all entitled persons used to receive UA, but when UA was abolished in 2001, the number of RSA recipients went up drastically. In 2007, 2.5% of the population received one of these four allowances, and 2% received RSA alone.

Ireland

The Irish welfare state is characterised by a relatively modest level of social expenditure and a high share of means-tested benefits of various kinds, including a large number of different categorical MIP schemes. One reason for this development is the relatively late introduction of social insurance and its implementation on the basis of mainly flat-rate and low benefits. As a consequence, social assistance has retained an important complementary function for uncovered needs and population groups to a degree that is exceptional in Western Europe. Another exceptional feature of the Irish MIP system is its categorical character, organised in 12 schemes that serve different population groups and one general scheme that serves as the residual last safety net for all.

Ireland gained independence from Britain in 1921. Until that time, social policy was shaped by British legislation, which left a long-lasting imprint. Early milestones of this legislation were the poor law of 1838 and the old-age pension system with non-contributory, means-tested, and flat-rate pensions introduced in 1909. These founding laws put the subsequent development of the Irish welfare state on track (Cousins, 2003). In addition, some specific features of the Irish Free State and its society contributed to the persistence of this track and included the long-lasting predominance of agriculture, the structure of the Irish party system, and the strong cultural and political influence of the Catholic Church (Daly and Yeates, 2003).

The predominance of agricultural employment and family farming until the 1950s retarded the development of earnings-related social insurance until the 1960s and

1970s. There was a sizeable Irish working class, but it lived and worked mainly abroad due to emigration and labour migration to the industrial centres of Britain and the US. The Irish party system emerged out of the struggle for independence and the civil war. This nationalistic cleavage has weakened the impact of class cleavages on party structures and voter alignments (Cousins, 2005). The major role of the Catholic Church has resulted in a traditional family model and a limited development of public social services. This pattern inhibited an early materialisation of the idea that the state has the duty to support all needy persons and that each individual has a subjective right to public support.

The welfare state context

The Irish welfare state has grown enormously over recent decades. Social expenditure has risen strongly due to the institutionalisation of earnings-related social insurance from the late 1960s and early 1970s onwards (Curry, 1998). The strong economic growth following EU membership also contributed to this development (McCashin and O'Shea, 2008).

In **old-age security**, the contributory flat-rate state pension forms a very important first pillar, providing a basic income for insured pensioners. The scheme goes back to the 1909 British legislation. In addition to this contributory benefit, there is a means-tested non-contributory pension for all those who have not been insured. This non-contributory means-tested pension (which is part of MIP) continues to play a far greater role in Ireland than in the UK for those without adequate insurance records.

The historical legacy of **unemployment insurance** is also visible. In 1911, British legislation introduced unemployment insurance, providing contributory flat-rate benefits. This system was supplemented by a non-contributory means-tested scheme during the Great Depression in the 1930s. Today, insured unemployed persons receive contributory flat-rate benefits at the level of social assistance for up to 15 months following loss of employment. For uninsured unemployed persons and those who have exhausted their contributory insurance claims, a means-tested scheme guarantees a minimum income. Since the insurance-based system is not very generous (flat-rate benefits) and limited in time, this means-tested unemployment assistance plays an important role.

With respect to **family policy**, the Irish welfare system is characterised by some universal and a myriad of categorical and means-tested benefits, especially for single parents and working families with low incomes. In comparative perspective, family policy is not highly developed in Ireland due partly to the strong influence of the Catholic Church, which firmly opposed a greater role of the state in relation to families, social services, and education. Universal child benefit was introduced in 1944, but most other family-related benefits are means-tested and focus on incomplete families and families with low earnings (Maguire, 1986). In addition, public childcare is very limited in Ireland, but there is a growing sector of private childcare that provides high-cost services for middle-class families.

The Irish system of MIP

As already mentioned, the present Irish MIP system is composed of 12 MIP schemes for different categorical groups and one general and truly residual last safety net for all persons in need who are not covered by any of the other schemes (see Table 3.9). A major characteristic of the system is that all of these benefits – except the very last safety net – are regulated by the central state and have nationally uniform entitlement conditions and benefit rates (Daly, 2009). However, there are some major variations in the strictness of the means test, in particular with respect to the value of exempted property. Within the scheme for disabled people, the most generous disregards are applied, whereas the disregards for unemployed people are the lowest.

The categorical benefits can be differentiated into four groups:

1) benefits for pensioners
2) benefits related to disability and long-term care
3) benefits for single parents and widowed women
4) benefits for the unemployed and persons on low wages.

In addition, the general supplementary welfare allowance is the very last safety net for all other needy persons. This scheme very often serves as a temporary buffer for recipients until a decision is made on claims for a specific categorical scheme.

Category 1), MIP for pensioners, has the longest tradition. Older people were the first group to be lifted out of the stigmatising system of the poor law. Already in 1909, British legislation introduced a non-contributory and means-tested flat-rate pension. Today the state pension guarantees a minimum income for all persons above 66 who are in need and do not qualify for the contributory pension. A non-contributory widows' pension was introduced in 1935. In 1997, it was extended to widowers, and today it covers all survivors who are not entitled to a contributory pension. Since 2006, claimants have been transferred to the non-contributory state pension from the age of 66. In 1990, a means-tested pre-retirement allowance was introduced for former employed persons between 55 and 65 to combat unemployment. This scheme was closed to new applicants in 2007.

The second group of benefits focuses on disabled persons and persons who take care of those with disabilities. The oldest of this kind of benefits is the blind pension from 1920, which guarantees blind persons and their families a minimum pension. There has been a means-tested income support since 1990 for persons caring for disabled, needy, or impaired persons (carer's allowance). A general disability allowance was introduced in 1995 for disabled persons between 16 and 65, and their dependants. The allowance is paid to those with a limited earnings capacity due to personal hardships.

In addition to widows' pensions, Ireland introduced a number of means-tested benefits for other groups of single parents or deserted wives (category 3). While public support for complete families remains limited, 'need' was translated as the

Table 3.9: MIP schemes in Ireland, around 2010

Year of introduction (abolition)	Name (in English)	Major target group	Main characteristics
1909	State pension (non-contributory); formerly old-age pension	People over 66 who do not qualify for contributory state pension	Minimum pension for older people
1935–1997	Widow(er)'s pension (non-contributory)	Widow(er)s below 66 who are without children and who do not qualify for contributory widow(er)s' pension	Minimum pension for widow(er)s
1990	Pre-retirement allowance (closed to new applicants in 2007)	Former workers between 55 and 65, and their dependants	Minimum pension for early retired workers
1970	Deserted wife's allowance (closed to new applicants in 1997)	Deserted wives below 66 who are without children and who do not qualify for deserted wives' benefit	Minimum income for deserted wives
1973–89	One-parent family payment (replaced deserted wife's allowance and prisoner's wife's allowance) (formerly lone parent's allowance)	Lone parents and their children (below 18 or 22 if in education)	Supplementary payment for lone parents and their children
1974	Prisoner's wife's allowance (closed to new applicants in 1997)	Women below 66 who are without children and whose husbands are in jail	Minimum income for wives with imprisoned husbands
1920	Blind pension	Blind or visually impaired people between 18 and 66, and their dependants	Minimum pension for blind people and their dependants
1990	Carer's allowance	People (and their children) who live with and care for a disabled, impaired, or needy person	Supplementary income support for people who care for others
1995	Disability allowance	Disabled people between 16 and 65, and their dependants	Financial support for people who do not receive a full income due to disability
1933	Jobseeker's allowance (formerly unemployment assistance (before 2006))	Jobless people (and their dependants) who are actively seeking work and between 18 and 66	Unemployment assistance for workless jobseekers and their families
1966	Farm assist (formerly smallholder's unemployment assistance)	Farmers between 18 and 66 on low income, and their dependants	Financial support for farmers on low income
1984	Family income supplement	Working couples on low income, and their children (below 18 or 22 if in education)	Financial support for working families on low income
1977	Supplementary welfare allowance	People without or on low income who do not work fulltime, and their dependants	Supplementary payment for people with low or no income, and their dependants

Source: Authors' compilation.

lack of a (male) breadwinner, and the state replaced the 'father' and husband as the main provider in cases of need. In the early 1970s, three different allowances were introduced that guaranteed a minimum income for deserted wives (1970), unmarried mothers (1973), and prisoners' wives (1974). Since 1997, the three benefits have been integrated into the one-parent family payment for new benefit claims.

The fourth group of schemes relates to the unemployed and low-wage workers. Today, the jobseeker's allowance (2006) covers jobless persons who are between 18 and 65, actively seeking work, and not entitled to insurance-based benefits. This is the case for persons who do not fulfil the minimum contribution requirements or who are unemployed for longer than 15 months.

A particular feature of the Irish employment structure is the long-lasting importance of agriculture. In this context, flat-rate benefits have played a strong role because earnings-related benefits have been largely irrelevant to smallholders. In Ireland, those benefits were mainly means-tested. In 1966, smallholders' unemployment assistance was introduced for farmers between 18 and 65 on low income, and their families. In 1999, this scheme was replaced by the present farm assist programme. The third benefit that falls into the category of work-related provisions is the family income supplement for working families on low income with children. This scheme began in 1984 and helps low-wage families secure a minimum income.

Finally, the supplementary welfare allowance (SWA) functions as a truly residual last safety net as it grants a subsistence minimum to needy persons who do not work and are not entitled to any of the categorical MIP benefits or who are waiting for a decision on their claims. In 1977, the SWA replaced the former home assist programme, which referred back to the old poor law. The SWA still applies a more severe means test and has no earnings disregard. Work requirements are also strongly enforced.

In addition to the guaranteed minimum income, housing benefits play a significant role. If they are included in the benefit package, Irish benefit levels are among the highest in Europe when compared with the national average income (see Chapter Four). Free access to healthcare is also available to poor people. Despite two seemingly contradictory features, a strong role of the state and a high proportion of 'private' supply, the majority of the private schools and hospitals are Catholic, but they are integrated into the public system and largely paid for by social insurance and the state. Even if 'private' agencies play an important role, access is guaranteed by the state, which is especially important for poorer persons.

Structural developments

Despite the numerous benefits described earlier, only four schemes clearly dominate the quantitative structure of Ireland's MIP: the non-contributory state pension, the jobseeker's allowance, the one-parent benefit, and the disability allowance. In 2007, each of these four benefits covered about 100,000 persons (recipients excluding dependent family members). The remaining nine schemes are far behind in terms of caseload (see Figure 3.9).

In the early 1990s, the jobseeker's allowance (then called unemployment assistance) was by far the most extensive scheme, including more than 200,000 persons. But with the subsequent steep decline in unemployment, the number of recipients decreased significantly. Behind this development stands the Irish 'economic miracle' in which unemployment rates fell from about 15% in 1992 to less than 5% in 2000. This downturn was especially marked between 1996 and 2000. While the jobseeker's allowance has followed labour market cycles, the stable figures for state pensions reflect a constant structural need for minimum pensions in the Irish old-age security system. Over the past 15 years, the number of recipients of means-tested minimum pensions has remained remarkably stable at around 100,000 persons.

Figure 3.9: MIP receipt in Ireland, 1992–2010[1]

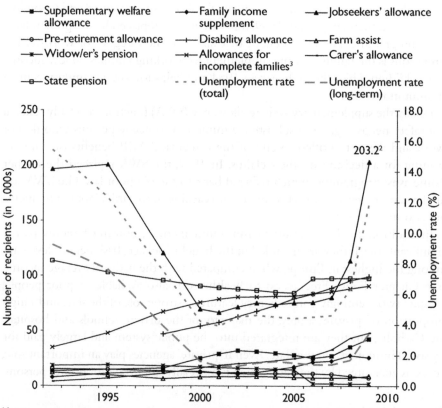

Notes:
[1] The number of MIP recipients is displayed by the solid lines which refer to the left vertical axis. The dashed lines depict the unemployment rates (total and long-term) and refer to the right vertical axis.
[2] By way of illustration, in 2009, 203,248 people received jobseekers' allowance which represents 4.57% of the total population.
[3] These include one-parent family payment, deserted wife's allowance and prisoner's wife's allowance.

Sources: EuMin database; Eurostat (2010); ILO (2010).

The other two main MIP schemes show a constant increase in recipients. The disability allowance covered fewer than 50,000 persons in 1996 but almost 100,000 in 2007. The one-parent family payment (formerly lone parent allowance) increased by about the same size. The growing significance of the one-parent benefit is based on changing family structures in Irish society. Due to the very low provision of affordable (public) childcare, single parents face considerable barriers when combining paid work and care for their children. MIP benefits thus play an important role in securing a living for this group, and activation policies targeted at single parents are confronted with huge structural problems. By contrast, the benefits for deserted wives and prisoners' wives have always covered few persons and were replaced by the one-parent benefit for all new claimants in 1997.

Farm assist and family income supplement each cover fewer than 30,000 persons. The support of low-income earners, be they employed families with children or agricultural workers, obviously has no priority in the Irish MIP system. This is perhaps surprising if one compares this situation with the UK working tax credit, which covers more persons than all other MIP schemes combined. The idea of 'welfare through work' is firmly established in the UK, but there is only a limited version of it in Ireland.

A final interesting feature of the Irish system is that the very last safety net (the supplementary welfare allowance) covers a low number of recipients. In 2007, fewer than 30,000 persons were covered, and figures have been low over the whole period. This suggests that the categorical schemes seem to operate quite well and cover most persons in need. But the low coverage rate of supplementary welfare allowance may also be an effect of a higher stigmatisation of these benefits compared with the categorical schemes and the stricter means test imposed on recipients.

Italy

Italy has no national MIP system for the whole population. Older and disabled persons in need are covered by nationally organised categorical MIP schemes, whereas the various general MIP schemes are regulated at the regional level and organised by local communities. This fragmented MIP system has led to strong discrepancies between different population groups and huge geographical variations.

The creation of a national public social assistance system was prevented by three main historical factors. First, there is the strong tradition of Catholic welfare institutions, which have been acknowledged and subsidised by the state since the late 19th century but continue to be controlled by religious congregations and the clergy. In 1890 these *opere pie* were given a juridical personality and a uniform system of administration imposed by the state. However, benefits and services were not regulated. Secondly, there is a strong tradition of local self-governance in Italy. Finally, the family has also always been an important social institution, providing help and assistance to its members in various circumstances and at different stages of life. These three factors have prevented the development of a strong role of the state in assisting the poor. Ferrera (2006) argues that the lack of administrative capacities also played an important role, because MIP systems need sophisticated mechanisms of government. Another important factor is certainly the high regional disparities in Italy (Saraceno, 2006).

At the same time, social insurance for workers and employees has developed on a national scale similar to that of other countries of the conservative welfare regime type. In addition, the state introduced public welfare schemes for specific population groups in need – particularly for mothers and children, blind people, and deaf people – who were not covered by social insurance. In 1937 public local welfare institutions, the *enti comunali di assistenza*, were introduced by the Fascist regime. They became responsible for various groups of poor and destitute persons at the local level. Since World War II, the regions and local communities have been responsible for social welfare.

The welfare state context

The Italian welfare state is characterised by a strong emphasis on pensions, a limited system of unemployment protection, and a rudimentary family policy.

Italy has a very generous **pension system**. Expenditure on old-age and survivors' pensions constitutes about 60% of total social expenditure, which is one of the highest shares in Europe. Employment-based old-age and invalidity pensions provide high average benefits. In addition, a minimum contributory pension has been provided for the insured population since 1952 (*integrazione al trattamento minimo*). This scheme provides a guaranteed minimum to old-age and invalidity pensioners who have fulfilled the required insurance period and whose pensions fall below the legally defined minimum. This pension supplement is paid by the state but provided under the pension insurance system. It depends solely on a test of individual income and is therefore not included in our definition of MIP (see Chapter One). The *integrazione al trattamento minimo* is suspended for all who entered employment after 31 December 1995. Where there is need, persons have to apply for the means-tested guaranteed minimum income benefit described later. In addition, since 2002 the *maggiorazioni sociali* have topped up all pensions (including the MIP benefits described later) to a certain minimum. It is considered MIP because it is means-tested at the household level and applies to all older persons (to be discussed later).

The Italian system of **unemployment protection** is limited and fragmented. Ordinary unemployment benefits are modest and only available for a short period of time. In 2007 the ordinary unemployment benefit (*indennità di disoccupazione*) provided payments for up to eight months for persons under 50 and up to 12 months for those over 50. The benefit was 60% of the previous wages for the first six months, 50% for the seventh month, and 40% thereafter. In addition, there are variations according to sector of employment and wage level. Protection is limited for persons who lost their job for 'individual' reasons, but it is much better for workers who lost jobs due to 'external' and 'objective' reasons. In cases of bad weather, temporary lay-offs, or reductions in working time due to industry crises or company restructuring measures, a temporary unemployment benefit is paid by the Cassa Integrazione Guadagni. Standing at 80% of the previous wages, these benefits are higher than in the case of ordinary unemployment compensation. The same is true for workers who definitely lost their job as a result of industrial or company restructuring and who receive unemployment mobility benefits (Strati, 2009; OECD 2007b). These mobility benefits are also paid at the level of 80% of previous wages. Given this limited and fragmented unemployment protection system, one would expect MIP to be very important to unemployed persons, but unemployment rates in Italy vary strongly by gender, age, and region. In fact, middle-aged men in the north have one of the lowest unemployment rates in Europe, whereas young persons and women in the south are highly disadvantaged. The high level of labour market segmentation leads to a situation where the majority of the unemployed are concentrated among the most vulnerable groups, who do not have access to adequate ordinary unemployment benefits. Some of these problems are perhaps mitigated by the strong family solidarity that plays an especially important role for young unemployed persons.

Besides the 'gerontocratic' character of social protection and the highly segmented labour market, the lack of a universal **family policy** is a third specific characteristic of the Italian welfare state. There is only an income-tested family allowance for dependent workers, providing benefits that depend on income and family size. In 2009, for example, a two-parent family with an annual income below €13,119 (the lowest income category) and only one child was entitled to an annual family benefit of €137.50; if they had two or three children, the amounts increased to €258.33 and €375.00, respectively. These payments are obviously very low and do not constitute an effective MIP for families. In addition, the Italian childcare system is not well developed; while the number of places is high for children between three and five years of age, the situation is worse for younger children. Only in recent years has the number of places for children below three grown.

Overall, the Italian welfare state is characterised by gross structural imbalances. It provides adequate protection for some groups but almost nothing for other populations at risk. One buffer to these structural imbalances is the elaborate family solidarity. Another potential buffer is the large size and high significance of the shadow economy. The Italian MIP system, however, is rather inadequate and imbalanced.

The Italian MIP system

Since the Italian last safety net is based on very different regional and even local schemes, it does not constitute a truly national MIP system. At present it consists of four types of benefits: a guaranteed minimum income for older persons, a similar benefit for disabled persons, a general means-tested guaranteed minimum for all types of pensioners on either contributory or non-contributory benefits,

Table 3.10: MIP schemes in Italy, around 2010

Year of introduction (abolition)	Name (in Italian)	Major target group	Main characteristics
1969	*Pensione sociale*	Citizens/residents 65+ with no or very low income	National guaranteed minimum for older persons
1995	Replaced by *assegno sociale*		
1971	*Pensione d'invalidità civile*	Full or partially disabled persons with no or very low income	National guaranteed minimum for disabled persons
2002	*Maggiorazioni sociali*	Recipients of contributory or non-contributory old-age or invalidity pensions and with an income below a threshold	National guaranteed minimum for all poor pensioners
(2000)	*Minimo vitale*	National framework law for general subsistence minimum (not implemented due to constitutional reform of decentralisation)	In practice only regional and local social assistance schemes

Source: Authors' compilation.

and the general last safety net, which covers various kinds of individual needs and risks. The first three benefits are legislated at the national level, while the fourth is legislated at the regional level and administered by local communities. However, the funding is granted by the state.

The guaranteed income for older persons was introduced in 1969 and reformed in 1995. In the same year, the *pensione sociale* was replaced by the *assegno sociale* for all new entrants. Those entitled to the benefit are Italian citizens aged 65 or older and those with permanent residence in Italy. In 2008 the *assegno sociale* amounted to €396 per month and was paid 13 times a year. The annual income limit was €5,143 for a single person and €10,285 for a couple. The amount paid out equals the difference between the income limit (the benefit) and the actual income of the person or couple.

The guaranteed income for disabled persons was introduced in 1971. Those entitled to this benefit are disabled persons between 18 and 65 who reside in Italy permanently and have a degree of invalidity between 75% and 100%. In 2007 the *pensione d'invalidità civile* amounted to €243 per month and was paid 13 times per year. In the same year, the income limits for the *pensione d'invalidità civile* were €4,171 per year for persons with a degree of invalidity between 74% and 99%, and €14,257 per year for those with a 100% degree of invalidity. In addition, persons with a degree of disability of 100% receive the *indennità di accompagnamento* (care allowance), amounting to €458 per month (paid 12 times per year).

The *maggiorazioni sociali* is a means-tested top-up to all contributory and non-contributory pensions, including the *pensione sociale* (*assegno sociale*) and the *pensione d'invalidità civile*. In 2002, when the scheme was introduced, the guaranteed monthly amount was equal to 1 million Italian lira (about €516 at that time). The level of this supplement has been augmented since then.

Apart from these categorical schemes, there is no national general last safety net in Italy. There was some experimentation with a national system starting in 1996, the *reddito minimo d'inserimento* (RMI) (minimum integration income), but it was terminated in 2001 because the constitutional reform in the same year defined social assistance as a competence of the regional governments (Saraceno, 2006). The regions (and the autonomous provinces) have introduced different schemes with widely varying regulations and benefits. The description of all these variations, however, is beyond the scope of this study, but an overview is given by Strati (2009). In addition to regional differences, administrative discretion is high at the local level (Saraceno, 2002).

In addition to these MIP benefits, a variety of other means- and income-tested benefits are granted by the Italian welfare state. Among these, only the pensions for blind or deaf persons can be considered MIP. The level of these pensions is similar to those for the *pensione d'invalidità civile*, but the additionally available *indennità di accompagnamento* is much higher for these special categories.

Structural developments

There are no national data on recipients of the regional schemes constituting the general last safety net in Italy. Only some data for the national experimentation period with the former RMI are available, and they show the very residual character of this scheme. According to a report published by the Ministero della Solidarità Sociale (2006), the share of families who received benefits was about 3.1% of all families in the communes that participated in the experimentation (referring to the year 2000).

Considering these low figures, the significance of the categorical MIP benefits for older or disabled persons is higher but still low compared to the legal minima provided for contributory pensions under social security (Figure 3.10).

MIP benefits constitute only about one quarter of all minimum benefits. The total number of MIP pensions for disabled persons (*pensione d'invalidità civile*) covered about 923,000 persons in 2005; in the same year, about 769,000 MIP pensions for older persons (*pensione sociale* or *assegno sociale*) were given out, and 404,000 victims of war received their respective pensions. More than 4,506,000 persons, however, received a minimum contributory pension. The latter figure includes 2,187,000 old-age minimum contributory pensions, representing more than one fifth of all contributory old-age pensions. Social spending on MIP for older persons and disabled persons amounted to €3.4 billion and €2.7 billion respectively in 2005. On average, MIP benefits for older persons are higher than for disabled persons, ignoring additional care allowances (*indennità di accompagnamento*). Compared with these figures, however, social spending on the contributory minimum pensions (not MIP) was much higher, with more than €24 billion in 2005. The prevalence of pensions in the Italian welfare state is also quite clearly reflected in the system of MIP, emphasising the gerontocratic character of this welfare system. In addition, the incidence of MIP benefits is much higher in the southern regions of Italy.

Figure 3.10: Categorical MIP and minimum contributory pensions, Italy 2005

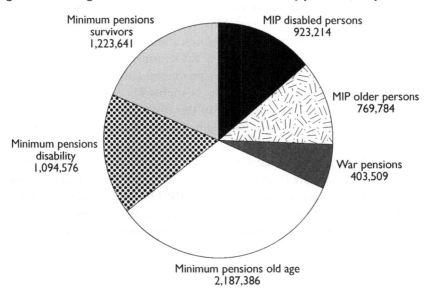

Source: Ministero del Lavoro, della Salute a delle Politiche Sociali (2008, p 3).

The Netherlands

In the post-war decades, welfare in the Netherlands was mainly focused on passive redistribution. The economic crisis of the 1970s resulted in massive cost pressure being put on unemployment insurance and even more so on disability schemes that were highly accessible and frequently used as routes to early retirement and an alternative to layoffs by employers. As a consequence of concerted reforms in all fields of social policy, this 'Dutch disease' was turned into a 'Dutch miracle', with unemployment rates falling from about 8% to 3% between 1990 and 2000 (Gerards et al, 2008; van Oorschot, 2008; Schmid, 2010). Ever since, Dutch unemployment rates have remained below the European average. The institutionalisation of flexible work arrangements and the introduction of activation measures in the 1990s, as well as the recent strengthening of self-responsibility and market principles in welfare production, have added a strong liberal dimension to the Dutch welfare mix, but the original insurance character of the overall system has not been renounced. The coexistence of social rights based on citizenship, employment status, and reciprocity makes the Dutch welfare state an exception in Western Europe; a hybrid, incorporating 'elements of all three of Esping-Andersen's [1990] "worlds of welfare capitalism" – liberal, conservative-corporatist and social-democratic' (Eardley et al, 1996, p 270). Under this very specific welfare arrangement, MIP plays a somewhat residual role that mostly mirrors gaps in the coverage of insurance.

The welfare state context

In its essence, social security in the Netherlands rests on insurance schemes, but these are based on different principles. The risks of unemployment, work incapacity, and sickness are covered by a system of employee insurances (*werknemersverzekeringen*). They have their origins in schemes that were introduced between 1901 and 1939 and strongly oriented on the German Bismarckian model. In the post-war decades, nationwide *volksverzekeringen* were installed in the areas of old-age, survivors', and child benefits. They were modelled after the British concept of national insurance after the important influence the Beveridge Plan had had an on social policy planning during the Dutch government's exile in London.

The Dutch public **pension system** (*algemene ouderdomswet*, AOW) was the first *volksverzekering* to be introduced, in 1957. It works as a pay-as-you-go system that provides basic retirement benefits that vary according to household situation and contribution years. Insurance contributions are paid by all residents aged between 15 and 65 who have an income (social benefits included) and by persons living abroad who are employed in the Netherlands and pay social security taxes. Residents with no incomes are exempted from contributions without being expelled from insurance. An insurance period of 50 years is needed in order to obtain a full pension, which amounts to 70% of the minimum wage for singles and 100% for married or cohabiting couples. Every missing year of insurance leads to a 2% reduction in the pension amount. For pensioners whose partner has not reached age 65 yet, the benefit is partially means-tested against the partner's work income (UWV, 2007; van Oorschot, 2008).

Apart from this basic tier of old-age security, about 90% of employees in the Netherlands are covered by occupational pensions. Most of these schemes are arranged at the sector level by collective agreements, making them quasi-mandatory for employers and employees. Other kinds of private arrangements, are of minor importance. For those pensioners whose total income falls below the social minimum, means-tested benefits are available that top up household incomes to the level of a full AOW. Until 2009, these benefits were granted by municipalities within the context of the Work and Benefits Act (WWB, discussed later), but in January 2010 a separate scheme for this target group was installed (*aanvullende inkomensvoorziening ouderen*, AIO), and responsibility was shifted to the centrally organised Social Insurance Bank (Sociale Verzekeringsbank, SVB), which also administers AOW and the other *volksverzekeringen* (SVB, 2010).

Unemployment protection is divided into two tiers: a short-term, basic benefit, which is paid for three months, and a prolonged benefit, given for a maximum period of 38 months. To obtain the basic benefit, a claimant must have worked for at least 26 of the previous 36 weeks. The replacement rate is 75% of the former daily wages for the first two months and 70% in month three. Afterwards, the benefit can be prolonged if the recipient has worked for at least 52 weeks per year for four of the five years prior to the unemployment spell. This benefit also amounts to 70% of former wages. The duration of this extension depends on the total working career of a person and cannot exceed 38 months (Schmid, 2010; UWV, 2010).

The unemployment law (*werkloosheidswet*, WW) of 1949 has undergone a series of reforms as a consequence of persistently high unemployment rates from the late 1970s up to the early 1990s. Conditions for access to benefits were tightened by linking eligibility more closely to individual work records, shortening reference periods, and introducing activation measures. More recent direct cuts in benefit duration include the shortening of the initial basic payment in 2006 from six to three months and the abolition of an unemployment assistance that had been paid for one year following wage-related payments until 2003 (van Berkel and de Schampheleire, 2001; van Oorschot, 2008).

The main elements of Dutch **family policy** are flat-rate child benefits, tax reductions, and an individualised system of care services and leave arrangements (Morel, 2007; van Oorschot, 2008). Universal child benefits were introduced in 1963 (*algemene kinderbijslagwet*, AKW) and supplement parents' wages and benefits until the children reach the age of 18. These benefits vary slightly by age, and until the mid-1990s the amounts also differed according to the number of children. Today, this regulation has been phased out almost completely since it remained applicable only to those children born before 1995, who will have reached age 18 by 2013 (European Commission, 2010). The resulting losses for larger families were partly smoothed out in 2008 and 2009 when the child tax relief of 2001 was transformed into a direct benefit that comes in different amounts for one, two, and three or more children (Rijksoverheid, 2010). Further tax relief is available to employed parents of children younger than 12 and to lone parents who have dependent children under 27.

As women's employment rose rapidly in the 1990s, childcare coverage for children younger than three expanded from only 3% in 1990 to 14.5% in 2004. The state heavily subsidised day care facilities at the beginning of this process, but childcare became more and more privatised. Since 2005, parents have been obliged to buy childcare services from private for-profit and non-profit providers. There are, however, special tax reductions for lone mothers and low-wage earners, and since 2007 employers have been obliged to contribute to the childcare expenses of their employees. The introduction of the life course savings scheme (*levensloopregeling*) in 2004 is another factor that individualises the risk of child rearing as well as of old age and sickness. Employees can save 12% of their gross annual earnings for different leave purposes (for example childcare, care of older people, or education). This arrangement can be problematic for low-wage workers and persons without regular employment, especially when they face the need for leave more than once during their career, which is often the case for women (Knijn, 2008).

The Dutch system of MIP

In the Netherlands, the MIP system is split into general social assistance, four categorical schemes, and a supplementary scheme in the scope of national insurance (Table 3.11). Most MIP benefits are oriented at the social minimum, which is nationally defined as 50% of the minimum wage for singles, 70% for single parents, and 100% for married or cohabiting couples. Child benefits are paid additionally and most schemes also have a vacation supplement.

The current legislation of general social assistance came into effect in 2004 with the law on work and income (*wet werk en bijstand*, WWB). Its precursor was the *algemene bijstandswet* (ABW) of 1965, which was reformed in 1996. Until 1995, a separate MIP scheme existed for the unemployed (*rijksgroepsregeling voor werkloze werknemers*, RWW), to whom job search requirements and other activation measures were already applied (UWV, 2007). The 1996 reform integrated this scheme into the ABW and extended activation to all recipients except persons temporarily unable to work and single parents of children under the age of five. Today, single parents are only exempted from work obligations in exceptional cases. The financial responsibility of municipalities has increased since 2001; until then, the central state reimbursed 90% of local ABW costs. This was lowered to 75% in order to intensify municipal efforts to reintegrate recipients into the

Table 3.11: MIP schemes in the Netherlands, around 2010

Year of introduction (abolition)	Name (in Dutch)	Major target group	Main characteristics
2004	Wet werk en bijstand (WWB), former algemene bijstandswet (ABW)	Persons aged 27–64	General social assistance and activation
1986	Wet inkomensvoorziening oudere en gedeeltelijk arbeidsongeschikte werkloze werknemers (IOAW)	Unemployed people over 50	Minimum income for older unemployed persons
1987	Wet inkomensvoorziening oudere en gedeeltelijk arbeidsongeschikte gewezen zelfstandigen (IOAZ)	Former self-employed people over 55	Minimum income for older self-employed who have to give up business
1986	Toeslagenwet (TW)	Recipients of employee insurance and wajong benefits	Top ups for benefits below the social minimum
2010	Wet werk en arbeidsondersteuning jonggehandicapten (wet wajong), formerly Wet arbeidsongeschiktheidsvoorziening jonggehandicapten (wajong)	Persons who became (partly) incapable of work in young age	Income guarantee and work incentives
1999	Wet werk en inkomen kunstenaars (WWIK), formerly Wet inkomensvoorziening kunstenaars (WIK)	Artists	Temporary assistance for working artists
2009	Wet investeren in jongeren (WIJ)	Persons aged 18–26	Labor market integration and supplements on work incomes
2010	Aanvullende inkomensvoorziening ouderen (AIO)	Persons aged 65+	Social assistance for older people

Source: Authors' compilation.

labour market. At the same time, the system of labour market service provision was privatised (van Berkel, 2010). The implementation of today's WWB in 2004 took these developments another step further; municipalities now receive a fixed yearly budget that is split into two parts: 'income' and 'work'. Costs exceeding the budget have to be settled mostly with the municipalities' own resources, while surpluses from one year can be carried over to the next (Ministerie van Sociale Zaken en Werkgelegenheid, 2008).

Until 2009, *bijstand* was paid out to persons between 18 and 65. For beneficiaries under 21, however, the benefit rates were lower while those over 65 received a slightly higher rate equal to the level of public pension. Since October 2009, young jobless persons under 27 have been excluded from WWB and subject to the law on investing in the young (*wet investeren in jongeren*; WIJ), which stipulates that, instead of granting benefits, municipalities are to allocate young persons to a job or an apprenticeship immediately. In January 2010, persons 65 and older were also excluded from the WWB with the creation of the AIO scheme (mentioned earlier).

As a complement to WWB, parts of work income can be spared from the means test, and there is a supplement (*langdurigheidstoeslag*) for long-term benefit recipients who have very little chances of getting reintegrated into the labour market. Singles and lone parents can request a 20% top-up to their benefit, and there are also extra payments (*bijzonere bijstand*) for exceptional expenses. These additional benefits, for example for school supplies or special healthcare expenses, are also available to persons who do not receive WWB but whose income lies close to the social minimum. Furthermore, citizens with very low incomes can claim rent supplements and apply for subsidies on compulsory healthcare contributions.

In 1986 and 1987, two categorical schemes were introduced for older or partly disabled workers (*inkomensvoorziening oudere en gedeeltelijk arbeidsongeschikte werkloze werknemers*, IOAW) and for the self-employed (*inkomensvoorziening oudere en gedeeltelijk arbeidsongeschikte gewezen zelfstandigen*, IOAZ). The age limits lie at 50 for IOAW and 55 for IOAZ. Access to these benefits is granted if the right to unemployment benefits has expired, if work incapacity benefits do not provide a sufficient income, or − in the case of the IOAZ − if a person's business generates revenue below the social minimum and therefore has to be given up. As a result of new regulations for work incapacity insurance for the self-employed in 2004 and for the employed in 2005, those partly unable to work are now gradually excluded from IOAW and IOAZ. As in the case of WWB, municipalities are in charge of the administration. Compared with WWB, means-testing is more generous. The IOAW levels do not take assets such as savings and housing into account at all. For IOAZ, total assets up to €120,408 are disregarded, contrasting with a maximum of €51,680 for WWB (including housing; values from 2010). Moreover, private pension savings are partly excluded from the means test in certain cases.

The 1998 law *wet arbeidsongeschiktheidsvoorziening jonggehandicapten* (*wajong*) provides income security to persons with disabilities who become partly or fully incapable of working before they have the chance to contribute to employee disability insurance. The Uitvoeringsinstituut Werknemersverzekeringen (UWV), which is in charge of these insurances, is also responsible for *wajong*. Eligibility conditions imply that the beginning of impairment must start before age 17 or age 30 if a person was enrolled in vocational or university education at least six months before the sickness or disability emerged. The upper age limit is 65. *Wajong* can be paid as a full benefit of 75% of the minimum wage in the case of total work incapacity. Students, in any case, are paid only 25% of the minimum wage. *Wajong* may also top up individual earnings from work. In 2010, work incentives were increased as integration planning and job search became obligatory for those partly capable of working. The resulting income for working '*wajongers*' can now amount to up to 100% of the minimum wage.

For some recipients of *wajong* (for example, students or parents), total income might still be below the social minimum. They are eligible to top-ups according to the law on income supplements (*toeslagenwet*, TW). TW was introduced in 1986 in order to guarantee sufficient income to beneficiaries of employee insurance; it is means-tested on the household level, but own housing and savings are not taken into account, as is also the case in IOAW. Moreover, 15% of work income is disregarded for a maximum of two years.

The smallest categorical scheme is very specifically targeted at artists. It was introduced in 1999 in the form of the *wet inkomensvoorziening kunstenaars* (WIK) and was replaced by the *wet werk en inkomen kunstenaars* (WWIK) in 2005. The benefit is granted for no longer than four years, while the disregarded work income gradually increases in order to stimulate future self-sufficiency of recipients (see Ministerie van Sociale Zaken en Werkgelegenheid, 2010).

Structural developments

Social assistance for able-bodied people has been the most important form of MIP throughout the period studied (Figure 3.11). The peak was reached in 1995, with a total of 489,000 ABW and RWW recipients. At the same time, unemployment rates reached their peak at 6.6%. Throughout both decades, the caseloads of ABW, RWW, and WWB fluctuated in parallel to labour market developments, but these reactions seem to have become more intense as a consequence of the 2003 and 2006 cuts in insurance benefit duration (UWV, 2009). After 1998, the number of benefiting households was in decline until 2009, when the current economic crisis reached labour markets. This constant decrease of ABW and later of WWB recipients over more than 10 years can be interpreted as a success of the organisational reforms that were implemented between 1996 and 2004, but it might also be a sign of increased non-take-up since the enforcement of activation requirements and sanctioning were central elements of these reforms (Blommesteijn and Malee, 2009).

Another factor that could have had a positive impact on ABW and WWB numbers is the fact that since 1998 *wajong* has given young persons with disabilities an alternative to *bijstand* if they lack the right to insurance benefits. In contrast to

Figure 3.11: MIP receipt in the Netherlands, 1992–2010[1]

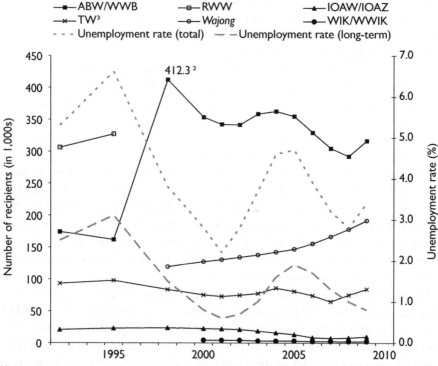

Notes:
[1] The number of MIP recipients is displayed by the solid lines which refer to the left vertical axis. The dashed lines depict the unemployment rates (total and long-term) and refer to the right vertical axis.
[2] By way of illustration, in 1998, 412,320 people received ABW which represents 2.63% of the total population.
[3] Excluding *wajong* recipients.

Sources: EuMin database; Eurostat (2010); ILO (2010).

other categorical benefits, TW reacts to labour market dynamics because it also tops up unemployment insurance. The remaining three schemes are of minor importance in the Dutch MIP system. The shrinking of IOAW and IOAZ over time can be ascribed to the reforms in disability insurance. WIK/WWIK is a very marginal scheme that shows an overall fall in recipient numbers, except for 2005 – the year of the reform – and 2009, when all MIP schemes experienced an increase in recipient numbers because of the economic crisis.

At the end of 2009 and the beginning of 2010, significant changes were made in several areas of MIP, most importantly the exclusion of younger and older age groups from WWB by creating separate schemes for them, as well as the introduction of new work incentives for '*wajongers*'. It is too soon to know if these measures will have an effect on the overall caseload of the MIP system or on its efficiency, but it is safe to say that the pressure on young recipients to find and keep work increases.

Poland

by Anna Baranowska and Katarzyna Piętka-Kosińska

Fundamental political, economic, and social transitions imposed reforms in all sectors of the welfare state in Poland at the end of the 1980s. Within this fundamental shift, MIP has evolved in a specific way. Although the basic idea of social assistance is to protect people from poverty, neither coverage nor the level of benefits seem sufficient to fulfil this goal. Some experts argue that this design is aimed at preventing people from receiving benefits, especially social assistance dependence, yet the specific development of MIP in Poland mainly results from the strong expansion of other types of social transfers such as old-age, disability, survivors', and pre-retirement pensions. These benefits were supposed to cushion the negative results of the transformation (Boeri and Edwards, 1998). The major causes of this change were the strong trade unions of the time and the 'Solidarity' heritage of the majority of the political elite.[7] As a consequence, the underlying assumption of all social policies was that the workers (who had contributed heavily to the fall of communism) should not be the victims of the transition to a market economy. The expansion of these cushioning social policies has contributed to a strong increase in social expenditure, posing a barrier to more generous social assistance.

The welfare state context

In 2007, social expenditure in Poland was moderate at 19.1% of the GDP, compared with 25.4% for EU-25. Expenditure was dominated by transfers targeted at older people – the share of expenditure for old-age, disability, and survivors' pensions was the highest among EU countries (70% of total social expenditure).

Bismarckian **old-age pension insurance**, established at the end of the 19th century (Müller, 2008), was integrated into the state budget after World War II (a pay-as-you-go scheme with defined benefits). In 1999, a major reform of the employee old-age pension system introduced a multi-tier, defined notional contribution system based on individual accounts (Chłoń-Domińczak, 2002). The early retirement schemes (for women/men younger than 60/65) expanded rapidly at the beginning of the transition (Chłoń et al, 1999) and expanded on old-age pension expenditure (Szumlicz, 2004; Piętka, 2005). Only recently were early retirement pensions restricted to a list of selected occupations. In 1997, pre-retirement allowances (special schemes for older workers who lost their jobs) were introduced; eligibility criteria included job tenure requirements and 50% of the minimum wage income threshold (up to 50% of the average wage as of 2004). Eligibility for disability pensions used to be determined by invalidity, very moderately assessed in the early 1990s (Polish Ministry of Economy, Labour and Social Policy, 2003). In 1996, the criterion of invalidity was replaced by inability to work (Piętka, 2009). The inflow of new disabled people has thereby decreased from nearly 300,000 per year in the early 1990s to around 50,000 in recent years.

There are separate schemes for farmers: the core eligibility criterion for old age and disability pensions for farmers is the long-term inability to work on a farm or retirement age (60/65) (Golinowska et al, 2003). The system, established only in the 1970s (Czepulis-Rutkowska, 1999; Pfeifer, 2004), is subsidised by the state up to 94%.

Minimum benefit levels have been defined in both old-age and disability pension schemes, and the state tops up an individual pension to the minimum level, provided the person is entitled to the pension and does not earn more than the amount of the supplement. The minimum disability and old-age pensions used to be defined at 75–90% of the minimum wage. In the early 1990s, these were related to the average wage and simultaneously decreased (Chłoń-Domińczak, 1999; Piętka, 2009), but they were later defined as fixed amounts in 1999 (at 49–64% of the minimum wage). The current rate is 48% of the minimum wage for old-age, full disability, and survivors' pensions, and 37% for partial disability pensions. All types of pensions are suspended if earnings from employment or economic activity exceed 130% of the average wage. The social pension is granted to individuals younger than 18 (or 25 if they continue their education) who became disabled, and stands at 84% of the minimum disability pension. After a month of receiving income from work exceeding two thirds of the minimum wage, the social pension is suspended.

Eligibility conditions for **unemployment benefits** were very relaxed in the early 1990s (Boeri and Edwards, 1998) and offered relatively generous compensation (Góra and Schmidt, 1998; Golinowska, 1999). Soon, a surge in the numbers of beneficiaries forced authorities to tighten the eligibility criterion and introduce a flat-rate scheme and a constraint on benefit duration (with a maximum of 12 months in standard situations; later cut down to six months, except in regions with unemployment rates higher than 150% of the national average, where the maximum remains 12 months). Unemployment benefits are not means-tested and cannot be combined with any other benefits apart from social assistance. Poland has never introduced any unemployment assistance scheme (Golinowska, 1999). Only unemployed people raising a child up to seven years old can receive a guaranteed temporary benefit (80–100% of the permanent benefit for a maximum 36 months). The other unemployed people who fulfil the income criteria can receive a temporary social assistance benefit. Older unemployed people can be protected with pre-retirement transfers.

Before the transition, **family policy** used to include many in-kind benefits that were reoriented towards universal cash benefits in the early 1990s (Golinowska et al, 2003). These benefits currently include a basic family allowance and several supplements. Family benefits have been kept at a very modest level of 2.5–3.5% of the average net wage (Piętka, 2009), but the income criterion and supplements are higher than for social assistance. The nursing benefit is reserved for poor parents who quit their jobs to take care of a disabled child. The pre-paid alimony benefit is for children whose second parent avoids paying alimony. It is means-tested and capped by the core family benefit level, but the cap is twice as high for the abjectly poor. Access to public childcare is limited and only partially free of charge. Moreover, childcare provided by private crèches and kindergartens is far from adequate, although they are very important in the process of 'closing the gap' (Piętka-Kosińska and Ruzik-Sierdzińska, 2010; Saxonberg and Szelewa, 2007; Pascall and Lewis, 2004; Pascall and Manning, 2000). Some local governments grant means-tested subsidies for monthly fees for public or private childcare.

The Polish system of MIP

Under communism, social assistance played a marginal role for ideological and structural reasons and was reserved mainly for older people and people with disabilities (Księżopolski, 1993). According to the new law (1991), entitlement to benefits, apart from the income criterion, was related to a list of problems such as joblessness, disability, homelessness, alcoholism, and helplessness (Warzywoda-Kruszynska and Grotowska-Leder, 1993). In 2004, the list was extended to include large families, refugees with adaptation problems, and people in crisis situations. Individuals (families) experiencing poverty and at least one of the listed problems (or similar, unspecified problems) are guaranteed support from local authorities (see Table 3.12).

MIP cash benefits include the permanent and the temporary benefit. The permanent benefit is available for poor people who are unable to work due to old age (above 60/65) or disability. It is computed as the difference between the income criterion and the family per capita income (minimum PLN30, maximum PLN444) and financed by the central budget. The duration is unlimited. Between 1996 and 2004 there were also benefits that covered adults whose disability started before the age of 18 and the poor who were taking care of a disabled child – both

Table 3.12: MIP schemes in Poland, around 2010

Year of introduction (abolition)	Name (in Polish)	Major target group	Main characteristics
1990	Permanent social assistance benefit (*zasiłek stały*)	Poor persons not able to work due to old age or disability, or those who stay out of the labour market to care for children or adults whose disability started before the age of 18	Income criterion based on household income per head; household resources can also be taken into account
1990	Temporary social assistance benefit (*zasiłek okresowy*)	Poor persons experiencing other social problem(s)	Entitlement in the form of the income criterion based on household income and experiencing at least one of the listed social problems; household resources can also be taken into account by the social worker

Source: Authors' compilation.

schemes were included in family protection schemes in 2004. Before 1996, there was only one permanent benefit for all these groups.

Temporary benefit is available for persons or families whose poverty is of a temporary nature, particularly due to unemployment, long-term illness, or the situation of awaiting another social security benefit. This benefit equals 50% (and up to 100%) of the difference between the income criterion for a household and the household income; 50% of the difference is guaranteed by the central budget, and the additional portion may be covered voluntarily by local governments at their discretion. The duration of the benefit is set by local authorities.

In addition, there is the targeted benefit, which is a one-off payment for specific needs (such as for schoolbooks, clothes or medication) and a special targeted benefit that can be granted in extraordinary situations in which the income criterion for an ordinary benefit is not fulfilled. Finally, there are a number of targeted allowances for specific life situations, such as allowances for becoming economically independent, continuing education, or covering costs of living and learning Polish by refugees. Non-monetary social assistance also includes many forms of material aid as well as services.

Social assistance is means-tested against family income (net of taxes and social security charges). Since 2006, the threshold has been PLN477 for a single person per month or PLN351 per person in a family (36% and 27% of the minimum wage, respectively). Households may include relatives or non-relatives, provided they manage the household together. The poverty line equals the value of a basket of goods and services in low-income households and should be recalculated every three years, although it is not guaranteed by law.

Each member of a family may apply for social assistance, even if the social problem concerns other family members. An application may be declined if the 'neighbourhood interview' reveals a large disproportion between the declared income and the family wealth. Since 2004, a social worker is entitled (but not required) to sign a social contract with an applicant, setting the rules of cooperation (including the requirement of accepting a job offer). If an applicant refuses to sign the contract or the rules are neglected, the allowance may be refused or suspended.

As well as social assistance, means-tested housing benefits are available. For eligibility, household income should not exceed 125% of the minimum pension level (175% for a single person). Healthcare services are provided on the basis of contributions, yet healthcare for the unemployed and social assistance clients is covered by the state if not by the insurance of the family members.

Structural developments

Poverty in Poland is strongly correlated with unemployment and the number of children in a family; older people are thereby not at the highest poverty risk (Piętka, 2008). Additionally, rural society, accounting for 38% of the population, used to record poverty rates more than twice those of the rest of society. The method of estimating farming income for social assistance purposes, however, takes into account lower costs of living in the countryside compared with urban areas.

Poverty in Poland started to increase before 1989 (Milanovic, 1991), but expenditure and the number of recipients of social assistance were very low. The number of beneficiaries (recipients plus dependent family members) of temporary benefits amounted to 4.5% of the population in 2007 (compared with 3.7% in 1992 and over 8% from 1993 to 1998). The rate of permanent benefits was 3.4% in 2007 compared with 0.8% in 1992.

The figures for recipients of monetary social assistance benefits showed a strong upward trend in the early 1990s (Figure 3.12). During the period 1992–2007 the number of recipients of the permanent benefit (and of all three permanent benefits added since 1996[8]) has increased more than fourfold, while the recipients of temporary benefits addressing social risks other than old age or disability decreased by only half. At the beginning of transition, temporary benefits were used to soften the first wave of poverty, and their recipients rose from 52,000 in

Figure 3.12: MIP receipt in Poland, 1992–2010[1]

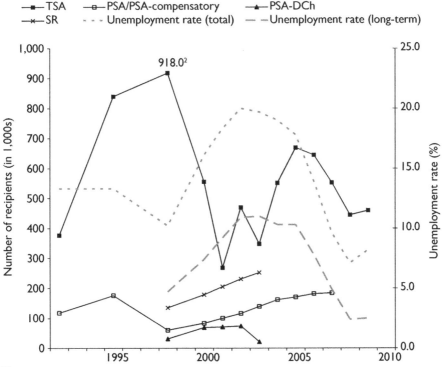

Notes:
[1] The number of MIP recipients is displayed by the solid lines which refer to the left vertical axis. The dashed lines depict the unemployment rates (total and long-term) and refer to the right vertical axis.
[2] By way of illustration, in 1998, 918,000 people received TSA which represents 2.37% of the total population.

Sources: EuMin database; Eurostat (2010); ILO (2010).

1985 and 1990 to over 1 million in 1993. Temporary benefits used to follow the subsistence poverty rate to a limited extent, being under strong pressure from public finances (apart from poverty), especially since the end of the 1990s. The launch of pre-retirement transfers (offering the long-term unemployed more generous protection) could have lowered the demand for temporary benefits since 1997.

Since 2004, the central budget has been covering only 50% of expenditure for 'own duties' of *gminas* (which include the payment of both temporary and targeted benefits). Local governments can increase expenditures on temporary benefits from their own resources by raising the income criteria or the benefit level above the national minimum, but this is not widely practised. In 2007, only 13% of the total costs of temporary allowances were covered by *gminas* (Sejm (Polish Parliament), 2008). In addition, the non-take-up rate and the ineffectiveness of benefits are very high in Poland. The role of social assistance in alleviating poverty is therefore very limited: for example, in 2003, 26% of the population fulfilled the income criteria based on consumption but nevertheless had no access to social assistance (Piętka, 2009). Benefits are low and far from adequate, representing less than 3.3% of poor households' expenditures on consumption[9] and they limit poverty to a very small extent (Piętka, 2007). This translates into low expenditures on social assistance. Throughout the period 1990–2007, benefits represented no more than 0.5% of the GDP (Golinowska et al, 2003; authors' calculations).

Regular monetary allowances accounted for 0.08% of the GDP in 1990. After they grew during the first years of transition (to 0.32% in 1993), they ranged between 0.21–0.27% of the GDP. During the period 1990–2007 the real[10] increase in expenditures was similar for permanent-type schemes (5.7 times) and temporary benefits (nearly 5 times). The expansion of temporary benefits in the early 1990s was achieved by lowering the average payment per person in real terms[11] (by half) and increasing coverage, while the real average permanent type benefit payment per person was kept at the same level. The share of temporary benefits in total expenditure grew from 23% in 1990 to 63% in 1995; later, the benefits were marginalised down to 11%. Further decentralisation of social assistance funding as well as shifting social pensions and benefits for parents taking care of disabled children to the family support system have contributed to an increase in resources for temporary benefits. During 2004–7 real expenditure on temporary benefits grew by nearly 200% (reflecting a 60% rise in the number of recipients and an increase of over 80% in average real payment per person).

Portugal

Portugal's total social expenditure averaged 23% of GDP between 2003 and 2005. It topped the OECD average of 20.6% of GDP in this period, but the country is certainly not among the most lavish spenders (OECD, 2010a). Benefit levels are low, and the family continues to play an important role. More than 80% of social expenditure goes towards pensions and healthcare (Pereirinha et al, 2008). In 2007, only 1.7% of total social expenditure was directed towards social assistance for the working-age population, and in the longer run, the figure is even lower, with 1.6% on average from 2000 to 2008 (Instituto de Gestao Financeira da Segurança Social (IGFSS), 2008, p 366).

In the first half of the 19th century, mutual aid societies organised social security schemes (Chulia and Arsensio, 2006). During the First Republic, the government legislated compulsory Bismarckian social insurance schemes but lacked the financial and administrative means to implement them. The voluntary schemes remained in place until 1935 (Capucha et al, 2005). Then the Salazar dictatorship provided a legal framework for the social insurance of employees in trade and industries, agricultural workers, and seamen, as well as schemes for specific industries, civil servants, and the existing mutuality associations (Pereirinha et al, 2008). Despite this considerable expansion of social protection both in terms of persons and risks covered, significant gaps remained. At the beginning of the 1960s, 80% of agricultural workers and 30% of the workforce in trade and industry were not covered by social security. After investigating the performance of the social protection scheme, the government set up an institution for the administration of pension benefits on a national scale, and the situation of agricultural workers improved (Capucha et al, 2005; Chulia and Arsensio, 2006).

After the Carnation Revolution in 1974, the expansion of social protection continued despite financial difficulties. Significantly, a non-contributory social pension for older people and people with disabilities was introduced in 1980 to prevent extreme hardship for groups who had insufficient contribution records and low wages during their employment career. Apart from these efforts, the government viewed its role in providing for the poor as entirely residual, and private not-for-profit organisations remained dominant in poor relief (Chulia and Arsensio, 2006). There was no general social assistance scheme in place. Only after EU accession in 1986 did the fight against poverty appear on the political agenda with the EU programmes of Poverty II and Poverty III, which were designed to facilitate research on both the incidence and the origins of poverty and helped raise awareness of the issue (Capucha et al, 2005; Bahle et al, 2010b). In 1996, a general assistance scheme was introduced in a trial phase under the name of *rendimento mínimo garantido* (RMG). From 1997 onwards, it became a regular benefit, guaranteeing those of working age an income at the level of the social pension.

The welfare state context

The first pillar of the Portuguese **pension system** has several tiers. Tax-financed and means-tested non-contributory pensions for old-age and disability pensioners aim to guarantee a minimum income. They are regarded as MIP schemes (discussed later). In terms of contributory pensions, the Portuguese system is of Bismarckian heritage. It provides old-age pensions in three different sub-schemes for occupational groups depending on both the duration of the contributory career and the wages throughout it. To be eligible for a contributory pension, contributions for 15 years for at least 120 days each year are necessary, and a full pension is available after 40 years of contributions. For each year of contributions, around 2% of the reference wage is accrued (European Commission, 2009).

As average Portuguese pensions are quite low due to low wages and short employment careers, there is a minimum threshold below which they are not allowed to fall. It is expressed as a percentage of the national minimum wage, also known as the reference index for social support (*indexante de apoios sociais*; IAS), and amounts to around €420 in 2009. Depending on the length of contributory career, low pensions are topped up to between around 60% and 90% of the IAS. These social supplements in the contributory scheme are not to be regarded as MIP schemes, because they are not means-tested and require prior contributions. Almost half of the 2.7 million contributory pensioners receive them (Chulia and Asensio, 2007; IGFSS, 2008). Even with these non-means-tested top-ups, the level of low contributory pensions was deemed insufficient. Therefore, in 2006 the solidarity supplement for older people (*complemento solidario para idosos*; CSI) was introduced, which guarantees an income equal to the IAS. It is means-tested at the family level and thus qualifies as a categorical MIP scheme with an increased level of benefits (discussed later).

The Portuguese **unemployment protection system** consists first of the unemployment insurance benefit (*subsidio de desemprego*) available to those involuntarily unemployed and with a contribution record of at least 450 days in the last two years. The benefit lasts for nine months for those under 30 and with a short employment history. With increasing age and contribution history, the benefit duration increases up to 30 months and more. The benefit grants 65% of the average salary of the last 12 months, starting two months before unemployment. It is capped at triple the national minimum wage. Second, unemployment assistance (*subsidio social de desemprego*) is available as a flat-rate benefit amounting to 80% of IAS for singles and 100% for families after a contribution history of 180 days in the year before unemployment or as a follow-up benefit on the exhaustion of the insurance benefit. Its duration is identical to that of the insurance benefit (halved for people who have exhausted the insurance benefit). The benefit is tested against the household income of the claimant, which may not exceed 80% of the national minimum wage for the claimant, and relatively generous percentages of this rate for each additional household member. Because of this per capita style of means testing on a very generous level, unemployment assistance is not considered an MIP benefit. It does not genuinely fulfil the function of guaranteeing a certain minimum amount of resources to the claimant (OECD, 2008b).

The system of **family benefits** consists of several benefits available to both parents and children. There is a cash benefit for mothers related to prior earnings (*subsido de maternidade*) and a parental leave of three months (*subsido por licenca parental*) connected to a cash benefit (OECD, 2008b). As of 2009, child benefits are means-tested and designed to filter out rich families. Families with household incomes below 50% of IAS received €170 for a child under one year of age and around €43 for a child over one year. The benefit is gradually phased out with rising reference income, ceasing at an income above five times IAS, currently around €2,100. The child benefit most strongly supports the poorest families, especially as it is not included in the means test for the RSI (Pereirinha et al, 2008).

The Portuguese system of MIP

The Portuguese system of MIP has several components (Table 3.13). A general scheme for those of working age has existed since 1996. Initially, the benefit introduced by the socialist government was called *rendimento mínimo garantido* (RMG). In 2003, the succeeding right-wing government renamed it *rendimento social de inserção* (RSI), increasing the emphasis placed on activation and the restriction of entitlements. While RMG had been available to all above 18 years of age, the new RSI benefit is only available to those aged 25 and over (Hespanha, 2007). The duration of benefit receipt is limited to 12 months, after which recipients have to prove their continued eligibility (Pereirinha, 2006).

The RSI amounts to the difference between the claimant's income and the non-contributory social pension, which is set at 44.7% of the IAS, around €187 in 2009 (European Commission, 2010). For the means test, all household resources are considered, but some benefits are exempt, for example, housing allowances, study grants, and family benefits. There is an income disregard of 20% for work income, and if claimants start working while on benefit, the disregard climbs to 50% for the first year on the new job. The first and second adults receive 100% of the benefit, the third adult in the household 70%. Both the first and second child receive 50% of the adult rate, the third child 60%. In specific circumstances – for

Table 3.13: MIP schemes in Portugal, around 2010

Year of introduction (abolition)	Name (in Portuguese)	Major target group	Main characteristics
1980	*pensão social de velhice*	People above 65 without a claim in the contributory pension scheme	The flat-rate benefit amounts to 30% of the national minimum wage
1980	*pensão social de invalidez*	Disabled people without a claim in the contributory scheme	As above
1980	*pensão social de sobrevivencia*	Widow(er)s without claims in the contributory scheme	As above
1996/2003	*rendimento mínimo garantido* (RMG) *rendimento social de inserção* (RSI)	Those over 18 without sufficient means; the general scheme.	The benefit tops up claimants' income to the level of the social pension. Recipients are activated
2006	*complemento solidario para idosos* (CSI)	Pensioners above 65 with an annual income below around €5,000 for a single person	The benefit topped up claimants' pension income to the level of around €420 in 2008

Source: Authors' compilation.

example, for pregnant women – somewhat higher rates apply (Capucha et al, 2005). Benefit receipt is conditional on the conclusion of an individual insertion contract, and the main tools of activating recipients are training, subsidised jobs, and self-employment schemes (Hespanha, 2007, p 211).

In addition to the RSI, there are means-tested social pensions for older people (*pensão social de velhice*), disabled people (*pensão social de invalidez*), and survivors (*pensão social de sobrevivência*) who have no or insufficient contributions to receive a pension from the contributory scheme. To be eligible for the benefit, the income of a single claimant may not exceed 30% of IAS (€126), and the joint income of couples may not be higher than 50% of IAS (€210). In contrast to RSI, the social pension is paid out at a flat rate, not as a differential amount. Therefore, as long as the income of a single pensioner does not exceed €126, the claimant will receive €187 as a social pension (60% of that, or €112, for survivors). The social old-age and invalidity pensions are topped up by a supplementary benefit (*complemento extraordinário de solidariedade*), which amounts to around €17 for those under 70 years and around €35 for those over 70. Due to the higher income threshold for the means test, the flat-rate benefit, and the supplements available to older people, the social pensions provide a more generous minimum income than for the working-age population, as recipients can reach an income of almost 75% of the national minimum wage.

Since 2006, the solidarity supplement for people above pensionable age (*complemento solidario para idosos*; CSI) has been phased in. This MIP scheme guarantees a higher amount of resources than either the social pensions or RSI. It provides a top-up for pensioners who do not qualify for social pensions because of high incomes and at the same time receive less than around €420 monthly as a (pension) income. It is also available to recipients of the lifetime subsidy for disabled persons (*subsídio mensal vitalício*). In 2006, only pensioners over 80 qualified for the benefit; in 2007, the reference age was reduced to 70, and since 2008, people 65 and over have been eligible for the benefit if they have insufficient means (IGFSS, 2008, p 373).

In 2010, an annual income below around €5,000 for a single person, or €8,780 for a couple, was considered insufficient and topped up to this level, leading to a monthly income of around €420. To receive the benefit, claimants need to be Portuguese citizens and have resided in the country for six years before filing the claim. Many kinds of income are taken into account in the means test. Moreover, the income of claimants' children in relation to their household size is also considered (even if they do not live in the same household as the claimant). If the child is married with two children, the older parent would lose the right to CSI benefit only if the child's household income were above €67,800. CSI functions mostly as a top-up to other benefits; the average benefit paid out equates to around €80, indicating that claimants usually have other sources of income that the CSI supplements.

MIP recipients are eligible to use the national health service. Exemptions from cost-sharing arrangements for consultations and medicines are available to them.

A means-tested housing benefit can be combined with the receipt of social assistance and social pensions. The means test is significantly less strict than with regard to RSI, for the benefit only ceases if the claimant's regular income is over three times the national minimum wage or if housing costs are extremely low.

Structural developments

In 2007, the Portuguese total population was around 10.6 million persons, and on average, approximately 196,000 households, or around 410,000 persons, including dependent household members, lived on MIP benefits – around 3.9% of the total population. The cost for MIP benefits added up to €0.7 billion, around 0.42% of the GDP. The most expensive MIP programme was the RSI, which accounted for 58% of the total expenditure.

The receipt of RMI/RSI peaked in 1999 with around 432,000 beneficiaries and sank to around 309,000 in 2006 (Figure 3.13). The number reached more

Figure 3.13: MIP receipt in Portugal, 1992–2010[1]

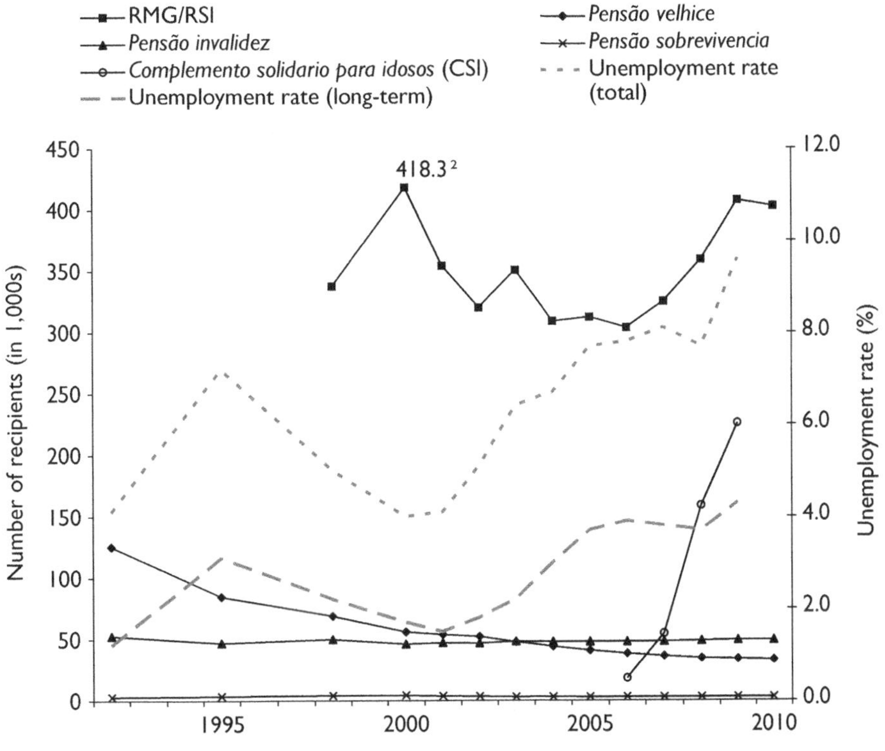

Notes:
[1] The number of MIP recipients is shown by the solid lines which refer to the left vertical axis. The dashed lines depict the unemployment rates (total and long-term) and refer to the right vertical axis.
[2] By way of illustration, in 2000, 418,256 people received RMG which represents 4.1% of the total population.

Sources: EuMin database; Eurostat (2010); ILO (2010).

than 407,000 in 2009; this development is closely coupled with changes in the Portuguese labour market, where unemployment climbed to 10.2% at the end of 2009 (OECD, 2010b). In May 2010 there were around 402,000 beneficiaries of RSI, potentially indicating a slight recovery of the Portuguese economy.

In 2008, 37% of beneficiaries were children under 18. Despite the comparatively generous provisions of the social pensions, 5% of beneficiaries were over 65, while the majority of beneficiaries – 58% – were of working age. Among those, 27% were between 18 and 29 years old, and 24% were between 30 and 39 (IGFSS, 2008, p 354). In 2008, 29% of recipient households were couples with children, while 21% were households headed by single parents; 9% of households were couples without children, 24% were single people, and 7% of recipient households were extended families (IGFSS, 2008, p 355).

The number of old-age social pensioners dropped from over 125,000 to around 40,000 persons, probably due to the younger cohorts claiming from contributory schemes. The high levels of employment among women since the 1960s may have played a role in the reduction in the number of social pensioners. For the social invalidity pension, the number of recipients has been almost constant at around 50,000 persons since 1992, and for survivors the count has been lower than 5,000 persons since 1992.

The number of claimants of CSI has increased rapidly since its introduction in 2006. Initially, only around 18,000 persons received the benefit, as it was limited to those over 80. When the age limit was reduced to 65 in 2008, around 110,500 topped up their income with CSI, and in 2009, the number of recipients reached around 257,000 persons, indicating that the benefit indeed tops up otherwise very low (contributory) pensions.

Slovakia

by Daniel Gerbery

After the state socialist regime collapsed in 1989, Slovakia experienced fundamental political, economic, and social changes that led to a readjustment of institutions in all areas of society. Though optimistic expectations prevailed at the beginning and unemployment was seen as a temporary problem, MIP has remained a constant part of the Slovak welfare state since the early 1990s, yet its institutional framework has changed several times. MIP has experienced three fundamental reforms up to now with a general trend towards increased conditionality and tightened eligibility rules, and these reforms have been accompanied by changes in active labour market policies, unemployment benefits, taxation, and social services.

Today, Slovakia is one of the EU countries with the lowest overall social protection expenditure, which was only 16% of the GDP (EU average 26%) in 2007. Expenditure on MIP (according to ESSPROS methodology, see Eurostat, 2010) represented only around 4% of the total, which is well below levels in Denmark, France, and the UK, but higher than in Poland, the Czech Republic, and Hungary.

The welfare state context

The new welfare state architecture in the post-communist era was based on principles that reflected the transition to the market economy. In Slovakia (which became an independent state in 1993), the Ministry of Labour, Social Affairs and the Family prepared a 'Strategy of transformation of the social sphere', which outlined the principles of social policy development. The transformation process was framed by various and often contradictory ideas. One of the main principles was subsidiarity, under which the family was regarded as the first channel of support where there are 'social problems'. At the same time, the document stressed the role of the state in providing adequate protection from social risks. The public policy discourse, however, was mainly influenced by liberal ideas regarding the role of the state (Kusá, 2008). The new design of the social protection system was built on three pillars: social insurance with benefits depending on income and contribution record (old-age, unemployment, and sickness insurance); state social support with benefits related to defined events during the life cycle (child allowances, parental leave benefits, or birth allowances); and social assistance providing means-tested benefits for poor persons. In addition, labour market policies and social services were strongly connected to MIP and provided opportunities for recipients to improve their standard of living.

In 2002, a radical change in the Slovak welfare state began. The new government, based on centrist and right-wing parties, introduced a series of changes not only in social policy but also in the tax system and labour market policies. Among the priorities were the creation of employment incentives, support of activation and tightening rules and benefit levels in targeted social policy programmes, and active labour market policies.[12] In line with these changes, the support of working families was increased, whereas eligibility conditions and benefit levels in unemployment insurance and in the last safety net became tighter. Together with the new flat tax rate, these changes indicate a shift towards a residual welfare regime. In the period 2002–5, such a shift can be identified, especially in MIP.

The Slovak system of MIP

The system of MIP has undergone significant changes since the early 1990s, including tightened rules, increased conditionality, and stronger work requirements (work test). Moreover, the structure of benefits has changed repeatedly. There are three periods can be seen in this development: 1) 1990–7, with the social care scheme; 2) 1998–2003, with the social assistance scheme; and 3) 2004–present, with the assistance in material need scheme (see Table 3.14).

During the first period (1990–7), MIP was provided as part of the general system of social care, which included various forms of benefits and services for different target groups – people in need, older people, unemployed people, disabled persons, and so-called socially non-adapted persons. The subsistence minimum was the main tool of MIP,[13] and was defined as the 'socially recognised minimum

Table 3.14: MIP schemes in Slovakia, around 2010

Year of introduction (abolition)	Name (in Slovak)	Major target group	Main characteristics
· 1990–7	Social care (sociálna starostlivosť')	General system for all needy population groups as part of social care system	Uniform for all recipients; no additional allowances
1998–2003	Social assistance (sociálna pomoc)	General system, but differentiated in two categories by reasons of need: 'objective' (impersonal; for example, age) and 'subjective' (personal; for example, voluntary unemployment). Special treatment of employed persons	For 'objective' reasons: 100% of the subsistence minimum; for 'subjective' reasons: 50% of the subsistence minimum; for employed persons: 120% of the subsistence minimum. No additional allowances
2004–	Assistance in material need (pomoc v hmotnej núdzi)	General system, but different categorical benefit levels for different family types. Allowances play an important role	Different benefits for: – single adult person – single person with 1–4 children – couple without children – couple with 1–4 children – single person with more than 4 children – couple with more than 4 children Additional (supplementary) allowances: activation, housing, protection, healthcare, parents with child older than 1, child attending compulsory school

Source: Authors' compilation.

level of a citizen's income'.[14] The subsistence minimum's role was twofold: first, it served as the income assessment level for eligibility to minimum income benefits; second, it defined the guaranteed minimum level below which other social benefits could not fall – for example, for unemployment benefits and old-age pensions (for more detailed information, see Kusá and Gerbery, 2009). The subsistence minimum consisted of two parts. One reflected the needs of individuals, the other the needs at the household level. The first covered food (nutrition) and personal needs with different levels of support for adults and children differentiated by age. The second part covered a household's (common) needs and depended on household size. The level of the subsistence minimum was adjusted over time due to changes in the living costs index calculated for low-earning households.

In 1998, a new minimum income scheme, social assistance, was introduced as part of an overall transformation of social policy. This reform introduced a new stage in the development of anti-poverty policies in Slovakia. With the new Act No 125/1998 on Subsistence Minimum, the distinction between individual needs and needs of the household was removed. The amounts of the new subsistence minimum took into consideration only the size and composition of the household. The subsistence minimum continued to act as an eligibility threshold for the new social assistance scheme, but this scheme underwent marked changes, which, according to policymakers, reflected a fundamental change in the relation between the state and poorer citizens.[15] The official aim of social assistance was to help persons who were living in material need, that is, those households with an income below the subsistence minimum threshold.

The most important new feature was that social assistance distinguished two causes of material need: objective and subjective. Objective reasons of need were related to an inability to maintain sufficient resources due to age, disability, health problems, or other factors. Subjective reasons referred to several situations, including rejection of cooperation with labour offices, leaving a job without good reasons, and so on. Later, this category also included all long-term unemployed persons. This distinction had direct consequences for benefit levels. Persons who were considered poor because of objective 'factors' were entitled to 100% of the subsistence minimum, whereas entitlement for subjective reasons was limited to 50% of the subsistence minimum. The concept of 'subjective reasons' was created as a form of sanction in order to eliminate behavioural patterns that differed from socially accepted standards. It was, however, very strange that long-term unemployed persons were also included in this category. In spite of the general high unemployment and especially the very high long-term unemployment rates in Slovakia, long-term unemployment was not seen as a result of structural factors. This approach implied an individualisation of the risk of long-term unemployment (Gerbery, 2009). By contrast, higher benefits – at the level of 120% of the subsistence minimum – were provided to poorer employed people.

During 1998–2002 the system was repeatedly modified, mainly due to state budget difficulties. New benefit ceilings were introduced, which especially worsened conditions for families with more children. Moreover, the relationship between benefit amounts and the subsistence minimum was abolished. Instead, the law defined these terms in absolute amounts without reference to the official poverty line.

In 2004, the current assistance in material need was introduced[16] as part of a radical reform in the design of the welfare state. The new scheme was established as a universal system for persons living in material need, meaning those living in a household with an income below the subsistence minimum.[17] The new scheme differs from previous programmes in three important ways: the general structure of benefits, a lower overall benefit level, and additional allowances based on various conditions. The distinction between objective and subjective reasons of material need has been removed. The system has one basic benefit (in material need) with six different levels, depending on household composition; the actual number of children thereby plays no role except for families with more than four children. For example, in 2009, benefit rates (rounded figures) for single persons were €61, for single parents with one to four children €115, and for couples with one to four children €158. Higher rates apply for single parents and couples with more than four children (Central Office of Labour, Social Affairs and Family, www.upsvar.sk).

The universal character of the last safety net is complemented by quasi-categorical allowances. In addition to the basic benefits, several special allowances (which are provided only within this scheme) cover various situations of need: an activation allowance, housing allowance, protection allowance, healthcare allowance, an allowance for parents who care for a child under one year old, and benefits for children who fulfil compulsory school attendance (Kalužná, 2008; Kusá and Gerbery, 2009).

Three of these allowances are very important: housing, activation, and protection allowances. Housing allowance is provided to poor people (persons living in material need) to help with housing costs. As Kusá and Gerbery (2009) point out, this is fundamental in preventing indebtedness because the basic benefit is set at a low level. Claimants must fulfil two conditions: they must declare legal relation to their house/flat, and they must show that they have no debts relating to housing (meaning that they regularly pay for electricity, water, and so on). Activation allowance is provided to poor people who are willing to actively solve their unfavourable situation (§12 in Act No 599/2003 on Assistance in Material Need) through means such as participating in training programmes,[18] completing community or volunteer work (based on an agreement with the municipality or labour office), qualification through part-time studies, and so on. The amount of the activation allowance is quite high in relation to the basic benefit and therefore creates a strong workfare bias to the minimum income system. Persons must be active in order to increase their very low basic benefits. For example, in 2009, the housing allowance (rounded figures) was €56 for a single person and €89 for households with two or more members; the activation allowance amounted to €63 (Central Office of Labour, Social Affairs and Family, www.upsvar.sk). The protection allowance is provided to persons who cannot support themselves through work due to age, health status, or participation in reintegration programmes. It is paid at the level of the activation allowance. The benefit for a child who fulfils compulsory school attendance is aimed at increasing the primary school enrolment rate of children in poor families. Subsidies for school meals and other supplies are provided in addition to this allowance. Benefit for parents who care for a child less than one year old is conditional on a paediatrician's confirmation that the child has undergone preventive medical examinations. This regulation has probably been introduced in order to compensate for the weak differentiation of the benefit in material need in relation to the number of children in households (Kusá and Gerbery, 2009). Healthcare allowance is paid to each member of a household at very low levels and should compensate for some costs relating to healthcare in a hospital or ambulance.

Structural developments

The three periods of MIP are reflected in the development of quantitative indicators. Expenditures (as % of the GDP) decreased during the first period (under the social care scheme) from 0.9% in 1994 to 0.65% in 1997 (Svoreňová and Petrášová, 2005, p 261). With the new social assistance, expenditure rose to 0.83% in 1999 and 1.14% in 1999. This proportion remained relatively stable until the end of the second period. Thereafter, with the new assistance in material need, expenditure declined sharply to 0.8% in 2003 and to 0.5% in 2004 and 2005.

This development was partly due to changing labour market conditions and particularly to trends in long-term unemployment. The overall unemployment rate grew very rapidly from 13% in 1998 to 19% in 2001, and the long-term unemployment rate increased significantly from 6.5% in 1998 to 12.2% in 2002. Long-term unemployed persons who had lost entitlement to unemployment insurance benefits became dependent on social assistance but received benefits of only 50% of the subsistence minimum level. This also led to an increased number of persons receiving minimum income benefits. While the share of the total population (including both recipients and members of their households) covered by the minimum income scheme decreased during the first period, the second period was characterised by the opposite trend. The share of the population depending on minimum income benefits increased from 1997. The peak was reached in 2001 with 11.7% of the total population (see Figure 3.14). The reform in 2003 brought a shift towards more tightened rules and resulted in lower recipient rates, which fell to 7.1% in 2004. Jobless adult children (between 18 and 25 years) living in a household with their parents were entitled to their own benefits before 2004, but since then, they have been treated as part of their parents' household. Since 2004, the share has remained more or less stable.

The breakdown of recipients also changed significantly over time. In 1999, most (64.8%) received benefits at the level of the subsistence minimum because the cause of poverty was regarded as 'objective' (Svoreňová and Petrášová, 2005). Benefits at the lower level were received by 27.9% of recipients. The situation changed in 2000 when the proportion of persons in need due to 'subjective' reasons rose to 46.6%, a shift that is mainly explained by the fact that long-term unemployed persons were only entitled to the lower benefit level (Kotýnková, 2003, p 4). In 2001, both recipient groups showed similar 'weight' (50.3% with 'objective' versus 49.7% with 'subjective' reasons). The share of recipients who had an income from work was 7% in 1999 and 15.4% in 2000. From 2004 onwards, roughly 60% of all recipients were single persons, about 10% were couples, and 30% were families with children.

As outlined earlier, the present system of assistance in material need consists of several partial allowances that are related to the fulfilment of various conditions. Researchers in Slovakia have pointed out that the design of some allowances could imply serious problems. For example, strict rules connected to the housing allowance have led to a low proportion of minimum income recipients who are eligible for it. In 2005, only 35.3% of all recipients also received housing allowances. The proportion increased as conditions for pensioners were eased to 59.3% in 2007 (Slovak Ministry of Labour, Social Affairs and Family (various years)). However, this is still quite a low percentage if the low level of the basic benefit is taken into account.

Figure 3.14: MIP receipt in the Slovakia, 1992–2010[1]

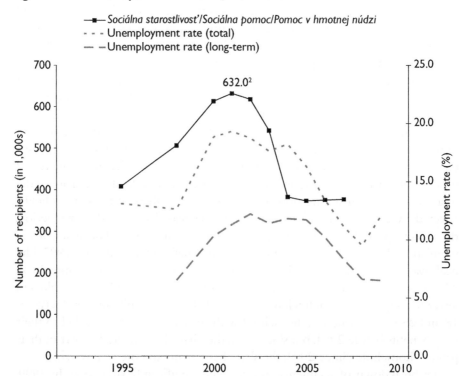

Notes:
[1] The number of MIP recipients is displayed by the solid line, which refers to the left vertical axis. The dashed lines depict the unemployment rates (total and long-term) and refer to the right vertical axis.
[2] By way of illustration, in 2001, 632,014 people received *sociálna pomoc* which represents 11.75% of the total population.

Sources: EuMin database; Eurostat (2010); ILO (2010).

There is empirical evidence of problems with entitlement among the most vulnerable groups in Slovakia. According to the UNDP *Report on the living conditions of Roma in Slovakia* (Filadelfiová et al, 2006), fewer than 16% of Roma households that received minimum income benefits also received housing allowances. This low proportion seems to be clearly linked to the parameters of the allowance. 'Many households fail to meet these conditions precisely because of the character of their housing – they often lack official approval, they are built illegally without formal recognition of ownership rights or they are unable to pay the accommodation costs regularly, which becomes a barrier to satisfying the second condition entitling a person to the allowance' (Filadelfiová et al, 2006, p 50). The situation among Roma households differs according to the type of settlement: 'While 22.8% of households living in mixed settlements received the housing allowance, the percentage for households living on the edges of towns and villages was 16.4 percent and in segregated settlements it was only 7.8 percent' (Filadelfiová et al, 2006, p 50).

Spain

Compared with those of other Western European countries, Spain's welfare state developed relatively late. Some measures of social security were created before and during the Franco era, but the redistributive effect of the instruments in place was limited due to very low benefit levels, a strong economic fragmentation into different insurance funds for more or less privileged professions, and considerable coverage gaps (Schmid, 2010). The foundation of Spain's present welfare state can be dated to 1978, when the newly adopted Spanish constitution defined the duty of public authorities to 'maintain a public social security system for all citizens which will guarantee adequate social assistance and benefits in situations of hardship' (Boletín Oficial del Estado, 2011: p 17).

The constitution also set the basis for regional autonomy and defined the role of different government levels whereby social assistance was defined as exclusive competence of the Autonomous Communities. First installed in 1989 in the Basque Country, regional MIP was a reaction to growing poverty levels caused by persistently high unemployment and gaps in the national social security system. Creating a last safety net was also an opportunity for regional governments to strengthen the public legitimacy of their autonomous status. Partly on their own initiative but also as a result of political pressure from opposition parties, trade unions, and NGOs, more and more regional governments followed the Basque example in the following decade (Rodríguez Cabrero, 2009). The resulting patchwork of MIP varies widely in terms of benefit levels and the conditions under which access to benefits is granted. The selectivity and variety at the different levels of governance involved in social protection pushes mostly women, young persons, immigrants, and minorities, such as the Roma population, to the margins of the welfare state, which is reflected by the high proportion of these groups among the beneficiaries of MIP.

The welfare state context

The Spanish welfare state incorporates status–oriented, targeted, and universal elements. While the latter dominate in healthcare and education, income protection is characterised by a heavy focus on employment-related social insurance (*seguridad social*). The system is fragmented into occupational branches[19] and strongly oriented at the male-breadwinner model. Citizens' social protection status therefore depends on the type of occupation,[20] the work history, and salary of the contributors, and derived rights for their dependants. Tax-financed MIP schemes are available for disabled, older, and widowed persons as well as orphans without sufficient insurance rights. Unemployment insurance also offers assistance-based benefits for a limited period of time. Those in need who are not eligible for the centrally organised social security benefits may apply for the *rentas mínimas* of the Autonomous Communities. Social services are mostly provided at the local level by municipalities and NGOs, most importantly the Spanish Caritas.

Furthermore, the family plays a central role as provider of childcare and long-term care and is also an important source of informal social protection (Villota Gil-Escoin and Vázquez, 2008).

The Spanish **pension system** consists of a general scheme and a special schemes for certain occupational branches. There is also the possibility of building up rights in a funded scheme of complementary pensions. In the general scheme, eligibility is given if a person at age 65 has a contribution record of at least 15 years, at least two of which must have occurred within the 15 years directly preceding retirement. Early, late, and flexible retirement arrangements are possible and vary by type of activity and occupational pension scheme. The pension amount is dependent on the contribution rates paid and the number of contribution years. The maximum pension that could be received per month in 2010 was €2,497.91 (for families with two or more children), and the minimum was €587.80 (for single people). The minimum is guaranteed by means-tested pension supplements (*complementos por mínimos*). Those not eligible for benefits in the contributory scheme have the option to claim non-contributory retirement pensions (*pensiones no contributivas de jubilación*) (Ministerio de Trabajo e Inmigración, 2011). The latter two schemes are discussed in further detail in the later sections on MIP benefits.

Unemployment protection is divided into wage-related and flat-rate benefits (*nivel contributivo* and *nivel asistencial*). At both levels, special schemes and conditions have been installed for agrarian workers in Extremadura and Andalusia. Eligibility depends on the contribution period achieved. Employees who have worked for at least 360 days within the six years prior to unemployment are eligible for wage-related benefits. The duration of payment also depends on the contribution record and lies between 120 and 720 days. Benefit levels are calculated on the basis of the contribution rates paid in the last 180 days before unemployment, but they cannot fall below or exceed certain limits in relation to the public revenue index (*indicador público de renta de efectos múltiples*, IPREM).[21]

Affiliated workers who fail to meet the requirements for wage-related benefits, as well as those who have exhausted their claims, may apply for unemployment assistance. Unemployment assistance benefits are flat-rate at 80% of the IPREM (€426 in 2010) and are means-tested. The sum of household incomes divided by the number of household members may not exceed 75% of the *salario mínimo interprofesional* (SMI), which stood at €475 in 2010. As a result of this mode of means-testing, the total income of recipients may be considerably higher than the benefit paid. Therefore, unemployment assistance in Spain is, as the main scheme's name (*subsidio de desempleo*) suggests, an income subsidy rather than an MIP benefit. The *subsidio* can be obtained by employees who have a contribution record of at least 180 days, or 90 days if there are dependent family members.

For unemployed persons above the age of 52 who have contributed to unemployment insurance for at least six years during their career, the benefits are unlimited. Long-term unemployed persons above 45 can obtain the *renta activa de inserción*, an activating benefit that is paid for 11 months. In 2009, in reaction to the massive impact of the global economic crisis on the Spanish market, a temporary unemployment benefit was introduced for those who exhausted their rights for other unemployment benefits between 1 January 2009 and 15 February 2011 (Servicio Público de Empleo Estatal, 2010).

While the budgets for Spain's pension and unemployment protection systems are comparatively high, public expenditure on **family policy** is among the lowest in Europe. Family benefits (*prestaciones familiares por hijo a cargo*) are targeted at low-income families or families with disabled children, and although there are tax reductions for working parents and persons caring for dependent relatives, these measures do not cover the expenses of child rearing or long-term care. Childcare for children under three is mainly provided informally or by private providers on the market. The provision of preschools for three- to six-year-olds, however, has been heavily expanded since the early 1990s and now reaches universal coverage. Today, enrolment is generally cost free. Until 2003 this had been the case only for public preschools (Delgado et al, 2008).

The Spanish system of MIP

Spain's MIP system consists of three institutional layers according to the level of social protection on which they are located. The contributory schemes of social security offer minimum income complements to old-age, survivors', and disability pensions. National social security also offers non-contributory pensions for older and disabled persons when they are not eligible for contributory pensions. While these categorical schemes are institutionalised by the central government, general social assistance is subject to the mesogovernments of the 17 Autonomous Communities and the Autonomous Cities of Cueta and Melilla (Martínez Torres, 2005; Moreno, 2007).

The contributory pensions (*complementos por mínimos*) are granted if pensioners' incomes, including earnings from work or capital income, are below a fixed amount. In 2010, the income limit was €6,923.90 per year for a single person or a person living with a non-dependent spouse. For persons living with a dependent spouse, the income limit was €8,076.80. The benefit paid out equals the difference between these thresholds and the minimum pension of the respective contributory scheme. These minimum amounts vary according to the type of pension and household constellation. For persons above 65, for example, the monthly minimum amount in 2010 was €570.40 for singles, €601.40 for persons with a non-dependent spouse, and €742 for family households. Widows younger than 60 were guaranteed €455.30 per month, and persons with severe disabilities (above 75%) could claim at least €855.60 (Instituto de Mayores y Servicios Sociales, 2011).

For older and sick or disabled persons, assistance pensions (*pensiones asistenciales de vejez y enfermedad*; PAS) were first introduced in 1962 (Arriba and Moreno, 2005). In 1982, a special law on the integration of persons with disabilities was adopted (*ley de integración social de las personas con discapacidad*, LISMI), granting different kinds of benefits for medical needs and care, and also a means-tested minimum

Table 3.15: MIP schemes in Spain, around 2010

Year of introduction	Name (in Spanish)	Major target group	Main characteristics
1960	Pensiones asistenciales (PAS) – de vejez – de enfermedad	Persons above 65 or disabled persons without sufficient resources	Expiring; benefit levels frozen since 1992
1978	Complementos por mínimos	Pensioners in the contributory system with household incomes below the official minimum pension	Minimum amounts vary by type of pension (old-age, disability, orphanage, widowhood) and by household constellation
1982	Subsidio de garantía de ingresos mínimos (SGIM)	Disabled persons without sufficient resources	Expiring; benefit level frozen since 1992
1990	Pensiones no contributivas (PNC) – de jubilación – de invalidez	Persons above 65 or disabled persons ineligible for contributory pensions and lacking sufficient resources	Household income and number of recipients per household define the amount paid; higher benefit level for persons with severe or absolute disability
1989 (Basque Country)– 1999 (Melilla)	Rentas mínimas de inserción (RMI)	Families with very low incomes and no (or very limited) access to the general system of social security	Benefit rates and eligibility conditions vary by region; schemes usually include measures of labour market insertion

Source: Authors' compilation.

income guarantee (*subsidio de garantía de ingresos mínimos*, SGIM). In 1990, a new system of non-contributory pensions was installed (*pensiones no contributivas de jubilación y invalidez*; PNC) with the objective of integrating the different schemes and universalising the right to a minimum pension.

In order to be eligible for PNC, claimants must have reached age 65 or have a disability of at least 65%. Furthermore, they have to have been residents of Spain for at least five years prior to applying for benefits. In 2010, the monthly pension was €339.70, with two additional payments per year of the same amount. Where more than one member of a household receives a PNC, the amount per person is 85% of the base amount if two recipients cohabit, and 80% if there are three or more recipients. As in the case of contributory pensions, the benefit for severely disabled persons who are in constant need of personal assistance is higher (€509.55 per month). Overall, recipients' yearly income may not exceed the yearly amount of the PNC. The means test also takes into account the incomes of other household members, depending on the number of cohabitants and their degree of kinship.[22] The expiring PAS and SGIM benefits are considerably lower (about €150 per month) than those of the PNC since the amounts were frozen in 1990 in order to stimulate the transition of recipients to the new system.[23] For the same reason, a PNC is incompatible with these benefits. Moreover, it may not be accumulated with contributory pensions. PNC is, however, compatible with regional MIP benefits to varying degrees.

The regional minimum income schemes constitute Spain's very last safety net to which people with insufficient resources can turn. Although the term *rentas mínimas de inserción* (RMI) is generally used when referring to these schemes, and most of them combine benefits with activation measures of some kind, not all are modelled as strictly on the French RMI as the term suggests. Only in the Basque Country, Navarre, Madrid, and Asturias, does the minimum income guarantee take the form of a subjective right. MIP is less protective in the remaining Autonomous Communities, some of which display restricted annual budgets for social assistance, or a limited number of places, as is the case in Valencia. Others, such as Castille and Leon, grant benefits only for a limited period of time (Laparra and Ayala, 2009).

In order to access benefits, claimants usually have to be aged between 18 and 64. All programmes require a period of registered residence prior to the application for benefits (6 to 12 months), a condition that aims to prevent 'welfare tourism' due to the varying benefit levels among regions. The medium benefit level in 2007 was €375.68 for single persons and €593.86 for a family, which is the typical benefit unit. However, different family concepts are applied in different programmes. In some cases, incomes of family members outside the household are taken into account for the means test. In others, households can consist of more than one family unit that can apply for benefits separately (Arriba and Moreno, 2005; Rodríguez Cabrero, 2009). In general, all the family's resources are subject to means-testing. Nevertheless, there are huge variations in terms of the treatment of different kinds of incomes. In many schemes, unemployment is a necessary condition for having access to benefits. But earnings from employment can also be compatible with a RMI and can even be spared to a certain extent, as is the case in Aragon, the Basque Country, and Navarre. Social benefits are also treated in different manners. With the exception of Castille–La Mancha and Murcia, households can combine RMI benefits with non-contributory and other assistance pensions. In most cases, the full amount of these pensions is taken into account when determining the household income. In Aragon, the Balearic Islands, Madrid, and Catalonia, they are partly disregarded. Family benefits can be a criterion for exclusion from RMI (as in Andalusia). In other regions, such as Castille and Leon, they are subject to the means test and are subtracted from the benefit. Only in Madrid, Catalonia, and Murcia, are these family benefits exempted entirely. In all cases, MIP recipients have access to the Spanish universal healthcare system and can generally claim additional targeted benefits such as scholarships, transport allowances, and emergency help. In some cases, such targeted benefits are also treated as alternatives for families that are not eligible for RMI (García Romero, 2005).

The aspects outlined in this description highlight only some facets of variance between regional schemes in Spain. They do, however, underscore the fact that (potential) MIP beneficiaries find themselves in very different situations depending on where they live. Some schemes are more accessible and less exclusive than others, and official benefit rates might look quite similar on paper, but the applied rules of means-testing can lead to considerable differences in the resulting household income of beneficiaries. Economically less prosperous regions tend to have more restrictive benefit schemes, leading to a widening of regional inequalities (Ayala and Rodríguez, 2007).

Structural developments

Figure 3.15 outlines the number of MIP recipients over time. Two limitations of the data should be noted when reading this graph. First, data on PAS and SGIM are missing for the 1990s, and the minimum complements of contributory pensions are only available from 1998. Second, the totals for regional MIP scheme recipients are taken from various sources for different years (for example: Moreno, 2007; Ministerio de Trabajo e Inmigración, 2008). Since the Autonomous Communities' social protection records apply different modes of data collection, it is not possible to reproduce how these data entered the final sums presented here. Therefore, the quantitative assessment of MIP developments has its limits, and the regional data should be seen as estimates.

Figure 3.15: MIP receipt in Spain, 1992–2010[1]

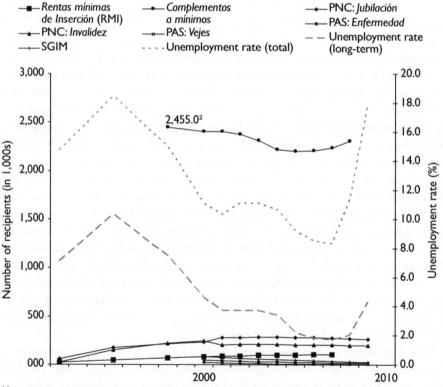

Notes:
[1] The number of MIP recipients is displayed by the solid lines which refer to the left vertical axis. The dashed lines depict the unemployment rates (total and long-term) and refer to the right vertical axis.
[2] By way of illustration, in 1998, 2,455,000 people received *complementos a mínimos de la seguridad social* which represents 6.19% of the total population.

Sources: EuMin database; Eurostat (2010); ILO (2010).

The complements to contributory pensions form Spain's largest MIP system, especially for the retired population, since the majority of beneficiaries are old-age pensioners (about 60% in 2008). The second-largest group consist of widows and widowers (about 30%). Orphans and other relatives who were economically dependent on a deceased person made up 6% of the beneficiaries in 2008, and persons with disabilities only 3%. Expenditure for these schemes confirms their quantitative importance in terms of beneficiaries. In 2006, €4,803 million were spent on the minimum complements, compared with €2,002 million for PNC schemes and only €369 million for the regional RMI programmes. Until 2005, the number of complementary pensions was in decline, but it began to increase again in 2006 at a growing rate. The PNC schemes show a different pattern. The PNC for older persons has particularly been on the rise since its introduction, while PAS and SGIM are expiring.

RMIs were also in constant increase, but their growth rate slowed down in the last decade, when all communities had installed their proper MIP scheme. Unfortunately, no data for RMI recipient numbers after 2007 were available at the time of writing, but a study for the Spanish Caritas offers information on the proportional changes in beneficiaries and expenditure between 2007 and 2008 (Laparra and Ayala, 2009). On average, the number of beneficiaries increased by about 11%, and expenditure by 6%. This development is rather meek given the fact that the number of households that can draw neither on benefits from work nor on some kind of central government social security benefit increased by 20% in the same period (from an estimated 300,000 to 360,000 households). In 2007, only around 100,000 households, or 0.6% of the total, received RMI benefits. On the other hand, the proportion of households in Spain that suffer from severe poverty is estimated to lie between 3% and 4%. The low significance of regional MIP schemes can thus not be ascribed solely to their residual role in the overall welfare system. It also indicates a low capacity in filling the gaps in Spain's last safety net. Nevertheless, three factors need to be mentioned that cannot be evaluated in detail here: first, it should be borne in mind that a certain number of persons theoretically eligible for benefits might not apply for them. For the PNC *de jubilación*, Matsaganis et al (2010) estimate a non-take-up rate of around 44%. Second, the shadow economy in Spain, the size of which is estimated to be about 20% of the GDP (Feld and Schneider, 2010), may alleviate some of the effects of the shortfall in social protection. Moreover, the extended role of family solidarity should be taken into account.

Sweden

Sweden is often referred to as the ideal typical case of the Scandinavian or social-democratic welfare state, characterised by generous and universal social services and benefits. State support for the poorest, however, has a tradition that precedes the institutionalisation of its present welfare system and can be traced back to the 16th century, when social functions that were formerly fulfilled by the Catholic clergy (such as poor relief) became the duty of the newly founded state Lutheran Church and thus public. Poor laws, for example those from 1847 and 1918, reaffirmed the right to poor relief and shifted responsibility from the parish to the municipalities, which had been founded on the basis of the church's territorial structures in the 19th century. In 1956, the Social Assistance Act replaced the traditional *fattigvård* (care for the poor) with the concept of *bistånd* (support), but only in 1982 was a universal right to social assistance installed. Aside from the existence of this centralised legal framework that was slightly reformed in 1998 and 2002, today's *ekonomiskt bistånd* still shares important attributes with its historical precursors: In contrast to the country's universalist main systems, social assistance is subsidiary and administered as well as financed by the local governments (Kaufmann, 2003; Andrén and Gustavsson, 2004; Wollmann, 2008).

The welfare state context

Income support for the poor, which plays a rather rudimentary role in Sweden's welfare state today, dominated local government's costs until the beginning of the 20th century. It lost its relevance with the introduction of universal insurance- and tax-based social security systems (Andrén and Gustavsson, 2004). In 2007, MIP made up only 1% of social expenditure and 1.9% of regular cash benefit payments.

In 1998, new **pension legislation** was passed, replacing the combination of the universal basic *folkspension* and income-related supplementary pension (ATP). The legislation was fully enacted in 2003, and the oldest cohorts of pensioners (born between 1938 and 1953) are now entitled to a supplementary pension (*tilläggspension*) that raises benefits to former pension levels. Such claims result from changes in the calculation basis of the pensions: ATP only took into account the best of 30 contribution years. After the reform, a person's whole working biography affects his or her pension level. This is a significant advantage for the low-wage workers with long-term employment careers but can lead to cutbacks for other groups with interrupted working biographies. On the other hand, career breaks due to childcare, education, and military service are now considered contribution periods.

Apart from these aspects, the central element of Sweden's pension reform is the transformation of its financial basis. While the tax-financed *folkspension* constituted the core of the old pension system, contribution-based pensions are the main element of today's old-age security, which is split into four tiers: the earnings-related *inkomstpension*, a funded supplementary pension (*premiereservsystem*), and two additional tax-financed schemes that guarantee a minimum standard of living for older people. Persons who have had no or a low income during their working age can apply for a guaranteed pension (*garantipension*), which can be granted when no contributory pension claims exist, but it also serves as a top-up when earnings-related pensions fail to provide the minimum income level. If a person's income after taxation, income-based and guaranteed pensions, as well as housing supplements is still below the social minimum, he or she can apply for the means-tested *äldreförsörjningsstöd*, Sweden's most residual benefit scheme for older people (Kaufmann, 2003; Palme, 2003). Only the latter benefit is considered part of MIP.

Unemployment protection in Sweden is organised as a Ghent system. Insurance is voluntary, covering 85% of the labour force, and coordinated mostly by fund associations with close institutional links to trade unions,[24] which offer their members public employment services and supplementary insurance programmes. Since 1974, two kinds of unemployment benefits have existed: the traditional, income-related type of benefit and a flat-rate, state-financed assistance paid to out-of-work persons who fail to meet the requirements of the first benefit. In order to qualify for income-based payments, one must have been member of an insurance fund for at least a year and have been employed for at least six months in the previous year.[25] The same working period condition holds for receiving the basic benefit, but fund membership conditions are irrelevant. Therefore, unless personal insurance entitlements[26] do not expire or previous ties to the labour market are not missing entirely (as in the case of young adults entering the labour market), unemployment insurance can be considered a central functional alternative to MIP (Clasen and Viebrock, 2008).

Family policy in Sweden is marked by well-developed childcare services and generous financial support for parents. Every child above the age of one has the legal right to public childcare. Universal child allowances, with supplementary support for larger families, were established in 1947 and still are based on the same legislation today. Additionally, Sweden has a well-developed parenthood insurance system warranting income-related parental leave benefits. Further financial support for families is available in the form of housing supplements and study allowance for children older than 16 (Hort, 2008; European Commission, 2010).

The Swedish system of MIP

In addition to Sweden's general social assistance, two other benefit types can be classified as MIP schemes. One is directly linked to *ekonomiskt bistånd* and aims at providing equivalent help for refugees and other social groups who fail to meet the legal requirements for receiving this kind of support. The other type is designed to avoid poverty in old age. A summary of all three benefit programmes is given in Table 3.16 (see Eardley et al, 1996; Hort, 2008; Halleröd, 2009; European Commission, 2010).

Sweden's main system of MIP is the *ekonomiskt bistånd*. Its current legal basis is the Social Services Act that came into effect in January 2002. The *ekonomiskt bistånd* replaced the *socialbidrag*, which had been regulated by the original 1982 Social Services Act. Social assistance is a subordinate aid granted to households that are unable to sustain their living costs. In principle, citizens should try to earn their living by their own means as long as they are capable of working and below the age of 65. Furthermore, all alternative resources need to be exhausted. Therefore, although assistance is an individual right, the overall household situation (for example, the partner's income, the number of children) is taken

Table 3.16: MIP schemes in Sweden, around 2010

Year of introduction (abolition)	Name in Swedish	Major target group	Main characteristics
1982	Ekonomiskt bistånd (former socialbidrag)	Individuals resident in Sweden and their household (mostly family) members who fall below a certain minimum	Legally guaranteed social assistance for persons/ households that are unable to maintain their livelihood
1993	Introduktionsersättning	Asylum seekers and refugees	Social assistance for refugees, asylum seekers and their families
2003	Äldreförsörjningsstöd	People 65+	Minimum income provision for older persons with very low or no pension income

Source: Authors' compilation.

into account when judging entitlement and benefit level. *Ekonomiskt bistånd* clearly serves as means of last resort and aims directly at activation and timely reintegration into the labour market – even if a beneficiary is highly qualified, he or she must accept every 'tolerable' job offer. Apart from these restrictions, payment duration is unlimited and oriented to people's support needs. There are no entitlement conditions concerning age or nationality. The main requirement is to be a registered resident of Sweden.

On a yearly basis, the Ministry of Health and Social Affairs publishes minimum levels for the benefit rates.[27] The actual amounts are set by the local authorities and vary accordingly. Administration and benefit grants are in the hands of communal social services that are supervised by the National Board of Health and Welfare. The monthly payments aim at covering the cost of living (such as food, clothing, and leisure) as well as rental costs. The needs of different household members are taken into account, with specific rates for children according to their age. Additional benefits – granted depending on municipality and case – can be claimed for housing, electricity, and social insurance, or even for trade union contributions. In the case of illness, beneficiaries (just as every citizen) are entitled to medical treatment, the costs of which are mainly financed publicly.

In 1993, the Introductory Allowance for Refugees and Certain Other Aliens Act established a separate social assistance scheme for immigrants, refugees, and asylum seekers. This *introduktionsersättning* provides an income guarantee that is equal to general social assistance and thus fills a legal gap that had existed for certain immigrant groups. This scheme's beneficiaries are usually included in the general statistics of the *ekonomiskt bistånd*, although the central state reimburses the municipalities for these costs.

In 2003 a third MIP scheme was introduced for pensioners (*äldreförsörjningsstöd*). The minimum pension age in Sweden is 65. In order to obtain the full basic pension (*garantipension*), applicants must have lived in the country for 40 years. Retirement payments from abroad or widows' allowances can reduce the minimum pension amount. To ensure an adequate standard of living, even if no or a very low regular pension is received, pensioners can claim *äldreförsörjningsstöd*. In contrast to *garantipension*, where only personal pension income is taken into consideration, the means test of the *äldreförsörjningsstöd* takes into account the total incomes of claimants' households.

Structural developments

Although trade union based insurances still cover the majority of Sweden's active population, unemployment can have a significant impact not only on the number of persons receiving insurance-based benefits but also on social assistance receipt. During the economic recession of the 1990s, Sweden's unemployment rate rose rapidly from less than 2% in 1990 up to around 8% in the mid-1990s (ILO, 2010). At the same time, beneficiary rates of *socialbidrag* reached a peak of 4.0% of the working-age population in 1995 compared with 2.6% in 1992. The parallels in the development of unemployment and social assistance receipt become even clearer when looking at the timeline of both plotted in Figure 3.16. The two

Figure 3.16: MIP receipt in Sweden, 1992–2010[1]

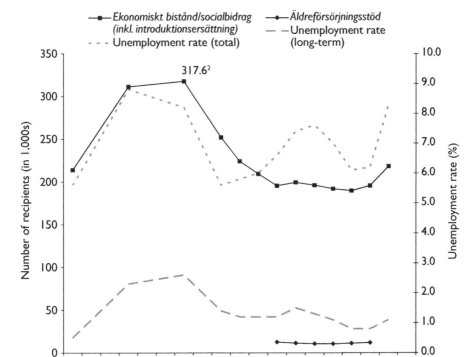

Notes:
[1] The number of MIP recipients is displayed by the solid lines which refer to the left vertical axis. The dashed lines depict the unemployment rates (total and long-term) and refer to the right vertical axis.
[2] By way of illustration, in 1998, 317,637 people received *socialbidrag* which represents 3.59% of the total population.

Sources: EuMin database; Eurostat (2010); ILO (2010).

groups seem to be linked, and the time lag between the curves' maxima points to an effect directing from unemployment to social assistance receipt, as suggested also by Brännström and Stenberg (2007).

Figure 3.16 also suggests a recent weakening of the relationship. The rise in unemployment between 2000 and 2005 produced only minimal increases in the number of *bistånd* recipients. This could be due to the reforms of social assistance between 1998 and 2002, which led to the introduction of various kinds of activation measures at the municipal level. Evaluation studies have proved these policies to be especially valuable for the groups in society that were hit hardest by the 1990s crisis, mainly young persons and immigrants (see, for example, Dahlberg et al, 2008). The new policies of labour market integration might have made these groups less vulnerable to market fluctuations, leading to a decline in the influence of unemployment rates on social assistance receipt. Overall, a steady decrease in the number of minimum income beneficiaries occurred until 2007. This picture, however, has changed in the course of 2008 and 2009 since the latest economic events led to a steep increase of recipients. This new reactivity to unemployment may be partly caused by developments in unemployment insurance and also sick pay. It is very likely that the recent tightening of eligibility conditions for these higher-tier benefits has intensified the current recession's influence on increasing *bistånd* claims (Larsson, 2004; Hall, 2008; Halleröd, 2009).

United Kingdom

MIP plays a very important role in Britain. In 2007, total social expenditure was 25.3% of the GDP, and about one third of it went to means-tested and income-related benefits (including tax credits). Within the European context, overall social spending is below average, but the share of means-tested benefits is among the highest. Though not all means-tested benefits are MIP, it is nevertheless an important element of the British welfare state.

Three major developments have contributed to this pattern in an historical perspective. First, the strong salience of means-testing fits very well with the long-standing tradition of British social policy, beginning with the Elizabethan poor law of 1601. In this tradition, still reaffirmed by the 1834 Poor Law, recipients of poor relief lost civil rights and were usually institutionalised in the workhouse. Yet there was also a considerable level of outdoor relief. In the 19th century, British poor relief (indoor and outdoor) was the most developed in Europe. Spending levels were higher than in any other European country or the US at that time (Lindert, 2004, vol 1, pp 46–7).

The old Poor Law institutions were eventually abolished after World War II. The new British welfare state, built upon the original plans of Lord Beveridge, introduced encompassing national insurance benefits, universal family allowances, and a National Health Service. In addition, full employment was a major aim. With this system, the expectation was that the vast majority of the population would be effectively protected against poverty and poor relief should be shifted into a residual position within social security. But the original promise was not kept due to inadequacies and failures of the insurance system and far-reaching social and economic changes in British society. From the beginning and in contrast to the original plans of Beveridge, contributory flat-rate insurance benefits were set at a very low level. In many cases they did not protect people against poverty effectively. At the same time, family stability and full employment (two structural preconditions of the system) soon eroded, leading to growing risks that were not covered by existing social insurance.

The more recent reforms introduced by Conservative governments from Margaret Thatcher onwards further undermined the protectiveness of social insurance, in particular for the unemployed (see the following section). Consequently, the role of MIP has grown ever more important.

The welfare state context

The failure of the social insurance system to protect the vast majority of the population effectively from falling into the last safety net can be attributed to four major reasons (Bradshaw and Bennett, 2009). In **old-age security**, the contributory basic state pension (non-means-tested) provides flat-rate benefits at a very low level, which does not take into account housing costs. Consequently, pensioners without additional pension claims or other significant incomes have to rely on MIP benefits in order to make ends meet. Since additional earnings-related pensions were introduced relatively late in Britain and do not yet cover the whole pensioner population many older persons depend on MIP. The poverty rate among older people in Britain has been one of the highest in Europe during the whole post-war period.

The present system of **unemployment compensation** is also not strongly protective (Mohr, 2007). Since 1996 the contributory jobseeker's allowance is paid only for six months and the benefit level is the same flat-rate amount as for the means-tested, non-contributory benefit (so-called income-related jobseeker's allowance) that is paid after six months and is also for jobless persons without contributory records. Income-related jobseeker's allowance is part of MIP.

Growing family instability and modest **family policy** in Britain are also reasons for the great salience of MIP. Marriage breakdown often leads to financial problems that are not covered by the insurance system because contributory social insurance is based on economic activity and provides mainly flat-rate benefits. Single mothers' labour force participation is not supported by the state because British childcare policy has been very reluctant to provide affordable places. Since Britain has one of the highest shares of single parenthood in Europe and family policies have remained limited, a very high number of single parents rely on MIP.

Similarly, national insurance pays contributory benefits to persons who are disabled due to work accidents or occupational diseases but does not provide for **civilian disability**. Hence, many disabled persons who did not work have to rely on the last safety net for their daily expenses, whereas benefits related to their special needs have been improved substantially in recent years.

Overall, the structure of social insurance and family policies does not provide a high level of protection. People on low pensions, single-parent households, many disabled persons, and the majority of the unemployed depend on MIP for their livelihood. In addition, a growing number of working persons with low wages (the working poor) rely on supplementary means-tested in-work benefits such as the working tax credit. Hence, the system of MIP has to shoulder a huge burden.

The British system of MIP

This largely ungenerous and limited social insurance system is mirrored in a highly developed and strongly institutionalised MIP system. In contrast to original expectations of post-war social reform, means-tested benefits of last resort have continued to play a major role in the British welfare state. At the same time, the MIP system is one of the most institutionalised in the world in terms of social rights, accessibility, and standardisation of rules and benefits. Non-take-up continues to be high, but is lower than in other countries due to the lower degree of stigmatisation, its rights-based character, and a low level of discretion. Indeed, all minimum income benefits are centrally regulated and a firmly established element of the welfare state.

National assistance was introduced in 1948 as a universal scheme covering the whole needy population (see Table 3.17). With this system, the poor law tradition of severe stigmatisation and loss of civil rights was completely abolished. The scheme was renamed supplementary benefit in 1966 and income support (the current name) in 1988. However, over the years, the originally unified system has become differentiated for various categorical groups, but the system as a whole covers all people in need.

The present MIP system consists of six schemes, but it is noteworthy that Britain has universal coverage, as opposed to many other countries that have categorical schemes.

Income support was originally open for all people in need, including pensioners and the unemployed with (low) flat-rate benefits. In addition, non-active people and persons who had exhausted claims to insurance-based benefits were among the main recipient groups.

Different groups of claimants were transferred to newly created categorical schemes of MIP in the 1980s and 1990s. income support (IS), itself, thereby became a benefit with a strong categorical character as well. Today, IS is only available for persons between 16 and 65 who do not work and are unable to work permanently or temporarily, such as disabled persons, single parents with young children, or family carers. Persons in work with low incomes can receive tax credits rather than IS, unemployed persons are entitled to the jobseeker's allowance (introduced in 1996), and older persons have a right to the pension

Table 3.17: MIP schemes in the United Kingdom, around 2010

Year of introduction (abolition)	Name	Major target group	Main characteristics
1948 (1988)	Income support (until 1988: supplementary benefit; 1948–66: national assistance)	Persons 16+ on low income who do not have to register as unemployed (pensioners, disabled people, lone parents, family carers) and their dependants. From 1999, minimum income guarantee (MIG) for older people	Social assistance for UK residents on low income
1996	Jobseeker's allowance (non-contributory) (until 1996: unemployment benefit and income support for the unemployed)	Unemployed workless persons 18+ who are actively seeking work or working fewer than 16 hours per week on low income	Financial support for jobless people who are actively seeking work
2000	Asylum support(before 2000, included in income support)	Refugees, asylum seekers and their dependants	Social assistance for refugees, asylum seekers and their dependants
2003	Pension credit (guaranteed credit); (1999–2003: minimum income guarantee within income support)	People 60+ living in the UK whose income is below a certain minimum	Means-tested basic pension for older people
2003	Working tax credit (WTC) (1988–98, family credit; 1999–2002: working family tax credit)	People 16+ working more than 16 hours per week, or families living in the UK on low income	Financial support in the form of tax credits for working persons or families on low income
2008	Employment and support allowance (ESA; part of income support)	For new claimants of IS who are sick or disabled and under 60	Orientation period for 13 weeks; thereafter, shift to either work-related component or support component with higher benefits

Source: Authors' compilation.

credit (introduced in 2003 following the minimum income guarantee, which was introduced in 1999 as part of IS).

As of 2008, new claimants of IS who are disabled or sick get an employment and support allowance (ESA) during an initial assessment period of 13 weeks. Thereafter, the claimant is shifted either to work-related activity or to permanent support – both components entail a higher benefit amount. The ESA is basically an instrument by which the employability of sick and disabled claimants is tested and client groups are clearly separated from one another according to their ability to work.

The first large group for whom a special categorical scheme was introduced was unemployed people. In 1996 the system of unemployment protection was reformed and the jobseeker's allowance introduced. Since then, there have been two benefits: an insurance-related contributory benefit, which is paid for six months, and a means-tested non-contributory benefit, which is paid thereafter or for all persons without insurance claims. Both benefits are paid at the same flat-rate level. The means test is only applied to the non-contributory benefit, however. Asylum seekers and refugees are another group for whom a special categorical benefit was introduced in 2000, yet this is a minor scheme with few beneficiaries (discussed later).

Pensioners have always been a major MIP recipient group due to the low level of flat-rate basic pensions in Britain. Within the IS scheme older people have been treated more favourably than other groups, for example with respect to the means test. A minimum income guarantee (MIG) for older persons was introduced in 1999 and replaced by the pension credit (guarantee credit) in 2003.

Another important means-tested benefit is provided for persons in work with low income. A family credit for working families was introduced in 1988 and reformed in 1999 by the working families tax credit (WFTC). In 2003 the WFTC was replaced by the present working tax credit (WTC), which covers more people, including families and persons without children. Over the years, entitlement to tax credits has been extended significantly. The major condition is that persons have to be in full-time work (more than 16 hours per week) and earn less than a certain amount, which varies by household size and income group. Hence, the working tax credit operates at different income levels with sliding scales and does not only include persons on a minimum income level. Therefore, the WTC cannot be regarded as a genuine MIP benefit; it is a borderline case.

All minimum income recipients have access to free healthcare through the National Health Service (NHS). The costs for dental care and glasses, normally not included in the NHS, are also covered to some extent. Additionally, cash housing benefits are an important element in the overall benefit package for poor people. Most minimum income schemes (except the WTC) have significant housing supplements, which cover almost all housing costs.

Structural developments

The British system of MIP covers a high percentage of the overall population. The share of all persons depending on MIP (including household dependants and children) fell slightly over the period, from 16.9% in 1995 to 12.9% in 2007 (estimated annual averages). Among the adult working-age population, the share was 8.8% in 2007, and for people older than 60 it was 18.9% (if calculated with reference to the population over 65 it was even 26.1%; see Chapter Four). The WTC is not even included in these figures.

Figure 3.17 shows the structural developments in the number of MIP recipients from the early 1990s until 2009. The data only include adults; dependent children are not taken into account because data are incomplete. The largest programme is IS. Income support for working-age adults mainly covers sick and disabled persons, single parents, and family carers. Until 1996 (when the jobseeker's allowance was introduced), the long-term unemployed also received IS. Today, single parents are

Figure 3.17: MIP receipt in the UK, 1992–2010[1]

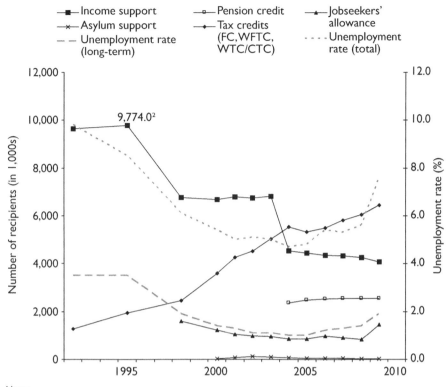

Notes:
[1] The number of MIP recipients is displayed by the solid lines which refer to the left vertical axis. The dashed lines depict the unemployment rates (total and long-term) and refer to the right vertical axis.
[2] By way of illustration, in 1995, 9,774,000 people received income support which represents 16.87% of the total population.

Sources: EuMin database; Eurostat (2010); ILO (2010).

one of the major groups in receipt of IS. In August 2008, about 750,000 single parents were on benefit.

The second major benefit for persons of working age is the means-tested jobseeker's allowance (JSA). Compared with the number of recipients of this benefit, the caseload of contributory (non-means-tested) jobseeker's allowance is very low; in 2007 it was around 130,000 on average, compared with more than 700,000 for the means-tested benefit. Quite clearly, the majority of the unemployed are no longer protected by insurance benefits but instead by MIP. In comparative perspective, however, the numbers (as a share of the adult population) are low due to the relatively low unemployment rates in Britain until the current crisis that began in 2008.

The most significant structural change with respect to working-age adults is the continuous increase in the number of persons who receive WTC. In absolute numbers, WTC has been the single largest programme since 2004. In 2007 around 2.9 million adults lived in households receiving WTC. This underlines a significant shift: a growing proportion of MIP goes to in-work benefits. However, this increase is not reflected in a parallel decline of inactive and unemployed recipients of MIP. In-work benefits have probably prevented a further increase of 'passive' MIP benefits but not solved the structural problems related to work incapacity and single parenthood. The inactive 'component' of the MIP caseload is still exceptionally high in Britain. Moreover, the number of means-tested JSA recipients has not fallen significantly in recent years despite a very low long-term unemployment rate by international standards. Therefore, the growth of the WTC is mainly explained by deteriorating employment and wage conditions rather than by the success of activation for recipients of 'passive' MIP benefits. Most WTC recipients have dependent children; in 2007 more than 3 million children lived in households with WTC.

Not only children but also many older persons depend on MIP. For this age group there was no major structural change over the period. The difference between the number of older IS recipients until 2003 (including the minimum income guarantee from 1999) and the number of pension credit recipients is partly due to a statistical break in the data series and does not necessarily reflect a substantial change in benefit dependency. In any case, older people are still over-proportionally dependent on MIP in comparison with almost all other European countries, except Ireland (see Chapter Four).

MIP in the UK continues to play a strong and exceptional role by international standards. The major problem is not unemployment as such, but inactivity due to disability, sickness, and single parenthood. Despite the existence of various activation programmes, this structural problem has not been solved, mainly because of the lack of services that would help a better combination of paid work and family duties. In parallel, another structural problem has grown: in-work poverty, which is especially relevant for families with children. The WTC tries to solve part of this problem and has become an alternative to 'passive' MIP benefits for many persons, especially families with children.

Notes

[1] Contributing authors, country sections on the Czech Republic, Poland, Hungary and Slovakia: **Tomáš Sirovátka** is Professor of Social Policy at the Faculty of Social Studies, Masaryk University in Brno. He has contributed to several international journals and comparative books on the issue on employment and social policies in post-communist countries and has co-edited the book *Governance of active welfare states in Europe* (Palgrave 2011). **Anna Baranowska** is a research fellow at the Institute of Statistics and Demography, Warsaw School of Economics. Her research interests include the transition to adulthood, 'atypical family forms' and the impact of family formation on individual-level well-being. **Katarzyna Piętka-Kosińska** is specialised in macroeconomis, social policy, and the analyses of industries in Poland and is currently the Vice-President of the Board of CASE-Advisors, Warsaw. **Mónika Bálint** and **Zsuzsanna Szabó** are research assistants

at the Institute of Economics of the Hungarian Academy of Sciences (IEHAS), while **Dániel Horn** is a research fellow at IEHAS and also at the Department of Economics, Eötvös University. **Daniel Gerbery** is a lecturer in sociology and statistics at the Faculty of Philosophy, Comenius University in Bratislava and a researcher at the Institute for Labour and Family Research. His research interests are poverty and social exclusion, consequences of social and family policies, social indicators, and theories of the welfare state.

[2] For this reason, RIS is oriented towards non-disabled persons above the age of 18, whereby citizens younger than 18 are also treated as adults if they are parents or married.

[3] Zákon o životním minimu (Act No 463/1991 Coll).

[4] Zákon ČNR o sociální potřebnosti (Act No 482/1991 Coll.).

[5] Most of these benefits do not match the MIP definition of this study.

[6] For example, participate in public work, and be available for the labour market.

[7] 'Solidarity', led by Lech Wałęsa at that time, is the trade union that opposed communist leadership for nearly 10 years before the communists were forced to accept their participation in political power (1989), which led to a change of the entire system.

[8] Social rent and permanent benefit for parents taking care of disabled children were shifted to the family protection system in 2004 but are included in the calculations for 2004–7 for the purpose of data comparability.

[9] Authors' calculations based on 2007 HBS; the poor consume less than the social assistance income threshold.

[10] Due to high inflation during the 1990s, the analysis of flows in current prices would be misleading.

[11] Authors' calculations; average payment of a benefit equals monthly cost of benefits divided by an average monthly number of recipients.

[12] Priorities of the social policy reforms were identified in several documents: 'Programme declaration of the government of the Slovak Republic for period 2002–6; (*Programové vyhlásenie vlády Slovenskej republiky 2002–06*) and 'Strategy of support of employment growth'.

[13] It was implemented by Act No. 463/1991 on Subsistence Minimum. According to Kusá (2006, p 30), this legislative norm was very important because it framed the idea of guaranteed minimum income by reference to the Human Rights Declaration. Compared with later periods, it was a unique situation.

[14] The expression 'material need' has a long tradition in Slovak social policy, and it connotes a similar meaning to 'poverty' (it indicates situations in which persons have income below a certain threshold that is perceived as a necessary minimum living standard).

[15] Here we can hear the 'echo' of the ideas embodied in the 'Strategy of transformation of the social sphere', such as the rejection of the state paternalism. The expression 'state

paternalism' is not explained in the document. Therefore, it has been used without any specific conceptualisation of the social policy regime before 1989.

[16] As the name of the scheme suggests, the new system should provide assistance only to people in poverty, and it is not expected to tackle poverty significantly. Benefits are aimed at 'providing basic living conditions'. As a result, the scheme protects people against extreme forms of poverty, but people are expected to solve their situations with their own resources.

[17] Despite a radical redesign of the minimum income scheme, the subsistence minimum has remained unchanged as an assessment criterion of eligibility.

[18] These programmes must be approved by the Ministry of Labour, Social Affairs and Family or by the Central Office for Labour, Social Affairs and Family, and eventually by labour offices.

[19] There are distinct social security schemes for self-employed persons, domestic employees, agricultural and marine workers, and coalminers.

[20] Although many special social insurance funds have been integrated into the general scheme of social insurance, the contribution rates still vary by type of occupation, leading to differences in the base used to calculate benefits.

[21] For singles, the minimum is 80% of the IPREM augmented by one sixth. The maximum a household with children can obtain is 225% of the IPREM, also augmented by one sixth.

[22] In 2010, for example, the joint household income of a recipient living with his or her spouse or a parent-in-law was not to exceed €8,084.86 per year. For a four-person household, on the other hand, with a recipient cohabiting with his or her children or parents, the annual income limit was €36,857.45.

[23] Nevertheless, the number of PAS and SGIM recipients decreased slowly, since access conditions to PNC are more restrictive. PAS *de enfermedad*, for instance, does not require a minimum disability level of 65% and means tests are on the individual level.

[24] Since 1998, an additional fund has been introduced that is not affiliated with trade unions: The Alfa-Kassan provides unemployment insurance for employees of all sectors of the economy.

[25] With a minimum of 80 working hours per month if the employment period was interrupted or, in the case of continuous employment, 50 hours per month.

[26] The income-related payments can, after the standard benefit duration of 300 days (or 450 for parents of children under the age of 18), be prolonged by another 300 days (or 450 days, respectively). Recipients may also be transferred to the activation guarantee programme (either after the initial period of 300 or 450 days or after an extension), which involves full-time coaching, subsidised work, and training for another 300 or 450 days while insurance payments continue.

[27] Until the mid-1990s, these were pure guideline values. Since 1998, they have been legally binding and operate as the national set social minimum.

FOUR

Comparative analyses

This chapter studies the MIP systems in the 17 European countries in comparative perspective. The first section analyses the MIP benefit levels for adults of working age and their families. The crucial aspect is how the generosity of needs-based social citizenship rights deviates from average incomes and other social benefits (see Chapter Two). The more deviation can be observed, the less are generous basic social citizenship rights institutionalised in society. The second section compares aggregate MIP caseloads (recipients) across countries for three population groups: the total population (including children), adults at working age, and persons at pension age. These figures indicate the salience of MIP within the overall welfare state and society. They relate to the issue of inclusiveness of social citizenship rights as outlined in Chapter Two.

Since higher-level social benefits usually operate as 'protective filters', a high salience of MIP indicates a concept of social citizenship that is more strongly based on need than on accrued or universal rights. In some countries, however, a low salience of MIP indicates a weak institutionalisation of basic social citizenship rights in terms of entitlement. The results show that MIP systems affect sizeable population groups in many countries while they play only a marginal role in some. Moreover, total recipient figures in some countries are significantly higher when the various categorical MIP schemes are added up than when only the last residual scheme is considered. The third section of this chapter analyses expenditure on MIP, which seems to be more closely linked to the number of beneficiaries than to generosity. Despite international differences, MIP spending tends to be rather modest in terms of the share of national GDP or share of total social spending.

The next section of this chapter studies the institutional differentiation of national MIP systems in various categorical schemes in a comparative-historical perspective. Categorical differentiation within MIP systems indicates an important dimension of the institutionalisation of basic social citizenship rights. The more important categorical differentiation between different population groups is, the less coherent and equal are social citizenship rights. In this respect, individual countries have followed different paths of development in their MIP systems, leading to different institutionalised forms of fundamental social citizenship rights in Europe. Some countries have nationally unified last safety nets while others have highly segmented MIP systems. The fifth and final section of this chapter provides a summarising cluster analysis of these patterns of variation. It shows how individual countries can be grouped into different families of nations on the basis of the previously analysed dimensions of MIP.

Benefit levels

Introduction

This section investigates the generosity of the last safety net for the working-age population. Generosity can be measured in different ways by selecting different household types and using different reference values. In the following part, the level of minimum income benefits is first compared with individual wages and unemployment benefits, based on previous employment. The aim is to show the difference of the guaranteed minimum to average wages and to social insurance benefits, based on employment. Since wages and unemployment benefits usually refer to individuals, the analysis also focuses on single persons. In the second part of the analysis, minimum income benefits for families are compared with the average family household incomes in society. In the third part, the development of minimum income benefits is analysed relative to price levels. In addition, the cross-national 'value' of benefits is studied by using purchasing power parities for two points in time: 1996 and 2007. Finally, the main findings are summarised in the conclusion.

The data for this section are primarily based on model calculations and do not show the real income situation of in-need population groups. Rather, they indicate how the MIP system in each country should ideally work for the selected cases if all legally available benefits are granted and taken up. Results, therefore, do not consider the possibly strong differences between countries in the scope of MIP, eligibility rules, or entitlement conditions. Additionally, the problem of non-take-up of benefits is neglected here. Various studies show that non-take-up of benefits is a serious problem and varies greatly between countries (see later in this chapter for further discussion).

There are a number of studies available on benefit levels, but often they use different data and apply different methods. While it is not the intent of this text to provide an overview of the various approaches, a few remarks are necessary before presenting the results. In general, there are two broad perspectives: one looks at minimum income benefits in relation to employment and work incentives; the other primarily studies their relation to poverty. The first perspective usually takes wages as a reference, while the second one refers to the relative poverty line. Our approach has a third focus, which is on institutional features of MIP benefits. In this perspective, minimum income benefit generosity is regarded as an indicator of institutionalised social citizenship rights that are based on need. This generosity is first compared with income from work and work-related benefits in society. Secondly, it is related to the average income among the total population. Both results are interpreted as indicators for the social inclusion of needy population groups.

The indicators for this analysis are based on two currently available major data sources that include comparative time series on benefit levels: the OECD Benefits and Wages data (including tax benefit models) (OECD, various years) and the SaMip database on social assistance and MIP, developed by Nelson at the SOFI in Stockholm (for the documentation, see Nelson, 2007a; also Nelson, 2008, 2010). The OECD data series begins in 2001 and Nelson's data in the early 1990s. OECD is usually better suited for cross-sectional comparative analysis, whereas the SaMip data series is better for longitudinal study. The two data sources differ in a variety of aspects, including terms of data collection, scope of data, and model assumptions that cannot be discussed here (see van Mechelen, 2009 for a thorough analysis). Before the results can be presented, the treatment of housing costs and housing benefits in these two datasets must be discussed.

Housing costs present a critical issue for needy population groups. Whether and to what extent these costs are included in the benefit package makes a big difference in guaranteed minimum income levels. Yet the basic problem for international comparison and even for within-country comparisons on benefit levels is that housing supplements usually vary with actual housing costs, which vary by locality. In addition, housing costs vary by tenure, family type, and size. For inter-country comparisons, one must therefore select typical cases for the analysis or estimate housing costs. The SaMip data are primarily based on a sample of typical housing arrangements for different family types in one specific local community in each country. The data were collected for one point in time, and the costs are adjusted for each year according to the development of the housing costs price index in each country. By contrast, the OECD data are based on a standard estimate for housing costs, which equals 20% of average gross wages in each country, irrespective of family type, locality, or time. Both solutions are imperfect and each has specific advantages and shortcomings. SaMip data give a more empirical picture but do not necessarily reflect national averages. OECD data reflect standard assumptions for all countries but are not based on real empirical cases.

There is no simple right or wrong solution to this problem. The variation that comes up when using these two data sets is therefore not simply a matter of more or less appropriate methods, but a substantial issue that reflects the real variations in benefit levels due to differences in housing costs in different localities. In most countries, strong elements of local benefit regulation or discretion in MIP exists; only some countries have comprehensive uniform national systems with standardised benefits and housing supplements across the whole territory. Therefore, some if not most of the variability in results that is shown in the following analysis indicates the degree of complexity and local variability in MIP within a country.

Benefit levels for single persons compared with individual wages

The generosity of minimum income benefits compared with wages is an indicator for the 'value' of social citizenship rights relative to income from work. In this perspective, minimum income benefits are usually compared to the OECD average (typical) worker's wage (AW) as a reference. Yet in many countries, this typical wage is not representative of real earnings among the total population. A more realistic reference is therefore the average empirical wage level in the total economy standardised for full-time and full-year dependent employment. These data are provided by both Eurostat (2010) and the OECD (various years).

In some countries, the difference between the two reference values is significant. For example, average total wages in the economy are more than 20% higher than the AW in Ireland, but 20% lower in Germany. This leads to significant differences in the calculation of minimum income benefit generosity. If the reference value is higher, the relative amount of minimum income is estimated lower, and vice versa.

In the following analysis, both references are used for different purposes. Figure 4.1 shows the relative value of minimum income benefits compared with average total wages in the economy (case a) and compared with a typical low-wage worker with 67% of the AW (case b). The first case gives a more representative picture of the total economy, and the second compares minimum income benefits with a typical low-wage worker.

Figure 4.1 shows three indicators: 1) the level of minimum income benefits for a single person; 2) the income of an individual who previously worked at the AW level and now receives unemployment insurance benefits; and 3) the income of a person who earns the legal minimum wage based on full-time employment. All amounts are provided after taxes and social security contributions and include eventual housing benefits. Individual countries are grouped into five clusters following the discussion in Chapter Two (included in all following graphs): 1) Northern Europe (including Denmark, Finland, and Sweden); 2) Anglophone countries (Ireland and the United Kingdom); 3) Continental Europe (Belgium, Germany, France, the Netherlands, and Austria); 4) Eastern Europe (Poland, Slovakia, the Czech Republic, and Hungary); and 5) Southern Europe (Italy, Portugal, and Spain).

Compared with net average total wages in the economy (case a), minimum income benefits are most generous in Denmark and the Netherlands, with more than 50% of the reference value. Levels are intermediate in Finland, Sweden, Ireland, Britain, Germany, Austria, and the Czech Republic, with figures between 40% and 50%. In Belgium, France, Eastern Europe (except the Czech Republic), and Southern Europe, levels are below 40%. Slovakia has the lowest level, with 17%. These figures deviate significantly in some cases from figures based on the AW as usually provided by the OECD (case b). In particular, UK and Irish benefit levels are significantly lower if compared with total economy average wages. By using this more empirical measure as reference, these two countries are also closer together.

In general, minimum income benefits are most generous when compared with individual wages in Northern Europe and the Anglophone countries. These benefits are quite generous in Continental Europe but have strong variations. In Eastern and Southern Europe, benefit levels are relatively low, except in the Czech Republic. This finding confirms the impression that social citizenship rights are more developed (compared with average wages) in the Nordic and Anglophone countries and in some other countries, especially in the Netherlands and the

Figure 4.1: MIP compared with unemployment benefits and minimum wage, 2007

Note: 'Minimum wage' in Germany is estimated at €7.50 per hour with 168 hours a month.

Source: OECD Benefits and Wages database (OECD, various years), Eurostat (2010).

Czech Republic. In these countries, social security benefits based on citizenship rights rather than employment records are also important in other social branches, such as in the pension system (see Chapter Two).

This finding is further supported by the difference between minimum income benefits and the level of unemployment compensation for a person who previously earned an AW. As argued previously, this distance is an indicator of the level of basic social rights compared with social rights based on employment. Moreover, from an individual worker's perspective, it shows the additional level of social protection that is due to work compared with the last safety net, which provides the social minimum in society. Hence, this difference is an indicator of the value that the social security system assigns to (previous) work relative to the needs-based guaranteed minimum for all members in society.

This difference is minimal in the Nordic countries, and there is not even a small difference in the Anglophone countries because the unemployed receive the same amount as minimum income recipients. On the negative side, there is no security 'buffer' between short-term unemployment and the receipt of MIP. However, this is solely true for benefit amounts, not for entitlement conditions or means-testing, which strongly distinguish these benefits from each other. On the positive side, persons in need are not treated worse in terms of income than the short-term unemployed. In all other European countries, the difference between the two benefit levels is much larger, confirming the generally preferential treatment of work and work-related benefits compared to purely needs-based social citizenship rights.

The perspective is different if one compares minimum income benefit levels with the net income of a person who is employed at the minimum wage level. The difference between these two levels indicates the 'value' of income from work from the perspective of a minimum income recipient looking for a job at minimum wage conditions, which may be a typical pathway out of welfare dependency for many. The assumption is that this job would be in full-time employment.

In most countries with a legal minimum wage, the net income in such a case is substantially higher than the guaranteed minimum income. Only in Ireland, Britain, and the Netherlands is there no great difference. The Nordic countries do not have a legal minimum wage but rather relatively high wage levels based on collective bargaining.

Benefit levels for families compared with average household income

The income level of families with children is quite different to the case of single persons because more factors enter into the equation. First, household income depends on employment patterns in households and earnings levels of individual household members. Second, minimum income benefits vary greatly by family type and size. Such variations show the 'implicit' equivalence scales used in MIP systems. Since all countries use their own methods for assessing the needs of different households, these implicit equivalence scales differ from country to country. Countries that provide relatively generous benefits for single persons may be less generous when families are compared, and vice versa. Third, in addition to earnings and minimum income benefits, a variety of other, mostly non-means-tested social and family benefits are added to household income. Wages are therefore not an appropriate reference for analysing the income position of families with children in receipt of MIP. Instead, the reference that is most often used for this purpose is the median total household income, adjusted for family size and composition (net equivalent household income). The approach is also used here. This method compares model calculations based on family types with empirical income survey data, and it has some methodological pitfalls. Most important, even if calculations are based on empirical survey data, one should not interpret the resulting figures as indicators of the real income situation of households. Again, the focus is on the comparative assessment of institutional arrangements rather than on income inequality or poverty.

In the following analysis, we use two different data sources in order to show the possible range of results and get a more robust picture. As discussed previously, the crucial issue is the treatment of housing costs, which is especially relevant for families. Figure 4.2 shows the net income of two-child families that receive minimum income benefits as a percentage of the national net median household income adjusted for family size and composition. The figure indicates the income position of minimum income recipients relative to the population average and can therefore be interpreted as an indicator of social inclusion. Data are presented both excluding and including housing supplements (cases a and b, respectively), while family benefits are always included in the calculation if they are disregarded in the means test for minimum income.

Luckily, the broad comparative picture that emerges from Figure 4.2 is fairly consistent if we ignore minor differences between the two data sources. First of all, housing supplements have a major impact on benefit levels, especially in Finland, Sweden, Germany, and the United Kingdom. For Poland, however, this result is only reported by OECD data. Second, only in three countries (Denmark, Germany, and Ireland) are benefit levels (including housing supplements) close to or slightly above the 60% of the median line that is the EU–defined risk-of-poverty threshold. This means that, in most countries, MIP fails to lift families with children out of (relative) poverty, even if the ideal model situation with full benefit packages and complete take-up of benefits is presumed. In some countries, benefit levels are placed in between the 50% and the 60% lines, signalling relative poverty: Finland, Sweden, the Netherlands (for both data sources unanimously), the United Kingdom and the Czech Republic (only OECD data), and Poland and Italy (only Nelson's data). In other countries, the situation is even worse: in Belgium, France, Austria, Slovakia, Hungary, and Portugal, figures are consistently below 50% of the median; in Spain, they are much below 40%, indicating real hardship. According to OECD data, hardship is also experienced in Slovakia, while Nelson's data produce somewhat better results. Yet the main and consistent finding among all countries is that minimum income benefits everywhere fail to

Figure 4.2: MIP compared with national median income, 2007[1]

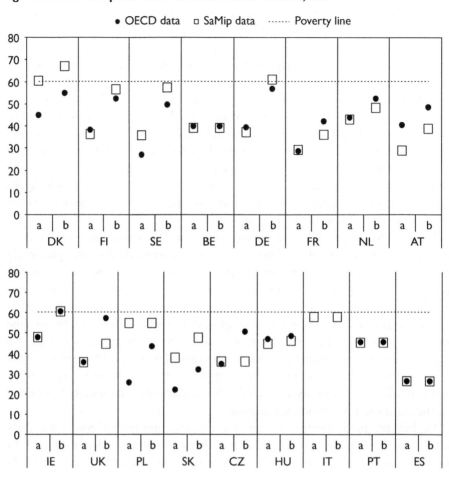

● OECD data   □ SaMip data   ┈┈┈ Poverty line

Notes:
[1] Benefit rates as % of median income.
a = excluding housing benefits
b = including housing benefits
Family consists of two adults and two children; weighting of median income by factor 2.1 (modified OECD-scale).

Sources: OECD Benefits and Wages database (OECD, various years); SaMip 2.0 (Nelson 2007a, 2010), Eurostat (2010).

lift people substantially above the relative poverty threshold. This also explains the empirical fact that (relative) poverty continues to exist even in countries with a comprehensive last safety net.

Some of the variations in the results produced by the two data sources can be explained by local differences in benefit levels within countries and by the selection of localities for the comparison. In the Austrian case, for example, Nelson's figures relate to Vienna, whereas OECD data refer to more generous Carinthia. For the United Kingdom, Nelson's data produce less generous benefits because they are based on (relatively low) housing costs referring to the situation in York, while the OECD standard assumptions produce a more generous benefit level.

Development of benefits, adjusted for prices and purchasing power parities

Even if minimum income benefits in all countries fail to lift people above the poverty line, do they at least compensate for increasing costs of living and rising prices over time? An argument that is often put forward in discussions about welfare state reform and retrenchment policies is that benefits for the poor are more likely than others to lose substance because they are not supported by powerful social and political groups. Though services for poor people always tend to be poor services, this problem may become more severe at times of welfare retrenchment policies and the financial crisis of the state.

In the Nordic and Continental European countries, the development of benefits adjusted for consumer price increases is surprisingly stable and does not show significant inter-country variations. Only in Sweden can one observe a small decline in real benefit levels. By contrast, in the Anglophone countries as well as in Southern and Eastern Europe, more change has occurred. In Ireland, a spectacular rise in price-adjusted benefit levels has taken place parallel to the high economic growth over this period. In the United Kingdom, benefit levels have followed a cyclical pattern, with strong increases during the late 1990s and a downturn from 2000 until 2007, when benefits reached the same level as at the beginning of the period. In Portugal benefit levels have slightly increased since the mid-1990s, whereas in Spain they have stagnated. Developments have also varied greatly among Eastern European countries. In the Czech Republic and Poland, benefit levels have been upheld, whereas they tended to decline in Slovakia and especially in Hungary.

Finally, we analyse the purchasing power that is guaranteed by MIP in each country. Of course, purchasing power mainly depends on national income and price levels. Yet benefit levels expressed in PPPs give at least an impression of the variation in real income standards of MIP in Europe. Since it is difficult to compare PPPs over time and internationally simultaneously, we focus on the latter perspective but look at two points in time. Figure 4.3 shows the PPP values (in US$) of minimum income benefits for a single person without housing supplements in 1996 and 2007.

In 2007, benefits were highest in the Netherlands, Ireland, Denmark, and Belgium, excluding the non-representative case of Milan, for which the Italian data stand. Not surprisingly, values are lowest for Eastern Europe, with Hungary at the bottom. In Southern Europe, Portugal is actually not much ahead of the Eastern countries, whereas Spain is closer to the European average. All other countries are close to the average and show quite similar benefit levels in terms of purchasing power: Germany, France, and Austria have almost similar levels, while the United Kingdom shows slightly lower values. What is perhaps surprising is the modest level of benefits in Finland and Sweden, which are even lower than in the UK.

Figure 4.3: MIP benefits for a single person (in PPPs), 1996 and 2007

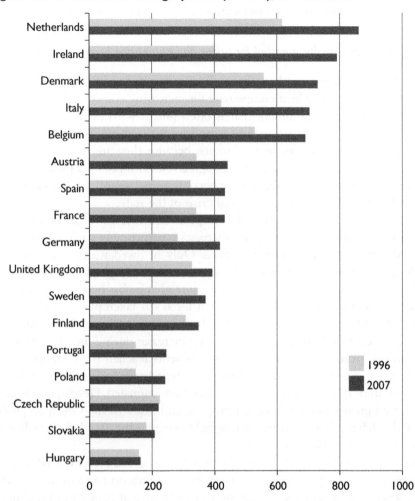

Source: SaMip 2.0 (Nelson, 2007a, 2010)

Hence, there is no consistent pattern in line with the five country groups that have guided the overall analysis. There is a big distance within the Nordic countries between generous levels in Denmark and very modest ones in Finland and Sweden. Ireland and the United Kingdom also differ from each other substantially, and among the Continental countries, Belgium and especially the Netherlands are distinguished from France and Germany by much higher benefit levels. Only the Eastern European countries are a quite homogeneous group due to their similar economic conditions. Over time, benefit levels increased in all countries except in the Czech Republic and Hungary, but the growth rate was very different. It was substantial in countries that already had high benefit levels 10 years ago: Ireland, the Netherlands, and Belgium. Again perhaps surprising, real benefit levels almost stagnated in Finland and Sweden.

Conclusion

When taking all the indicators presented in this section together and interpreting the overall result comparatively, one finding stands out: the comparative pattern of minimum income generosity does not fit with the usual welfare state regime types and country clusters.

The **Nordic countries** show relatively but not exceptionally high benefits compared with average total wages in the economy and with a typical low-wage worker. The same holds for families with children compared with the median household income. The Nordic countries have lifted benefit levels above at least 50% of the median household income when housing supplements are included, meaning that the systems tend to eliminate at least severe poverty. These countries furthermore show a great stability in benefit levels over time when adjusted for price increases, but their value in purchasing power parities is rather low, perhaps due to higher price levels. Another consistent finding across all indicators is that Denmark is doing comparatively better than Finland and Sweden. In terms of social citizenship, the Nordic countries show a pattern of relatively generous needs-based MIP benefits, which are not significantly below common minimum standards. The focus is clearly on the inclusion, rather than the exclusion, of in-need population groups.

The two **Anglophone countries** are characterised by relatively generous benefits compared with individual wages, and these benefits are indeed exceptionally high when compared with the insurance benefits of a typical low-wage worker. In both countries, therefore, needs-based social rights have a strong standing and fulfil an important task in the whole social security system. Benefits are also generous for families with children compared with average household income if housing supplements are added, although the two data sources differ in this respect for the United Kingdom. Across all indicators and sources, Ireland is consistently more generous than the UK and has significantly increased price-adjusted benefit levels over the past 10 years. Irish benefits are much higher than the British ones, especially in terms of purchasing power.

The **Continental European countries** are more heterogeneous but also show some common characteristics. Benefits vary from very modest (France) to rather high (the Netherlands) compared with individual wages, but are more similar in a middle position if a typical low-wage worker is taken as reference. For families with children compared with average household income, differences are again huge, ranging from less than 40% of the median in Belgium and France to more than 60% in Germany. Benefit rates have kept pace with rising prices in all Continental countries, but PPP values differ greatly. They are highest in the Netherlands and Belgium but rather modest in Germany, France, and Austria. Overall, among the Continental group, the Netherlands consistently stands out in terms of benefit generosity, and France is typically at the bottom. Compared with the situation in the Nordic and the Anglophone countries, social citizenship rights based on need in Continental European countries are less homogeneous and usually less generous than benefits based on desert and employment. This pattern clearly reflects the strong impact of the inheritance of Bismarck-type social insurance in which last resort benefits have occupied a residual place. In institutional terms, social citizenship rights based on need clearly constitute a less generous residual basement of the welfare state.

Benefits in **Eastern European countries** are usually well below those in the other countries, except for Southern Europe. This is particularly true if benefit levels are compared with individual wages, but is also the case for families in relation to the average household income. With respect to price levels, benefits have developed rather differently in individual Eastern countries. In Poland and the Czech Republic, the price-adjusted value was basically preserved (despite stronger fluctuations), whereas in Slovakia and particularly in Hungary, the benefit dropped in value. Given the low wealth in terms of the GDP in these countries, it is no surprise that benefit levels in Eastern European countries have the lowest purchasing power in Europe and are close to one another in this respect. Among the Eastern nations, the Czech Republic generally shows the most positive feature in terms of benefit generosity. Social rights based on need are relatively uniform, but the generosity of benefits is deplorably low and fails to secure a decent livelihood for the most needy population groups. In practice, therefore, MIP systems in Eastern Europe tend towards social exclusion, rather than inclusion, of the poor.

Finally, the **Southern European countries** do not perform well either, in terms of benefit generosity. Leaving aside the atypical Milan example of Italy, benefits are generally very low compared with individual wages. For families, however, Portugal provides rather generous benefits in contrast to Spain, which has the lowest level in Europe. Portugal also shows an increase in price-adjusted benefits, while the Spanish figures stagnate. The purchasing power of Spanish benefits is still significantly higher than in Portugal due to the stronger Spanish economy. The relative situation of minimum income recipients is thereby better in Portugal than in Spain, whereas the reverse is true for 'absolute' benefit levels in terms of purchasing power. It remains to be seen whether the financial crisis and its consequences will change this overall picture. By and large, social citizenship rights seem to be weaker in Southern Europe than in any other group of countries, including Eastern Europe. The gap between insurance-based and needs-based benefits is particularly high, indicating a very weak institutionalisation of basic social citizenship rights. Although MIP benefits are even lower in some Eastern European countries, their systems are less patchy in terms of entitlement, and the low benefits are partly explained by the worse economic conditions prevailing in these countries. In Southern Europe, by contrast, the low value of MIP indicates a clear institutional deficiency: the lack of a coherent concept of social citizenship (Saraceno, 2010).

Beneficiaries

Introduction

This section analyses the comparative number and structure of MIP recipients. It shows how extensive these systems are and how many persons depend on MIP benefits. The significance of MIP goes far beyond this simple measure, however. MIP institutionalises the social minimum below which nobody in society should be allowed to fall, at least for those groups that are entitled to benefits. Hence, MIP constitutes the ground floor of the welfare state edifice. At the same time, MIP benefits set an effective minimum wage threshold for working-age adults. Therefore, MIP is a significant institutional reference for both social security systems and the labour market. When compared with the size of the overall welfare state, the salience of MIP indicates how important the dimension of needs-based social rights in a country effectively is. A high salience usually indicates that the other two principles of social distribution (desert and equality) are less important. A low salience, however, can be seen alongside both a well-developed overall welfare state and a rudimentary welfare system. In the first case, social rights are strong but depend more on accrued rights or citizenship rather than need. In the second case, social citizenship is weak and often incomplete because it excludes sizeable populations in need of any form of benefit.

The focus of this section is on the share of MIP recipients among the population as an institutional indicator for the salience of these systems. This share cannot be interpreted as an indicator for need in a straightforward way, however, because the number of beneficiaries depends on a variety of factors: socioeconomic problem pressures, the protectiveness of social security benefits above the MIP level, the institutionalisation of MIP, itself, and finally, the take-up of MIP benefits by entitled persons (Behrendt, 2002). All these factors vary between countries.

Pressure comes primarily from high unemployment rates, low participation rates in the labour market, and low incomes. In addition, demographic and family changes are important, foremost the growth of migrant populations and single parenthood. Although individual countries vary in the level of these problem pressures, the general trend is towards increasing problems that are often not adequately protected by existing social security systems (Marx, 2007). Nonetheless, in some countries, part of these problems is solved better than it is in others by non-means-tested benefits 'above' the MIP level. These benefits then operate as a kind of filter for MIP systems (see Chapter Two).

Since countries vary in the protectiveness of their social insurance systems, the relevance of MIP systems also differs greatly. If social insurance provides adequate protection for large population groups, MIP is, *ceteris paribus*, less relevant, and vice versa. Yet if social security is inadequate or has serious gaps in coverage, MIP systems do not necessarily provide a viable last safety net either (Ferrera, 2005). Access to MIP may indeed be difficult or limited to certain categorical groups; some groups may even be completely excluded from any form of social security.

The theoretically possible combinations of the 'protectiveness' of social security and the 'openness' of MIP systems are shown in Table 4.1. The protectiveness of social insurance mainly depends on benefit levels and coverage among the population. The lower coverage rates or benefit levels are, the more persons may fall back into the last safety net in case of need. At the same time, access to MIP can vary independently. Some MIP systems may be open to all persons in need, but in other cases, access may be restricted to categorical groups or provided only under specific circumstances. The actual salience of MIP then depends on variations in both dimensions.

A low protectiveness of social insurance combined with open access to MIP should lead to the highest extension (salience) of MIP among the population if pressures of problems are held constant. Conversely, a high protectiveness of social insurance combined with closed or very limited access to MIP should result in the lowest MIP extension. The other possible combinations should fall in between, as shown in Table 4.1. This analytical framework can be applied either to the overall population or to categorical groups such as older persons or unemployed people.

Moreover, actual benefit receipt does not only depend on objective problem pressures, institutional social security filters, and access conditions to MIP. Beyond these structural and institutional factors, individual and more subjective factors are also highly relevant. First, the take-up of benefits by needy and eligible persons may vary significantly internationally. Many eligible persons in need might not claim benefits due to fear of stigmatisation or future reclaims. In other cases, potential claimants may not even know that they are entitled to benefits due to non-transparent regulations or complicated administrative procedures. These problems are usually very important for means-tested benefits. Secondly, local welfare officers may have a high level of discretion in deciding on benefit claims. This is especially relevant for means-tested benefits for which the specific circumstances of each individual case need to be considered. These more case-specific variations may occur even if MIP in legal terms seems to be accessible.

Empirical studies have repeatedly shown that non-take up of means-tested benefits is very high. For instance, Fuchs (2009) reported that in Austria, Germany, and Finland, about 50% of eligible households fail to take up benefits. Earlier studies reported that non-take-up varied from 30% to 50% in the United Kingdom and France, over 50–60% in the Netherlands, and more than 60% in Germany

Table 4.1: The salience of MIP

Access to social assistance	Social insurance protection		
	High	Medium	Low
Open	O	+	++
Medium	–	O	+
Closed	– –	–	O

Source: Authors' depiction.

(Hernanz et al, 2004). Behrendt (2002, p 191) reported non–take-up rates of 10–25% in the United Kingdom and around 50% in Germany for the early 1990s.

Comparative figures of benefit receipt are not available in international data sources as social expenditure data usually are, even though people on benefits is a crucial indicator. For example, Eurostat and OECD do not regularly collect information on benefit receipt. Although some selective studies are available, they do not focus on MIP (see OECD, 2003). In principle, there are two different approaches to studying benefit receipt: on the basis of survey data and based on administrative data. However, survey data are usually not detailed enough for a study of MIP benefits, and low-income groups are usually underrepresented in the survey population. By contrast, administrative data are published regularly on the basis of a complete 'institutional' sample but are usually not provided in a comparable structure. These data are based on institutional regulations and are therefore preferable for the institutionally oriented analysis of this book.

The following data are taken from diverse national administrative sources, giving the advantage that they are linked to institutional structures. Yet there are limits with respect to their comparability over time and between countries. Data are not provided in a standardised form internationally, sometimes not even within a country. Therefore, we had to make a number of adjustments in order to estimate comparable figures. This adjustment is fairly well possible for an overall estimate of MIP recipients across all programmes within countries but more problematic when analysing recipient structures across all individual programmes. A more detailed analysis relating to specific institutional structures is therefore provided in the country sections in Chapter Three. For the comparative analysis, we look at main aggregates only.

For this purpose, we collected data on MIP recipients in each individual scheme within a country and aggregated the figures for each country. Then we estimated annual averages that can be interpreted as average man years of benefit receipt (see Cluitmans et al, 2001; OECD, 2003). On this basis, two major distinctions were made. First, we made a distinction between recipients (individuals receiving benefits) and beneficiaries (recipients plus dependent household members). This distinction is relevant because MIP benefits are often provided to individuals but cover the needs of the complete household. The salience of MIP among the population is better understood if one includes all persons depending on them. Secondly, among individual recipients we distinguish between adults of working age (20–64) and the older population (above 65). This distinction is largely possible with the available data for most countries, but some estimates had to be made in this case.

Beneficiaries among the total population

Table 4.2 gives a first broad overview. It shows the percentage of the population that receives MIP benefits among three demographic groups: 1) the total population (beneficiaries including dependent household members); 2) adults at working

Table 4.2: Percentage of population receiving MIP, 1995 and 2007

Country	Total population[1] 1995	Total population[1] 2007	Population 20–64[2] 1995	Population 20–64[2] 2007	Population 65+[2] 1995	Population 65+[2] 2007
Nordic						
Denmark	6.1	4.2	4.4	3.4	0.0	0.0
Finland	5.1	3.2	4.9	3.3	0.0	0.6
Sweden	3.5	2.2	4.0	2.3	0.7	1.0
Anglophone						
Ireland	[f]19.8	18.4	[f]15.2	13.4	[f]22.9	20.9
United Kingdom[a]	16.9	12.9	11.5	8.8	19.1	26.1
United Kingdom[b]	20.2	22.5	14.3	16.7	19.1	26.1
Continental						
Austria[e]	[e]5.3	[e]5.1	[e]5.0	[e]5.5	15.2	10.2
Belgium	5.8	6.5	2.1	3.0	7.2	5.9
France	[f]9.2	9.3	[cd]6.7	[d]7.8	[f]10.6	5.8
Germany	3.9	9.6	3.9	11.3	2.5	2.4
Netherlands	7.9	5.4	6.3	5.1	[f]0.7	1.3
Southern						
Portugal	1.4	4.4	0.9	2.6	5.8	5.0
Spain	[g]7.9	6.9	[g]1.9	1.9	[g]39.2	31.4
Eastern						
Czech Republic	4.9	0.9	5.0	1.1	0.0	0.0
Hungary	2.3	2.5	4.0	3.3	0.0	2.3
Poland	9.6	5.3	4.6	3.1	0.0	0.0
Slovakia	7.6	7.0	5.8	5.7	0.0	0.0

Notes:
[1] Including dependent children.
[2] Excluding dependent children.
[a] Excluding working tax credit and similar earlier programmes.
[b] Including working tax credit and similar earlier programmes.
[c] 8.3% for population 25–59.
[d] 9.6% for population 25–59.
[e] Cumulative annual figures including children for population below 65.
[f] 1998.
[g] 1998; missing data for *pensiones asistenciales*.

Source: EuMin database. No data for Italy available.

age (recipients aged 20–65 plus their adult partners, but excluding children); and 3) older people (recipients aged 65+ and their partners, but excluding children). The indicators are shown for 1995 and for 2007, and the countries are grouped in the familiar territorial clusters.

These data are estimates, all of which are 'conservative' in the sense that they tend to underestimate benefit receipt because the number of dependent partners and children is not always provided in the statistics, especially for benefits provided as part of social insurance. This is most relevant for Continental and Southern European countries, which follow this tradition in welfare policy. Data are limited in this respect for Belgium, France, Austria, and Portugal. We have tried to overcome this problem by making estimates whenever possible. Nonetheless, the real salience and significance of MIP is even higher than the figures show in most cases. In the case of Spain, the scope of MIP might be underestimated for yet another reason: due to lack of data, the expiring assistance pensions for old-age and disability are not included in the figures for 1995.

With these caveats in mind, the table reveals significant differences between countries that do not fit nicely into the typical country clusters. At the same time, it is obvious that MIP in most countries is not residual in terms of the population affected by these schemes, but that beneficiaries represent sizeable proportions of the population.

The highest proportion among the total population can be found in Ireland in 1995, when one fifth of the population depended on MIP. More than one fifth of older people in both Ireland and the United Kingdom depended on MIP in 2007. The share of MIP beneficiaries is generally high in the two Anglophone countries, but with some variation. By contrast, the Scandinavian countries show much lower ratios, but they also differ strongly. In Sweden, for example, the situation looks better than in Finland or Denmark. Variation is also high within the Continental European group of countries. Figures are modest in Belgium and the Netherlands but higher in France and Germany. The two Southern European countries show a quite diverse pattern as well. The salience of MIP in Portugal is limited, while the system in Spain includes a significant share of the population. Eastern Europe looks more homogeneous on the whole, but even here – where ratios are at a medium to low level – countries are not similar.

A closer look at the different demographic groups (the recipient structure) reveals further important variations. Among the working-age population, benefit receipt is highest in the two Anglophone countries and in Germany (in this case only in 2007, however, because of institutional changes in 2005). This high ratio is due to the fact that unemployment protection in the Anglophone countries is rather limited both in time and benefit levels, meaning that most unemployed persons need MIP benefits after a short time. This is also the case in Germany, where people have had to claim MIP benefits after 12 months of unemployment since the reform of 2005 (see Chapter Three).

Recipient ratios, by contrast, are generally low in the Nordic states, except in Finland, where the economic crisis during the early 1990s hit many people and the unemployment rate climbed to levels around 20%. Taking this into account, the Finnish MIP recipient figures for 1995 look rather modest. In the Continental European countries, the figures are at a medium level with two exceptions: Germany (to the negative side) and Belgium (to the positive side). The German case is described above; the low MIP receipt among working-age adults in Belgium is due to a specificity in unemployment insurance. Belgium is the only country in Europe in which unemployment insurance pays unlimited benefits, although the replacement rate is significantly lower after the first year (see Chapters Two and Three). Still, the Belgian system prevents most unemployed persons from becoming dependent on MIP. The MIP systems in Eastern European countries are surprisingly small given the huge structural difficulties in these countries during the transition. Though the systems show some fluctuations in line with unemployment figures, their size is very limited. This shows the still highly exclusive character of most of these systems and the very low benefits they provide.

Looking at developments over time, there are only a few cases of significant change that are due mainly to institutional reforms. The outstanding example for such a change is the German reform in 2005, after which MIP recipient figures climbed extraordinarily. In most countries, unemployment rates – the most important indicator for problem pressure – went down significantly between the early 1990s and 2007, which was the last year before the crisis and a relatively favourable year in economic terms in most countries. This decline in problem pressure can be clearly seen in the Scandinavian countries and in the two Anglophone countries, where MIP systems have tended to react most visibly to this trend by a decline in salience. However, in most other countries in this study, recipient ratios have remained surprisingly stable and relatively high despite declining unemployment rates. This shows that structural problems and institutional inefficiencies are themselves responsible for this pattern.

For the older population, the situation is completely different. Again, the two Anglophone nations show the highest salience of MIP because a significant part of old-age security is organised as MIP. It is therefore not residual, but as integral a part of the whole system as unemployment protection. By contrast, very low or even non-existent recipient ratios among the older population are reported for the three Scandinavian countries as well as for the Netherlands, the Czech Republic, and Poland. In these countries, relatively effective and comprehensive basic pension systems exist that provide minimum pensions without a means test and without MIP-type benefits. Even though Finland and Sweden introduced major changes in their pension systems in the early 2000s, their basic character as systems providing guaranteed minimum pensions to all citizens has not changed (see Chapter Two). The share of older persons depending on MIP is medium in most Continental European countries and fairly low in Eastern European countries. These variations are clearly linked to institutional differences in pension systems. Portugal's share of old-age MIP recipients was similar to those in Continental Europe until recently. The situation has changed significantly since 2006, when a new MIP scheme for older persons was introduced, which grants a means-tested top-up to contributory pensions (see Chapter Three). The institutional picture now resembles the Spanish case, where a high share of older persons receives MIP benefits that are provided in two forms: as means-tested supplements to social insurance pensions (contributory schemes) and as non-contributory social pensions for other groups of older persons.

In general, the differences between countries have remained fairly stable, and no convergence has occurred. There has also been no general trend towards a decline or a growth in MIP receipt among countries and recipient groups. This underscores the fact that institutional differences between countries have persisted and that MIP systems continue to play specific roles within different social security systems despite similar structural changes in the economy and society.

Recipients at working age

Benefit dependency on all kinds of income-replacing measures among working-age adults increased from the early 1980s until the mid-1990s, when it started to decline (Cluitmans et al, 2001). This cyclical trend was mainly due to the development of unemployment benefits (Immervoll et al, 2004). By 2000, overall dependency rates varied from about 11% of the population aged 15–64 in Spain to 24% in France and Belgium (OECD, 2003, chapter 4). There was no similar cyclical pattern in social assistance, nor has there has been a downward trend since the mid-1990s, too.

For social assistance specifically, the ratios reported by Immervoll et al (2004) are very low compared with the figures presented in this section. Ratios varying from less than 1% of the population aged 15–64 in Spain and Austria, 3% in the United Kingdom, and 4% in Ireland to about 10% in Slovakia have been reported for the year 2000 (Immervoll et al, 2004, p 57). These low figures are explained by the narrow definition of social assistance employed in this study, which excluded all categorical schemes except benefits for lone parents. Moreover, MIP benefits provided on top of social insurance benefits were also excluded from their definition of social assistance. By contrast, our definition of MIP is broader and includes both categorical and top-up benefits. This seems to be a more reasonable approach for studying the overall salience of MIP systems. In a cross-national comparison, one should take into account all relevant 'functional' and categorical equivalents to the general social assistance scheme.

Therefore, the figures presented here are significantly higher. Figure 4.4 shows the percentage of adults below pension age who received MIP benefits for each year since 1992. The figure confirms persisting differences between countries but shows some significant changes, which are related to major institutional reforms.

Persistently low recipient ratios are reported for Sweden and Denmark due to their open access and generous unemployment protection systems and the low level of inactivity among single-parent households. In Denmark, figures have been stable over time while Sweden had a small peak in the mid-1990s due to exceptionally high unemployment rates at that time. For both Nordic countries, open and generous social security systems for the working-age population have shifted MIP into a residual role. At the same time, MIP systems themselves are open to all needy population groups, but in comparative terms only a few people need or claim them.

Figure 4.4: MIP recipients at working age (as % of population 20–64), 1992–2010

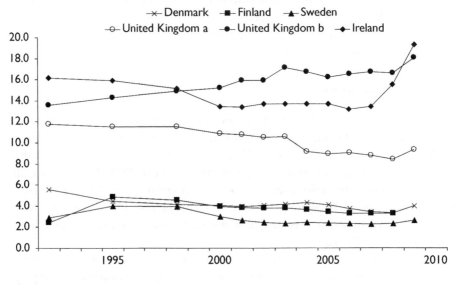

a) Nordic and Anglophone countries

—×— Denmark   —■— Finland   —▲— Sweden
—○— United Kingdom a   —●— United Kingdom b   —◆— Ireland

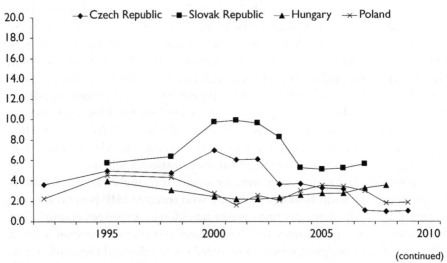

b) Eastern Europe

—◆— Czech Republic   —■— Slovak Republic   —▲— Hungary   —×— Poland

(continued)

A similar pattern holds for Belgium and Austria, which, in this respect, are exceptions among Continental European countries. In Belgium, unemployment insurance is unlimited, which explains why the size of MIP is small for adults at working age. However, the wage replacement rate is significantly lowered after one year. Moreover, unemployment insurance is also accessible for persons without previous work experience, particularly the young unemployed. In addition, Belgium has one of the most developed systems of childcare and preschools in Europe, providing favourable conditions for working families and single parents.

Figure 4.4: MIP recipients at working age (as % of population 20–64), 1992–2010 (continued)

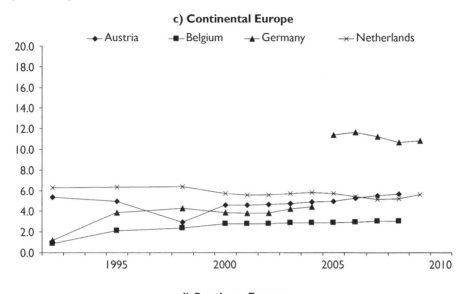

c) Continental Europe

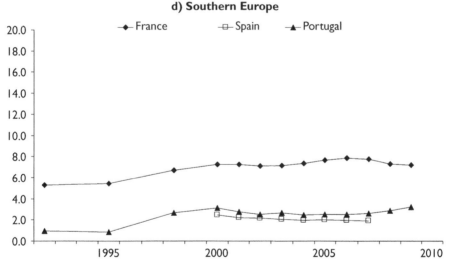

d) Southern Europe

Source: EuMin database; authors' depiction.

Austria is one of the few countries that still have unemployment assistance that provides wage-related benefits for the long-term unemployed. Therefore, as in Belgium, the pressure of long-term unemployment is solved mainly by policies above the MIP level, although the situation is worse for labour market entrants and single parents.

Low recipient ratios also characterise Portugal and Spain. In Portugal, the ratio varies between 1% and 3% and is mainly made up of the general, nationally enacted MIP scheme. In Spain, about half of MIP recipients in this age group are included in the regional last safety nets, and half in disability schemes and schemes topping up insurance benefits to a minimum level.

On the opposite end, very high recipient ratios characterise the United Kingdom and Ireland. Including the working tax credit (WTC) for the UK, the ratio was 16.7% in 2007 and even exceeded the Irish level. This high ratio is exceptional in the European context and comes close to the earned income tax credit (EITC) in the US. Including the WTC, the ratio of MIP recipients has not declined with the decreasing unemployment rates since the mid-1990s, even though by 2007 both the UK and Ireland had very low unemployment, which can only be explained by the fact that MIP does not play a residual role in these countries but provides the only benefit available in the social security system in many cases. Flat-rate and means-tested benefits are crucial elements in their social security systems. For example, the whole system of unemployment protection in the UK is organised on this basis. In addition, the rise of the WTC is an indicator for an increasing number of poor working households, although the income level provided by WTC is higher than the minimum. In some other countries, working households can also receive MIP benefits on top of their earnings, and this group is also growing in these other countries, as in the UK.

Continental countries show a diverse pattern. Austria and Belgium have low MIP recipient ratios due to their inclusive social insurance systems. The Netherlands also ranks low when we exclude the supplementary means-tested benefits topping up social insurance provisions. France and Germany have medium levels. The French ratio has remained relatively stable at around 7 and 8%. The German ratio went up significantly from about 4% to more than 11% due to the abolition of unemployment assistance in 2005 and the subsequent inclusion of long-term unemployed in the new MIP scheme.

Eastern European countries show strongly fluctuating figures of MIP recipients, closely in line with developments in unemployment. In the Czech Republic and Slovakia, MIP recipient ratios climbed in the early 1990s, reaching a peak around the early 2000s, and have since levelled off.

Older recipients

For the older population, the country clusters show a clearer pattern of variation because the situation of this group is mainly influenced by one institution: the public pension system, particularly the first tier, providing basic pension income (see Chapter Two for more detail). One can distinguish between two different historical types of pension systems: the Beveridge type and the Bismarck type. In the Beveridge type, public pension systems provide a ground floor for all insured persons with flat-rate benefits. Insurance coverage is usually comprehensive, including all economically active persons (as in the United Kingdom) or all citizens (residents) in a country (as in the Netherlands and Denmark). In the Bismarck-type systems, public pensions aim to secure individual income standards through earnings-related benefits. In most cases, insurance is limited to employed (and sometimes economically active) persons.

At first sight, the basic logic of the Beveridge-type system should make additional MIP for older people unnecessary because a basic pension for all is guaranteed by the pension system. Conversely, in Bismarck-type systems, one may expect a high and actually growing proportion of persons who are not adequately secured in old age due to low lifetime earnings or short and interrupted working careers. Hence, in Bismarck-type systems, one should expect a higher share of older MIP recipients.

Despite expectations, empirical data actually show a different pattern (Figure 4.5). Indeed, the share of older persons depending on MIP is very high in two Beveridge-type cases – the United Kingdom and Ireland. In Ireland, the ratio declined from around 30% in 1992 to 20% in 2007, while in the UK figures actually climbed due to the change from income support to pension credit. Obviously, the original promise of these two Beveridge-type pension systems – to secure a decent income floor in old age for everybody – has never been fulfilled in practice in these two countries.

Yet there have been more successful Beveridge-type pension systems, too, such as the Dutch and Danish systems as well as those in Sweden and Finland. Denmark and the Netherlands are not included in the figure because their pension systems grant basic pensions to all residents. Consequently, there are almost no older persons needing to claim MIP. Finland and Sweden, however, introduced income testing into their basic pension tiers in the early 2000s. Only the recipient numbers for those schemes where overall household income is taken into account for the means test are included in Figure 4.5 (see Chapter Three).

The Bismarck-type pension systems fall between these extremes and do comparatively well on average. MIP recipients in some countries represent less than 10 % of the older population while in others the share is higher. In Spain and France MIP has constituted an important element in the social protection of older persons. In both countries, however, there has been a slight downward trend. In Portugal, a means-tested top-up to contributory pensions was introduced in 2006, comparable to the complementary pensions in Spain. Since then, recipient rates among older persons are steeply climbing. In Austria, figures have been relatively high, too, but show a slight downward trend. In Germany MIP plays a minor role.

However, one has to be cautious. On the one hand, the low MIP dependency among older people certainly indicates a great historical achievement of some Bismarck-type pension systems, not only in securing individual living standards but also in providing a ground floor for large population groups. Three different institutional mechanisms are responsible for this achievement. First, a calculation of pension credits on the basis of the 'best' instead of average income years; second, the recognition of time spent in education, as a family carer, or unemployed as relevant to accrue pension rights; and third and most notably, the existence of survivors' pensions for non-working spouses. On the other hand, one should be aware that this overall positive picture may only be correct for the present generation of

Figure 4.5: MIP recipients at pension age (as % of population 65+), 1992–2010

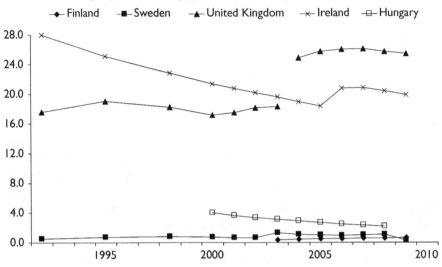

a) Nordic and Anglophone countries plus Hungary

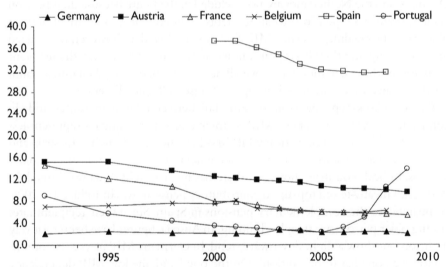

b) Continental and Southern European countries

Source: EuMin database; authors' depiction.

pensioners and not for coming pensioner cohorts. Present pensioners grew old under three exceptionally favourable conditions: strong economic growth, low unemployment, and a relatively generous pension system. Future pensioner cohorts have already experienced lower growth and higher unemployment during their working lives and will strongly feel the impact of recent pension reforms that have left older pensioner cohorts largely unaffected.

Moreover, in Bismarck-type countries, the problem of non-take-up of MIP benefits may be especially high among older people because pension systems and MIP are often institutionally disconnected. The pension system has a high level of legitimacy because it is strongly related to work and achievement, often regarded as a strong 'earned' social right. By contrast, the legitimacy of MIP is much lower. MIP is often institutionally completely separate from social insurance because it is regulated and provided by local welfare authorities, in contrast to national social insurance. Lower legitimacy often results in lower take-up rates, especially among older people. In Beveridge-type countries, the distance between insurance and assistance is smaller, probably making access to MIP easier. Hence, it can be argued that social citizenship rights are more integrated in Beveridge-type systems, while they are more fragmented in Bismarck-type countries.

Conclusion

There are huge differences in MIP receipt between countries, and there is no general trend. The impact of institutional arrangements is strong, especially with respect to pensions and the role of MIP among older people. For the working-age population, diverse institutional contexts play a role because the population is heterogeneous and exposed to a variety of risks, such as long-term unemployment single parenthood, or disability.

The picture with respect to country clusters is rather differentiated and does not fit nicely with the dominant welfare regime types. There is strong variation in all these groups, suggesting that specific institutional arrangements in individual countries have a profound impact on the implementation of social citizenship.

The **Nordic countries** constitute a relatively homogeneous group. Sweden and Denmark have a consistently low number of MIP recipients among both working-age adults and older people due to their generous unemployment protection systems, extensive family-related services, and effective basic pensions for all citizens. Consequently, few people fall back into the last safety net. Social citizenship is highly inclusive and mainly based on residence and accrued rights, linked to the basic concept of the citizen–worker. Needs-based citizenship rights also have an inclusive and universal character but play a residual role in the overall welfare system. In Finland, the situation is a little worse for working-age adults but similar for pensioners.

By contrast, the two **Anglophone countries** rely more heavily on needs-based benefits. Both the United Kingdom and Ireland are characterised by high levels of MIP recipients in both age groups due to very limited social security in general. As noted by Gough et al (1997), social assistance in these countries is not residual but an integral part of the welfare state edifice, particularly for older people.

The **Continental European countries** show a strongly varying pattern. For working-age adults, Belgium and Austria provide extensive social security above the MIP level. In Germany, the situation was not so different until the major reform of unemployment assistance in 2005. Since then, Germany has had one of the highest levels of MIP receipt among the working-age population. France and the Netherlands show medium figures. As argued earlier, the situation for older people is still relatively favourable in most Continental countries but will certainly deteriorate in the coming years. This is especially true for Germany, whose pension insurance does not have a minimum pension. Social citizenship is still largely based on desert in the Continental European countries due to the strong employment relatedness of their social security systems. The significance of needs-based benefits varies between different population groups. Universal components of social citizenship are only relevant for the older Dutch population due to the residents' pension system (see Chapter Three). At the same time, with the exception of France, all population groups are covered by one of the elements in the social citizenship package.

This almost universal coverage does not exist in **Southern Europe**, even though the two countries for which we have data show a rather diverse picture that needs to be qualified. The impression of severely underdeveloped systems of welfare, particularly for needy population groups, dominates the common view on these countries. This is certainly true when considering solely the very last residual social assistance scheme, which is most often organised on a regional or even local basis (Portugal is the only Southern European country with a national system). When including categorical MIP benefits, which are often attached to social insurance, the picture changes. In Spain, about 7% of the population receives some form of MIP, a sizeable proportion in comparison with other European countries. The MIP system is hence predominantly based on categorical benefits and obviously has great gaps, but it clearly exists, in particular for older persons. Social citizenship in these countries is certainly more narrowly defined and not fully developed when compared with the other European countries. A universal concept of basic social citizenship rights is missing, and MIP has a patchy and incomplete character. This fact is even more significant for the two Southern European countries without data here: Italy and Greece. In most of these countries, it is still the family that fills in the huge gaps in social protection of those in need.

This might also be the case in **Eastern European** countries, although MIP systems here are mainly based on a general last safety net without categorically defined schemes. MIP in Eastern Europe has remarkably few recipients when taking into account the fact that the general schemes have to shoulder the whole burden and are highly reactive to labour market developments. The surprisingly small size of these systems may be explained by three factors. First, there is considerable stigmatisation in MIP, and minority ethnic groups such as the Roma population are often excluded from access to welfare. Second, benefit levels and income thresholds are very low, which means that only the really poor have access. Third, the size of the shadow economy probably has a positive impact on problem pressure and may offer many a viable alternative to the stigma of welfare benefits. Since access to benefits is strongly restricted in practice and benefit levels are extremely low, Eastern European MIP systems are actually highly exclusive and often do not effectively guarantee basic social citizenship rights.

Expenditure

Introduction

The analyses of this chapter so far reveal that MIP constellations do not fit the usual welfare state regime typologies. The ideal typical groups show great internal variation in terms of benefit rates and recipient numbers. This raises the question of whether the observed diversity is also reflected by MIP expenditure. If so, Denmark and Finland should spend higher amounts on MIP than Sweden does because of higher benefit rates in the case of Denmark and higher beneficiary numbers in Finland. Ireland and the UK should both be among the top spenders, but Ireland should show greater expenditure levels because of more generous benefits. The Continental countries should show great variation as a result of their differences in recipient rates, pushing costs in France, the Netherlands, and – since 2005 – Germany above the levels of Belgium and Austria. On the other hand, the Dutch outlier position in terms of generosity should also have an effect on MIP spending. MIP expenditure in Spain is most likely higher than in Portugal because of higher recipient numbers and benefit levels. Low expenditure in the Eastern European countries can be expected, although it might be higher for the Czech Republic, where benefit levels are more generous, and for Slovakia, where a larger proportion of the population is dependent on MIP.

The EuMin database allows for setting public spending on MIP in relation to benefit levels and recipient numbers, which is crucial for interpreting expenditure data correctly. When financial data on MIP are compared without taking these factors into account, MIP's relevance can easily be underestimated. Guaranteed minimum income levels are rather low when compared with universal or wage-related benefits, making MIP 'cheaper' than other types of social benefits. Moreover, MIP often only makes up for the difference between a recipient's own resources and the official social minimum because it is needs based. Additional allowances such as housing or family benefits often come from parts of public budgets other than MIP. The actual amounts paid therefore frequently fall below the guaranteed minimum, which itself is already at a very low level. As a consequence, expenditure purely on MIP usually plays a minor role in the welfare state. This can lead to false conclusions about its social relevance if the total number of beneficiaries and their share in the whole population is not taken into account, too. Further, breaking expenditure down to these two variables helps in identifying the average costs arising per beneficiary and the average amount every member of society has to come up with to ensure a last safety net. The significance of MIP for citizens and its role within the overall welfare state context are furthermore influenced by a country's economic situation and this situation's effects on the labour market. Therefore, the GDP and total social expenditure are important reference indicators when comparing the role of MIP among countries with diverse welfare state settings and different economic backgrounds.

On the basis of this discussion, the analyses of this section look at MIP expenditure as a percentage of the GDP and of total social expenditure, as well as per capita of population. As reference parameters, the GDP and social spending give a better view of the significance of MIP in different economic and welfare state contexts. Per capita spending measures the cost intensity of the last safety net for the population and can thus be interpreted as an indicator for the costs of national solidarity. When comparing developments over time, there are several possible reasons for change in these indicators that need to be borne in mind. For example, the extent of MIP might rise although expenditure relative to the GDP decreases over time. This can easily happen in times of strong economic growth. Areas of social security other than MIP could gain importance in the course of policy reforms or changing eligibility patterns when labour market conditions change. Thus, the absolute scope of MIP does not necessarily change when relative expenditure indicators change. When looking at the costs per citizen, modest rises do not necessarily point to a higher burden of MIP for society since they might be a result of changing price levels.

In order to assess these potential interactions, this chapter explores MIP expenditure in four steps. First there is a general comparison between countries and over time, using the three aforementioned indicators for the years 1995, 2000, and 2007. Subsequently, the variation within country groups found in Chapter Four so far is reassessed by relating MIP to the number of citizens dependent on MIP schemes and to their generosity. This helps to evaluate whether developments in spending relative to the GDP and social expenditure can be ascribed to dynamics within the MIP systems themselves or if they are caused by contextual factors that mainly affect reference parameters. The last part of the analysis serves the same purpose for nominal cost developments by relating schemes' guaranteed income levels to the amounts actually spent on every beneficiary.

Spending on MIP, 1995-2007

Table 4.3 presents MIP spending for 1995, 2000, and 2007 in relation to three reference parameters in order to evaluate inter-country differences and developments over time from various angles.[1] The first column identifies and compares the absolute level of MIP expenditure relative to countries' wealth, represented by the GDP. The middle part of the table displays MIP's share in total social spending, portraying its salience within welfare states. For the third column, population size is used as reference value in order to measure the costs of MIP allocated to citizens. The values are given in purchasing power standards (henceforth EUR PPS, see Eurostat, 2010) in order to correct for varying price levels across countries.

In most countries, expenditure decreased between 1995 and 2007 relative to both the GDP and social spending. In Denmark and Sweden, the nominal costs for citizens also decreased, and after 2000 the same happened in the UK, which had shown growing costs for the population before. In France, Hungary, Ireland, and the Netherlands, sinking relative costs were accompanied by rising nominal

Table 4.3: Expenditure on MIP, 1995, 2000 and 2007[1]

Country	Percentage of GDP			Percentage of social expenditure[2]			Per capita of population[3]		
	1995	2000	2007	1995	2000	2007	1995	2000	2007
Nordic									
DK	1.14	0.97	0.69	3.68	3.46	2.48	221.1	243.4	210.3
FI	0.45	0.32	0.28	1.48	1.33	1.12	74.6	72.4	81.3
SE	0.60	0.42	0.30	1.80	1.43	1.04	109.6	102.3	92.9
Anglophone									
IE	4.07	2.24	2.68	22.62	16.92	15.26	591.5	562.9	999.4
UK	2.23	1.52	1.18	8.46	5.98	4.77	370.7	346.1	345.1
Continental									
AT	0.89	0.69	0.60	3.19	2.49	2.21	184.2	172.0	184.1
BE	0.48	0.47	0.54	1.85	1.90	1.91	94.9	113.8	155.0
FR	0.96	0.97	0.92	3.34	3.50	3.18	164.2	213.8	249.6
DE	0.65	0.56	0.99	2.39	2.00	3.73	128.3	127.4	286.6
NL	1.61	1.31	1.08	5.56	5.30	4.04	306.4	336.2	357.0
Southern									
PT	0.31	0.36	0.44	2.06	1.91	1.93	43.8	55.1	85.1
ES	0.88	0.94	0.73	4.20	4.74	3.58	120.7	175.1	193.9
Eastern									
CZ	0.15	0.36	0.09	0.88	1.93	0.51	16.0	47.5	18.6
HU	0.35	0.26	0.27	n.a.	1.36	1.21	26.2	27.5	41.3
PL	0.26	0.09	0.10	n.a.	0.45	0.55	16.1	7.8	13.2
SK	0.82	1.10	0.42	4.58	5.87	2.71	44.5	74.5	62.7

Notes:
[1] AT 1995: *Sozialhilfe der Länder* values from 1998. PT 1995: MIP expenditure and GDP values from 1998. ES: data for non-contributory pensions for 1995 and 2000 taken from 1992 and 2001; regional RMIs for 2007 adopted from 2006.
[2] Data on social expenditure taken from the EUROSTAT ESSPROS database (spr_exp_eur) (Eurostat, 2010).
[3] In purchasing power standards.

Sources: EuMin database; EUROSTAT (2010); authors' calculations.

costs throughout the whole period studied, although to a very different extent. France remained fairly constant compared with the other countries in this group, while in Ireland the contrast between declining relative expenditure and steeply rising nominal costs is striking. Between 1995 and 2000, Austria, Finland, and Germany followed the trend of Denmark and Sweden. In the first two cases, costs per citizen began to grow thereafter. In Germany, all indicators increased between 2000 and 2007. The only countries that showed a rise in MIP expenditure relative to their GDP throughout the whole period were Belgium and Portugal. In Belgium, all indicators actually increased, although at a relatively low rate. In Portugal, increases of spending relative to the GDP and population size went along with a drop in MIP expenditure as a share of total social spending. The relative importance of the Spanish MIP system also increased until 2000 but then slowed down again, while nominal costs continued to grow over time. Slovakia and the Czech Republic had increasing values in all indicators until 2000, but they dropped remarkably thereafter until 2007. In Poland, a sharp drop in the MIP–GDP ratio was already visible between 1995 and 2000, but MIP's share of social expenditure and spending per citizen began to increase after 2000.

The widespread phenomenon of MIP expenditure decreasing relative to the GDP can mostly be ascribed to periods of economic growth in the late 1990s and mid-2000s, leading to a decrease in the weight of MIP spending compared with countries' overall wealth. In some countries, such as Sweden, the Netherlands, Ireland, and the UK, falling unemployment had a strong impact on the caseloads of the MIP system as a whole, leading to a loss in relevance for total welfare state spending. In other countries, however, MIP's role within the welfare state increased. This was the case for Spain, Slovakia, and the Czech Republic in the 1990s, as well as for Germany after the year 2000. In Slovakia and the Czech Republic, MIP plays a crucial role for the working-age population, and its share in social expenditure therefore increased as unemployment rose strongly in the 1990s. In Spain, on the other hand, unemployment was less of an influencing factor. The 1990s was a period of reconstruction and expansion for the Spanish MIP system. From the beginning of the decade, assistance pensions for older and sick persons began to be gradually replaced by new non-contributory pension schemes that provide significantly higher income levels than their precursors. At the same time, more and more regional MIP schemes were introduced that nowadays serve as Spain's very last safety net. Hence, the rise of MIP's financial importance in the Spanish welfare state of the 1990s is a direct consequence of improvements in basic social citizenship rights. The introduction of a new benefit scheme recently caused MIP to gain importance in the German welfare state arrangement. Germany reformed its unemployment benefit system in 2005, leading to a fundamental loss of importance of insurance benefits and a rise in the significance of needs-based MIP for the unemployed (see Chapters Two and Three).

So far, the countries form relatively stable groups across all three indicators, and as in the preceding sections of this chapter, countries belonging to the same welfare state type do not always cluster together. The Czech Republic and Poland have the lowest values for all three indicators, with MIP spending being only 0.1% of the GDP and accounting for only 0.5% to 0.6% of social expenditure, costing citizens less than 20 EUR PPS. In a second group of countries, MIP spending lies between 0.2% and 0.5% of the GDP and makes up 1% to 2% of total social expenditure, whereas citizens' yearly costs remain below 100 EUR PPS. This cluster consists of Hungary, Finland, Sweden, Slovakia, and Portugal. Slovakia is a bit of an outlier since it has a higher share of social spending (2.71%). With regard to this indicator, the country changes positions with Belgium, where MIP spending amounts to 1.91% of social expenditure. Based on the other two indicators, Belgium can be allocated to the same group as Austria, Denmark,

Spain, France, and Germany. MIP expenditure relative to the GDP is between 0.5% and 1%, its share in social spending 2% to 4%, and inhabitants' costs of solidarity between 150 and 300 EUR PPS. The highest spenders on minimum income benefits are the Netherlands, the UK, and Ireland. The first two of these countries are rather similar, having MIP shares of about 1% of the GDP and 4% to 5% of social expenditure. The expenses per citizen are at 345 EUR PPS in the Netherlands and 357 EUR PPS in the UK. Ireland can be classified as an outlier in terms of MIP expenditure, for MIP amounts to almost 2.7% of the GDP and plays a more important role within the welfare state than in any other country studied. 15.3% of social spending is allocated to MIP, which costs citizens almost 1,000 EUR PPS a year. Although these nominal costs have increased significantly in Ireland since 1995, the analysis of all indicators for 1995 and 2000 indicates that Ireland had been an outlier all along. MIP has always played an important part in the Irish welfare state arrangement (see Chapter Three). In relative terms, MIP expenditure has even dropped over the past decades. This is certainly an effect of economic growth, higher wages, and of more people being on contributory benefits rather than social assistance due to rising employment levels and shorter unemployment spells. The rising nominal costs may also be a consequence of Ireland's rapid economic development since benefit levels have kept pace with rising price and wage levels, as seen above. The same interrelationships can be assumed for the other countries that show a decrease in the relative importance of MIP spending combined with rising per capita costs, namely for Finland, France, the Netherlands, and Hungary.

In order to understand the influencing factors on the scale of MIP spending better, the following subsections address the relationships between expenditure, caseloads, and the guaranteed minimum income level. The countries are compared with each other and over time by looking at scatter plots for the years 2000 and 2007.[2] This will shed light on the question of whether increasing or decreasing values of expenditure indicators are merely effects of changing contexts or if they are, in fact, caused by developments in the MIP systems, namely changing beneficiary numbers and generosity. Because the benefit rates available in the EuMin database refer to the countries' main MIP schemes, they are related solely to the expenses that occurred in these systems[3]. In the final step of the analysis, benefit levels are compared with the main scheme's expenditure per capita of beneficiaries. This serves two purposes. First, a central question that arises when looking at social expenditure data in general is whether more generous systems are also more expensive. This is not necessarily the case if, for example, most benefits are paid as top-ups or if only a small number of persons fall into the last safety net and benefit spells are short. Second, looking at the relationship between both variables over time helps to solve the puzzle concerning the rising or falling nominal costs of MIP. Does a general decline in the relevance of the last safety net, accompanied by increasing costs for the population, in fact speak for the adaption of benefit rates to rising prices and wages? If so, benefit levels relative to median income should not fall significantly while per capita expenditure rises.

Total expenditure and overall caseload

The number of beneficiaries as a share of the total population is plotted against MIP spending as a percentage of the GDP in Figure 4.6. The plot clearly demonstrates a positive relationship between the number of people dependent on MIP and expenditures on their behalf. In 2000, Hungary had the lowest values in both dimensions, for about 0.3% of the GDP was spent on 2.1% of the

Figure 4.6: MIP spending and number of beneficiaries, 2000 and 2007

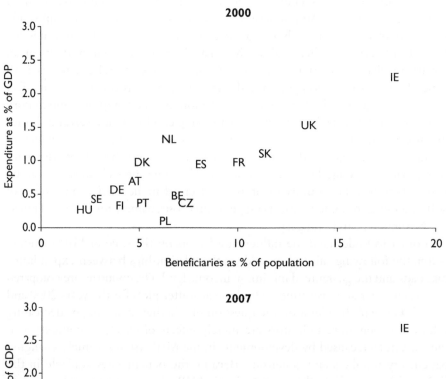

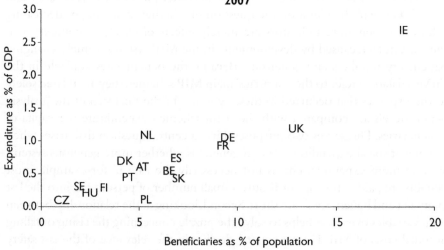

Notes: ES 2007: data for *rentas mínimas de inserción* from 2006. HU: only recipients, no data available for dependent beneficiaries.

Sources: EuMin database; EUROSTAT (2010).

population. Ireland's outlier position in terms of high spending is also reflected by a high significance of MIP in the population: Almost 18% received some benefit of this kind in 2000. The UK follows in second place, quite far behind, with 13.5% of the population on MIP benefits receiving amounts that add up to 1.5% of the GDP.

Despite the almost linear distribution of the data points in the diagram, there are some countries that spend more or less of their GDP on beneficiaries than do other countries with a comparable share of persons in the population receiving MIP. In 2000, the Netherlands and Denmark had comparatively high expenditure. This could be an effect of benefit levels being higher compared with those in other countries. Poland, on the other hand, stands out with very low spending in contrast to countries with comparable beneficiary rates, such as the Czech Republic, Belgium, and Portugal. Poland and the Netherlands keep their exceptional positions until 2007, while Denmark moves closer to the centre of the distribution. The bottom field is now headed by the Czech Republic, which spends only 0.1% of GDP on 0.9% of the population, while in 2000, 7.2% of the inhabitants claimed MIP and expenditure amounted to about 0.4% of the GDP. A similar decrease in recipient numbers can be observed in Slovakia, whose share of recipients dropped from 11.4% to 7% of the population and which had an even steeper fall in expenditure from 1.1% of the GDP to 0.4%. In both cases, this significant decline in MIP relevance is due to reforms that tightened entitlement conditions and lowered benefit levels (see Chapter Three). In most of the remaining countries, the share of beneficiaries in the population decreased as well, but only slightly (by no more than 2%) in most cases. Only in Austria, Hungary, Ireland, and Germany, did benefit receipt increase. In the latter case, the vast increase from 3.8% of the population to 9.6% was caused by the 2005 reform that shifted the German system from the group of countries with a rather low salience of MIP, such as Austria or Sweden, to the group that has a high impact in terms of expenditure and recipient numbers, slightly exceeding the levels reached in France. In contrast to the German case, the rises in beneficiary numbers of Austria, Ireland, and Hungary were rather modest. In Ireland and Hungary, the increases of less than 1% of the population are in clear contrast with the rises in costs per citizen between 50% and 80% observed in Table 4.3. It is unlikely that a small increase in beneficiaries can lead to such a sharp rise in costs. A more probable cause would be a significant rise in benefit levels for the same time period. Other countries might have experienced a strong rise in benefit levels as well, especially those that combine decreases in relative costs and caseloads with increasing MIP expenditure per capita of population. This scenario can be observed in the Netherlands, Spain, Finland, and France.

Expenditure and generosity

In Figure 4.7, an individual's net benefit level serves as an indicator for the very basic level of income granted to beneficiaries. The benefit rates are adapted from

Figure 4.7: Expenditure on main system and benefit rates, 2000 and 2007

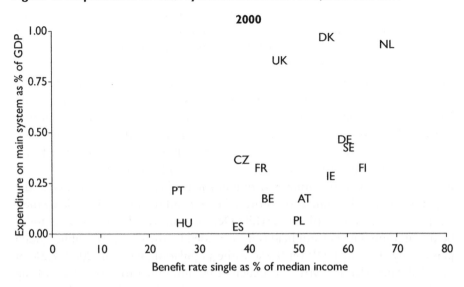

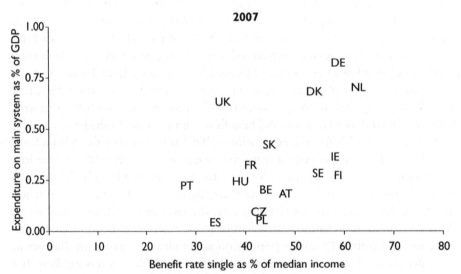

Notes: ES 2007: data on expenditure from 2006. CZ and DK 2000: data on median income from 2001 and 2003. SK 2000: missing due to lack of data on median income.

Sources: EuMin database; SaMip 2.5 (Nelson, 2007a, 2010); Eurostat (2010), personal information by Statistics Sweden (for Swedish median income).

SaMIP (Nelson, 2007a, 2010) and for matters of comparability housing benefits are included. Benefit levels are given as a percentage of median income to detect the relative financial situation of beneficiaries in society in a comparable manner and to evaluate changes over time. Expenditure in the countries' main systems is given as a percentage of the GDP. For the Czech Republic and Slovakia, this indicator is equal to the one for total expenditure since there is only one benefit scheme in place that corresponds to our definition of MIP. In other cases, such as Belgium, Spain, Ireland, and France, differences between both variables are stronger because MIP systems are more fragmented and their relative significance for the working age population is smaller.

The interpretation of schemes' expenditures and benefit rates is not as straightforward as in the case of expenditure and caseload. Although higher spending tends to come with generous benefits, the data points are more dispersed than in Figure 4.6. Interestingly, Ireland is not an outlier in this graph. The UK, the Netherlands, and Denmark deviated from other countries in 2000. Expenditure on their main systems was significantly higher than in other countries, lying between 0.8% and 1% of the GDP. The values were very close to those of total expenditure on MIP, indicating that the WWB, *kontanthjælp*, and income support were of high importance in the national MIP systems. Nevertheless, the countries' benefit levels differed considerably. In the UK, they reached only 46% of median income, while they were at 56% in Denmark and 68% in the Netherlands. For the Netherlands, this speaks for the assumption that generous benefit rates result in higher expenditure compared with other Continental European countries. Similar discrepancies such as those in the group of high-spending countries can be observed in the countries with the lowest expenditure rates of less than 0.1% of the GDP. Hungary offered beneficiaries only 27% of the population's median income; Spain, 38%; and Poland, 50%. Likewise, systems with very similar levels of expenditure can be quite different in terms of generosity. Benefits in the UK, for example, were comparable to those in France and Belgium in 2000. The variation of the indicator on spending in these three countries is not an effect of differences in their economic prosperity since the French level of the GDP in 2000 was closer to that of the UK, but expenditure relative to the GDP was nearer to Belgium. Higher expenditure in the UK is caused by higher numbers of beneficiaries (see Figure 4.6). The same effect could underlie differences between other countries as well. In 2000, Germany, Sweden, Ireland, and Finland all clustered around 60% of median income but differed in their level of spending. The schemes in Austria and Portugal were as generous as those in Poland and Hungary but had higher spending at around 0.2% of the GDP.

Comparing the graph for the year 2000 with the one for 2007 makes clear another difference to Figure 4.6: not only do countries spread wider across the diagram, but the changes over time are more pronounced. The distribution for 2007 is much more limited compared to that for 2000. In all countries except Belgium, the Czech Republic, Hungary, Ireland, and Portugal, benefit levels relative to median income decreased. The UK, Denmark, and the Netherlands still are at the top of the group in terms of spending, but spending nevertheless decreased to between 0.6% and 0.7% of the GDP, and benefit levels relative to median income declined, too – most remarkably in the UK by 10.9 percentage points. The Netherlands is still the highest-ranking country in terms of generosity (with 62.6% of median income). The highest costs in 2007 were incurred in Germany, where the main system changed from the now very residual *Sozialhilfe* to the new *Grundsicherung für Arbeitssuchende*. Spain and Poland are still the lowest-ranking countries concerning expenditure, whereas the indicator for Hungary increased, shifting the country closer to France and Belgium. Meanwhile, Czech expenditure dropped significantly from 0.4% to 0.1% of the GDP.

Regarding the distribution of countries in 2007, there is a country cluster consisting of Germany, Denmark, and the Netherlands that has relatively high benefits, between 50% and 60% of median income and high expenditure of 0.7% of the GDP or above. Ireland, Sweden, and Finland show comparable benefit levels but lower expenditure of around 0.3% of the GDP. Expenditure in the UK almost equals that in Denmark and the Netherlands, but the benefit level is comparable to that of Spain (about 35% of median income), the country where the main system's expenditure relative to the GDP is the lowest. The Portuguese main scheme is the least generous, with only 22% of median income, but relative costs are comparable to those in Belgium, Hungary, and Austria. These last three countries, together with France and Slovakia, make up the centre field of the distribution, where benefit levels lie at around 40% to 50% of median income and expenditure varies between 0.2% and 0.4% of the GDP. This wide variation, as seen for the year 2000, can be only partly explained by differences in the GDP. For some countries, different expenditure at similar benefit levels can result from differences in beneficiary numbers. This might be the case for Germany when compared with Finland, and the UK compared with Spain. The following section looks at expenditure per beneficiary to evaluate this assumption.

Expenditure per beneficiary

The benefit levels of Figure 4.8 are plotted against the expenditure per beneficiary in the years 2000 and 2007. As in Table 4.3, per capita expenditure is given in EUR PPS. The country cases that were previously identified as having exceptionally high total expenditure on their main systems in the year 2000 do not spend above-average amounts on every single claimant, indicating that the high levels of overall spending were an effect of higher beneficiary numbers. The UK now lies even closer to the Southern and Eastern European countries. This group of low-spending countries has furthermore been joined by the Czech Republic and Portugal. The Netherlands is still among the higher-ranking countries, indicating that generous benefit levels are indeed a factor that could explain why the country deviated from the centre of distribution in Figure 4.6. Nevertheless, Belgium, Denmark, and Ireland have the highest per capita expenditure of all the countries, although relative benefit rates are not exceptionally high. This is probably due to the comparatively high value of benefit levels in absolute terms and in purchasing power parities, as seen in Figure 4.3.

While the distribution of data points in the 2000 plot is rather flat in terms of expenditure and wide on the dimension of benefit rates, the opposite is true for 2007. As already discussed, the variation of relative benefit levels decreased during this period. Per capita expenditure, in contrast, increased in variety. All countries

Figure 4.8: Expenditure per beneficiary of main system and benefit rates, 2000 and 2007

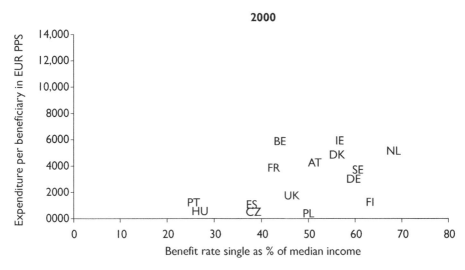

2000

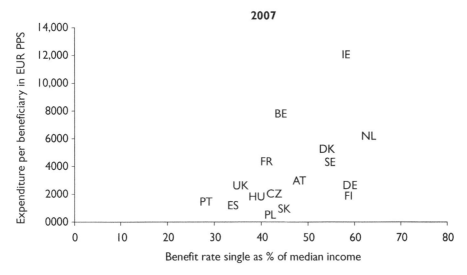

2007

Notes: ES 2007: data on expenditure and beneficiaries from 2006. BE, FR and HU: only recipients, no data available for dependent beneficiaries. CZ and DK 2000: data on median income from 2001 and 2003. SK 2000: missing due to lack of data on median income.

Sources: EuMin database; SaMip 2.5 (Nelson, 2007a, 2010); Eurostat (2010), personal information by Statistics Sweden (for Swedish median income).

that increased relative benefit rates also had significant increases in per capita costs. This is the case for Portugal and Belgium, which show an overall increase in the salience of MIP expenditure in this analysis. The strongest increase in spending per beneficiary can be observed in the Czech Republic, although all other indicators investigated so far fall in value. Hungary and Ireland also have strongly increasing expenditure per beneficiary. This is congruent with the assumptions made on the basis of Table 4.3 and Figure 4.6: the strong rises in expenditure per capita of population are, in fact, a consequence of rising benefit levels and the adjustment to increasing wages and prices. Other countries in which the relative indicators of expenditure fell while per capita spending rose include Finland, France, the Netherlands, and Spain. But overall, these countries are characterised by a greater level of stability. The rising per capita indicators should stand for adjustment to economic development, but on a rather low level since the relative income position of benefit recipients compared with the rest of the population decreased. This is even more true for Denmark, Sweden, and the UK, where MIP costs per citizen decreased along all other indicators of Table 4.3, and spending per beneficiary was the only value that increased over time.

The only countries in which expenditure for beneficiaries decreased are Austria and Germany. In Austria, the levels of other expenditure indicators hardly changed between 2000 and 2007, although the share of beneficiaries in the population increased slightly. In this case, dropping benefit levels and expenditure per beneficiary indicate that benefit rates were practically not adjusted to price levels. In Germany, by contrast, all three indicators on expenditure as well as benefit levels and receipt increased. Only expenditure per capita of beneficiaries decreased. A possible explanation is the change of rules concerning extraordinary payments in the course of the 2005 reform of the German MIP system. While the old system allowed recipients to apply for various kinds of tied supplements, these supplements are now abolished and meant to be balanced out by higher benefit rates. Another reason for the decrease might be the growing number of income-earning recipients who actually work and therefore only need an MIP top-up to their own earnings.

Conclusion

The analysis reveals some broad cross-national patterns. In the group of **Nordic countries**, decreasing numbers of beneficiaries are reflected by falling expenditure. In Sweden and Denmark, this development has been more pronounced than in Finland. The more generous benefit levels of Denmark in terms of purchasing power parities have a visible impact on expenditure, both in relative terms and in the costs per citizen and per beneficiary.

The **Anglophone countries** both have a high salience of MIP expenditure, but Ireland's outlier position in terms of beneficiaries is clearly confirmed by MIP spending. Per capita costs further highlight Ireland's marked adjustment of benefit rates to rising living costs and wages. A similar observation cannot be made for the UK.

The **Continental European countries** form a heterogeneous group. While the relative impact of MIP remained rather constant in France and Belgium, it decreased in Austria and the Netherlands and increased strongly in Germany. In Austria and Belgium, expenditure is lower than in the remaining three countries.

In France and in Germany (in 2007), higher expenditure is caused by a bigger scope of MIP in terms of beneficiaries, whereas in the Netherlands, the very generous benefit level causes costs to be higher.

The **Southern European countries** vary in terms of expenditure as they do for generosity and caseloads. Spain has higher expenditure than Portugal, but in the latter case, MIP spending is still on the rise while it seems to stagnate in Spain. Portugal has increased the amounts allocated to MIP relative to both the GDP and population size. Losses of MIP's financial relevance in the overall welfare state context could indicate that the Portuguese social protection system is still in a phase of expansion. Rising benefit levels and expenses for beneficiaries support this argument.

On average, the **Eastern European countries** are the group with the lowest salience of MIP spending, whereby the Czech Republic and Poland have the lowest values in all comparative indicators. Regarding expenditure relative to the GDP, welfare state spending, and spending on the countries' main system, Hungary and Slovakia stand out as having significantly higher indicators than the other two group members, but while Hungary increased its spending by improving generosity, this cannot be assumed for Slovakia, where MIP has witnessed a very strong loss of significance, much as in the Czech Republic.

This section highlights some patterns and influences of MIP expenditure, but the approach used certainly has its limitations. Benefit rates for singles, for example, are not the only possible indicator for looking at generosity as a cost driver. Another possible explanation for differences in expenditure might be families being treated more or less generously. Some countries with significantly lower costs per capita of beneficiary compared with total spending on their main scheme treat families considerably more generously than singles (the Czech Republic, Denmark, Portugal, and the UK, see earlier in this chapter). Another cause of variation might be differences in the number of benefits being paid as top-ups instead of in full. No data is available for the latter effect, but differences in the treatment of household types flow into the cluster analysis in the final section of this chapter.

Categorical differentiation

Introduction

Minimum income protection is the last safety net in the welfare state. The density and strength of this net, however, varies both over time and internationally. In many countries, MIP is not unified but consists of several categorical schemes for certain population groups, often with varying entitlement conditions and benefit levels, indicating that basic social citizenship rights are not uniform for the whole population in a given country. These different schemes of the last safety net partly reflect culturally embedded perceptions of desert of recipient groups that have also informed the old poor laws. These laws often divided people in need into different categories distinguished by a publicly acknowledged status of desert. Older and disabled people were treated with less harshness and stigmatisation than people of working age, and we can observe to some degree similar differentiations in today's MIP schemes.

Public perceptions of desert, however, are not the only reason that MIP systems in some countries are differentiated by population categories. Another major factor is that the link between social insurance protection and MIP has developed differently for different population groups, as described in Chapter Two. The situation of older people, for example, largely depends on the development of pension systems. The situation of unemployed people is mainly affected by unemployment insurance and assistance programmes, and single parents are strongly influenced by different family policy patterns.

While there are various reasons for categorical differentiation in MIP systems, for a comparative assessment all categorical schemes making up a country's MIP system are indispensible in obtaining a comprehensive view of the whole system. All categorical schemes are functional equivalents that need to be taken into account for measuring and understanding MIP systems internationally; focusing on the residual last safety net alone would neglect this dimension. Moreover, categorical differentiation as such is an indicator for the segmentation of social citizenship.

Accounting for categorical schemes is also crucial from a statistical point of view because persons in need may be shifted from one scheme to another or may try to enter a less stigmatising scheme providing higher benefits. In this respect, there are often fluid and changing boundaries between different schemes. One such boundary, for example, concerns persons with disabilities. Persons with lower grades of disability who are able to work for a limited number of hours may be shifted from a categorical scheme for disabled people to the general last safety net or to a scheme for employable people, or vice versa, depending on varying regulations. In Germany, for example, access to the existing special scheme for the disabled and older people (*Grundsicherung im Alter und bei Erwerbsminderung*) is very restrictive. All persons who are able to work more than three hours per day are automatically included in the scheme for unemployed people (*Grundsicherung für Arbeitsuchende*). This demarcation is obviously arbitrary and thus often contested in individual cases. Moreover, individual health conditions and ability to work can change over time. More important here, the border is drawn differently in different countries. This example shows that only a full account of all MIP schemes provides a reliable assessment of the situation in each country. Such a comprehensive account, to our knowledge, has not been systematically and comparatively undertaken before.

The crucial question is, of course, what categorical differentiation means for the concept of fundamental social citizenship rights granted to all members of society. Are these common rights of membership eroding as a result of increased differentiation of benefits? Is there indeed a trend towards more targeting even within MIP systems? If so, the concept of social citizenship may become more conditional and less universal, raising the issue of the foundation of the welfare state.

Overview of categorical differentiation

At present (2010), most European countries have more than one MIP scheme. Two of our 17 countries – the Czech Republic and Slovakia – have only one general last safety net. Measured by the pure number of schemes, France (with 10 schemes) and Ireland (with 13) have the most categorically differentiated MIP systems in Europe. In most countries, the various categorical schemes coexist with a general last safety net covering people not entitled to one of the categorical benefits. In this sense, these general systems function as a residual last safety net in MIP systems. This residual scheme, however, demonstrates varying degrees of strength and coherency in individual countries.

In France and Southern Europe, the residual scheme either has larger holes, or is not nationally standardised, or does not exist at all. In some countries, therefore, the concept of social citizenship is very limited and does not cover all people in need. Greece (not under study) does not have a MIP scheme at all. Italy is also an extreme case because the last safety net is a patchwork of regional and local schemes that operate quite differently. At the same time, the patchwork is full of holes because not all communes have established effective MIP programmes. There is practically no guaranteed, enforceable social right to MIP for all residents in Italy. In Spain, the last safety net is institutionalised at the regional level with varying conditions, but in contrast to Italy it covers the whole country. Portugal and France do have nationwide general last safety nets, but these do not cover the whole population. In Portugal, the general scheme was introduced in 1996 for those in need and over 18, but the scheme was reorganised in 2003 and young people below 25 were excluded. The young have also always been excluded from last resort benefits in France. There are two exceptions to this: adults below 25 are entitled to these benefits if they care for a child or (since 2009) if they have worked for two years during the three years prior to their benefit claim. The exclusion of young people in France and Portugal shows that the idea of reciprocity also has a bearing on MIP schemes: The young have not yet contributed much to society in terms of tax payments and social insurance contributions, and their right to benefit receipt has therefore been restricted. Another major reason for the exclusion of the young from MIP in these countries is the legally and socially regulated responsibility of the family for this group.

In all other countries of our study, there is a general and residual last safety net for all population groups that are not covered by a categorical MIP scheme. Major target groups for categorical schemes include older and disabled persons in need. In addition, some countries also have special schemes for long-term unemployed people, single parents, refugees, or asylum seekers, and even for a few other special categories such as victims of war and crime (see Table 4.4).

Table 4.4: Overview of categorical differentiation (first laws for respective category)

	Old age	Disability	Unemployment	Single parenthood	Refugees	Other categories	General scheme	Number of schemes in 2010[1]
AT	1955		(Special assistance)	None	None	1947	(1971) 2010[2]	3
BE	1969	1969	(Unlimited insurance)	None	None	None	1974	6
DK	(Basic pension)	(other)	(Long insurance)	None	1983	None	1974	4
DE	2003		2005	None	1993	1950	1961	5
FR	1956	1957	1984	1976–2009	None	1980	1988	10
HU	1990	None	1992–2000	None	None	None	1997	2
IT	1969	1971	None	None	None	None	(2000)[3]	6
ES	1962	1962	(Special assistance)	None	None	1985	(1989)[4]	7
PT	1980	1980	(Special assistance)	None	None	None	1996	5
SW	(Basic pension)[8]	(other)	(Long insurance)	None	1993	None	1982	3
UK	1999[5]	(other)	1996	None	2000	1988[6]	1948	5
IE	(State pension)[7]	1995	2006	1973	None	1984[6]	1977	13
SK	None	(other)	None	None	None	None	1990	1
CZ	(Basic pension)	(other)	None	None	None	None	1991	1
NL	(Basic pension)[8]	1998	1964–95	None	None	1998	1965	6
FI	(Basic pension)[8]		None	None	None	None	1984	2
PL	1990		None	None	None	None	1990	2

Notes:
1 Figure in some cases includes several schemes of the same category.
2 First regional law in parentheses. In 2010, establishment of national minimum standards.
3 *Minimo vitale.* Only framework law, not enforced at the local level.
4 First regional law (Basque Country).

5 Beside: basic state pension (basic law in 1909).
6 Tax credits for persons at work.
7 Non-contributory state pension. Basic law (as in the United Kingdom): 1909.
8 In these countries, very small schemes exist for older people who do not fulfil the residency requirements for the guaranteed basic pension.

In addition to these categories of MIP schemes, some countries have some very special programmes that are not considered here.
Source: Authors' depiction.

Older people and (to some degree) people with disabilities are generally the recipient groups that most easily meet criteria for deservingness. They often have contributed to society throughout their working lives and have thus 'earned' a benefit. They are not in control of their ageing process nor their disability and therefore cannot be blamed for needing help; moreover, they usually belong to the same (national) group as the people paying for their benefits. It has clearly been shown that public opinion throughout Europe deems older persons most worthy of support, closely followed by people with disabilities (van Oorschot, 2006). The perceived high level of deservingness of older people is partly reflected in the institutional design of categorical MIP schemes as well as certain pension system designs. Where older persons are covered by a separate categorical MIP scheme, this scheme in most cases provides higher benefits and applies a means test that is less strict than that of other schemes, particularly those for the working-age population or the general last safety net. In addition to MIP, a number of countries even provide relatively generous, non-means-tested basic pensions for long-term older residents. This arrangement makes MIP only necessary for a small minority of older people with shorter residence histories. Denmark, the Netherlands, Sweden, Finland, and to some extent the Czech Republic belong to this group of countries. They all have pension systems that (in one way or another) provide a basic pension above the MIP level for the vast majority of older people (see Chapter Two for a detailed analysis).

The United Kingdom also provides a basic national contributory pension to all insured, formerly economically active persons, but its level is actually below the MIP level, especially if housing costs are taken into account. This means that those older people who only have a basic pension need to claim additional last resort benefits following a means test. Until 1999, these older persons had been included as a special target group within the general income support benefit. Since then, the minimum income guarantee for older persons (1999–2002) and the pension credit (2003–) have fulfilled this function. The situation differs in Ireland, as the coverage of the contributory pension is smaller, and older people in need can receive a non-contributory and means-tested state pension, which is a categorical MIP scheme. As a consequence, a large share of older people in both the UK and Ireland depend on means-tested categorical MIP benefits.

In the Continental and Southern European countries, older people in need are also often covered by categorical MIP schemes. This is true for Austria (but only for insured persons who receive an old-age pension), Belgium, Germany, France, Italy, Spain, and Portugal. In addition, most of these countries have non-means-tested minimum pensions for persons with long insurance records, Germany being the main exception. Among the Eastern European countries, Poland and Hungary have special MIP benefits for older people in need, whereas in Slovakia, benefits are included in the general MIP scheme.

Disabled persons also often receive categorical MIP benefits. Such schemes exist in most countries, except in the Nordic nations and in Britain, where disabled people often receive non-means-tested benefits not included in our study. In countries without either categorical MIP programmes for disabled persons or general non-means-tested benefits, there are special conditions for this group in the general last safety net. In countries with a social insurance tradition, a distinction is often made between disabled former workers and disabled people who never had the ability to work. The first group is protected by social insurance benefits (often without applying a means test), the latter by categorical MIP schemes. These examples show that older and disabled people in most countries are protected by special arrangements that either belong to MIP (including a relaxed means test) or are institutionalised at a 'higher' protection level in the welfare state via non-means-tested benefits. In this sense, social citizenship rights for these groups are well developed almost everywhere in Europe.

Compared with this situation, categorical MIP schemes for long-term unemployed persons, single parents, or refugees and asylum seekers are less frequent. For the group of the long-term unemployed, the design of 'upstream' social insurance schemes is especially important. One group of countries stands out as providing relatively good protection for formerly employed unemployed persons. In Belgium, for example, unemployment insurance benefits are unlimited in time, even though they are reduced for those without children after the first year. In Denmark, unemployment insurance benefits are paid for four years. The long duration of the insurance benefit means that only the very long-term unemployed and those who are not members of unemployment insurance (which is not mandatory) actually need social assistance. Another group of countries (France, Spain, Portugal, and in part also Italy and the Netherlands) provides longer or higher payments to older, unemployed former workers with longer work histories (see Chapter Two). In some cases, unemployment insurance benefits also provide a minimum flat-rate amount that does not usually take into account actual family and household needs.

At the time of writing (2010), Austria is the only country that provides a special wage-related unemployment assistance benefit (*Notstandshilfe*) for those long-term unemployed who have exhausted their rights to unemployment insurance benefits. Since this scheme does not guarantee a social minimum but pays out wage-related amounts, it is not included in our MIP definition. In fact, the number of unemployment assistance recipients in Austria who have claimed additional social assistance has grown significantly in recent years. The *Notstandshilfe* is mainly an individual benefit and does not take into account the needs of the whole family or household group.

In Germany, a similar system of unemployment assistance existed until 2005, when the new *Grundsicherung für Arbeitsuchende* was introduced in the so-called Hartz reforms. This new scheme provides a last resort benefit for all people in need who are able to work (see Chapter Two); it guarantees a social minimum depending on family size and composition rather than on previous wages as was the case before. The same is true for the means-tested jobseeker's allowance (JSA) in the United Kingdom and Ireland. These two schemes include former recipients of contributory (non-means-tested) unemployment benefits as well as new entrants into the labour market and people without insurance claims (see Chapter Two). Moreover, the level of benefits in the scheme for the unemployed in these three countries (Germany, the UK, and Ireland) is the same as in the general last safety net.

Additionally, the French ASS is a means-tested MIP benefit for long-term unemployed people who have formerly received wage-related insurance benefits. The benefits are higher and the means test is less strict than in the general last safety net (RMI). Therefore, the formerly employed long-term unemployed receive better protection than labour market entrants and those who do not fulfil the insurance condition. ASS is only available to those unemployed who have worked at least five years within the ten years prior to unemployment (see Chapter Three).

In Hungary, Slovakia, the Czech Republic, and Poland long-term unemployed people are covered mainly by the general last safety net. This implies strict access conditions, harsh means-testing, and low benefits, resulting in very low take-up rates. In the other countries, there is no special MIP scheme for the unemployed.

In most MIP systems, single parents are also treated as a special category with specific needs. This is also true for the majority of countries that do not have a separate categorical scheme for them. In fact, only two countries (France and Ireland) institutionalised special MIP schemes for single parents. The French API was introduced in 1976 and abolished by (or integrated into) the new RSA, established in 2009. From the beginning, the API was limited to single parents with very young children. The child's age limit was set at below three, with a possible maximum extension of 11 months. Single parents in need with older children have always had to apply for the RMI, instead. As of 2009, all single parent families in need have been integrated into the new RSA, which replaced both RMI and API. The aim is to offer single parents the possibility of combining MIP benefits and income from work, thereby bridging the gap between unemployment and paid work. At the same time, single parents still receive a higher benefit level and are not forced into work. In Ireland, single parents are still covered by a separate MIP scheme with less strict work requirements. Benefit levels, however, are the same as in all other MIP systems in Ireland. This is a substantial difference to France (the country with the second most categorically differentiated system, after Ireland), where benefit rates widely vary between schemes.

As argued earlier, single parents have often been treated differently to single persons or other family types, even in those countries without categorical MIP benefits for single parents. While this is not necessarily true with respect to benefit levels (which take into account household size and composition anyway), it applies mostly with respect to work requirements and activation policies.

Finally, a number of countries have established special MIP schemes for refugees or asylum seekers with no full legal residence, or for persons who have just immigrated to the country. This group of recipients faces the greatest reservation from public opinion. When asked which group they view as the most deserving of support, Europeans first named older people, followed by ill and disabled people, and then unemployed people. Only after naming unemployed people did the people name immigrants, and this pattern holds throughout Europe (van Oorschot, 2006). This disinclination to support immigrants may be inspired by the perceived lack of desert: Immigrants have not yet contributed in any way to their host society; they have decided to leave their home country and migrate, which means that they are in control of their situation (except in the case of asylum seekers); and they do not belong to the 'in group' of those paying for the benefits. These doubts are partly reflected by the design of categorical MIP schemes intended to support immigrants. In contrast to most of the other categorical schemes described so far, the conditions in these schemes are always worse than in the general last safety net. Again, special regulations exist in almost all MIP schemes, but only a few countries have introduced separate schemes for this group.

Interestingly, those countries with a strong concept of social citizenship rights and without much categorical differentiation were the first to introduce special schemes and thereby excluded refugees from the existing general schemes. This was the case in Denmark (1983), Sweden (1993), Germany (also 1993), and Britain (2000). Denmark was the forerunner and meanwhile has three different schemes for refugees and immigrants, each of which varies in its work and activation requirements. Benefit levels in all three schemes are below the general last safety net for the (longer) resident population. Besides the general scheme and the schemes for refugees, the Danish MIP system has no other categorical benefits because it mainly relies on non-means-tested basic social security benefits.

In Sweden and Germany, the special schemes for asylum seekers and refugees were introduced on the basis of a contemporaneous, unified MIP system. While Sweden has stuck to its uniform system (except for refugees), the German system has become categorically differentiated. In Germany, the introduction of the scheme for asylum seekers was part of immigration policies aiming to restrict the inflow of refugees. At the beginning of the 1990s, large numbers of refugees and asylum seekers came to Germany; the government tried to prevent this development by forbidding this group from paid work and at the same time reducing their social assistance benefits. Since 1993, the major part of the benefit has been given in kind (food stamps and provision of public housing); only a small amount is paid out as pocket money. Moreover, asylum seekers are not allowed to work or to choose their place of residence. The ban on work is the opposite of the situation in Denmark, where the aim is to improve, indeed enforce integration into the labour market. Benefits are also low, with the aim of increasing work incentives.

Historical trajectories and comparative patterns of categorical differentiation

In a historical–comparative perspective there have been three paths to categorical differentiation and two paths that have led to a general last safety net without significant special MIP schemes (see Table 4.5).

The first path to a system of MIP benefits with significant categorical differentiation is the latecomer trajectory. The countries that have been following

Table 4.5: Historical paths to social citizenship and categorical differentiation

Type of trajectory to social citizenship	Categorical differentiation	Countries included	Main characteristics
Latecomer (Southern European)	Strong	France, Portugal, Spain, Italy	– late development of social insurance and the general last safety net; – diverse and incomplete social citizenship rights.
Forerunner (Liberal plus Germany)	Strong	United Kingdom, Ireland, Germany	– early development of social insurance and the general last safety net; – late differentiation related to labour market needs but based on universal concept of social citizenship.
Partial categorisation (Advanced continental welfare states)	Medium	Belgium, the Netherlands, Austria	– highly developed social insurance systems with strong minimum protection elements; – limited differentiation based on the existing general last safety net
Non-categorical protective (Nordic welfare states)	Very weak	Sweden, Denmark, Finland	– highly developed encompassing social security systems; – late introduction of residual and universal last safety net.
Non-categorical, not protective (Eastern Europe)	Weak	the Czech Republic, Slovakia, Poland, Hungary	– general last safety net established after transformation; – close link to labour market and highly restrictive access.

Source: Authors' depiction.

this path have introduced general social citizenship rights either late or not at all. The path usually began with categorical MIP schemes for the most deserving population groups. Later, coverage was completed in some cases by a final general last safety net. This is the pattern that can be found in France, Portugal, Spain, and Italy (and also Greece, which is not studied in this book) – the Southern European country cluster. In this group, a general last safety net was introduced either late or not at all. All these countries have been following the social insurance tradition, but social insurance coverage has grown later than elsewhere and has often remained incomplete, leaving substantial parts of the 'deserving' population groups unprotected. These gaps in social protection for 'deserving' groups were then filled by categorical MIP schemes, in particular for older and disabled persons. The categorical schemes were mainly introduced for those (inactive) population groups who were deemed deserving of help. They thereby compensated for the lack of a general last safety net.

When a general MIP scheme was eventually introduced, as in France in 1988 and in Portugal in 1996, the benefits of this residual scheme were kept lower than in the existing categorical schemes. In this group of countries, the differences between MIP schemes regarding access, benefit levels, and means–testing are indeed still huge. In France, for example, the basic benefit level for an older person is almost twice as high as for a person of active age who receives RMI, the general last safety-net benefit. In Portugal, the means test connected to the receipt of the social pension for old age and disability is less strict than for the RSI, which leads to benefit recipients' income levels that may reach almost twice the level of the RSI. This incompleteness of the MIP system in terms of coverage and the vast differences between the categorical schemes and the general last safety net, not to mention the lack of such a last resort benefit, indicate a serious weakness in the implementation of fundamental social citizenship rights.

The second path to a comprehensive and categorically differentiated net of MIP is the forerunner trajectory. This pattern can be found in Britain, Germany, and partly in Ireland. Even though Germany is the odd man out in this group, the group can be called the 'liberal' cluster. In these countries, the historical development has been almost the opposite of that in the Southern European country cluster. Britain and Germany were among the first countries to introduce comprehensive and integrated MIP systems. Only later did they opt for a categorical differentiation that is mainly related to the issue of unemployment and labour market integration. Parallel to the increased categorical differentiation of MIP, these countries reformed their unemployment protection systems in such a way that a large number of unemployed people, above all the long-term unemployed, became dependent on MIP benefits. Categorical MIP schemes for unemployed people were introduced in Britain in 1996 and in Germany in 2005, and have become mass social transfer programmes.

A second similarity between these countries is a limited institutional protection of older people through the pension system, which has made MIP very important for this group. This has always been the case in Britain since the basic pension was introduced. The original idea of guaranteeing a pension level above the social assistance threshold has never been realised. In Germany, by contrast, the pension system so far has effectively protected most of present pensioners even though the system is still strongly based on the principle of equivalence and does not have a minimum pension. This favourable situation was mainly the result of the relatively good economic and labour market conditions under which present pensioner cohorts have spent their active working lives. This situation has changed with reunification and rising unemployment, however, especially among older industrial workers in the new Eastern European states. Future pensioner cohorts will clearly not have such good pensions as were available in the past because the reforms in the pension system that reduce the replacement level and increase pensionable age will become effective. In this changed institutional and structural context, the new MIP scheme for older and disabled persons, effective as of 2003, is a significant new element of the German MIP system that will surely gain in importance.

The 'liberal' countries, including Germany, share major characteristics. They all have sizeable MIP systems in terms of recipients and distinguish between inactive population groups (among whom older people are the largest group) and persons who are able to work, including the longer-term unemployed. Social protection above the MIP level is rather limited for both groups. For older people, there is no effective minimum pension; for the unemployed, there is only short-term protection through non-means-tested unemployment insurance benefits. Thereafter, unemployed people fall immediately into MIP.

At the same time, however, these countries have well-integrated and comprehensive MIP systems based on a long-established and firmly institutionalised concept of social citizenship that distinguishes them sharply from the Southern European cluster. Their categorical systems were introduced on the basis of an existing comprehensive general last safety net. The social citizenship rights have existed for a long time, and the MIP system was differentiated later without abolishing the common foundation. This can also be seen in the basic benefit rates of the different schemes. Despite some variations, the benefit rates of all schemes are at a similar or even the same level as in the general last safety net, which is in sharp contrast to the situation in France and Southern Europe.

The third path has led to a limited or 'partial' categorical differentiation. This trajectory is based on relatively inclusive and protective social insurance systems that have left less room for MIP benefits. This pattern can be found in Austria, Belgium, and the Netherlands, the group of advanced continental welfare states. These three countries have developed relatively inclusive social insurance systems that also guarantee a basic floor to the main insured population groups. The countries differ from one another, however, with respect to the groups that are actually protected in this way. Therefore, the mix of MIP schemes is different.

In Austria and Belgium, the long-term unemployed are mainly protected by schemes that are not part of MIP. In the Netherlands, by contrast, unemployment protection is more limited, especially for young people with short work histories. Claimants must have worked for at least 52 weeks in four of the five years prior to unemployment in order to get an extension of the initial three-month contributory benefit (OECD, 2008c). Therefore, a higher number of unemployed people need MIP benefits. At the same time, however, the need for such benefits is not exceptionally high because unemployment rates in both Austria and the Netherlands decreased significantly over the last decades and are among the lowest in Europe today. Long-term unemployment, in particular, has been very low in these two countries. In Belgium, the situation is worse with respect to unemployment levels, but the social protection of the unemployed is not a concern of MIP.

The three countries also have categorical MIP schemes for older people, but these play different roles. In the Netherlands, the basic non-means-tested citizenship pension (based on longer-term legal residence) protects the vast majority of older people effectively from poverty and social assistance need. Only a small number of older persons fall back on MIP due to shorter residence in the country. Belgium and Austria, by contrast, have employment-based and earnings-related pension systems. Here, the situation for older persons is different from that in the Netherlands. In the Belgian case, a minimum pension in the pension system provides an effective income floor for the long-term insured population; in Austria, the means-tested pension supplement (*Ausgleichszulage*) fulfils this function. The latter is part of MIP; the former is not. In Belgium, however, older persons not adequately protected by the pension system can receive a means-tested categorical MIP benefit, too (GRAPA). In both countries, therefore, categorical MIP plays a significant role for older people.

At the same time, there is a general last safety net for all residents in all three countries. Due to the protective function of social insurance and the existing categorical schemes, the relevance of this residual scheme is rather limited in quantitative terms, but stands for a comprehensive last safety net with established social citizenship rights. In Austria, however, this state was only achieved with the reform in 2010, by which a new system was introduced with national minimum standards. Before, the Austrian last safety net was characterised by huge regional differences (see Chapter Three).

The three clusters described so far have more or less developed and differentiated categorical MIP systems. However, there are also countries that do not have significant categorical differentiation. Instead, there is only one basic MIP scheme that includes almost all persons in need. In this case, one can also distinguish between two historical pathways: an inclusive protective pathway and an exclusive non-protective one.

The protective path to 'unity' is 'dualistic' in the sense that the vast majority of the population is well protected above the MIP level by encompassing social insurance and non-means-tested benefits, whereas MIP is a residual general scheme for a small minority of people but in principle covers the whole population. This pattern is found most predominantly in Sweden and with some qualifications in Finland and Denmark. Historically, social assistance in the Nordic countries long remained a local and often discretionary benefit. While Britain, for example, introduced a modern national MIP system on the basis of social citizenship rights in 1948, and Germany and the Netherlands followed suit in 1961 and 1965, respectively, the Finnish and Swedish systems became more rights-based and nationally harmonised only in the early 1980s (1984 and 1982, respectively; Kuivalainen, 2004a). This indicates that social assistance played a marginal role within the firmly institutionalised Nordic welfare states.

The situation changed significantly with the major economic crisis that hit Sweden and especially Finland in the early 1990s. With unemployment rates climbing to unprecedented levels in the Nordic context, MIP schemes became important as the last safety net for larger numbers of people. In Finland, the recipient rate grew to almost 5% among the working-age population in the mid-1990s, a figure that is still low in the overall European spectrum but very high in the Nordic experience. When the economic situation improved, the last safety net was again shifted into a residual position in the social security system. Moreover, the Nordic MIP systems still allow for more local discretion than most other European systems, in particular when compared with the highly centralised systems of the United Kingdom, Ireland, and Germany.

In contrast to this Nordic path, there is also an exclusive non-protective path that has led to very limited and ineffective MIP systems that are not embedded in a protective welfare state environment. This pattern characterises the Eastern European countries. Historically, the origins of this pattern go back to the shock of transformation, but in part also before that, to the time of socialism when MIP played an ambiguous and rather special role. Officially, there was no strong need for a last safety net because everyone was expected to work, and unemployment did not officially exist. Social assistance existed only for marginalised population groups and was not at all based on a concept of social rights. By contrast, it had strong elements of social control and stigmatisation. With the transition to democracy and a market economy, the situation changed fundamentally. Unemployment and poverty became major social problems, and the establishment of a last safety net became crucial. Such schemes were also strongly recommended by the World Bank and the EU. The establishment of a last safety net was even a condition for later EU membership.

Since most Eastern European countries tried to protect pensioners through the pension system, the last safety net was mainly considered for the working-age population and especially unemployed people, although their coverage was very broad. The last safety net was a general system, but in practice it focused on some main population groups. Due partly to their close link to unemployment and the labour market, strict benefit conditions were set in order to prevent too large numbers of recipients and welfare dependency. Over time, and with economic improvement, the MIP schemes became even stricter. In some cases, elements of at least implied stigmatisation were introduced, as in Slovakia and the Czech Republic. Strong conditionality elements and work requirements were also implemented. Therefore, the social–rights character of the last safety net has been weak, and the systems have shifted back to a residual position.

Quantitative assessment of categorical differentiation

As the preceding discussion has shown, categorical differentiation is embedded in very different MIP systems in which the role of the residual scheme varies greatly. This can also be seen by looking at the main quantitative dimension of categorical differentiation, which is summarised in Table 4.6. The countries in the table are grouped as described in the previous section.

The Southern European country cluster (including France) is characterised by the late introduction of a general last safety net. Despite this major similarity, the quantitative significance of MIP and of the last safety net in particular varies greatly in this group. In France, the residual scheme (the RMI) covers about one third of all MIP recipients, whereas the majority are served by nine other categorical schemes, among which the scheme for older people is the most important in quantitative terms. In Portugal, the overall recipient rate of MIP among the total population is relatively low, but the share of the residual scheme is almost 70% of the total recipient population. In Spain, by contrast, the residual scheme plays a marginal role because the vast majority of MIP recipients are covered by categorical schemes, among which the supplementary means–tested benefits for

Table 4.6: The size of residual and categorical schemes, 2007

Trajectory to social citizenship	Country	Number of schemes	Recipient ratio (% of population)	Share of residual scheme	Share of largest scheme	Type of largest scheme	Share of second scheme	Type of second scheme
Latecomer[1]	FR	10	9.3	36.6	36.6	Residual	17.1	Old age
	PT	5	4.4	69.6	69.6	Residual	11.7	Old age
	ES	7	6.9	9.7	73.0	Supplementary[2]	6.9	Residual
Partial	AT	3	5.1	36.0	53.1	Old age + disability	36.0	Residual
	BE	6	6.5	27.0	33.8	Disability	29.7	Old age
	NL	6	5.4	69.5	69.5	Residual	19.0	Disability
Forerunner	IE	13[3]	18.4	6.1	28.3	Single parents	16.9	Unemployed
	UK	4[3]	12.9	55.3	55.3	Residual	32.5	Old age
	DE	5	9.6	1.1	89.3	Unemployed	7.0	Old age + disability
Protective	SE	3	2.2	94.5	94.5	Residual	5.5	Old age
	FI	2	3.2	97.1	97.1	Residual	2.9	Old age + disability
	DK	4	4.4	94.8	94.8	Residual	3.5	Refugees
Not protective[4]	HU	2	2.5	84.9	84.9	Residual	15.1	Old age
	PL	2	5.3	84.8	84.8	Residual	15.2	Old age

Notes: CZ and SK have only one (general) residual scheme.
[1] Includes Italy and Greece, which have no general system of last resort.
[2] Means-tested supplements to social insurance benefits.
[3] Excluding tax credits for the working population.
[4] Includes the Czech Republic and Slovakia, which do not have categorical schemes.

Sources: EuMin database; Eurostat (2010).

social insurance recipients are the most extended. This means that the majority of socially insured persons in need are, in fact, protected by national legislation linked to social insurance, while only a small minority of persons are covered by the regional residual MIP schemes.

The highly inclusive social insurance systems with limited MIP schemes existing in Austria, Belgium, and the Netherlands show a relatively similar pattern. In these countries, the overall MIP recipient rate among the total population is at a medium to low level, and only in the Netherlands does the general last safety net dominate the MIP system quantitatively. This domination is explained by the fact that the Netherlands has a contributory basic pension for all residents (which is not part of MIP), whereas Austria and Belgium have larger categorical MIP schemes for older people due to their earnings–related pension systems. Nonetheless, the overall MIP recipient rate in the Netherlands is not lower than in the two other countries as longer–term unemployed people in both Austria and Belgium are protected above the MIP level, while they mainly depend on MIP in the Netherlands. Hence, the situation is almost the opposite with respect to target groups: In Austria and Belgium, the main target groups of MIP are older and disabled persons; in the Netherlands, the unemployed. All three countries have good social protection above the MIP level for one of the major groups at risk.

By contrast, the liberal cluster including Germany has sizeable MIP systems covering large population groups, because the protection provided by social insurance is very limited for major groups at risk, the unemployed, and partly also older people. All three countries have large MIP systems for unemployed people because social insurance only covers short unemployment spells. In Germany, this scheme clearly has the most recipients, whereas the residual scheme covers less than 2% of the caseload. In Britain and Ireland, the situation is different, owing primarily to the pension system. In both countries, a high share of older people depend on means–tested benefits, either because contributory pensions are too low (as in Britain) or because they do not cover the whole population (as in Ireland). Hence, the system of MIP is characterised by a large share of older people, which is not the case in Germany, where the earnings–related pension system has so far protected present pensioner cohorts quite well due to favourable economic conditions during their active working years.

Another interesting point is that, despite these features, the residual MIP scheme in Britain is the largest. In fact, the categorical scheme for older persons in Britain covers about 33% of all MIP recipients, while the share of the residual scheme is above 50% and the remaining share goes mainly to the non-contributory jobseeker's allowance (JSA). This anomaly in comparison with Ireland and Germany is explained by the shift in Britain to the residual scheme of income support by many population groups who are considered not to be actively searching for work. This is true of persons with disabilities who are not fully employable, for family carers, and for single parents. These groups have also not been activated, as is the case for recipients of the JSA. Hence, Britain still has a high number of MIP recipients who are considered 'inactive' for various reasons.

In Ireland, single parents are not included in the residual scheme but receive a special categorical benefit, explaining a large part of the difference to Britain. In Germany, most population groups that would be included in income support in Britain are covered by the scheme for the unemployed (*Grundsicherung für Arbeitsuchende*). Only persons who are permanently not able to work at least three hours per day can receive MIP payments under the scheme for older and disabled people. All other groups, including single parents, partly disabled persons, family carers, and sick persons, are included in the scheme for the unemployed and can also be activated (Eichhorst et al, 2008).

This example shows that the division between 'employable' and 'not employable' MIP recipient groups is made quite differently in Britain and Germany. In Britain, most boundary cases are shifted to the residual scheme (therefore considered unemployable), whereas almost all persons of active working age in Germany are included in the scheme for those seeking for work.

Compared with these three country groups, the last two groups have less differentiated and smaller MIP systems in terms of population coverage, but for different reasons. In the Nordic countries, overall MIP recipient rates are low and the share of the general residual scheme is very high, at about 95%. This clearly shows that most persons are well protected by the overall social security system rather than by MIP and that the few categorical schemes that exist besides the residual safety net are indeed very small and focus on very special target groups, such as refugees. The Nordic countries can be considered latecomers with respect to the institutionalisation of a general last safety net, but due to their encompassing and highly protective social security systems, this situation has not led to the development of categorical MIP schemes of significant size, as was the case in Southern Europe and France.

Categorical differentiation is also very limited in Eastern Europe. In fact, there is only one general MIP scheme in the Czech Republic and in Slovakia, while Hungary and Poland also have categorical benefits for a small minority of older people. Eastern European countries introduced their general last safety nets during the transition period, but despite the huge social problems (which are still present to some extent), the overall recipient rate of MIP has remained surprisingly low. This seemingly paradoxical pattern may be explained by the fact that pensioners have been protected by social insurance rather than by MIP or that the MIP schemes themselves have set very strict conditions. Income thresholds and benefits are very low, and the list of conditional requirements is long. In addition, there is room in most countries for local discretion in deciding on access and benefit levels. All this taken together means that these schemes most probably cover only very few of those who are actually in need. An especially problematic aspect of this issue is the treatment of the Roma people, who often do not fulfil the strict entitlement conditions (see country sections on Slovakia and the Czech Republic in Chapter Three).

Differences in treatment

Categorical differentiation may only be the result of history and institutional inertia, on the one hand, for differences along the dimensions of access, eligibility criteria (including the strictness of the means test), and the level of benefits can be weak; in these cases, categorical differentiation matters only from an organisational and administrative point of view, as different groups have different needs, and different forms of help and treatment are appropriate. On the other hand, categorical differentiation may have a high social relevance if the various groups allocated to different schemes actually receive a differential treatment in terms of access, eligibility conditions, and benefit levels.

Table 4.7 provides basic information on the treatment of three main target groups that are often covered by categorical schemes. The table compares treatment in these categorical schemes (if existing) with the conditions applying to the general last safety net. The focus is on the three groups studied in Chapter Two with respect to overall social protection arrangements: older people, unemployed persons, and single parents. Information is given on three dimensions: access to schemes, the strictness of the means test, and benefit levels.

Conditions are usually better for older people in special schemes than in the general scheme since benefits are higher and the means test less strict than for the working-age population. Differences between countries exist with respect to access conditions. In some countries, the main conditions are residence and age, as is the case in Germany, Ireland, and Britain. In other countries, access to the special scheme for older people is linked to insurance record (pension insurance), as is the case in Austria and partly in France and Italy. Overall, however, if one also takes the non-means-tested benefits granted through pension systems into account, the situation of older people is certainly better than for most people of working age. The same is true, though no evidence is provided here, for disabled persons. Both groups are considered more 'deserving' than other persons in need.

For the long-term unemployed, the situation is different and varies more between countries. In some cases, they are protected by insurance-based benefits for a longer time or by special unemployment assistance schemes that continue to provide wage-related benefits. In most of these cases, there is no special MIP scheme for the unemployed, which is the situation in the Nordic countries, Belgium, and Austria. In other countries, special categorical MIP schemes for unemployed people exist. These systems usually provide similar benefit levels to those that exist in the residual schemes, but the means test is often not as strict. For example, a partner's income in these categorical programmes is considered to a lesser degree than it is in the residual scheme. Access, in contrast, is sometimes more difficult because benefits in some countries are only provided if former insurance benefits are exhausted. Hence, the receipt of these categorical benefits depends on previous employment and insurance records. This is the case in France, whereas in Germany, Britain, and Ireland, MIP systems for the unemployed

Table 4.7: Conditions in categorical schemes compared with the general last safety net, 2007[1]

Country	Old persons				Unemployed				Single parents			
	Scheme	Access	Test of means	Benefits	Scheme	Access	Test of means	Benefits	Scheme	Access	Test of means	Benefits
AT	Yes	Difficult	Relaxed	Higher	(None; unemployment assistance)				(None; included in other schemes)			
BE	Yes	Difficult	Same	Higher	(None; unlimited unemployment insurance)				(None; included in other schemes)			
DK	(None; basic pension)				(No: long unemployment insurance)				(None; included in other schemes)			
DE	Yes	Difficult	Relaxed	Same	Yes	Easy	Same	Same	(None; included in other schemes)			
FR	Yes	Easy	Relaxed	Higher	Yes	Difficult	Relaxed	Higher	Yes	Same	Relaxed	Higher
IT	Yes	Easy	Relaxed	Higher	(None; included in other scheme)				(None; included in other scheme)			
ES	Yes	Difficult	Same	Similar	(None; special unemployment assistance)				(None; included in other scheme)			
PT	Yes	Easy	Relaxed	Higher	(None; special unemployment assistance)				(None; included in other scheme)			
SE[2]	(No: basic pension)				(None; long unemployment insurance)				(None; included in other scheme)			
UK	Yes	Same	Relaxed	Similar	Yes	Same	Same	Same	(None; included in other scheme)			
IE	Yes	Same	Same	Same	Yes	Same	Same	Same	Yes	Same	Same	Same
NL[2]	(None; basic pension)				(None; included in other scheme)				(None; included in other scheme)			
FI[2]	(None; basic pension)				(None; included in other scheme)				(None; included in other scheme)			
PL	Yes	Difficult	Relaxed	Higher	(None; included in other scheme)				(None; included in other scheme)			
HU	Yes	Difficult	Relaxed	Higher	(None; included in other scheme)				(None; included in other scheme)			

Notes:
The Czech Republic and Slovakia are not included in the table because they both have only one scheme.
[1] Conditions in cells are always compared with respective conditions applying to the general scheme.
[2] In these countries, very small schemes exist for older people who do not fulfil the residency requirements for the guaranteed basic pension.
Source: Authors' depiction.

are open to all unemployed people, including persons with no employment or insurance records.

While single parents are often treated differently from other groups within the same MIP scheme, only Ireland and France have special benefits for them. In Ireland, there is not much of a difference from the residual scheme with respect to the three dimensions considered here. In France, however, benefit rates are significantly higher and the means test is less strict, but the scheme provides only for single parents with children younger than three. When children reach the age of three, recipients are shifted to the general scheme. In all other countries, single parents are included either in other categorical schemes (such as those for the unemployed) or in the residual scheme. Single parents are also often treated as a special category in these other schemes. In most cases, their benefits are higher and take into account their difficult household situation and childcare needs. In addition, work requirements are less strict than for single persons or even couples with children (at least for one of the partners).

The special treatment of single parents in MIP systems in most of Europe has raised a great deal of discussion. On the one hand, it is argued that their particular situation and difficulties in entering the labour market require special treatment. On the other hand, it is feared that this special treatment may result in higher welfare dependency among single parents and may prevent their return to the labour market over a prolonged period of time. In recent years, arguments have shifted towards a more critical view of special treatment. In many countries, a considerable shift in MIP policies towards single parents has taken place. At the same time, some countries have tried to improve the labour market chances of single parents by extending affordable childcare facilities.

Single parents with younger children have often been exempted from conditionality requirements that have gained ground in most MIP systems in recent years. In the UK, single parents were not required to work until their children reached the age of 16, which has more recently been reduced to 12. In the Netherlands, single parents were completely exempted from the requirement to work until 1995. Since then, the exemption has been first limited to single parents with children under five years old. In 2004 this exemption has been abolished but is still applicable if no external childcare is available to the parent. In France and Germany, single parents are increasingly considered employable. In Germany, the Hartz reform in 2005 was a major step towards employability, and in France, the recent introduction of the RSA (replacing the RMI) in 2009 will have similar consequences for the activation of single parents. Single parents in Germany are now normally included in the MIP system for the unemployed, but they still face fewer requirements to work than other recipients, at least until the child reaches the age of three. In Britain and Germany, the number of single parents receiving MIP is therefore very high, especially in Britain. However, policies have begun to change in order to prevent long-term benefit dependency, which has been a major problem in Britain. This policy shift is accompanied by a better childcare infrastructure and other measures of support. In the Scandinavian countries, the context conditions for single parents have been better for a longer time. The good supply of affordable childcare enables single parents to take up paid employment much more easily than is the case in Britain or Germany.

In some countries, young people also face differential treatment in MIP schemes. In France and Portugal, people under 25 are excluded from benefit receipt altogether, with exceptions for young people with a family of their own or pregnant women, among others. Moreover, young people in France who have already worked for two years also have the right to claim benefits. In Denmark, those under 25 have the right to receive *kontanthjaelp*, the general MIP benefit, but benefit levels equal those of *starthjaelp*, the programme intended for recent immigrants to Denmark, which offers benefits about 35% lower than those of the regular *kontanthjaelp* (in 2010). Moreover, young people have to be offered some form of activation or training much sooner during benefit receipt than older people. These younger people face sanctions in the form of reduced benefit levels if they refuse to participate in these measures. Such measures and sanctions also apply for young benefit recipients in Belgium and Germany. The Netherlands even installed a separate MIP scheme for persons younger than 27 in 2009.

The differential treatment of young people in MIP schemes by no means holds true for all countries under analysis. Where young people do face different conditions to other groups, however, their exclusion from benefits, or harsher conditions of access and lower benefit levels clearly aim at preventing welfare dependency and create incentives to participate in the labour market. Problems of youth unemployment are shifted back to the families in France and Portugal, where people under 25 do not have the right to receive MIP benefits. The Danish approach, in contrast, emphasises employability and the value of reciprocity: only if young people participate in training measures do they remain entitled to full benefits, and the main aim is to make these young people fit for labour market participation as quickly as possible.

Refugees, asylum seekers, and immigrants in general often face differential treatment in categorical schemes, with harsher access conditions and lower benefit levels. Once immigrants have gained a residence permit, they are mostly treated as the citizens of the country in question with regard to their right to receive MIP benefits. Recently, however, immigrants in Denmark have to fulfil one additional condition to receive *kontanthjaelp*. While benefits from this programme are available for all residents of Denmark who have lived there for seven out of the last eight years, immigrants must also have worked in the country for at least two and a half years to be eligible for benefits (Anker et al, 2009, p 12). Again, this measure emphasises the values of reciprocity: Only if immigrants have done something for their host society are they entitled to receive support.

Overall, the patterns of categorical differentiation and the special treatment of certain groups within the general last safety net tend to follow an implicit ranking of the perceived deservingness of particular recipient groups. While not all countries under analysis distinguish between benefits for older people, the long-term unemployed, single parents, young people, and immigrants within the system of MIP schemes, it is evident that older persons often do enjoy more generous access conditions and higher benefit levels, while groups whose deservingness may be perceived as doubtful, such as the unemployed, young people, and immigrants, are treated more harshly.

Conclusion

Overall, categorical differentiation has different meanings in different contexts. It plays a considerable quantitative role in about half of the countries, but it has serious consequences for the institutionalisation of social citizenship in all countries. Moreover, different population groups are often treated unequally in more broadly defined or general MIP schemes.

The assignment of different population groups to different schemes is done in diverse ways. In many instances, there are critical 'boundary' cases, as between 'employable' and 'non-employable' population groups. Persons with different grades of disability can be assigned to different schemes depending on many factors. The same is true for single parents. Moreover, these borderlines have changed in most countries over time, in particular for single parents, who are increasingly included in schemes for unemployed people because the major aim has become their integration into the labour market.

Not only are individual MIP schemes changing, but the number and the boundaries between different schemes have always been in flux. Moreover, the boundaries between social insurance and MIP systems are also shifting. Is there a general trend in these various changes? Of course, the answer is difficult to assess. From the perspective of MIP systems, countries still vary a great deal in all of these respects.

As far as the boundary between social insurance and MIP systems is concerned, some countries have successfully stabilised insurance-based protection and thus prevented MIP from gaining ground. This is especially the case in the Nordic countries and Belgium. In other countries, the protectiveness of social insurance has been reduced, providing MIP with more space. This has been the case for the unemployed in Britain, the Netherlands, and Germany. In other countries, changes to this dimension have remained more limited.

With regard to the comprehensiveness of the MIP system itself, there have also been some major changes that do not follow a common trend. In some countries, entitlement conditions have become stricter, and systems have remained very limited and stigmatising; this is the case in Eastern Europe. Moreover, Greece and Italy still lack a comprehensive general last safety net. In contrast, some MIP systems have become denser and more coherent. Portugal, for example, introduced a nationally regulated last safety net in 1996. In Spain, regional systems were introduced, and in Austria the minimum income security scheme of 2010 set national minimum standards for the regionally based general MIP schemes. In these three countries, the institutionalisation of the last safety net was substantially improved.

Countries still differ greatly with regard to the boundary between 'employable' and 'non-employable' population groups among MIP recipients, but there is a clear common trend. In general, the access conditions to non-employable MIP schemes (except for older persons) have become stricter, and more people have been shifted towards employability. This is quite obvious for single parents but is also the case for people with partial disability in some countries.

Taken together, the distinction between different recipient groups has grown everywhere, either through institutionalised categorical differentiation or through the different treatment of target groups in broader MIP schemes. This is perhaps no surprise in a period in which the activation paradigm has gained ground almost everywhere. If activation is a major goal and policy element of MIP, the distinction between 'employable' and 'non-employable' population groups is crucial. The more labour market integration is emphasised in general, the greater the need for categorical differentiation within and between schemes may become. Paradoxically, the idea of social inclusion through activation and labour market integration may thereby lead to a weaker, less general, and less comprehensive concept of social citizenship and to an erosion of equal social rights as the main foundation of the European welfare state.

Clustering MIP schemes

Introduction

While the previous sections of this chapter analysed benefit rates, the number of beneficiaries, expenditure levels, and categorical differentiation, this section investigates whether there is evidence for certain elective affinities between the MIP systems of different countries when taking all these dimensions of MIP systems into account simultaneously. Our goal is to establish certain 'families of nations', as Castles (1998) described them for the development of public policy in countries with cultural and historical similarities and geographical proximity (Castles and Mitchell, 1993; Castles, 1998).

Earlier studies of MIP have made similar efforts to group countries according to various characteristics. Based on an analysis of legal texts, Lødemel and Schulte (1992) identified the 'poverty regimes' of the UK, Norway, Germany, and Southern Europe, taking into account MIP systems' degree of centralisation, the discretion of case workers, the existence of institutionalised appeals procedures, the provision of a transfer income and social integration services, and the role of these services vis-à-vis insurance. The authors classified the UK as an 'institutionalised poverty regime', where social insurance mainly aimed to prevent poverty but did not always succeed at doing so. Therefore, the role of MIP was highly institutionalised and very important, and recipients were not automatically a client group for social work. Germany's 'differentiated power regime', with a stronger division between social insurance and MIP, differentiated between various categories of benefit recipients within MIP; social work did not play a huge role in the treatment of beneficiaries. Norway, in contrast, was a 'residual poverty regime' in which encompassing social insurance provision left only a marginal role for MIP. In addition to transfer income, benefit recipients received assistance to facilitate social inclusion. Southern Europe constituted an 'incomplete differentiated' regime and was characterised by a high degree of categorical differentiation for 'deserving' recipient groups, while general assistance did not exist or was underdeveloped (see also Gough et al, 1997, p 34).

On the basis of the data gathered in their seminal OECD study, Eardley et al (1996) suggested several typologies. Initially, they distinguished seven groups (Eardley et al, 1996, p 168 et seq), two of which comprised Anglo-Saxon welfare states not included in the present study. The first 'European' cluster of 'integrated safety nets' consisted of Great Britain, Ireland, Canada, and Germany. These countries shared general national programmes with generous and regionally invariant benefit levels, high spending, large numbers of beneficiaries, and well-established appeals procedures. Ireland stuck out of the group to some degree because of its strong emphasis on categorical benefits. France, Belgium, the Netherlands, and Luxembourg formed a group of 'dual assistance' characterised by categorical benefits for special groups and the comparatively late introduction of a general last safety net, although benefit levels varied between the countries. A third European cluster with 'rudimentary assistance' was made up of Southern Europe and Turkey. These countries shared an emphasis on nationwide categorical schemes for older people and disabled people, but they lacked general national schemes and had rather local, discretionary forms of relief in place. Benefit levels were low. In the Nordic countries (that is, Denmark, Finland, Sweden, and Norway), assistance schemes were classified as 'residual'. Benefit levels were generous and means tests relatively strict, although both were centred on the individual. Norway constituted a special case within this group, as it did not have a well-established system of appeals procedures. Finally, 'highly decentralised schemes with local discretion' were identified in Austria and Switzerland, characterised as a combination of the Nordic and Southern models, with generous benefits but a high degree of local discretion and low levels of take-up because of a high degree of stigma.

In a paper published one year later (Gough et al, 1997), the initial typology was slightly modified. Germany was now classified with France, Belgium, and Luxembourg as a 'dual assistance' country with a comparatively recent tendency to develop similarities to the British system. The Netherlands, which was initially placed within the 'dual assistance' cluster, now came to be in the same group as the Nordic countries, with 'residual' social assistance. Norway, initially a special case in the group of Nordic countries, was grouped together with Austria and Switzerland because of the strong emphasis on local discretion in a decentralised system.

In 2001, Gough reanalysed the data underlying the previous classifications using cluster analysis. His results confirmed a solution with seven clusters; changes mainly affected the non-European Anglo-Saxon nations not included in this study. The Nordic cluster, with residual but rights-based assistance, was preserved, as was the highly decentralised cluster with local discretion consisting of Austria, Switzerland, and Norway. The UK and Ireland remained united in one cluster, although joined by Australia. The rudimentary assistance cluster in Southern Europe was now made up only of Greece and Portugal, neither of which had a general nationwide assistance scheme in 1995. Spain and Italy joined the dual assistance cluster with Belgium, France, Germany, Japan, and Luxembourg.

Hölsch and Kraus (2004) grouped countries according to which government level funded benefits and set the benefit rates, and according to the degree of regional variations in benefit levels. Based on data drawn from MISSOC (European Commission, 2010) and Eardley et al (1996) for the mid-1990s, a ward cluster analysis revealed three distinct groups: The first group consisted of Germany, Sweden, Spain, Italy, and Austria, all of which were highly decentralised in all measures. Belgium, Denmark, France, and Finland formed a second cluster in which the central government set regionally invariant benefit levels but regional or local authorities were responsible for funding. In the third group, Ireland, the UK, and the Netherlands represented highly centralised systems with central determination of benefit levels, no regional variation, and almost exclusive central funding.

In a later study, Hölsch and Kraus (2006) built another typology based on indicators of expenditure, generosity, coverage, regional differentiation of benefit levels, benefit duration, and the number of recipients. As in Gough's (2001) study, Greece and Portugal formed a group without nationwide social assistance (in 1995). Spain, France, and Italy emerged as a second group because they had MIP schemes, but they either granted benefits only for limited time periods or were regionally fragmented. A large cluster comprised two subgroups, the first including Belgium, the Netherlands, Ireland, and Austria, which shared the characteristics of general nationwide schemes, indefinite benefit duration, and low numbers of recipients. Germany, Sweden, Finland, and Denmark formed the second subgroup, which was distinguished from the first by having higher numbers of recipients.

These examples illustrate that the classification of MIP schemes according to a predefined set of characteristics is by no means an easy endeavour. Moreover, the characteristics or dimensions of MIP schemes that constitute the most important elements and should be taken into account are debatable, and there may be different research questions that demand the inclusion of varying dimensions of MIP in the analysis. To some degree, the results of any comparative analysis are a product of decisions made by researchers based on their judgement, and these results also depend on the set of countries that is included in the analysis and the measurements used. Keeping these caveats in mind, this section classifies 16 countries according to their 2007 benefit generosity, number of beneficiaries, expenditure levels, and the degree of categorical differentiation. Italy is not included as we lack the relevant data for analysis. The indicators are taken from the descriptive comparisons in the previous sections of this chapter and depict various dimensions of MIP in the light of social citizenship rights (see Chapter Two). A firmly established right to a minimum income is likely to be implemented in a highly unified system with generous benefit levels. A strong role of such benefits in guaranteeing basic social rights might also be reflected by a high proportion of citizens on MIP benefits and a large share of MIP in social expenditure. More fragmented MIP systems with moderate or varying benefit levels point to a weaker standing of MIP in the welfare state context.

Indicators and data used for the analysis

Table 4.8 shows the data used to classify countries according to the specific characteristics of their MIP systems.

Benefit generosity. The generosity of the MIP benefit is one of the most important aspects for the scheme's recipients because it determines whether benefits succeed in lifting them out of poverty. As was shown earlier in this chapter, the analysis of benefit rates is highly complex and the results depend to some degree on the assumptions used in gathering the model data, especially if housing benefits are included. Here, the SaMIP data (Nelson, 2007a, 2010) on benefit levels are used, and they include housing benefits and family benefits in those cases where the latter are disregarded by the means test in the MIP benefit and thus improve household income (for the implications of this choice of indicators, see earlier in this chapter; see also van Mechelen, 2009). Net benefits for three family types – a single person, a lone parent with two children, and a couple with two children – are each related to 60% of the net median income of the household type in question. The resulting percentages are then divided by three to depict the average generosity of benefits across the different family types. The use of a relative poverty measure as a reference parameter helps to detect the equalising effect of MIP benefits. It shows that – using this measure – benefits are sufficient to lift recipients out of relative poverty only in two countries (Denmark and Germany). In Spain and Portugal, benefit levels only reach around 55% and 63% of the poverty threshold, respectively.

A second indicator of benefit generosity measures the degree to which the needs of households are assessed in a differentiated manner by specifying how families are treated in relation to single persons. Here, the benefit rate for a couple with two children is divided by the benefit rate for a single person, thus showing the approximate equivalence scale implicit in the benefit levels (because of the inclusion of housing and family benefits, this rate might differ from the one that can be derived from the 'pure' benefit levels). Portugal, with its low benefit levels for single persons and comparatively higher levels for families, tops the ranking of this indicator, while the Netherlands differentiates least in respect to the greater needs of families on the backdrop of comparatively generous benefits for single persons.

Both indicators of benefit generosity use the benefit rates of the residual MIP scheme and not for categorical schemes, which may have higher benefit levels in some instances (for example, in France, Spain, or Portugal). Moreover, the

Table 4.8: Characteristics of MIP schemes, 2007

	Generosity		Scope		Expenditure	Differentiation
	Average benefit rates in relation to 60% poverty threshold	Treatment of families in relation to a single person	Working-age recipients as % of working-age population	Recipients above 65 as % of population 65+	As % of total social expenditure	Number of schemes
Austria	81.30	2.06	5.5	10.2	2.21	3
Belgium	74.60	1.86	3	5.9	1.91	7
Czech Republic	76.56	2.36	1.1	0	0.51	1
Denmark	104.07	2.83	3.4	0	2.48	5
Finland	99.86	2.09	3.3	0.6	1.12	2
France	65.68	1.85	7.8	5.8	3.18	10
Germany	102.56	2.18	11.3	2.4	3.73	5
Hungary	84.31	2.62	3.3	2.3	1.21	3
Ireland	98.90	2.19	13.4	20.9	15.26	13
Netherlands	92.45	1.60	5.1	1.3	4.04	6
Poland	81.38	2.12	3.1	0	0.55	1
Portugal	63.66	3.37	2.6	5	1.93	5
Slovakia	81.53	2.21	5.7	0	2.71	1
Spain	54.83	1.84	1.9	31.4	3.44	7
Sweden	95.01	2.19	2.3	1	1.04	3
United Kingdom	71.53	2.65	8.8	26.1	4.77	4
Range	49.24	1.77	12.3	31.4	14.75	12
Median	81.46	2.18	3.35	2.35	2.34	3.34
Mean	83.01	2.25	5.1	7.06	3.13	4.75
SD	14.87	0.44	3.53	10.06	3.47	3.34
CV	0.18	0.2	0.69	1.43	1.11	0.70

Sources: SaMip (Nelson, 2007a, 2010), Eurostat (2010); EuMin database.

indicators do not take into account if and how benefit receipt can be combined with income from work. Therefore, the indicators do not depict actual average income levels of households on benefits; these income levels may be influenced by the design of means tests and tapers that aim to facilitate the transition from benefit receipt to paid work. Nevertheless, they provide information about the principles of social justice applied within MIP. While some countries provide generous benefit rates to all recipients, others differentiate more between families with higher needs and care responsibilities on the one hand and single people on the other. These single people would do better – at least in theory – to enter the labour market.

Scope. Another important aspect of MIP schemes is how many persons actually live on these benefits. To depict this dimension, two indicators are used: The first relates the number of recipients in working age to the overall population in working age (aged between 20 and 65 years); the second states how many persons aged 65 and over rely on MIP benefits in relation to the population above 65. The significance of MIP for these two age groups is an indication of MIP's position in relation to other forms of social protection that are primarily based on contributions and citizenship. For the number of recipients of working age, the existence and design of unemployment insurance benefits, as well as the situation in the labour market, are important (see Chapter Two and earlier in this chapter). In the set of countries analysed, the number of working-age recipients is highest in Ireland, with 13.4% of the working-age population, and lowest in the Czech Republic, with 1.1% of the reference group.

For the second indicator (the number of recipients above pensionable age), the institutional setup of the pension systems is of crucial importance (see Chapter Two and earlier in this chapter). Among the countries analysed, Spain has the highest proportion of older benefit recipients, with 31%, and there are no recipients above 65 in the Czech Republic, Denmark, Poland, or Slovakia.

Expenditure in relation to total social expenditure. The expenditure on MIP schemes constitutes another important dimension. Again, various alternative indicators are conceivable, such as expenditure as a percentage of the GDP or total social expenditure, or alternatively, as spending per capita of the population or per benefit recipient (see discussion earlier in this chapter). Here, expenditure levels are related to total social expenditure. This indicator has the advantage of representing the weight and importance of MIP systems within the overall welfare state. It is also a raw indicator for how much is spent on needs-based benefits in relation to benefits that are primarily based on desert or equality. While median spending on MIP schemes in the countries under analysis amounts to around 2.3% of total social expenditure, Ireland with its strong reliance on MIP benefits by far outspends the other countries, for it constitutes around 15.3% of total social expenditure. The figure is lowest in the Czech Republic and Poland, with around 0.5% and 0.6% of total social expenditure, respectively (see Table 4.8; see earlier in this chapter).

Degree of differentiation. The number of MIP schemes is used as an indicator for the degree of categorical differentiation of MIP systems. It ranges from only one scheme in the Czech Republic to as many as 13 in Ireland. While it shows how many different programmes exist, it neglects aspects such as benefit levels and entitlement conditions, which vary from scheme to scheme in some countries (see earlier in this chapter). Still, the sheer number of schemes can serve as a basic indicator for distinctions made between different social groups. Such a differential treatment can be due to the acknowledgement of distinct needs, but it may also point to a priority of desert over equality.

Analysis

Cluster analysis is used to discover similarities among the countries studied. This method has become increasingly popular in comparative welfare state research during the last decade (for example Obinger and Wagschal, 1998, 2001; Gough, 2001; Jensen, 2008; Wendt, 2009; Reibling, 2010; Pfeifer, 2011). It is especially suited to the research questions of this field as it is able to classify the units of analysis – usually, countries – by taking several of their characteristics into account simultaneously. The method thus highlights elective affinities of certain characteristics. In the analysis at hand, agglomerative hierarchical methods were used. They maximise the similarity of countries in one cluster while minimising the overlap between different clusters (Everitt et al, 2001). For the first step in the iteration procedure, each country forms its own cluster; gradually, countries are joined in groups. Once they have been allocated to a cluster, they do not change their affiliation any further. Once all countries have been united in one cluster, the procedure ends. Similarity or distance measures help to identify the optimal cluster solution that maximises homogeneity of the countries within the clusters while maximising the differences between the clusters (for a similar application, see Wendt, 2009; Pfeifer, 2011). As the method of cluster analysis is sensitive to the scales of the variables included in the analysis, the data were standardised between 0 and 1 according to the minimum and maximum of the distribution of each variable. Where there may be some noise in the data, this method of standardisation has been shown to be superior to z-standardisation (Milligan and Cooper, 1988).

Figure 4.9 shows the result of a ward cluster analysis using the squared Euclidean distance measure. Other analyses using single, complete, average, and weighted average linkage produced similar but not identical results. First of all, some countries proved difficult to classify for all procedures. The single linkage algorithm, which is specifically used to identify outliers, shows that Ireland is the most distinct country, its MIP system having little in common with those of the other countries. Spain and the United Kingdom join the other countries at somewhat earlier stages than does Ireland in the single linkage solution, but they are also distinct on at least some dimensions, making their placement in another group of countries difficult. Both the average and the weighted average procedures identify some core groups of countries, such as the four Central and Eastern European countries as well as the Nordic countries, whose core group is Finland and Sweden. Moreover, Belgium and the Netherlands are always placed close to each other and often joined by France and Germany. The solution of the complete linkage procedure is very close to the one shown in Figure 4.9; only Austria is placed in the cluster of Central and Eastern European countries.

The ward analysis yields the following cluster solution (see Table 4.9): cluster 1 consists of Austria, Belgium, the Netherlands, and France; Germany joins this cluster at a later step in the iteration procedure. This cluster is characterised by medium generosity (which increases by 5% when Germany joins the cluster),

Figure 4.9: Hierarchical cluster analysis: dendrogram using ward linkage and min–max standardisation

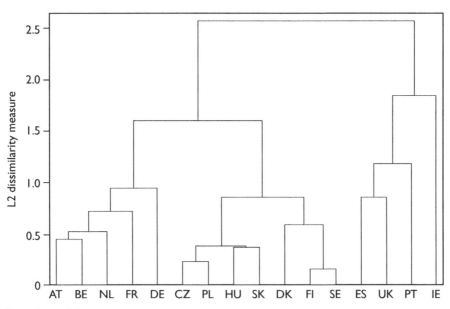

Source: Authors' depiction

less generous treatment of families in relation to single persons, and medium to high numbers of recipients (both in and above working age). Spending levels are medium and the number of schemes is quite high, with more than six on average.

Cluster 2 consists of the Czech Republic, Poland, Hungary, and Slovakia. Benefit levels lift recipients' incomes to around 80% of the poverty threshold. Families are treated more generously than in cluster 1. There are very few recipients both in and above working age, and expenditure amounts to around 1.2% of total social expenditure. On average there are fewer than two MIP schemes on average.

Cluster 3 covers Denmark, Finland, and Sweden. These countries are remarkably similar to the ones in cluster 2 in terms of expenditures, the number of recipients, and the treatment of families. They are much more generous, however, with benefit levels almost reaching the poverty threshold on average, and they also show a somewhat greater degree of categorical differentiation, with around three schemes on average.

Cluster 4 consists of Spain, the UK, and Portugal. These countries, which already proved hard to classify using the single linkage algorithm, are only joined in one cluster at a very late stage of the iteration process and should therefore be treated as a 'proto-cluster'; they are certainly not the most similar countries in the sample, even though they do share certain characteristics. To facilitate the interpretation, they are still treated as if they were joined at a somewhat earlier stage in the clustering process. They are characterised by relatively low benefit levels but generous treatment of families in comparison with the benefit rates for single persons. While the number of recipients of working age is at a medium

Table 4.9: Description of clusters

	Generosity		Scope		Expenditure	Differentiation
	Average benefit rates in relation to 60% poverty threshold	Treatment of families in relation to a single person	Working-age recipients as % of working-age population	Recipients above 65 as % of population 65+	As % of total social expenditure	Number of schemes
Cluster 1						
AT, BE, NL, FR, [DE]	Medium generosity (78.5%) [83.3%]	Low generosity (1.84) [1.91]	Medium to high (5.35%) [6.54%]	Medium to high (5.8%) [5.12%]	Medium (2.83%) [3.01%]	High (6.5) [6.2]
Cluster 2						
CZ, PL, HU, SK	Medium generosity (80.9%)	Medium generosity (2.33)	Extremely low (3.3%)	Extremely low (0.58%)	Extremely low (1.24%)	Extremely low (1.5)
Cluster 3						
DK, FI, SE	Very generous (99.6%)	Medium generosity (2.37)	Extremely low (3%)	Extremely low (0.53%)	Extremely low (1.55%)	Low (3.33)
[Cluster 4						
ES, UK, PT]	Relatively ungenerous (63.3%)	Very generous (2.61)	Medium (4.43%)	Extremely high (20.83%)	Medium to high (3.38%)	High (5.3)
Ireland	Very generous (98.9%)	Medium generosity (2.19)	Extremely high (13.4%)	Extremely high (20.9%)	Extremely high (15.26%)	Extremely high (13)

Note: Figures in brackets are the mean; square brackets indicate that the clustering or the joining of a cluster only happens at a later stage of the iteration process.

level, they all share a high number of recipients above 65, averaging more than 20% across the cluster. Portugal is an outlier, for it had only a 5% rate of older benefit recipients in 2007; however, because of the introduction of means-tested top-ups to low social insurance pensions in 2006, the number of older benefit recipients has been climbing steeply since then. Their average spending is also higher than in any of the other clusters described so far, and they show a high degree of categorical differentiation, with an average of more than five schemes.

Finally, Ireland constitutes an extreme case that is an outlier in almost all dimensions – with extremely high spending and a high number of beneficiaries, generous benefit levels and an extreme degree of categorical differentiation. Therefore, the country cannot be classified with any of the other groups, although it does join 'cluster 4' at a very late stage.

Conclusion

Depicting European MIP schemes with indicators of generosity, scope in terms of beneficiaries, expenditure, and categorical differentiation yields a classification that partly corresponds to earlier typologies and the country groupings that informed the comparative analyses of this chapter. We find Scandinavian-type welfare states with generous provisions and a marginal role for MIP, and we also identify a core group of Continental European countries with medium spending levels and a high degree of differentiation (Belgium, the Netherlands, France, Austria, and to some degree, Germany).

Table 4.10 compares the findings of earlier studies with the present ones. From the table, it is clear that, with the exception of Hölsch and Kraus (2004) – which focuses solely on the dimension of decentralization – all studies find a core group of Nordic countries consisting of Denmark, Finland, and Sweden. These countries share extensive social insurance provision, a residual role of MIP schemes, and comparatively generous benefit rates. Denmark has introduced categorical benefits intended to cover the needs of recent immigrants and has thus grown somewhat dissimilar to the other countries. However, the distinctive makeup of the Nordic welfare states continues to be present in their MIP systems, and we can safely conclude that these countries share characteristics that still strongly distinguish them from others included in our sample, rendering them a genuine Nordic family of nations.

Table 4.10: Typologies of MIP schemes

Study	Dimension(s)	Year	Types of MIP systems	Classification of countries
Lodemel and Schulte (1992)	– degree of centralisation – extent of discretion of case workers – institutionalised rights of appeal – income security vs treatment	Late 1980s/ early 1990s	1. institutionalised poverty regime 2. differentiated power regime 3. residual poverty regime 4. incomplete differentiated regime	1. UK 2. DE 3. NO 4. Southern Europe
Eardley et al (1996) (slightly changed country groupings of Gough et al (1997) in brackets)	– extent – structure – generosity	1992	1. public assistance state 2. selective welfare systems 3. integrated safety nets 4. dual assistance 5. rudimentary assistance 6. residual assistance 7. highly decentralized schemes with local discretion	1. US 2. AU, NZ 3. UK, IE, CA, DE (GB, IE, CA) 4. FR, BE, NL, LU (FR, BE, DE, LU) 5. Southern Europe, Turkey 6. DK, FI, SE, NO (DK, FI, SE) 7. CH, AT, NO

(continued)

Table 4.10: Typologies of MIP schemes (continued)

Study	Dimension(s)	Year	Types of MIP systems	Classification of countries
Gough (2001, based on Eardley et al. (1996); non-European clusters not included)	– extent – structure – generosity	1992	1. extensive, inclusive, above-average benefits 2. low extent, exclusive, above-average benefits 3. below-average extent, average inclusion/exclusion, average benefits 4. minimal extent, very exclusive, very low benefits 5. average extent, average inclusion/exclusion, generous benefits	1. IE, UK 2. AT 3. BE, FR, DE, ES, IT? 4. GR, PT 5. DK, FI, SE, NL?
Hölsch and Kraus (2004)	– degree of centralisation – funding – determination of benefits – regional benefit differentiation		1. high degree of decentralisation 2. medium decentralisation 3. highly centralised systems	1. DE, SE, ES, IT, AT 2. BE, DK, FR, FI 3. IE, UK, NL
Hölsch and Kraus (2006)	– expenditure – generosity – degree of targeting – duration		1. no assistance 2. regionally fragmented benefits 3a. nationwide schemes with indefinite duration and few beneficiaries 3b. as in a, but more beneficiaries	1. GR, PT 2. ES, FR, IT 3a. BE, NL, AT, IE 3b. De, SE, FI, DK
Types in *The last safety net* (2011)	– generosity – expenditure – scope – differentiation	2007	1. highly differentiated MIP with residual last safety nets 2. patchy safety nets in rudimentary MIP 3. residual citizenship-based MIP 4. extensively differentiated MIP with insurance substitute functions 5. highly institutionalised extensive MIP with categorical differentiation	1. AT, BE, NL, FR, DE 2. CZ, PL, HU, SK 3. DK, FI, SE 4. ES, UK, PT 5. IE

Note: Question marks indicate that a country is difficult to classify.

Source: Authors' compilation

Our analysis also identifies a group of Continental countries that share well-developed social insurance systems and comparatively fragmented MIP systems with medium scope, both in terms of expenditure and beneficiaries. In comparison with earlier findings, France and Belgium constitute the core of this cluster, while Germany, the Netherlands, and Austria proved either difficult to group or ended up in very different clusters in other analyses.

Regarding Germany, Eardley et al (1996) already saw a development in the British direction. Since then, ALG II, a highly centralised means-tested benefit at the social assistance level, replaced the unemployment assistance benefit in 2005, and the new scheme was modelled after the example of the British jobseeker's allowance (Fleckenstein, 2008). Due to these institutional changes, the total number of MIP benefit recipients at working age climbed steeply, and the residual scheme, *Sozialhilfe*, lost importance. The fact that Germany is the country that joins the Continental cluster last may point to the conclusion that its similarity to the core group of this cluster is limited; however, it is not grouped with the UK, for MIP benefits play a much smaller role in protecting the population above 65 in Germany. In Hölsch and Kraus's study (2006), Germany was placed with the Nordic countries due to their very high number of beneficiaries in the mid-1990s. In 2007, however, the Nordic countries had much lower caseloads than Germany because of the positive developments in their labour markets. The similarities with that group were therefore limited in 2007.

Likewise, the Netherlands was often seen as part of the Nordic family of nations due to the residual nature of MIP, but it is part of the Continental group in the present analysis. Compared with Denmark, Finland, and Sweden, the number of working-aged recipients and expenditure levels are higher, benefits are slightly less generous, and there is also a higher degree of fragmentation in the Dutch MIP system. The latter characteristic is especially significant in rooting the Netherlands firmly in the Continental group.

Austria also joins the cluster of Continental countries in our analysis. It was placed with Norway and Switzerland in a cluster characterised by a highly fragmented provision of MIP benefits and strong discretionary elements in a residual framework, especially in the groupings connected to the Eardley study. Neither Norway nor Switzerland is part of the country sample in our study, and we have not included measures of decentralisation and discretion. Austria resembles the other Continental countries in terms of benefit levels, caseloads, expenditure, and fragmentation. In addition to these aspects, Austria's closeness to the Continental group may also be due to the rise in the number of beneficiaries – their number has almost tripled since the early 1990s, rendering *Sozialhilfe*, the regionalised MIP benefit for the working-age population, much less residual than it used to be. In 2010, Austria introduced national minimum standards for the regional schemes, and – while not yet reflected in the 2007 data – the greater homogeneity across regions will also make the country more similar to its Continental siblings.

In contrast to other scholars' findings, there is no genuine Southern European cluster in our analysis. This conclusion is based on several factors. First, Southern

Europe as a region is somewhat underrepresented, for Greece was not analysed in this book and we lack the necessary data for Italy with its regionally fragmented MIP scheme. Second, the Portuguese MIP system has seen profound institutional change, because Portugal introduced a general nationwide MIP scheme in 1996 (not reflected in the OECD study with data from 1992). In addition, since 2006, a new means-tested scheme to top up low contributory pensions has been in operation. These institutional changes may lead to a different grouping of this country in relation to the other countries involved in this study. It now forms a proto-cluster together with Spain and the UK, all of which support a considerable number of people above 65 with MIP benefits.

Next came our placement of the UK, which has often been closely associated with Ireland in earlier analyses. However, Eardley et al (1996) have pointed out that Ireland was to some degree different from the UK because it placed a much greater emphasis on categorical differentiation. This difference has persisted since the early 1990s, and Ireland has additionally increased its benefit levels and the scope of its MIP schemes so that its expenditure levels are unparalleled, even in the UK. Therefore, Ireland is now an outlier, and the UK is associated with Portugal and Spain.

Finally, our analysis also includes the four Visegrad countries (the Czech Republic, Hungary, Poland and Slovakia), which have not been part of the earlier efforts. These countries are apparently more similar to each other than to any other European country in our sample. Therefore, they cluster together, forming another genuine family of nations characterised by similar developments in MIP systems and geographical proximity.

In the light of the existing typologies discussed, the 'families of nations' of MIP that are found in this analysis can be interpreted in the following way (see Table 4.9).

1. **Highly differentiated MIP with residual last safety nets.** The Continental European countries in this family (Austria, Belgium, the Netherlands, France, and Germany) use categorically differentiated MIP schemes that are supplemented by a general and residual last safety net. Here, MIP developed to complement a comprehensive social insurance system. Medium levels of generosity and expenditure reflect this subsidiary role of MIP. Nevertheless, more than 5% of the population both in and above working age depend on MIP schemes. This type closely corresponds to Eardley et al's (1997) 'dual assistance' type, and it also shows up in the analyses of Hölsch and Kraus (2006) when they classify countries according to their extent and the degree of targeting.

2. **Patchy safety nets in rudimentary MIP.** The Central and Eastern European countries included in this type (the Czech Republic, Poland, Hungary, and Slovakia) have very low levels of expenditure and low numbers of recipients, both in and above working age, and in that way resemble the cluster described

under (3). Their generosity, however, only reaches around 80% of the poverty threshold, and the degree of categorical differentiation is lower. Although not contained in the indicators used in this analysis, the MIP benefits in these countries are only accessible after a strict means test and benefit receipt involves a high degree of stigmatisation (see Chapter Three). Other mechanisms of social protection, such as pensions and disability benefits, may have acted as a buffer against the most severe effects of transition, and the shadow economy may provide potential benefit recipients with a sensible alternative way of making a living. While alternatives to MIP receipt in early retirement or disability schemes certainly continue to exist, they are gradually becoming less accessible. We can therefore safely assume that existing poverty is probably not tackled effectively in this group of countries with regard to both benefit generosity and the coverage of people in need, who lack the generalised citizenship right to appeal to MIP.

3. **Residual citizenship-based MIP.** In this Nordic family of nations (Denmark, Finland, and Sweden), MIP plays a residual role due to the extensive protection provided by social insurance and other citizenship-based benefits such as the national pensions. The existing MIP protection is highly unified. Benefits are generous, and both expenditure levels and the number of recipients are quite low. This type is closely matched by the Nordic cluster in all the typologies based on Eardley et al (1996), and it is also identified by Lødemel and Schulte (1992) as 'residual poverty regime'. While it does resemble the 'patchy safety nets in rudimentary MIP' type in some indicators, the welfare state context is very different and needs to be considered if we are to interpret this cluster properly. Not only do the Nordic welfare states extensively protect their citizens in all kinds of contingencies, they also have functioning labour markets with a large sector of public employment. Citizens are citizen-workers (Leibfried, 1993), and unemployment is usually temporary. Long-term reliance on MIP is therefore rare, and MIP schemes truly act as last safety nets to ensure 'equality at the bottom'.

4. **Extensively differentiated MIP with insurance substitute functions.** As stated earlier, the countries in this cluster (Spain, the United Kingdom, and Portugal) are not as closely matched as the countries making up clusters 1 to 3. Due to the structure of the MIP systems, they resemble the countries in the first cluster with their highly differentiated MIP, which has residual general safety nets. In contrast to these countries, however, in cluster 4 MIP benefits for the older population are of even greater importance, for these schemes not only supplement other pensions but also substitute them to some degree. Thus, MIP schemes patch holes in the provision of social security through higher-tier protection mechanisms, which often provide insufficient benefits. Additional common features of this cluster include relatively low benefit levels

with comparatively generous treatment of families, indicating that principles of need and desert have priority over equality.

5. **Highly institutionalised, extensive MIP with categorical differentiation.** The Irish situation is unparalleled in the countries under analysis in this book. Ireland cannot be grouped with any of the other countries since it is unique in its strong reliance on means-tested benefits for ensuring social citizenship rights. High numbers of beneficiaries, a large share in social spending, and a high degree of categorical differentiation are combined with a great uniformity of comparatively generous benefit levels both geographically and across the different categorical schemes.

The typology presented here depicts the situation in 2007 – it is a snapshot of the situation at that time. Moreover, a limited range of indicators has been used for the formation of the different types of MIP. It is possible that countries which combine the characteristics of several types of welfare states are especially susceptible to the various indicators used in comparative analyses.

Furthermore, institutions as well as economic and labour market contexts do, of course, change, as the cases of Portugal, Germany, Austria, and Denmark show. In addition to changes deeply affecting the institutional structures of MIP, there are certainly other, more subtle institutional changes that still influence the way in which MIP systems work, and there are many qualitative aspects of MIP schemes that 'can be so important in their implementation and effects' (Gough, 2001, p 169) but cannot be considered in this type of analysis. Additionally, the inclusion of other countries – such as more Anglo-Saxon nations, countries of the European Free Trade Area, or new OECD member states and additional Central and Eastern European countries – may lead to the formation of further or different types.

At the time of writing (2010), many countries face the need to adopt austerity measures in the wake of a sovereign debt crisis caused by the larger economic downturn in 2008, resulting in a rise in the number of claimants of social assistance. It is possible that both the need to economise and the demand for social protection will trigger further institutional changes in European welfare states, possibly leading to a larger role for means-tested benefits. While this road may prove beneficial to the fiscal budget, it shifts the balance between needs-, desert- and equality-based social rights and might cause a deterioration of the social situation in the long term. We know that many of the means-tested benefits analysed in this book are unable to lift recipients out of poverty, and it is this trade-off between fiscal considerations and the poverty of large population groups that policymakers need to keep in mind when reforming both social insurance and social assistance benefits.

Notes

[1] Due to missing values, the 1995 indicators for Portugal reflect 1998 values. Information for the Austrian *Sozialhilfe der Länder* has also been taken from 1998. In the Spanish case, data for the non-contributory pensions had to be taken from 1992 for 1995 and from 2001 for the 2000 aggregate. Furthermore, regional RMI expenditure of 2007 is adopted from 2006. Due to additional missing values for the expiring assistance pensions, the approximated Spanish values tend to be underestimated.

[2] In some cases, data on median income were not available for the 1990s. In order to investigate changes over time in as many countries as possible, the year 2000 was chosen as a starting point.

[3] A country's main system is defined as the most relevant benefit scheme for the able-bodied working-age population (see Chapter One). In the Spanish case, all regional programmes are included in expenditure and beneficiary data. The benefit rates of Madrid are used as an example for an average regional MIP scheme (see Ayala and Rodríguez, 2007).

Conclusion

More than 15 years ago, the seminal study by Eardley et al (1996) observed great differences between OECD countries' social assistance schemes. The analyses provided in our book show that MIP systems in Europe continue to vary substantially between countries. This conclusion summarises the findings in line with the three research questions that were defined in the Introduction. First, the similarities and differences between European MIP systems are evaluated in light of different welfare state contexts. Second, the issue of changes over time is discussed. Finally, the short-term impact of the current economic crisis is assessed. While it is too early to present a thorough analysis of these consequences due to the lack of up-to-date data in many countries, a few preliminary observations can be made in order to provide an impression of the interactions between long-term trends in MIP and the short-term impact of the crisis on the economic and societal conditions of social citizenship rights.

Comparative patterns of MIP systems

A few country groups that share basic characteristics in MIP systems can be identified in a comparative perspective. However, there are still significant variations within these groups. Both the observed similarities and differences can be traced back to the broader contexts of national welfare states that partly share ideological and structural characteristics but are also unique for each country in many ways (see Chapter Two). Individual countries vary greatly in their specific arrangements for socially vulnerable groups, such as older persons, unemployed people, and single-parent families. Accordingly, the analyses in this book have shown that the comparative pattern of MIP does not always match the broad welfare regime types.

The Nordic countries form a relatively homogeneous cluster, yet with some qualifications for MIP. In these countries, the welfare state was set up in a universal manner for citizen-workers and has covered most social risks comprehensively and generously. MIP has therefore always played a residual role, although the more prominent aim of basic social security in Denmark has provided more room for MIP. The last safety net in the Nordic countries covers relatively few people, and older persons are particularly well protected by basic pensions.

The remaining country groups that were identified are more heterogeneous. MIP systems in Continental Europe, for instance, can all be characterised as 'dual assistance' systems (Eardley et al, 1997), with categorical benefits supplemented by a general MIP benefit of last resort. But the degree of differentiation and the quantitative importance of MIP, both in general and for specific target groups, vary considerably. Austria and Belgium show the most protective social security systems, in which MIP stands behind a highly developed welfare state that is particularly strong in the areas of unemployment protection and family support. The Netherlands also provides generous social security for older persons but has tighter conditions for the working-age population. France and Germany are at opposite ends of the Continental group of nations. France shows similarity to Southern Europe because of its categorically fragmented MIP system. As in Southern Europe, this pattern is the outcome of a historically belated development of both social insurance schemes and general social rights for all citizens (see Chapter Four). Germany has shown a similarity to the Anglophone nations since the major reform in 2005 shifted large parts of unemployment protection from a desert-oriented concept to needs-based MIP benefits.

Unlike in Germany, social security as a whole rests to a large extent on needs-based benefits in the Anglophone countries, which often provide the only type of social protection available. MIP is therefore an integral part and main component of social security because of the lack of more generous arrangements. While it is very similar to Britain in a structural perspective, Ireland is an extreme case and outlier in many perspectives. Although it has the most strongly differentiated MIP system, the treatment of different target groups is very egalitarian, and benefits rates are among the highest in Europe. This is not the case for the UK, where benefit levels are lower and some recipient groups, such as older persons and families, are treated more generously than, for example, single unemployed persons.

In this respect, the MIP system in the UK resembles the two Southern European countries in our sample. Another aspect shared by all three countries is that many persons at pension age depend on MIP. Portugal and Spain differ, however, from the UK with regard to their welfare state context. Social citizenship rights are weaker in Southern Europe, where access to higher-tier benefits is more restricted and the achievable level of protection depends more heavily on the type and status of employment than in any other region of Europe. This leads to huge gaps in social security that are filled by an MIP system that mirrors the status differences between more and less 'deserving' population groups. As a consequence, MIP is quite extensive in categorical schemes, which are often part of social insurance, but it is very limited in the general last safety net among all residents.

The Eastern European countries form a group of their own because of their small-scale and ungenerous MIP systems. These countries introduced MIP systems at the beginning of the transition to democracy and a market economy. MIP schemes were quite important, especially at a time of strongly rising unemployment, but were later restricted. Older persons in these countries are protected by alternative institutional arrangements, whereas there is often virtually nothing for younger population groups in need except the very exclusive system of MIP.

Changes over time

In many of the countries described, reforms undertaken over the past 15 years have not changed the basic character of existing MIP systems. This finding is not surprising, for the welfare state and the institutionalisation of the last safety net have remained a national competency in the context of the EU. On the other hand, poverty and social exclusion have been major issues in EU activities for many years, and MIP itself has been a part of the OMC for more than 10 years. In the course of these long-term activities, EU-wide social surveys have been undertaken, extensive national reports on social inclusion have been produced, and peer reviews for the Commission have been prepared by distinguished scholars and experts. The expectation of a convergence of MIP policies in the EU from these activities would be naive given the vast differences among member states' social security systems and labour market arrangements, but a substantial improvement of the basic social protection of Europe's most vulnerable citizens could have been hoped for.

A few positive developments in MIP over the past 15 years can indeed be reported. Among the most important are Portugal's introduction of a general, nation-wide last safety net in 1996 (the first Southern European country to do so); Austria's significant improvement of its regionalised system of last resort in 2010; and Spain's introduction of regionally-based MIP schemes that cover the whole territory. Compared with the situation in Italy or Greece, these positive developments certainly represent a major step forward. In France, the change from RMI to RSA in 2009 improved the situation for younger adults and for those who combine paid work with MIP receipt. Hence, in some countries, MIP systems have become stronger and more inclusive than before.

However, a number of countries still do not have a comprehensive last safety net for the whole resident population. In most countries, the last safety net fails to lift persons out of poverty. Europe, which is proud of its social model containing strong social cohesion and comprehensive social protection, has so far failed to institute a viable and effective last safety net for all its citizens. This failure is not only an issue for socially excluded minority groups among the population. The last safety net includes large population groups in many countries, consisting in some cases of more than 10% of the working-age population or more than 20% of older persons. Such high figures indicate a deliberate 'overstretching' of MIP's role within social security systems. This pattern is structurally prevalent in the Anglophone countries and has also recently gained ground in Germany due to a major shift in unemployment policy. It is, however, questionable whether MIP can reasonably close the huge gaps in general social protection systems because it was not originally designed to handle these gaps.

Moreover, access to MIP schemes has become more difficult in recent years in quite a few countries, especially for the working-age population. An extreme example is provided by the Eastern European countries, where MIP has been shifted towards a more residual position, made less accessible and less generous in order to prevent long-term benefit dependency. The decline in MIP caseloads in these countries has been accompanied by a fall in unemployment rates. Still, recipient numbers are very low given the extent of social problems in the Eastern European countries.

In many countries, the distinction between different target groups is strongly institutionalised in different categorical MIP schemes. The more 'deserving' population groups are then often treated significantly better than those persons that are sometimes blamed for being in need, which is regarded as a result of their own individual faults and failures. Problems of non-take-up are certainly linked to such factors. Persons in need face different problems of access to MIP: lack of information, fear of stigmatisation, problems of residence, and proofs of household or income situations. MIP is therefore often 'underdeveloped' in many countries compared with the level that would be required to match the need for it.

The capability of MIP to secure basic social citizenship rights is furthermore challenged in times of major economic downturns. An important issue is therefore the way in which MIP schemes reacted to the recent economic crisis when it hit labour markets in 2008 and 2009.

The impact of the crisis on MIP

The impact of the crisis has been very different in individual countries because unemployment developed quite differently and because the role of MIP varies between countries, as the analyses presented in Chapter Two and Chapter Four have shown. The following preliminary overview is based on unemployment data provided by Eurostat (2010) and on MIP recipient numbers taken from the EuMin database for the 12 countries for which such data is available for 2009. Unemployment rates refer to men because they have been hit harder by the crisis than women and because variations between countries are less influenced by different levels of activity than is female employment (Eurostat, 2010). The comparison refers to the situations in 2007 and 2009, which represent the last year before and the first year after the beginning of the crisis. Data are annual averages.

The countries in the sample can be roughly divided into four groups. The first group consists solely of Poland and Germany, which are the only two EU countries in which unemployment rates for men actually fell during the crisis. One reason for this success was the relatively protected labour market. The German government made extensive use of the instrument of subsidised shortened working hours (*Kurzarbeit*) in order to prevent layoffs. Employers readily participated in this measure and kept their labour force in light of the already-dawning and expected labour-supply shortage. Nonetheless, the success of this instrument in avoiding rising unemployment was by no means foreseeable at the beginning of the crisis. In 2009, the German economy had already returned to an unexpected growth, as had Poland. Therefore, Germany is the only country in our sample for which the number of MIP recipients for working-age adults in the main scheme actually declined between 2007 and 2009. Still, with more than 6.7 million beneficiaries (including dependent children), the figure remains high. Recent data are not available for Poland.

In the second group of countries, the rise in male unemployment was relatively small. Between 2007 and 2009, male unemployment rates increased from 4.2%

to 5.9% in the Czech Republic, 2.8% to 3.4% in the Netherlands, and 6.7% to 7.8% in Belgium. Apart from Belgium, the countries in this group had the lowest unemployment rates of all EU member states before the crisis began. This book identifies two of these countries as well-protecting Continental European welfare states. The Czech Republic, the positive outlier among Eastern European nations, is close to this pattern. The growth in MIP recipient numbers in the main schemes for the working-age population was also modest but clearly visible in the data: Between 2007 and 2009, these numbers increased from about 80,000 to 91,000 in Belgium, 72,000 to 90,000 in the Czech Republic, and 304,000 to 317,000 in the Netherlands (only WWB; see Chapter Three). The relative increase in Belgium was low due to the specific features of unemployment insurance (as described in Chapter Two and Chapter Three), while in the Netherlands, shorter working-hour arrangements quite similar to those in Germany were used to buffer the impact of the crisis in labour markets.

Both unemployment rates and MIP recipient numbers increased strongly in a third group of countries, but starting levels differed. Male unemployment between 2007 and 2009 increased from 3.5% to 6.5% in Denmark, 5.6% to 8.6% in the United Kingdom, 5.8% to 8.6% in Sweden, and 7.8% to 9.2% in France. Portugal can also be included in this group, as it experienced an increase in male unemployment from 6.7% to 9.0%. With the exception of France and Portugal, the countries in this group have very flexible labour markets. It is therefore no surprise that unemployment rates strongly react to economic cycles and crisis events. The Danish level of unemployment is still modest, but Sweden and the UK had higher unemployment rates in 2009 than did Belgium or Germany, countries that are often regarded as having inflexible labour markets with high structural unemployment. Though the growth in unemployment rates did not vary much among these countries, the impact of this growth on MIP systems has been dramatically different. In Sweden, one of the extreme cases, the number of MIP recipients in the main scheme rose from 190,000 in 2007 to only 218,000 in 2009. The growth in MIP receipt was also modest in Denmark, rising from 107,000 to 125,000 (only *kontanthjælp*; see Chapter Three). At the other extreme, recipient numbers in the UK increased from 914,000 to 1,460,000 (only JSA; see Chapter Three). These differences clearly mirror varying levels of protectiveness of employment and of unemployment insurance systems. The rise in MIP receipt in France was very high compared with the country's unemployment rates, increasing from 1,279,000 in 2007 to 1,730,000 recipients in 2009. However, there was a substantial institutional reform in the MIP system in this case. The shift from RMI to RSA in 2009 significantly widened the scope of the MIP scheme (see Chapter Three). The increase in MIP receipt was also strong in Portugal, where it rose from 325,000 to 407,000 recipients (RMG/RSI; see Chapter Three).

Finally, an exceptional growth in unemployment occurred in two countries. Between 2007 and 2009, male unemployment rates climbed from 4.9% to 14.9% in Ireland and 6.4% to 17.7% in Spain. These two countries were hit hardest by the crisis. No recent data are available for the regional MIP schemes, but a study by

Laparra and Ayala (2009) on the basis of 2008 data suggests that the crisis' effects vary strongly by region and are rather weak on average, with an overall increase in recipients of 11% between 2007 and 2008. This confirms the impression of a fairly low significance of MIP for the unemployed in Spain. In Ireland, on the other hand, the combined caseload of both JSA and SWA (see Chapter Three) climbed from 182,000 recipients in 2007 to more than 420,000 in 2009.

The figures presented must, of course, be read with caution because data are incomplete and do not cover the entire spectrum of benefits available in each country. Moreover, the situation can change rapidly as the crisis develops further. Some countries seem to have passed their lowest points and begun to grow out of the crisis, as is the case for Germany, whereas others may not yet be out of the eye of the storm, as is likely the case for Ireland and Spain. Irrespective of the varying degrees of problem pressure, the development of MIP in the crisis seems to be coherent with the patterns found in the preceding chapters of the book. The two Northern European countries have experienced substantial increases in the number of MIP recipients, but given the strong rises in unemployment, needs-based benefits are still in a residual position in the welfare state. Economic policy and unemployment insurance seem to have buffered the impact of the crisis very well in all Continental European countries with the exception of France, were reforms made MIP more accessible in 2009. Spain and Portugal differ in the fact that MIP's reaction to labour market developments is slower in Spain, where unemployment assistance plays a stronger role and the regional fragmentation of the very last safety net emphasises its residual role in social protection. The strongest increases of MIP recipients due to unemployment can be observed in the two Anglophone countries, confirming the high structural importance of needs-based benefits in these welfare states and the low availability of other (better) forms of social protection.

The analyses presented in this book reveal that MIP systems do not only matter for marginalised population groups but are also very important for the population as a whole. They have become a very important instrument of social protection in most countries. MIP has been shifted towards the centre of the welfare state, and this shift has serious consequences for the population and social policy in general. Many countries have in recent years cut or limited those social protection systems that are based on accrued or universal rights, resulting in the growth of MIP's structural relevance. But while such needs-based benefits play a significant quantitative role in many welfare systems today, MIP does not exist in every country as a firmly established right that is of equal status with other citizenship rights. Not only are many MIP systems weak and patchy, but they often do not effectively protect those persons who are most in need. This point is crucial from a European perspective because it directly applies to migrant workers and ethnic or national minorities in the European nation states. The EU cannot allow a minimum standard of living not to be effectively guaranteed for a growing number of its citizens. If 'Social Europe' has any significant meaning for Europeans, the guarantee of a decent minimum in each member state should have first priority. One of the priorities of the EU's Europe 2020 strategy, under the title 'inclusive growth', contains the policy targets of ensuring social cohesion and lifting at least 20 million persons out of poverty. From our data and results as well as those of many other comparative analyses undertaken in this field, the most solid conclusion is that most countries and the EU have a long way to go in order to achieve this eminent goal.

Bibliography

Abrahamson, P. (1999) 'The welfare modelling business', *Social Policy and Adminimstration*, vol 33, no 4, pp 394–415.

Adema, W. (2006) 'Social assistance policy development and the provision of a decent level of income in selected OECD countries', *OECD Social, Employment and Migration Working Papers*, no 38, Paris: OECD.

Alber, J. (1982) *Vom Armenhaus zum Wohlfahrtsstaat: Analysen zur Entwicklung der Sozialversicherung in Westeuropa*, Frankfurt a.M.: Campus.

Albert, F. (2009) 'Minimum income schemes: a study of national policies: Hungary', *Peer Review in Social Protection and Social Inclusion and Assessment in Social Inclusion*, available at www.peer-review-social-inclusion.eu, accessed 12 April 2010.

Alesina, A. and Glaeser, E.L. (2004) *Fighting poverty in the US and Europe: A world of difference*, Oxford: Oxford University Press.

Andrén, T. and Gustavsson, B. (2004) 'Patterns of social assistance receipt in Sweden', *International Journal of Social Welfare*, vol 13, no 1, pp 55–68.

Andreß, H.J. and Lohmann, H. (eds) (2008) *The working poor in Europe: Employment, poverty and globalization*, Cheltenham: Edward Elgar.

Anker, J., Lindén, J., Wegner, M.H. and Holch, J.A. (2009) 'Overview and analysis. Minimum income schemes in Denmark: a study of national policies', *Peer Review in Social Protection and Social Inclusion and Assessment in Social Inclusion*, available at www.peer-review-social-inclusion.eu, accessed 19 May 2010.

Apospori, E. and Millar, J. (eds) (2003) *The dynamics of social exclusion in Europe: Comparing Austria, Germany, Greece, Portugal and the UK*, Cheltenham: Edward Elgar.

Armingeon, K. and Bonoli, G. (eds) (2006) *The politics of post-industrial welfare states: Adapting post-war social policies to new social risks*, London: Routledge.

Arriba, A. and Moreno, L. (2005) 'Spain: poverty, social exclusion and "safety nets"', in M. Ferrera (ed) *Welfare state reform in Southern Europe: Fighting poverty and social exclusion in Italy, Spain, Portugal and Greece*, London and New York: Routledge, pp 141–203.

Atero Escartín, I. (1997) 'Las políticas sociales de garantía de rentas', *Acciones e investigaciones sociales*, no 6, pp 83–108.

Atkinson, A.B., Cantillon, B., Marlier, E. and Nolan, B. (2002) *Social indicators: The EU and social inclusion*, Oxford: Oxford University Press.

Aurich, P. (2011) 'Levels, directions and divisions of change towards activation in Europe', *European Journal of Social Security*, vol 13, no 3.

Aust, A. and Arriba, A. (2005) 'Towards activation? Social assistance reforms and discourses', in P. Taylor-Gooby (ed) *Ideas and welfare state reform in Western Europe*, Basingstoke: Palgrave Macmillan, pp 100–23.

Ayala, L. and Rodríguez, M. (2007) 'What determines exit from social assistance in Spain?' *International Journal of Social Welfare*, vol 16, no 2, pp 168–82.

Bäckman, O. (2005) 'Welfare states, social structure and the dynamics of poverty rates: a comparative study of 16 countries, 1980–2000', *Institute for Futures Studies Working Paper*, no 7/2005, Stockholm: IFS.

Bahle, T. (2008) 'Family policies in the enlarged European Union', in J. Alber, T. Fahey and C. Saraceno (eds) *Social conditions and quality of life in the enlarged Europe*, London: Routledge, pp 100–26.

Bahle, T. (2009) 'Public childcare in Europe: historical trajectories and new directions', in K. Scheiwe and H. Willekens (eds) *Childcare and preschool development in Europe*, Basingstoke: Palgrave Macmillan, pp 23–42.

Bahle, T., Kohl, J. and Wendt, C. (2010a) 'Welfare state', in S. Immerfall and G. Therborn (eds) *Handbook of European societies*, New York: Springer, pp 571–628.

Bahle, T., Pfeifer, M. and Wendt, C. (2010b) 'Social assistance', in F.G. Castles, S. Leibfried, J. Lewis, H. Obinger and C. Pierson (eds) *The Oxford handbook of the welfare state*, Oxford: Oxford University Press, pp 448–61.

Bálint, M. and Köllő, J. (2008) 'A gyermeknevelési támogatások munkaerő-piaci hatásai', *Esély*, vol 19, no 1, pp 3–27.

Barbier, J.C. (2005) 'Citizenship and the activation of social protection: a comparative approach', in J. Goul Andersen, A.M. Guillemard, P.H. Jensen and B. Pfau-Effinger (eds) *The changing face of welfare: Consequences and outcomes from a citizenship perspective*, Bristol: The Policy Press, pp 113–34.

Bargain, O., Morawski, L., Myck, M. and Socha, M. (2007) 'As SIMPL as that: introducing a tax-benefit microsimulation model for Poland', *IZA Discussion Paper*, no 2988, Bonn: IZA.

Barrientos, A. and Holmes, R. (2006) *Social assistance in developing countries database, version 2.0*, London: DFID, available at www.ids.ac.uk, accessed 21 March 2010.

Baštýř, I., Chomátová, L. and Kotýnková, M. (2003) *Revize věcné náplně a konstrukce životního minima a stanovení minima existenčního: Závěrečná zpráva, sv. 1*, Prague: VÚPSV ČR/RILSA, available at www.vupsv.cz/index.php?p=publikace&klasif=&kateg=91&pracovnik=vse&rok=2003, accessed 10 April 2009.

Beblo, M., Golinowska, S., Lauer, C., Piętka, K. and Sowa, A. (2002) 'Poverty dynamics in Poland: selected quantitative analyses', *CASE Network Reports*, no 54, Warsaw: CASE.

Becker, I. and Hauser, R. (2005) *Dunkelziffer der Armut: Ausmaß und Ursachen der Nicht-Inanspruchnahme zustehender Sozilhilfeleistungen*, Berlin: edition sigma.

Behrendt, C. (2000) 'Do means-tested benefits alleviate poverty? Evidence on Germany, Sweden and the United Kingdom from LIS', *Journal of European Social Policy*, vol 10, no 1, pp 23–42.

Behrendt, C. (2002) *At the margins of the welfare state: Social assistance and the alleviation of poverty in Germany, Sweden and the United Kingdom*, Aldershot: Ashgate.

Benner, M. and Bundgaard Vad, T. (2000) 'Sweden and Denmark: defending the welfare state', in F.W. Scharpf and V.A. Schmidt (eds) *Welfare and work in the open economy: Diverse responses to common challenges*, Oxford: Oxford University Press, pp 399–466.

Blommesteijn, M. and Malee, L. (2009) 'The Netherlands. Minimum income scheme: Work and Social Assistance Act', *Peer Review in Social Protection and Social Inclusion and Assessment in Social Inclusion,* available at www.peer-review-social-inclusion.eu, accessed 19 May 2010.

Boeri, T. and Edwards, S. (1998) 'Long-term unemployment and short-term unemployment benefits: the changing nature of non-employment subsidies in Central and Eastern Europe', *Empirical Economics,* vol 23, no 1/2, pp 31–54.

Boletín Oficial del Estado (2009) *Ley 14/2009, de 11 de noviembre, por la que se regula el programa temporal de protección por desempleo e inserción,* available at www.boe.es/boe/dias/2009/11/12/pdfs/BOE-A-2009-18003.pdf, 3 accessed December 2010.

Boletín Oficial del Estado (2011) *The Spanish Constitution (English Version),* available at www.boe.es/aeboe/consultas/enlaces/constitucion.php, accessed 21 March 2011.

Bonoli, G. (2006) 'The politics of the new social policies: providing coverage against social risks in mature welfare states', in K. Armingeon and G. Bonoli (eds) *The politics of post-industrial welfare states: Adapting post-war social policies to new social risks,* London: Routledge, pp 3–26.

Borger.dk (2009), 'Introduktionsydelse', available at www.borger.dk, accessed 28 May 28 2010.

Bradshaw, J. and Bennett, F. (2009) 'United Kingdom. Minimum income schemes in the UK: a study of national policies', *Peer Review in Social Protection and Social Inclusion and Assessment in Social Inclusion,* available at www.peer-review-social-inclusion.eu, accessed 19 May 2010.

Bradshaw, J. and Finch, N. (2002) 'A comparison of child benefit packages in 22 countries', *Department for Work and Pensions Research Report,* no 174, London: Department for Work and Pensions.

Bradshaw, J. and Finch, N. (2010) 'Family benefits and services', in F.C. Castles, S. Leibfried, J. Lewis, H. Obinger and C. Pierson (eds) *The Oxford handbook of the welfare state,* Oxford: Oxford University Press, pp 462–78.

Brandolini, A., Saraceno, C. and Schizzeroto, A. (eds) (2009) *Dimensioni della disuguaglianza in Italia: povertà, salute, abitazione,* Bologna: Il Mulino.

Brännström, L. and Stenberg, S.A. (2007) 'Does social assistance recipiency influence unemployment? Macro-level findings from Sweden in a period of turbulence', *Acta Sociologica,* vol 50, no 4, pp 347–62.

Brutovská, G. (2006) 'Pôsobenie aktívnej politiky trhu práce na zamestnanos', in T. Sirovátka (ed) *Sociální vyloučení a sociální politika,* Brno: FSS MU.

Busch, K. (ed) (2008) *Wandel der Wohlfahrtsstaaten in Europa,* Baden-Baden: Nomos.

Cantillon, B. and Marx, I. (2008) 'Auf der Suche nach einem Weg aus der "Wohlfahrt ohne Arbeit": das belgische Wohlfahrtssystem', in K. Schubert, S. Hegelich and U. Bazant (eds) *Europäische Wohlfahrtssysteme: Ein Handbuch,* Wiesbaden: Verlag für Sozialwissenschaften, pp 71–87.

Cantillon, B., Marx, I. and van den Bosch, K. (2003) 'Welfare state protection, labour markets and poverty: lessons from cross-country comparisons', in G. Standing (ed) *Minimum income schemes in Europe*, Geneva: ILO, pp 11–28.

Cantillon, B, van Mechelen, N. and Schulte, B. (2008) 'Minimum income policies in old and new member states', in J. Alber, T. Fahey and C. Saraceno (eds) *Handbook of quality of life in the enlarged European Union*, London: Routledge, pp 218–34.

Capucha, L., Bomba, T., Fernandes, R. and Matos, G. (2005) 'Portugal – a virtuous path towards minimum income?', in M. Ferrera (ed) *Welfare state reform in Southern Europe: Fighting poverty and social exclusion in Italy, Spain, Portugal and Greece*, London: Routledge, pp 163–209.

Carcillo, S. and Grubb, D. (2006) 'From inactivity to work: the role of active labour market policies', *OECD Social, Employment and Migration Working Papers*, no 36, Paris: OECD.

Castles, F.G. (1998) *Comparative public policy: Patterns of post-war transformation*, Cheltenham: Edward Elgar.

Castles, F.G. and Mitchell, D. (1993) 'Worlds of welfare and families of nations', in F.G. Castles (ed) *Families of nations: Patterns of public policy in Western democracies*, Aldershot: Dartmouth.

Cerami, A. (2006) *Social policy in Central and Eastern Europe: The emergence of a new European welfare regime*, Berlin: LIT Verlag.

Cerami, A. and Vanhuysse, P. (eds) (2009) *Post-communist welfare pathways: Theorizing social policy transformations in CEE*, Basingstoke: Palgrave Macmillan.

Chłoń, A., Góra, M. and Rutkowski, M. (1999) 'Shaping pension reform in Poland: security through diversity', *Social Protection Discussion Paper Series (World Bank Pension Primer)*, no 9923, Washington, DC: World Bank.

Chłoń-Domińczak, A. (2002) 'The Polish pension reform of 1999', in E. Fultz (ed) *Pension reform in Central and Eastern Europe, Volume 1: Restructuring with privatization*, Budapest: ILO, pp 95–205.

Chulia, E. and Arsensio, M. (2006) 'Portugal: in search of a stable framework', in E.M. Immergut, K.M. Andersen and I. Schulze (eds) *The handbook of West European pension politics*, Oxford: Oxford University Press, pp 605–59.

Civil Affairs Agency (2009) *Bekendtgørelse om nedsættelse og efterregulering af den samlede hjælp efter § 25 b i lov om aktiv socialpolitik*, available at www.retsinformation. dk/forms/r0710.aspx?id=29930, accessed 29 April 2010.

Clasen, J. and Clegg, D (2006) 'Beyond activation: reforming European unemployment protection systems in post-industrial labour markets', *European Societies*, no 8, vol 4, pp 527–53.

Clasen, J. and van Oorschot, W. (2002) 'Work, welfare and citizenship: diversity and variation within European (un)employment policy', in J. Goul Andersen, J. Clasen, W. van Oorschot and K. Halvorsen (eds) *Europe's new state of welfare: Unemployment, employment policies and citizenship*, Bristol: The Policy Press, pp 233–45.

Clasen, J. and Viebrock, E. (2008) 'Voluntary unemployment insurance and trade union membership: investigating the connections in Denmark and Sweden', *Journal of Social Policy*, vol 37, no 3, pp 433–51.

Cluitmans, M., Moor, I. and Arents, M. (2001) 'Benefit dependency ratios differentiated by age-groups: an international comparison', *NEI Working Paper*, Rotterdam: NEI Labour and Education.

Cook, L.J. (2010) 'Eastern Europe and Russia', in F. Castles, S. Leibfried, J. Lewis, H. Obinger and C. Pierson (eds), *The Oxford handbook of the welfare state*, Oxford: Oxford University Press, pp 671–88.

Cousins, M. (2003) *The birth of social welfare in Ireland, 1922–52*, Dublin: Four Courts Press.

Cousins, M. (2005) *Explaining the Irish welfare state: A historical, comparative, and political analysis*, Lampeter: Edwin Mellen Press.

Curry, J. (1998) *Irish social services* (3rd edn), Dublin: Institute of Public Administration.

Czech Ministry of Labour and Social Affairs (various years) *Basic indicators of labour and social protection (yearly publication)*, Prague: Czech Ministry of Labour and Social Affairs, available at www.mpsv.cz/files/clanky/6050/casove_rady_en.pdf, accessed 10 April 2009.

Czepulis-Rutkowska, Z. (1999) 'The Polish pension system and its problems', in K. Müller, A. Ryll and H.-J. Wagener (eds) *Transformation of social security: Pensions in Central-Eastern Europe*, Heidelberg: Physica, pp 143–58.

Dahlberg, M., Johansson, K. and Mörk, E. (2008) 'On mandatory activation of welfare receivers', *IFAU Working Paper Series*, no 24/2008, Uppsala: IFAU.

Daly, M. (2009) 'Ireland. Minimum income schemes: a study of national policies', *Peer Review in Social Protection and Social Inclusion and Assessment in Social Inclusion*, available at www.peer-review-social-inclusion.eu, accessed 19 May 2010.

Daly, M. (2010) 'Families versus state and market', in F.C. Castles, S. Leibfried, J. Lewis, H. Obinger and C. Pierson (eds) *The Oxford handbook of the welfare state*, Oxford: Oxford University Press, pp 139–51.

Daly, M. and Yeates, N. (2003) 'Common origins, different paths: adaptation and change in social security in Britain and Ireland', *Policy and Politics*, vol 31, no 1, pp 85–97.

Danish Ministry of Employment (2009) *450-timers-reglen*, Copenhagen: Danish Ministry of Employment, available at www.bm.dk/Beskaeftigelsesomraadet/Ydelser/Kontanthjaelp/450timersreglen.aspx, accessed 17 April 2010.

de Montalembert, M. (ed) (2008) *La protection sociale en France*, Paris: La documentation française.

Delgado, M., Meil G. and Zamora López, F. (2008) ,Spain: short on children and short on family policies', *Demographic Research,* vol 19, art 27, pp 1059–104.

DG Personnes handicapées (2006) *Rapport annuel 2005*, Brussels: SPF Sécurité sociale, available at http://handicap.fgov.be/fr/toolbox/publications/autres/rapport_annuel.htm, accessed 17 December 2010.

Dingeldey, I. (2007) 'Between workfare and enablement. The different paths to transformation of the welfare state: a comparative analysis of activating labour market policies', *European Journal of Political Research*, vol 46, no 6, pp 823–51.

Dlouhý, J. (1997) *Životní minimum*, Prague: Socioklub.

Dziennik Ustaw no 87, poz 505-6 (1990) *Ustawa o pomocy społecznej z 29 listopada 1990*, available at http://isip.sejm.gov.pl/, accessed 5 November 2010.

Dziennik Ustaw no 100, poz 459 (1996) *Zmiana ustawy o pomocy społecznej oraz ustawy o zatrudnieniu i przeciwdziałaniu bezrobociu z 14 czerwca 1996 r*, available at http://isip.sejm.gov.pl/, accessed 5 November 2009.

Dziennik Ustaw no 64, poz 593 (2004) *Ustawa o pomocy społecznej z 12 marca 2004*, available at http://isip.sejm.gov.pl/, accessed 5 November 2010.

Eardley, T., Bradshaw, J., Ditch, J., Gough, I. and Whiteford, P. (1996) *Social assistance in OECD countries: Synthesis report*, London: HMSO.

Ebbinghaus, B. (2006) *Reforming early retirement in Europe, Japan and the USA*, Oxford: Oxford University Press.

Eichhorst, W., Grienberger-Zingerle, M. and Konle-Seidl, R. (2008) 'Activation policies in Germany: from status protection to basic income support', in W. Eichhorst, O. Kaufmann and R. Konle-Seidl (eds) *Bringing the jobless into work? Experiences with activation schemes in Europe and the US*, Heidelberg: Springer, pp 18–67.

Eichhorst, W., Kaufmann, O. and Konle-Seidl, R. (eds) (2008) *Bringing the jobless into work? Experiences with activation schemes in Europe and the US*, Heidelberg: Springer.

Esping-Andersen, G. (1990) *The three worlds of welfare capitalism*, Cambridge: Polity Press.

Esping-Andersen, G. (1999) *Social foundations of postindustrial economies*, Oxford: Oxford University Press.

Esping-Andersen, G. and Korpi, W. (1987) 'From poor relief to institutional welfare states: the development of Scandinavian social policy', in R. Erikson, E.J. Hansen, S. Ringen and H. Uusitalo (eds) *The Scandinavian model: Welfare states and welfare research*, Armonk: Sharpe, pp 39–74.

European Commission (2007a) *Joint report on social protection and social inclusion 2007*, Luxembourg: Office for Official Publications of the European Communities.

European Commission (2007b) *Study on poverty and social exclusion among lone-parent households*, Luxembourg: Office for Official Publications of the European Communities.

European Commission (2008) *Child poverty and well-being in the EU: Current status and way forward*, Luxembourg: Office for Official Publications of the European Communities.

European Commission (2009) *Joint report on social protection and social inclusion 2009*, Luxembourg: Office for Official Publications of the European Communities.

European Commission (2010) *Mutual information system on social protection (MISSOC): Comparative tables on social protection*, Brussels: European Commission, available at www.ec.europa.eu/employment_social/missoc/db/public/compareTables.do?lang=en, accessed 20 May 2010.

Eurostat (2009) *Statistics in focus*, no 24/2009, Luxembourg: Office for Official Publications of the European Communities.

Eurostat (2010) Statistics website, available at www.epp.eurostat.ec.europa.eu/portal/page/portal/statistics/themes, accessed 22 September 2010.

Everitt, B.S., Landau, S. and Leese, M. (2001) *Cluster analysis*, London: Arnold.

Feld, L.P. and Schneider, F. (2010) 'Survey on the shadow economy and undeclared earnings in OECD countries', *German Economic Review*, vol 11, no 2, pp 109–49.

Ferrera, M. (1986) 'Italy', in P. Flora (ed) *Growth to limits: The Western European welfare states since World War II. Volume 2: Germany, United Kingdom, Ireland, Italy*, Berlin and New York: de Gruyter.

Ferrera, M. (1996) 'The "southern model" of welfare in social Europe', *Journal of European Social Policy*, vol 6, no 1, pp 17–37.

Ferrera, M. (ed) (2005) *Welfare state reform in Southern Europe: Fighting poverty and social exclusion in Italy, Spain, Portugal and Greece*, London: Routledge.

Ferrera, M. (2006) *Le politiche sociali*, Bologna: Il Mulino.

Fideler, P.A. (2006) *Social welfare in pre-industrial England*, Basingstoke: Palgrave Macmillan.

Filadelfiová, J., Gerbery, D. and Škobla, D. (2006) *Report on the living conditions of Roma in Slovakia*, Bratislava: UNDP Regional Bureau for Europe and Commonwealth of Independent States.

Filipová, J. and Valná, S. (1999) *Životné minimum: Výskumný ústav práce, sociálnych vecí a rodiny*, Bratislava: VÚPSVR/RILSA.

Fink, M. and Grand, P. (2009) 'Austria. Minimum income schemes: a study of national policies', *Peer Review in Social Protection and Social Inclusion and Assessment in Social Inclusion*, available at www.peer-review-social-inclusion.eu, accessed 12 May 2010.

Fleckenstein, T. (2008) 'Restructuring welfare for the unemployed: the Hartz legislation in Germany', *Journal of European Social Policy*, vol 18, no 2, pp 177–88.

Flora, P. (ed) (1986–7) *Growth to limits: The Western European welfare states since World War II*, 2 volumes, Berlin: de Gruyter.

Flora, P. and Heidenheimer, A. (eds) (1995) *The development of welfare states in Europe and America*, London: Transaction.

Frazer, H. and Marlier, E. (2009) 'Minimum income schemes across EU members states: synthesis report', *Peer Review in Social Protection and Social Inclusion and Assessment in Social Inclusion*, available at www.peer-review-social-inclusion.eu, accessed 12 April 2010.

Fuchs, M. (2007) 'Social assistance – no thanks? Empirical analysis of non-take-up in Austria 2003', *EUROMOD Working Paper*, no EM4/07, Colchester, Essex: ISER.

Fuchs, M. (2009) 'Nicht-Inanspruchnahme von Sozialleistungen am Beispiel der Sozialhilfe', in N. Dimmel, K. Heitzmann and M. Schenk (eds) *Handbuch Armut in Österreich*, Innsbruck: Studien Verlag, pp 290–301.

Gallie, D. and Paugam, S. (2000a) 'The experience of unemployment in Europe: the debate', in D. Gallie and S. Paugam (eds) *Welfare regimes and the experience of unemployment in Europe*, Oxford: Oxford University Press, pp 1–22.

Gallie, D. and Paugam, S. (eds) (2000b) *Welfare regimes and the experience of unemployment in Europe*, Oxford: Oxford University Press.

García Romero, M.B., Losa Carmona, A. and Esteban Yago, M. (2005) *El ingreso mínimo de inserción en la Región de Murcia*, Murcia: Consejo Económico y Social de la Región de Murcia.

Gerards, R., Müllers, M. and Muysken, J. (2008) 'Institutional reforms that really matter: OECD institutional indicators vs. Dutch reform history', *Working Paper No.08-02*, Maastricht: Center of Full Employment and Equity (CofFEE Europe), Maastricht University.

Gerbery, D. (2009) 'Chudoba ako object sociálno-politických itnervecnií: Ochranná a aktivačná funkcia garancie minimálneho príjmu', PhD thesis, Bratislava: Comenius University.

Gerbery, D. and Kvapilová, E. (2006) 'Nové kontúry sociálneho štátu na Slovensku: inštitucionálne základy sociálnej súdržnosti', in Inštitút pre vyskum práce a rodiny (ed) *Premeny sociálnej politiky*, Bratislava: Inštitút pre vyskum práce a rodiny, pp 9–37.

Goedemé, T. and Van Lancker, W. (2009) 'A guaranteed minimum income for Europe's elderly: options and pitfalls in the design of a harmonised basic pension scheme in the European Union', *CSB Working Paper Series*, no 2009/01, Antwerp: University of Antwerp.

Golinowska, S. (1999) 'Ochrona socjalna bezrobotnych w Polsce oraz w innych krajach', *CASE Network Studies and Analyses*, no 201, Warsaw: CASE.

Golinowska, S., Balcerzak-Paradowska, B., Machol-Zajda, L. and Ruzik, A. (2008) *Decent work country report: Poland*, Geneva: ILO.

Golinowska, S., Piętka, K., Sowada, C. and Zukowski, M. (2003), *Study on the social protection systems in the 13 applicant countries. Poland. Country Study: Report for the European Commission – DG Employment and Social Affairs*, Brussels: European Commission.

Góra, M. and Schmidt, C.M. (1998) 'Long-term unemployment, unemployment benefits and social assistance: the Polish experience', *Empirical Economics*, vol 23, no 1/2, pp 55–85.

Gough, I. (2001) 'Social assistance regimes: a cluster analysis', *Journal of European Social Policy*, vol 11, no 2, pp 165–70.

Gough, I., Bradshaw, J., Ditch, J., Eardley, T. and Whiteford, P. (1997) 'Social assistance in OECD countries', *Journal of European Social Policy*, vol 7, no 1, pp 17–43.

Goul Andersen, J. (2011) 'Denmark: the silent revolution toward a multipillar pension system', in B. Ebbinghaus (ed) *The varieties of pension governance: Pension privatization in Europe*, Oxford: Oxford University Press, pp 183–209.

Green-Pedersen, C. (2006) 'Denmark: a "World Bank" pension system', in E.M. Immergut, K.M. Anderson and I. Schulze (eds) *The handbook of West European pension politics*, Oxford: Oxford University Press, pp 454–95.

Green-Pedersen, C. and Baggesen Klitgaard, M. (2008) 'Im Spannungsfeld von wirtschaftlichen Sachzwängen und öffentlichem Konservatismus: das dänische Wohlfahrtssystem', in K. Schubert, S. Hegelich and U. Bazant (eds) *Europäische Wohlfahrtssysteme: Ein Handbuch*, Wiesbaden: VS Verlag für Sozialwissenschaften, pp 149–68.

Haan, P. and Myck, M. (2007) 'Safety net still in transition: labour market incentive effects of extending social support in Poland', *IZA Discussion Paper*, no 3157, Bonn: IZA.

Hall, K. (2008) 'Do interactions between unemployment insurance and sickness insurance affect transitions to employment?', *IFAU Working Paper Series*, no 18/2008, Uppsala: IFAU.

Halleröd, B. (2009) 'Sweden: minimum income schemes', *Peer Review in Social Protection and Social Inclusion and Assessment in Social Inclusion*, available at www.peer-review-social-inclusion.eu, accessed 19 May 2010.

Handler, J.F. (2003) 'Social citizenship and workfare in the US and Western Europe: from status to contract', *Journal of European Social Policy*, vol 13, no 3, pp 229–43.

Heady, C. and Room, G.(2003) 'Tackling poverty and social exclusion', in E. Apospori and J. Millar (eds) *The dynamics of social exclusion in Europe: Comparing Austria, Germany, Greece, Portugal and the UK*, Cheltenham: Edward Elgar, pp 164–77.

Heikkilä, M. and Kuivalainen, S. (2004) *Using social benefits to combat poverty and social exclusion: Opportunities and problems from a comparative perspective. European synthesis report*, Strasbourg: Council of Europe.

Heikkilä, M., Moisio, P., Ritakallio, V.M., Bradshaw, J., Kuivalainen, S., Hellsten, K. and Kajanoja, J. (2006) *Poverty policies, structures and outcomes in the EU 25: Report for the 5th European round table on poverty and social exclusion, 16–17 October 2006, in Tampere, Finland*, Helsinki: STAKES.

Hernanz, V., Malherbet, F. and Pellizzari, M. (2004) 'Take-up of welfare benefits in OECD countries: a review of the evidence', *OECD Social, Employment and Migration Working Papers*, no 17, Paris: OECD.

Hespanha, P. (2007) 'The activation trend in Portuguese social policy: an open process?', in A. Serrano Pascual and L. Magnusson (eds) *Reshaping welfare states and activation regimes in Europe*, Brussels: P.I.E. Peter Lang, pp 207–40.

Hölsch, K. and Kraus, M. (2004) 'Poverty alleviation and the degree of centralization in European schemes of social assistance', *Journal of European Social Policy*, vol 14, no 2, pp 143–64.

Hölsch, K. and Kraus, M. (2006) 'European schemes of social assistance: an empirical analysis of set-ups and distributive impacts', *International Journal of Social Welfare*, vol 15, no 1, pp 50–62.

Holzer, P. (ed) (2010) *Jelentés A nyugdíj és időskor kerekasztal tevékenységéről; a jelenlegi nyugdíjrendszerről, a közelmúlt (2006–2009) szabályozási változásairól és 2013-ról*, Budapest: Prime Minister's Office.

Hort, S.O.E. (2008) 'Sklerose oder ständig in Bewegung? Das schwedische Wohlfahrtssystem', in K. Schubert, S. Hegelich and U. Bazant (eds) *Europäische Wohlfahrtssysteme: Ein Handbuch*, Wiesbaden: VS Verlag für Sozialwissenschaften, pp 525–47.

Horusitsky, P., Julienne, K. and Lelièvre, M. (2006) 'Un panorama des minima sociaux en Europe', *Études et Résultats*, no 464, Paris: La documentation française.

Hungarian Central Statistical Office (HCSO) (2007a) *Társadalmi ellátórendszerek 2006*, Budapest: HCSO.

Hungarian Central Statistical Office (HCSO) (2007b) *Társadalmi helyzetkép 2005*, Budapest: HCSO.

Hungarian Central Statistical Office (HCSO) (2008) *Társadalmi jellemzők és ellátórendszerek 2007*, Budapest: HCSO.

Hungarian Central Statistical Office (HCSO) (2009) *Társadalmi jellemzők és ellátórendszerek 2008*, Budapest: HCSO.

Huster, E.U., Boeckh, J., Bourcade, K. and Schütte, J.D. (2009) 'Analysis of the situation in relation to minimum income schemes in Germany: a study of national policies', *Peer Review in Social Protection and Social Inclusion and Assessment in Social Inclusion*, available at www.peer-review-social-inclusion.eu, accessed 19 May 2010.

Hvinden, B. and Johansson, H. (eds) (2007) *Citizenship in Nordic welfare states: Dynamics of choice, duties and participation in a changing Europe*, London: Routledge.

IEHAS and NEF (2002a) *Munkaerőpiaci Tükör 2002*, Budapest: Institute of Economics of the Hungarian Academy of Sciences (IEHAS) and National Employment Foundation (NEF).

IEHAS and NEF (2002b) *The Hungarian labour market: Review and analysis 2002*, Budapest: Institute of Economics of the Hungarian Academy of Sciences (IEHAS) and National Employment Foundation (NEF).

Immervoll, H. (2010) 'Minimum income benefits in OECD countries: policy design, effectiveness and challenges', *OECD Social, Employment and Migration Working Papers*, no 100, Paris: OECD.

Immervoll, H., Marianna, P. and D'Ercole, M.M. (2004) 'Benefit coverage rates and household typologies: scope and limitations of tax-benefit indicators', *OECD Social, Employment and Migration Working Papers*, no 20, Paris: OECD.

Inglot, T. (2008) *Welfare states in East Central Europe, 1919–2004*, Cambridge: Cambridge University Press.

Instituto de Gestao Financeira da Segurança Social (IGFSSS) (2008) *Conta da Seguaranca Social 2008*, Lisbon: IGFSSS.

Instituto de Mayores y Servicios Sociales (2011) *Prestaciones y subvenciones*, available at www.imserso.es, accessed 21 March 2011.

International Labour Organization (ILO) (1942) 'Approaches to social security: an international survey', *Studies and Reports*, Series M, no 1, Geneva: ILO.

International Labour Organization (ILO) (2004) *The fight against poverty and social exclusion in Portugal: Experiences from the national programme of fight against poverty*, Geneva: ILO.

International Labour Organization (ILO) (2010) *ILO Laborsta database*, Geneva: ILO, available at http://laborsta.ilo.org/, accessed 29 November, 2010.

IPSS (2007) *Social Security in Japan 2007*, Tokyo: National Institute of Population and Social Security Research (IPSS), available at www.ipss.go.jp, accessed 12 November 2009.

Jahoda, R., Kofroň, P. and Šimíková, I. (2009) *Změny v oblasti pomoci v hmotné nouzi a jejich dopady (příjemci a dávky, aplikace nových institutů)*, Prague: VÚPSV/RILSA, available at www.vupsv.cz, accessed 10 December 2009.

Jensen, C. (2008) 'Worlds of welfare services and transfers', *Journal of European Social Policy*, vol 18, no 2, pp 151–62.

Jensen, Per H. (1999) 'Activation of the unemployed in Denmark since the early 1990s: welfare or workfare?', *CCWS Working Paper*, no 7/1999, Aalborg: CCWS.

Jonasen, V. (2009) *Dansk Socialpolitik: Menneske, økonomi, samfund og socialt arbejde 1708–2008*, available at www.viggojonasen.dk, accessed 12 February 2010.

Kalužná, D. (2008) 'Main features of the public employment service in the Slovak Republic', *OECD Social, Employment and Migration Working Papers*, no 72, Paris: OECD.

Kangas, O. (2007) 'Finland: labour markets against politics' in E.M. Immergut, K.M. Andersen and I. Schulze (eds) *The handbook of West European pension politics*, Oxford: Oxford University Press, pp 248–96.

Kangas, O. and Luna, P. (2011) 'Finland: from statutory pension dominance towards voluntary private schemes', in B. Ebbinghaus (ed) *The varieties of pension governance: Pension privatization in Europe*, Oxford: Oxford University Press, pp 210–39.

Karamessini, M. (2008) 'Continuity and change in the southern European social model', *International Labour Review*, vol 147, no 1, pp 43–70.

Kaufmann, F.X. (2003) *Varianten des Wohlfahrtsstaates. Der deutsche Sozialstaat im internationalen Vergleich*, Frankfurt a.M.: Suhrkamp.

Keane, M.P. and Prasad, E.S. (2002) 'Inequality, transfers, and growth: new evidence from the economic transition in Poland', *Review of Economics and Statistics*, vol 84, no 2, pp 324–41.

Keane, M.P. and Prasad, E.S. (2006) 'Changes in the structure of earnings during the Polish transition', *Journal of Development Economics*, vol 80, no 2, pp 389–427.

KELA (2010) *National pensions*, Helsinki: KELA, available at www.kela.fi/in/ internet/english.nsf/NET/100702121508MH?OpenDocument, accessed 4 May 2010.

Knijn, T. (2008) 'Private responsibility and some support: family policies in the Netherlands', in I. Ostner and C. Schmitt (eds) *Family policies in the context of family change: The Nordic countries in comparative perspective*, Wiesbaden: VS Verlag für Sozialwissenschaften, pp 155–74.

Kogan I., Gebel, M. and Noelke, C. (eds) (2008) *Europe enlarged: A handbook of education, labour and welfare regimes in Central and Eastern Europe*, Bristol: The Policy Press.

Konle-Seidl, R. (2008) 'Hilfereformen und Aktivierungsstrategien im internationalen Vergleich', *IAB-Forschungsbericht*, no 7/2008, Nuremberg: IAB.

Korpi, W. and Palme, J. (1998) 'The paradox of redistribution and strategies of equality: welfare state institutions, inequality, and poverty in the Western countries', *American Sociological Review*, vol 63, no 5, pp 661–87.

Kotýnková, M. (2003) 'Diferencovná úroveň dávek sociální pomoci na Slovensku', *Sociální politika*, vol 29, no 9, pp 2–5.

Księżopolski, M. (1993) 'Social policy in Poland in the period of political and economic transition: challenges and dilemmas', *Journal of European Social Policy*, vol 3, no 3, pp 177–94.

Kuivalainen, S. (2004a) 'A comparative study on last resort social assistance in six European countries', *Research report*, no 146, Helsinki: National Research and Development Centre for Welfare and Health.

Kuivalainen, S. (2004b) 'Production of last resort support: a comparison of social assistance schemes in Europe with the notion of welfare production and the concept of social right', *Luxembourg Income Study Working Paper Series*, no 397, Luxembourg: LIS.

Kuivalainen, S. (2007) 'Toimeentulotuen alikäytön laajuus ja merkitys', *Yhteiskuntapolitiikka*, vol 72, no 1, pp 49–56.

Kusá, Z. (2008) 'Diskurz a zmeny sociálneho štátu', *Sociológia*, vol 40, no 1, pp 5–34.

Kusá, Z. and Gerbery, D. (2009) 'Slovakia. Minimum income schemes: a study of national policies', *Peer Review in Social Protection and Social Inclusion and Assessment in Social Inclusion*, available at www.peer-review-social-inclusion.eu, accessed 9 November 2009.

Laparra, M. and Ayala, L. (2009) *El sistema de garantía de ingresos mínimos en España y la respuesta urgente que requiere la crisis social*, Madrid: Fundación Foessa.

Larsson, L. (2004) 'Harmonizing unemployment and sickness insurance: why (not)?', *IFAU Working Paper Series*, no 8/2004, Uppsala: IFAU.

Legros, M. (2009) 'Minimum income schemes: the French experience of means-tested benefits', *Peer Review in Social Protection and Social Inclusion and Assessment in Social Inclusion*, available at www.peer-review-social-inclusion.eu, accessed May 19, 2010.

Leibfried, S. (1992) 'Towards a European welfare state? On integrating poverty regimes into the European Community', in Z. Ferge and J.E. Kolberg (eds) *Social policy in a changing Europe*, Frankfurt a.M.: Campus, pp 245–79.

Leisering, L. (2008) 'Social assistance in the global south: a survey and analysis', *Zeitschrift für ausländisches und internationales Arbeits- und Sozialrecht*, vol 22, no 1/2, pp.74–103.

Leitner, S. (2005) 'Conservative familialism reconsidered: the case of Belgium', *Acta Politica*, vol 40, no 4, pp 419–39.

Lelièvre, M. and Nauze-Fichet, E. (eds) (2008) *RMI, l'état des lieux 1988–2008*, Paris: La Découverte.

Leschke, J. (2008) *Unemployment insurance and non-standard employment: Four European countries in comparison*, Wiesbaden: VS Verlag für Sozialwissenschaften.

Lindert, P.H. (2004) *Growing public: Social spending and economic growth since the eighteenth century*, 2 vols, Cambridge: Cambridge University Press.

Lindquist, G.S. (2007) 'Unemployment insurance, social assistance and activation policy in Sweden', *Peer Review Programme of the European Employment Strategy*, available at www.mutual-learning-employment.net, accessed 17 December 2010.

Lødemel, I. (2004) 'The development of workfare within social activation policies', in D. Gallie and S. Paugam (eds) *Resisting marginalization: Unemployment experience and social policy in the European Union*, Oxford: Oxford University Press, pp 197–222.

Lødemel, I. and Schulte, B. (1992) 'Social assistance: a part of social security or the poor law in new disguise?', in European Institute of Social Security (EISS) (ed) *Yearbook: Reforms in Eastern and Central Europe: Beveridge 50 years after*, Leuven: Acco, pp 515-43.

Lødemel, I. and Trickey, H. (eds) (2001) '*An offer you can't refuse': Workfare in international perspective*, Bristol: The Policy Press.

Lohmann, H. (2007) *Armut von Erwerbstätigen in europäischen Wohlfahrtsstaaten: Niedriglöhne, staatliche Transfers und die Rolle der Familie*, Wiesbaden: VS Verlag für Sozialwissenschaften.

Lubyová, M. (2000) 'Trh práce', in A. Marcinčin and M. Beblavý (eds) *Hospodárska politika na Slovensku 1990–1999*, Bratislava: Centrum pre spoločenskú a mediálnu analýzu, Slovak Foreign Policy Association, INEKO, pp 161–201.

Maguire, M. (1986) 'Ireland', in P. Flora (ed) *Growth to limits: The Western European welfare states since World War II. Volume 2: Germany, United Kingdom, Ireland, Italy*, Berlin, New York: de Gruyter, pp 241–384.

Magyar-Nemzetközi Kék Szalag Bizottság (1994) *A jóléti rendszer átalakulása Magyarországon: Felépítése, a kezdeti reformok és javaslatok*, Budapest: Magyar-Nemzetközi Kék Szalag Bizottság.

Mahon, R. (2002) 'Child care: toward what kind of "social Europe"?', *Social Politics*, vol 9, no 3, pp 343–79.

Markkola, P. (2007) 'Changing patterns of welfare: Finland in the nineteenth and early twentieth centuries', in S. King and J. Stewart (eds) *Welfare peripheries: The development of welfare states in nineteeth and twentieth century Europe*, Brussels: P.I.E. Peter Lang, pp 207–30.

Marlier, E., Atkinson, A.B., Cantillon, B. and Nolan, B. (2007) *The EU and social inclusion: Facing the challenges*, Bristol: The Policy Press.

Marshall, T.H. and Bottomore, T. (1992) *Citizenship and social class*, London: Pluto Press.

Martínez Torres, M. (2005) 'Las rentas mínimas autonómicas desde una perspectiva comparada', *Cuaderno de Relaciones Laborales*, vol 23, no 2.

Marx, I. (2007) *A new social question? On minimum income protection in the post-industrial era*, Amsterdam: Amsterdam University Press.

Matsaganis, M., Ferrera, M., Capucha, L. and Moreno L. (2003) 'Mending nets in the south: anti-poverty policies in Greece, Italy, Portugal and Spain', *Social Policy and Administration*, vol 37, no 6, pp 639–55.

Matsaganis, M., Levy, H. and Flevotomou, M. (2010) 'Non-take up of social benefits in Greece and Spain', *Social Policy & Administration*, vol 44, no 7, pp 827–44.

McCashin, A. (2004) *Social security in Ireland*, Dublin: Gill and Macmillan.

McCashin, A. and O'Shea, J. (2008) 'Unter Modernisierungsdruck: das irische Wohlfahrtssystem', in K. Schubert, S. Hegelich and U. Bazant (eds) *Europäische Wohlfahrtssysteme: Ein Handbuch*, Wiesbaden: VS Verlag für Sozialwissenschaften, pp 355–78.

McLaughlin, E. (2001) 'Ireland: from Catholic corporatism to social partnership', in A. Cochrane, J. Clarke and S. Gewirtz (eds) *Comparing welfare states* (2nd edn), London: Sage, pp 203–24.

Milanovic, B. (1991) 'Poverty in Poland: 1978-88', *World Bank Policy Research Working Paper Series*, no 637, Washington, DC: World Bank.

Milanovic, B. (1990) 'Poverty in Poland, Hungary, and Yugoslavia in the years of crisis, 1978–87', *World Bank Policy Research Working Paper Series*, no 507, Washington, DC: World Bank.

Miller, D. (1999) *Principles of social justice*, Cambridge, MA: Harvard University Press.

Miller, D. (1976) *Social justice*, Oxford: Clarendon Press.

Milligan, G.W. and Cooper, M.C. (1988) 'A study of standardization of variables in cluster analysis', *Journal of Classification*, vol 5, no 2, pp 181–204.

Ministerie van Sociale Zaken en Werkgelegenheid (2008) *The Work and Social Assistance Act (WWB) in a nutshell: From social assistance to work in the Netherlands*, The Hague: Ministerie van Sociale Zaken en Werkgelegenheid.

Ministerie van Sociale Zaken en Werkgelegenheid (2010) *Stand van zaken van de sociale zekerheid. Overzicht 1 juli 2010*, The Hague: Ministerie van Sociale Zaken en Werkgelegenheid.

Ministerio de Trabajo e Inmigración (2008) *Informe nacional de estrategias para la protección social y la inclusión social del Reino de España (2008–2010)*, available at www.seg-social.es/Internet_1/LaSeguridadSocial/DocumentacionGeneral, accessed 14 March 2011.

Ministerio de Trabajo e Inmigración (2011) *Jubilación*, available at www.seg-social.es/Internet_1/Trabajadores/PrestacionesPension10935/Jubilacion, accessed 14 March 2011.

Ministero del Lavoro, della Salute e delle Politiche Sociali (2008) *Rapporto di monitoraggio sulle politiche sociali, parte seconda – sezione I: i trasferimenti monetari per invalidità, pensioni sociali, integrazoine al minimo, pensioni di guerra e ai superstiti,* Rome: Ministero del Lavoro.

Ministero dell'Economia e delle Finanze (2008) *Relazione generale sulla situazione economica del paese – (2007), volume II: le analisi,* Rome: Ministero dell'Economia.

Ministero della Solidarità Sociale (2006) *Rapporto di monitoraggio sulle politiche sociali, parte II, sezione II: i servizi sociali territoriali,* Rome: Ministero della Solidarietà.

Mitra, P. and Yemtsov, R. (2006) 'Increasing inequality in transition economies: is there more to come?', *World Bank Policy Research Working Paper Series,* no 4007, Washington, DC: World Bank.

Mohr, K. (2007) *Soziale Exklusion im Wohlfahrtsstaat: Arbeitslosensicherung und Sozialhilfe in Großbritannien und Deutschland,* Wiesbaden: VS Verlag für Sozialwissenschaften.

Moilanen, M. (2009) *Financial recession increases need for social assistance,* Helsinki: Finnish Ministry of Social Affairs and Health, available at www.stm.fi/en/focus/article/view/1423339, accessed 6 June 2010.

Moniteur Belge (1976) *8 Juillet 1976.– Loi organique des centres publics d'aide sociale,* available at www.just.fgov.be, accessed 17 December 2010.

Moniteur Belge (2002) *26. Mai 2002. – Loi concernant le droit à l'integration sociale,* available at www.just.fgov.be, accessed 17 December 2010.

Moor, I., Vossen, I. and Arents, M. (2002) 'Benefit dependency ratios by gender: an international comparison', *NEI Working Paper,* Rotterdam: NEI Labour and Education.

Moreira, A. (2008) *The activation dilemma: Reconciling the fairness and effectiveness of minimum income schemes in Europe,* Bristol: The Policy Press.

Morel, N. (2007) 'From subsidiarity to "free choice": child- and elder-care policy reforms in France, Belgium, Germany and the Netherlands', *Social Policy and Administration,* vol 41, no 6, pp 618–37.

Moreno, L. (2007) 'Europa social, bienestar en España y la "malla de seguridad"', in Á. Espina (ed), *Estado de bienestar y competitividad. La experiencia Europea,* Madrid: Fundación Carolina-Siglo XXI, pp 445–511.

Müller, K. (2008) 'The politics and outcomes of three-pillar pension reforms in Central and Eastern Europe', in C. Arza and M. Kohli (eds) *Pension reform in Europe: Politics, policies and outcomes,* London: Routledge, pp 87–106.

Nauze-Fichet, E. (2008) 'Le système français de minima sociaux', *Recherches et Prévisions,* no 91, Paris: CNAF, pp 85–91.

Nelson, K. (2004) 'Mechanisms of poverty alleviation: anti-poverty effects of non–means-tested and means-tested benefits in five welfare states', *Journal of European Social Policy,* vol 14, no 4, pp 371–90.

Nelson, K. (2005) 'The last resort: determinants of the generosity of means-tested minimum income protection in welfare democracies', in E. Carroll and L. Eriksson (eds) *Welfare politics cross-examined: Eclecticist analytical perspectives on Sweden and the developed world, from the 1880s to the 2000s*, Amsterdam: aksant, pp 85–116.

Nelson, K. (2007a) 'Introducing SaMip: The social assistance and minimum income protection interim dataset', *S-WoPEc*, no 11/2007, Stockholm: Swedish Institute for Social Research.

Nelson, K. (2007b) 'Universalism versus targeting: the vulnerability of social insurance and means-tested minimum income protection in 18 countries 1990–2002', *International Social Security Review*, vol 60, no 1, pp 33–58.

Nelson, K. (2008) 'Minimum income protection and European integration: trends and levels of minimum benefits in comparative perspective 1990–2005', *International Journal of Health Services*, vol 38, no 1, pp 103–24.

Nelson, K. (2010) 'Social assistance and minimum income benefits in old and new EU democracies', *International Journal of Social Welfare*, vol 19, no 4, pp 367–78.

Nelson, K. (2003) *Fighting poverty: Comparative studies on social insurance, means-tested benefits and income redistribution*, Stockholm: Stockholm University Press.

Obinger, H. and Tálos, E. (2006) 'Sozialstaat Österreich: historische Entwicklung und internationaler Vergleich', in H. Obinger and E. Tálos (eds) *Sozialstaat Österreich zwischen Kontinuität und Umbau Bilanz der ÖVP/FPÖ/BZÖ-Koalitionen*, Wiesbaden: VS Verlag für Sozialwissenschaften, pp 51–80.

Obinger, H. and Wagschal, U. (1998) 'Drei Welten des Wohlfahrtsstaates? Das Stratifizierungskonzept in der clusteranalytischen Überprüfung', in S. Lessenich and I. Ostner (eds) *Welten des Wohlfahrtskapitalismus: Der Sozialstaat in vergleichender Perspektive*, Frankfurt a.M.: Campus, pp 109–35.

Obinger, H. and Wagschal, U. (2001) 'Families of nations and public policy', *West European Politics*, vol 24, no 1, pp 99–114.

Observatoire National de la Pauvreté et de l'exclusion sociale (2008) *Les travaux de l'Observatoire 2007–2008*, Paris: La documentation française.

OECD (1998a) *The battle against social exclusion. Volume 1: Social assistance in Australia, Finland, Sweden, and the United Kingdom*, Paris: OECD.

OECD (1998b) *The battle against social exclusion. Volume 2: Social assistance in Belgium, the Czech Republic, the Netherlands, and Norway*, Paris: OECD.

OECD (2003) *Employment outlook 2003: Towards more and better jobs*, Paris: OECD.

OECD (2007a) *Pensions at a glance 2007: Public policies across OECD countries*, Paris: OECD.

OECD (2007b) *Benefits and wages 2007: OECD indicators*, Paris: OECD.

OECD (2008a) *OECD benefits and wages. Country chapters: Finland*, Paris: OECD.

OECD (2008b) *OECD benefits and wages. Country chapters: Portugal*, Paris: OECD.

OECD (2008c) *OECD benefit and wages. Country chapters: The Netherlands*, Paris: OECD.

OECD (2009a) *Employment outlook 2009: Tackling the job crisis*, Paris: OECD.

OECD (2009b) *Pensions at a glance 2009: Retirement income systems in OECD countries*, Paris: OECD.

OECD (2010a) *OECD social expenditure database 1980–2005*, Paris: OECD.

OECD (2010b) *OECD main economic indicators: Harmonised unemployment rates*, available at http://stats.oecd.org/mei/, accessed 19 May 2010.

OECD (2010c) *Net replacement rates (NRR) during the initial phase of unemployment*, available at www.oecd.org/els/social/workincentives, accessed 3 June 2010.

OECD (various years) *Benefits and wages database*, Paris: OECD.

ONAFTS (2005) *Cinq générations d'allocations familiales 1930–2005*, Brussels: ONAFTS.

ONAFTS (2007) *Le régime des prestations familiales garanties*, Brussels: ONAFTS.

ONEM (2009) *Mieux comprendre la législation chômage*, available at www.onem. be/Frames/frameset.aspx?Language=FR&Path=D_documentation/&Items=5, accessed 17 December 2010.

ONP (2010) *La Garantie de revenu aux personnes agées*, available at www.rvponp. fgov.be/onprvp2004/FR/I/IE/IE_00.asp, accessed 18 December 2010.

Österle, A. and Heitzmann, K. (2009) 'Welfare state development in Austria: strong traditions meet new challenges', in K. Schubert, S. Hegelich and U. Bazant (eds) *The handbook of European welfare systems*, London: Routledge, pp 31–48.

Palme, J. (1990) *Pension rights in welfare capitalism: The development of old-age pensions in 18 OECD countries 1930 to 1986*, Stockholm: Swedish Institute for Social Research.

Palme, J. (2003) 'Die "große" schwedische Rentenreform', *Zukunft,* no 6/2003, pp 8–13.

Pascall, G. and Lewis, J. (2004) 'Emerging gender regimes and policies for gender equality in a wider Europe', *Journal of Social Policy*, vol 33, no 3, pp 373–94.

Pascall, G. and Manning, N. (2000) 'Gender and social policy: comparing welfare states in Central and Eastern Europe and the former Soviet Union', *Journal of European Social Policy*, vol 10, no 3, pp 240–66.

Pearson, M. and Whitehouse, E. (2009) 'Social pensions in high-income countries', in R. Holzmann, D.A. Robalino and N. Takayama (eds) *Closing the coverage gap: The role of social pensions and other retirement income transfers*, Washington, DC: World Bank.

Pereirinha, J.A. (2006) 'Poverty and anti-poverty policies in Portugal: the experience of the guaranteed minimum income', in M. Petmesidou (ed) *Poverty and social deprivation in the Mediterranean: Trends, policies and welfare prospects in the new millenium*, London: Zed Books, pp 117–41.

Pereirinha, J.A., Arcanjo, M. and Nunes, F. (2008) 'Von einem korporativen Regime zu einem europäischen Wohlfahrtsstaat: das portugiesische Wohlfahrtssystem', in K. Schubert, S. Hegelich and U. Bazant (eds) *Europäische Wohlfahrtssysteme: Ein Handbuch*, Wiesbaden: VS Verlag für Sozialwissenschaften, pp 483–501.

Pfeifer, M. (2004) 'Neue Wege der Wohlfahrtsstaatlichkeit? Esping-Andersens Typologie der Wohlfahrtsstaaten und ihre Anwendbarkeit auf mittel- und osteuropäische Transformationsländer am Beispiel des polnischen Rentensystems', unpublished manuscript.

Pfeifer, M. (2009) 'Public opinion on state responsibility for minimum income protection: a comparison of 14 European countries', *Acta Sociologica*, vol 52, no 2, pp 117–34.

Pfeifer, M. (2010) 'Comparing unemployment protection and social assistance in 14 European countries: four worlds of protection for people of working age', *International Journal of Social Welfare*, DOI: 10.1111/j.1468-2397.2010.00765.x.

Piętka K. (2005) 'Transfery społeczne: problemy zakresu i trafności', *Third Stage of Reforms Series*, Warsaw: CASE.

Piętka, K. (2007) *Social protection in Poland: Background paper prepared for the EU8 social inclusion study*, Washington, DC: World Bank.

Piętka, K. (2008) 'Poland', in J.C. Vrooman (ed) *The elderly poor in the EU's new member states, ENEPRI Research Report, no 60*, Brussels: ENEPRI.

Piętka, K. (2009) 'Polityka dochodowa a ubóstwo i wykluczenie społeczne', in B. Balcerzak-Paradowska and S. Golinowska (ed) *Polityka dochodowa, rodzinna i pomocy społecznej w zwalczaniu ubóstwa i wykluczenia społecznego: Tendencje i ocena skuteczności*, Warsaw: Instytut Pracy i Spraw Socjalnych.

Piętka-Kosińska, K. and Ruzik-Sierdzińska, A. (2010), 'Żłobki w Polsce. Badanie empiryczne i jakościowe', Warsaw: CASE.

Plantenga, J., Remery, C., Siegel, M. and Sementini, L. (2008) 'Childcare services in 25 European Union member states: the Barcelona targets revisited', *Comparative Social Research*, vol 25, pp 27–53.

Polish Ministry of Economy and Labour (2004) *Report on Labour Market and Social Security System*, Warsaw: Polish Ministry of Economy and Labour.

Polish Ministry of Economy, Labour and Social Policy (2003) *Zielona Księga: Raport Racjonalizacja Wydatków Społecznych*, Warsaw: Polish Ministry of Economy, Labour and Social Policy.

Polish Ministry of Labour and Social Policy (2008) *Report on labour market and social security system*, Warsaw: Polish Ministry of Labour and Social Policy.

Pratscher, K. (2009) 'Sozialhilfe, Behindertenhilfe und Pflegegeld der Bundesländer im Jahr 2007 und in der Entwicklung seit 1997', *Statistische Nachrichten*, 12/2009, Vienn a: Statistics Austria, pp 1117–32.

Pratscher, K. (2010) 'Sozialhilfe, Behindertenhilfe und Pflegegeld der Bundesländer im Jahr 2008 und in der Entwicklung seit 1998', *Statistische Nachrichten*, 6/2010, Vienna: Statistics Austria, pp 468–83.

Reher, D. (1998) 'Family ties in Western Europe: persistent contrasts', *Population and Development Review*, vol 24, no 2, pp 203–34.

Reibling, N. (2010) 'Healthcare systems in Europe: towards an incorporation of patient access', *Journal of European Social Policy*, vol 20, no 1, pp 5–18.

Rijksoverheid (2010) *Vraag en antwoord: Wat is het kindgebonden budget?*, available at www.rijksoverheid.nl/onderwerpen/kindgebonden-budget/vraag-en-antwoord/wat-is-het-kindgebonden-budget.html, accessed 17 December 2010.

Ringold, D. and Kasek, L. (2007) 'Social assistance in the new EU member states: strengthening performance and labor market incentives', *World Bank Working Paper Series*, no 117, Washington, DC: World Bank.

Rodriguez Cabrero, G. (2009) 'Spain. Assessement of minimum income schemes in Spain', *Peer Review in Social Protection and Social Inclusion and Assessment in Social Inclusion* available at www.peer-review-social-inclusion.eu, accessed 19 May 2010.

Rosholm, M. and Vejlin, R.M. (2010) 'Reducing income transfers to refugee immigrants: does start-help help you start?', *Labour Economics*, vol 17, no 1, pp 258–75.

Ruoppila, S. and Lamminmäki, S. (2009) 'Finland. Minimum income schemes: a study of national policies', *Peer Review in Social Protection and Social Inclusion and Assessment in Social Inclusion*, available at www.peer-review-social-inclusion.eu, accessed 29 May 2010.

Sainsbury, D. and Morissens, A. (2002) 'Poverty in Europe in the mid-1990s: the effectiveness of means-tested benefits', *Journal of European Social Policy*, vol. 12, no. 4, pp 307–27.

Saraceno, C. (ed) (2002) *Social assistance dynamics in Europe: National and local poverty regimes*, Bristol: The Policy Press.

Saraceno, C. (2006) 'Social assistance policies and decentralization in the countries of Southern Europe', *Revue Française des Affaires Sociales*, 1 (January-March), pp. 97-118.

Saraceno, C. (2010) 'Concepts and practices of social citizenship in Europe: the case of poverty and income support for the poor', in J. Alber and N. Gilbert (eds) *United in diversity?*, Oxford and New York: Oxford University Press, pp 151–75.

Saxonberg, S. and Sirovátka, T. (2009) 'Neo-liberalism by decay? The evolution of the Czech welfare state', *Social Policy and Administration*, vol 43, no 2, pp 186–203.

Saxonberg, S. and Szelewa, D. (2007) 'The continuing legacy of the communist legacy? The development of family policies in Poland and the Czech Republic', *Social Politics: International Studies in Gender, State and Society*, vol 14, no 3, pp 351–79.

Scarpa, S. (2009) 'The scalar dimension of welfare state development: the case of Swedish and Finnish social assistance schemes', *Cambridge Journal of Regions, Economy and Society*, vol 2, no 1, pp 67–83.

Schmid, J. (2010) *Wohlfahrtsstaaten im Vergleich: Soziale Sicherung in Europa: Organisation, Finanzierung, Leistungen und Probleme*, Wiesbaden: VS Verlag für Sozialwissenschaften.

Schmidt, M.G. (2005) *Sozialpolitik in Deutschland. Historische Entwicklung und internationaler Vergleich*, Wiesbaden: VS Verlag für Sozialwissenschaften.

Schubert, K., Hegelich, S. and Bazant, U. (eds) (2009) *The handbook of European welfare systems*, London: Routledge.

Schulten, T., Bispinck, R. and Schäfer, C. (eds) (2006) *Minimum wages in Europe*, Brussels: ETUI-REHS.

Sejm (Polish Parliament) (1999) *Wystąpienie poseł Jolanty Banach, w ramach 50 posiedzenia Sejmu 21.05.1999, po przedstawieniu informacji przez rząd o sytuacji finansowej i prawnej systemu pomocy społecznej*, Warsaw: Sejm, available at http://orka2.sejm.gov.pl/Debata3.nsf/main/3E8F5D92, accessed 13 November 2009.

Sejm (Polish Parliament) (2001) *Kronika Sejmowa Nr 150 (454) III kadencja period: 31.01–6.02.2001*, Warsaw: Sejm, available at http://kronika.sejm.gov.pl/kronika.2001/text/ks-150.htm, accessed 13 November 2009.

Sejm (Polish Parliament) (2008), *Wystąpienie Minister Pracy i Polityki Społecznej Jolanty Fedak w odpowiedzi na interpelację poselską, May 20, 2008*, Warsaw: Sejm, available at http://orka2.sejm.gov.pl/IZ6.nsf/main/4786DC79, accessed 12 November 2009.

Serrano Pascual, A. (2007) 'Reshaping welfare states: activation regimes in Europe', in A. Serrano Pascual and L. Magnusson (eds) *Reshaping welfare states and activation regimes in Europe*, Brussels: P.I.E. Peter Lang.

Serrano Pascual, A. and Magnusson, L. (eds) (2007) *Reshaping welfare states and activation regimes in Europe*, Brussels: P.I.E. Peter Lang.

Servicio Público de Empleo Estatal (2010) *Información sobre prestaciones por desempleo*, available at www.redtrabaja.es/es/redtrabaja/contenidos/infoPresta.do, accessed 3 December 2010.

Sirovátka, T. and Mareš, P. (2006) 'Poverty, social exclusion and social policy in the Czech Republic', *Social Policy and Administration*, vol 40, no 3, pp 288–303.

Slovak Ministry of Labour, Social Affairs and Family (various years) *Správy o sociálnej situácii obyvateľstva SR 1998–2009*, Bratislava: Slovak Ministry of Labour, Social Affairs and Family.

Social Protection Committee (SPC) (2006) *Minimum income provision for older people and their contribution to adequacy in retirement, SPC special pension study*, Brussels: European Commission, available at www.ec.europa.eu/employment_social/social_protection, accessed 15 May 2010.

Sociale Verzekeringsbank (SVB) (2010) *Jaarverslag 2009: Zicht op zekerheid*, Amstelveen: SVB.

SPF Emploi, Travail et Concertation Sociale (2008) *Clés pour devenir parent tout en travaillant*, Brussels: SPF Emploi, Travail et Concertation sociale.

SPF Sécurité Sociale (2008) *Tout ce que vous avez toujours voulu savoir sur la sécurité sociale*, Brussels: SPF Sécurité sociale.

SPP Intégration Sociale, Lutte contre la Pauvreté, Economie Sociale et Politique des Grandes Villes (2003) *Loi du 26 mai 2002 concernant le droit à l'intégration sociale et arrêté royal du 11 juillet 2002 portant règlement général (R. G.) en matière de droit à l'intégration sociale*, available at www.mi-is.be/be_fr/01/integratie/Leefloon, accessed 17 December 2010.

SPP Intégration Sociale, Lutte contre la Pauvreté, Economie Sociale et Politique des Grandes Villes (2009) *RMI: Het leefloon – DIS Le revenu d'intégration Sociale*, available at www.mi-is.be/Statistieken/Samenvatting/beleidsnota%20RMI%20 -%20Leefloon.pdf, accessed 11 November 2010.

STAKES (National Institute for Health and Welfare) (2008) *Social assistance 2007: Statistical summary*, no 38/2008, Helsinki: STAKES.

Standing, G. (ed) (2003), *Minimum income schemes in Europe*, Geneva: ILO.

Staręga-Piasek J., Golinowska, S. and Morecka, Z. (2009) 'Pomoc społeczna: ocena działania instytucji', in B. Balcerzak-Parandowska and S. Golinowska (ed) *Polityka dochodowa, rodzinna i pomocy społecznej w zwalczaniu ubóstwa i wykluczenia społecznego. Tendencje i ocena skuteczności*, Warsaw: Instytut Pracy i Spraw Socjalnych.

Staręga-Piasek, J., Matela, P., Wóycicka, I. and Piotrowski, B. (2006) *Rescaling social welfare: Policies in Poland: Country report provided for a comparative study on the path towards multi-level governance in Europe*, Warsaw: European Centre for Social Welfare Policy and Research.

Stephens, J.D. (2010) 'The social rights of citizenship', in F. Castles, S. Leibfried, J. Lewis, H. Obinger and C. Pierson (eds), *The Oxford handbook of the welfare state*, Oxford: Oxord University Press, pp 511–25.

Strati, F. (2009) 'Minimum income schemes in Italy', Peer Review in Social Protection and Social Inclusion and Assessment in Social Inclusion, available at www.peer-review-social-inclusion.eu, accessed 19 May 2010.

Svoreňová, M. and Petrášová, A. (2005) *Social protection expenditure and performance review: Slovak Republic*, Geneva: ILO.

Szumlicz, T. (2004) 'Reforma systemu zabezpieczenia społecznego: ku rozwiązaniom ubezpieczeniowym', in M. Rymsza (ed) *Reformy społeczne: Bilans dekady*, Warsaw: Instytut Spraw Publicznych.

Tálos, E. (ed) (1998) *Soziale Sicherung im Wandel: Österreich und seine Nachbarstaaten im Vergleich*, Vienna: Böhlau.

Tálos, E. (ed) (2003) *Bedarfsorientierte Grundsicherung*, Vienna: Mandelbaum Verlag.

Tálos, E. (2005) *Vom Siegeszug zum Rückzug: Sozialstaat Österreich 1945–2005*, Innsbruck: Studienverlag.

Taylor-Gooby, P. (ed) (2004) *New risks, new welfare: The transformation of the European welfare state*, Oxford: Oxford University Press.

Titmuss, R.M. (1974) *Social policy. An introduction*, London: Allen and Unwin.

Topińska, I. (2008) *Housing benefits in Poland: Current rules and implementation process*, Warsaw: CASE.

Torfing, J. (1999) 'Workfare with welfare: recent reforms of the Danish welfare state', *Journal of European Social Policy*, vol 9, no 1, pp 5–28.

Uitvoeringsinstituut Werknemersverzekeringen (UWV) (2007) *Kroniek van de sociale verzekeringen 2007: Wetgeving en volume-ontwikkeling in historisch perspectief*, Amsterdam: UWV.

UWV (2009) *Kennis voor beleid en uitvoering van Sociale Zekerheid*, available at www.uwv.nl/overuwv/kennis-publicaties/kennis/kenniscahiers.aspx, accessed 17 December 2010.

UWV (2010) 'Werkloos', available at www.uwv.nl/Werkloos, accessed 17 December 2010.

van Berkel, R. (2010) 'The provision of income protection and activation services for the unemployed in "active" welfare states: an international comparison', *Journal of Social Policy*, vol 39, no 1, pp 17–34.

van Berkel, R. and de Schampheleire, J. (2001) 'The activation approach in Dutch and Belgian social policies', *Journal of European Area Studies*, vol 9, no 1, pp 27–42.

van Mechelen, N. (2009) *Barriers to adequate social safety nets*, Antwerp: Universiteit Antwerpen, Faculteit Politieke en Sociale Wetenschapen.

van Oorschot, W. (2006) 'Making the difference in social Europe: deservingness perceptions among citizens of European welfare states', *Journal of European Social Policy*, vol 16, no 1, pp 23–42.

van Oorschot, W. (2008) 'Von kollektiver Solidarität zur individuellen Verantwortung: der niederländische Wohlfahrtsstaat', in K. Schubert, S. Hegelich and U. Bazant (eds) *Europäische Wohlfahrtssysteme: Ein Handbuch*, Wiesbaden: VS Verlag für Sozialwissenschaften, pp 465–82.

Veit-Wilson, J. (1992) *Setting adequacy standards: How governments define minimum incomes*, Bristol: The Policy Press.

Villota Gil-Escoin, P. and Vázquez, S. (2008) 'Work in progress: Das spanische Wohlfahrtssystem', in K. Schubert, S. Hegelich and U. Bazant (eds) *Europäische Wohlfahrtssysteme: Ein Handbuch*, Wiesbaden: VS Verlag für Sozialwissenschaften, pp 169–85.

Víšek, P. (1998) 'Hmotná nouze (material need)', *Sociální politika*, vol 24, no 6, pp 4–5.

Vládní návrh zákona o pomoci o pomoci v hmotné nouzi (2005), last revision 31 March 2006, available at www.psp.cz/sqw/text/orig2.sqw?idd=14460, accessed 8 January 2009.

Warzywoda-Kruszynska, W. and Grotowska-Leder, J. (1993) 'Poverty and social conditions in Poland during the transformation to a market economy', *International Journal of Social Welfare*, vol 2, no 3, pp 115–27.

Weigel, W. and Amann, A. (1987) 'Austria', in P. Flora (ed) *Growth to limits. The Western European welfare states since World War II. Volume 4: Appendix (synopses, bibliographies, tables)*, Berlin: de Gruyter, pp 529–610.

Wendt, C. (2009) 'Mapping European healthcare systems: a comparative analysis of financing, service provision, and access to healthcare', *Journal of European Social Policy*, vol 19, no 5, pp 432–45.

Whiteford, P. and Adema, W. (2007) 'What works best in reducing child poverty: a benefit or work strategy?', *OECD Social, Employment and Migration Working Papers*, no 51, Paris: OECD.

Wollmann, H. (2008) *Comparing local government reforms in England, Sweden, France and Germany. Chapter 4: Country report Sweden*, available at www.wuestenrot-stiftung.de/download/local-government, accessed 17 December 2010.

World Bank (1996) 'Hungary: poverty and social transfers', *Sector Report*, no 14658, Washington, DC: World Bank.

World Bank (2002) *Slovak Republic: Living standards, employment, and labour market study*, Washington, DC: World Bank.

Wóycicka, I. (2009) 'Poland. Minimum income schemes: a study of national policies', *Peer Review in Social Protection and Social Inclusion and Assessment in Social Inclusion*, available at www.peer-review-social-inclusion.eu, accessed 12 December 2009.

Zeitlin, J., Pochet, P. and Magnusson, L. (eds) (2005) *The open method of co-ordination in action: The European employment and social inclusion strategies*, Brussels: P.I.E. Peter Lang.

Index

The letter f indicates a figure and t a table

Printed and bound by CPI Group (UK) Ltd, Croydon, CR0 4YY

23/04/2025

14661026-0002